THE PLAY

ETHIC

www.theplayethic.com

THE PLAY ETHIC

PAT KANE

A MANIFESTO FOR A DIFFERENT WAY OF LIVING

MACMILLAN

First published 2004 by Macmillan
an imprint of Pan Macmillan Ltd
Pan Macmillan, 20 New Wharf Road, London N1 9RR
Basingstoke and Oxford
Associated companies throughout the world
www.panmacmillan.com

ISBN 0 333 90736 1

9 8 7 6 5 4 3 2 1

A CIP catalogue record for this book is available from
the British Library.

Typeset by IntypeLibra London
Printed and bound in Great Britain by
Mackays of Chatham plc, Chatham, Kent

CONTENTS

to the net

she's everything 2 me

We refuse a world where the guarantee that we will not die of starvation entails the risk of dying of boredom . . . We can escape the commonplace only by manipulating it, controlling it, thrusting it into our dreams or surrendering it to the free play of our subjectivity.

– Raoul Vaniegem, *The Revolution of Everyday Life*, 1967

It doesn't matter what I think – it *plays*.

– John le Carré, *Tailor of Panama* (film), 2001

INTRO / 1
TOWARDS THE
PLAY ETHIC

Surely by now we know what play is: what it means, when it happens; what it means *when* it happens.

The puritans have been telling us since the Reformation that play is at best trivial, at worst demonic and at the very least *not work*. And if we use the word to describe the boundary-challenging, reality-defying, insanely optimistic, relentlessly experimental activity of children, then we usually think we know what we mean by 'play'.

Play can be beautiful, silly, perplexing, simple, funny, surreal. It can be distracted or obsessed; and it always seems to slip away from the standard rules of measurement, through being either too inconsequential or too diffuse. But we usually trust that it has been *confined*, at least; kept to the margins of our competently functioning adult society. Play is something childish, something we have put behind us, and something we only allow ourselves to recover in moments of permissible excess.

And when we do play – enjoying it, not regretting it, letting it take us over – we make our excuses. Surely play is so exceptional, so beyond the everyday norm, that it can have only a temporary rather than a permanent effect. Surely this is where (and when) we're allowed to *break free* from the ethical, the humdrum – from the anxiety of 'how we should live our lives now'. Surely we should be thankful that play can do that for us, at least. Can't we just leave it there?

Why do we need a 'play *ethic*' of all things?

A play day

It only takes one day of considered reflection – as we move through our city streets and surf our cultural resources, as we converse intimately and impersonally with others, as we dream and scheme, plan and imagine –

to realize that this account of play is deeply impoverished. The earliest etymology of the word gives us our cue to move onwards. The Indo-European root behind the Old English *plegian*, a root also found in Celtic, Germanic, Slavic and possibly Latin, is *dlegh,* meaning 'to engage oneself'.[1]

To play is to engage oneself. As a first step to seeing beyond the trivial, that sounds about right. Let's take this particular day – 28 April 2003, spent mostly at home, in my neighbourhood in the West End of Glasgow – to briefly measure the presence of play in my own daily experience as a writer, musician, father and citizen.

The most obvious way to begin is to do what I've been doing for years now – by noting the way that the concept of play, even the word itself, seems to be one of the great unarticulated metaphors of our times, informing public discourse of all kinds, from the most apparently substantial to the most obviously trivial. From the start, this day has been a richly ludic Tuesday indeed. In fact, it's easier to begin my search for examples of play at the grandest levels of power, money and realpolitik, than in the foothills of fun. War games, at the moment, are not hard to come by.

The recent conquest of Iraq by a non-UN-mandated alliance of the US, UK and a motley crew of other suppliant nations still mostly dominates my morning papers.[2] The lead story on the front page of the *Financial Times* (which joins the UK's *Guardian* and the Scottish national the *Herald* as my usual daily newspapers of choice) is this: 'Blair warns Chirac on the future of Europe'. The headline leads to a wide-ranging interview conducted with the British Prime Minster. Blair's warning is that the French 'vision of a multipolar world' (President Chirac's notion that Europe should be a rival to the US) is 'dangerous and destabilizing . . . You would end up reawakening some of the problems that we had in the cold war, with countries playing different centres of power off each other . . . [it is better] to have it out in the open.'[3]

The *Guardian* runs two stories on the same geopolitical theme, both hingeing on ludic metaphors. In an analysis on the divisions between 'old' Europe and 'new' Europe (US Secretary of Defense Donald Rumsfeld's attempt to distinguish post-communist European states from France and Germany), a Czech foreign minister comments that 'there has to be an integration in Europe, but an integration built by all the players, not by one or two'.[4] The journalist Ian Traynor notes that Eastern Europe 'was turned into a playground for the feuding Americans and West Europeans'.

An Op-Ed piece in the same paper puts into perspective the Bush administration's unwillingness to use economic benefits to curb rogue nations (like North Korea): 'A UN-brokered economic assistance and security package, such as might have been negotiated by other US presidents, is not in George Bush's political playbook.'[5]

Now one could note other structuring metaphors in today's papers, but what I want to emphasize with these examples is the *non-triviality* of certain kinds of play. The scholarship of play can readily support this. Johan Huizinga wrote his masterwork *Homo Ludens*, while being held in detention by the Nazis from 1942 till his death in 1945. Huizinga claimed that philosophy, law and politics were all born out of 'agonism' – the contesting of viewpoints and positions in the public sphere, which needs a spectating audience to guarantee its credibility.[6] As political leaders and military strategists deploy their 'game plans' over the heads of terrified civilian populations, we might lament our ineffectuality, and rail at their irresponsibility. But they are being players, nonetheless. A fastidious disdain for the ludic, in this context, doesn't take us very far.

There are humbler versions of this political agonism knocking around the broadsheets today. In the same edition of the *Guardian*, the coming leader of a British trade union is described as 'a new player at the centre of things, and everyone is struggling to work out who he really is': Mr Kevin Curran, for his part, 'has a stark analysis of the state of play between the unions and the government'.[7] A *Financial Times* headline, covering the UK local and Scottish elections, has a different nuance: 'Labour and Tories vie to play down expectations'.[8] The usual political tussling, then – but also with a sense of play as a *display*: the management of feeling and perceptions through language or spectacle.

And one extra detail of political play: a small piece reporting an interview with Tony Blair's brother Bill who claimed that 'people have tended to underestimate the role my mother played in forming Tony's view of life' (she died when the future Prime Minister was twenty-two, after prolonged periods in hospital).[9] So yet another example of play inserts itself into the political process – the psychology of a powerful global politician being shaped by the dramatis personae of his childhood, that inescapable cast of characters called 'family'. The picture at the top of the piece is of young Bill and Tony Blair in their shorts and pudding-bowl haircuts, proudly playing on their pushbikes. For the record, Tony looks the more joyous and blissful, clearly showing off.

Cue the psychohistory, if you wish.[10] But all this is to say, once again, that play enters into our lives in much more profound and constitutive ways than as merely the stuff of recreation or leisure, idleness or diversion. Indeed, the most chilling story in today's *Guardian* conjoins play in its most acceptable, heart-warming form – the experiments and fantasies of the young child – with the consequences of power play at its most shocking and awesome. The international pages lead with the picture of a winsome Iraqi boy holding a mortar bomb. With a rapt expression, the boy is prising loose its booster charge. In a deadly game called 'genie', reports the paper, 'children empty out the gunpowder and light it . . . Satair Ahmed Abbas, fifteen, had been playing with explosives on wasteground near the military camp. He sat stoically as the doctor examined his charred face. "He's lost one eye: we may be able to save the other," Dr Hussein Khalifa said.'[11]

It's a truism among aid workers that when traumatized children of war start to play again, they have begun the process of managing their grief. The basic psychology of childhood play, as most of the standard texts will tell you, is that it's a way to safely master the complexities of the world.[12] Yet here we see a darker element of child's play: war children consciously playing with the very technological violence that has turned their towns to rubble, killed their relatives and battered their psyches. Playing, as it were, with the very chaos, instability and fatedness of their lives – with their very lives.

So we think we know what play is? If we truly listened to the culture around us, we'd understand it a lot better.

We can allow play to be play, of course – to let it simply do its subversive, turn-the-world-upside-down thing, joyously refusing (or refuting) all utility and practicality. But even that is never quite as simple as it looks.

Having escaped from the flat for provisions this afternoon, I return home with two presents and one drop-jaw memory. The two presents were bought from one of these super-girly accessory shops that are opening up around here – little oases of super-hip kitsch, inspired as much by downtown Soho as downtown Tokyo (except they're located in Byres Road, outside the gothic ruin of Glasgow University). The presents are two red plastic purses called Pucca Funny Love: she is 'a sweet daughter of owner of the Chinese restaurant', and the purses depict 'a Funny Love story of the tomboy Pucca and her eternal love Garu' – who Pucca has just socked with her boxing glove. They are for my two daughters, who have been abandoned by me as this book intensifies, but who I will see next week, when things ease off. The purses are daft enough for them to love, which I hope will instantly trigger all the love they have inside for me. There is no sophistry or feinting in this play. It's a toy arrow, travelling from heart to heart.

And the drop-jaw memory? A defaced sign on a park fence that I have been passing for months, unread until this moment. The fence encloses one of these vast unused private gardens that cover this neighbourhood. They are pristine and clipped, and from winter to summer I've never seen them occupied or played in, and certainly not by any children. The original words on the sign were:

STRICTLY UNAUTHORIZED
PERSONS WILL BE
PROSECUTED
NO
BALL GAMES

Some genius kid, with the truancy habits of a delinquent but the soul of a sixties' situationist, has whited out or scraped off some letters, obliterated some words and spray painted on his or her own additions. I'm looking at it, and Rabelais, Laurence Sterne, André Breton and Valerie Solanas would undoubtedly approve:

STRICTLY AUTHORIZED
PERSONS WILL
SHAG
NO
ALL GAMES

From 'no ball games' to 'no, *all* games'. Not that this kid would necessarily know it, but that's one of the core ideas in this book. Rather than disdain the ludic as something that disrupts all social order, we need to realize that it's the richness and variety of our human games which make for a healthy and vibrant society. We need to become literate in all the forms of play that humans pursue. This can help us to describe our civilizations better – and then begin to prescribe some of the directions they should be heading in. It's possible that play will have as much to tell us about those major keywords of our lives – like 'productivity', 'labour', 'creativity' – as work does. Could we use a full understanding of play as a critique, helping us to liberate our best capacities from unnecessary control and regimentation?

We may go to work: but we are always in play, or at play. Which is also to say that we are always, no matter how determining our context, free humans. To quote the great play scholar James Carse: 'Whoever must play, cannot play'.[13] And to quote the miscreant kid's handiwork on the wall, our lives are always 'STRICTLY AUTHORIZED'. Even if the storyline and the staging keeps changing, players always compose and perform their own script. This is one smart kid.

It would be easy to go on listing examples of the immanent nature of play that I'm picking up on today: the play of forms, and the forms of play, looping into each other like a Moebius strip. To see all this play, and all this *as* play, is partly a perception issue, of being able to flow through a city, rather than peer out at it for most of the daylight hours – and perhaps also an issue of not being in an office, school or some other disciplinary institution. In terms of the playful variability of the everyday, you can't see what you're simply not *there* to see. To flower and burgeon, play needs its 'third spaces', the debatable lands between work and home. My brief visit today to my local wireless cafe – where giant leather sofas are occupied by nannies bouncing toddlers, or crop-headed infonauts picking up their emails on iBooks; where lovers and professional rivals and profoundly inactive slackers all buzz with caffeine – is proof of that.

But there's another level of play going on around me today – which is neither the metaphors of play as used by politicians and generals; nor the spontaneous, impish play that can enchant a disenchanted world; nor the play that you can see all around you, symbolic animals simply being their natural selves.[14]

This new level is play that knows, self-consciously, that it's *important* and *significant* to play. The super-girly shops are on the first rung of this level, which usually goes by the name of 'camp', 'postmodern' or 'ironic'. They're glorying in the very excess of a Japanese manga character, or a fifties' cheesecake graphic, because of the ways these signs and symbols wantonly play around with reality: they are, in Susan Sontag's terms, the 'lies that tell the truth' about how unstable and open our cultural frameworks are.[15]

As we know by now, this mentality is a notorious intellectual dead end: and play understood as merely the mutability of a sign or image is hardly anything to get excited about. But there are cultural and social spaces opening up, right in the heart of the mainstream, which are tentatively acting as if play was the accepted norm of human behaviour, not its perma-nent exception or subversion. The television I've snacked on throughout this day, partly through choice and partly by chance, has been a weird exemplar of all this.

Click: last night's recorded video of a BBC1 series on Leonardo da Vinci. The portion I'm watching seems to render da Vinci as the world's most intelligent dilettante ever – only ever playing with knowledge, pursuing an area of study (whether anatomy, architecture or avionics) to the extent that it kept his passion alive. 'He may have looked like a flake, never finishing anything,' said one of the experts. 'But at the end of a life, he turns out to have achieved an incredible amount.' Clearly, da Vinci could never stop taking the opportunity to engage with the world. Playful genius celebrated on prime-time television? Some things are changing.

Click: I'm trying to catch the six o'clock news, and just before it there is a promotional sequence for something called 'innovation nation'.[16] It's a campaign organized by the BBC and NESTA (The National Endowment for Science, Technology and the Arts) to encourage young inventors: the sequence is an exciting montage of multi-ethnic young men and women tinkering with materials, punching computer keyboards, musing on what could be in their hands. NESTA is another sign that things are changing: a government willing to set up a well-funded agency whose brief is to subsidize creativity and experiment across, and between, the arts and sciences.

I regularly receive their email newsletter, and I print out the last one received. If one wanted an official commitment to a multiplicity of ways to engage with the world, here it is, funded and noted; £53,650 to a Jamaican poet to produce her first novel; £98,000 to a company that wants to make dairy farm robots 'that can milk cows without the presence of a farmer, by working similarly to an elephant's trunk'; £150,000 to a film company that allows a savage satirist to make uncensored short films; £77,212 to a participative dance company that uses digital technology . . .

There is always the question of how one gets this money – who you know, how to fill in the forms, the bureaucratic-corridor politics of arts funding – but it would be churlish not to affirm the nobility of their inten-tion. One of the later Latin roots of play is *plevium*, to pledge; an earlier Latin derivation of the Indo-European root *dlegh* is *indulgere*, to indulge. So NESTA are pledging funds to indulge creatives in order that they may engage the world? Seems like the very model of a playful institution. Yet the question still lingers: does everyone who wants to play, at the level they want to play, actually get to play?

Click: before I switch off to phone the kids, I watch ten minutes of the beginning of a show called *I'm A Celebrity, Get Me Out Of Here!* Two confident and consummately ironic young men are taking us through what looks like an elaborate jungle compound. The premise of the show is to dump a collection of B- and C-list 'celebrities' (the term itself invites endless deconstruction) into a harsh tropical environment, and record their every interaction, every crisis. Then the audience votes to keep them in or out.

What the two young men are doing is gleefully showing all the apparatus of this situation: the filthy toilets, the hidden cameras, the insect-laden sleeping berths; a camp for concentrated scrutiny. Their attitude towards the celebrities – two sportsmen, two presenters, a singer, a dancer, a cook and a model – is unrepentantly sadistic. 'You can watch as their pampered little lives just fall apart,' says one, as the other mimics an emotional breakdown in the middle of the compound.

I've always found the savagery of these 'reality' shows to be disturbing and excessive, and right now I've figured out why. Showing at 7 p.m., the commencement hour of standard leisure time (crap job/course finished, meal eaten, hit the couch), this is a theatre of hateful catharsis. The show is mostly watched by those whose options to be a full player – meaning full engagement with the world, full commitment to one's actions, full mental and spiritual flexibility – are severely limited. They're watching the humiliation of those whose options for full play would seem to be much less limited: at least that's the standard fantasy of celebrity, where it appears that simply being oneself to an intense level can bring you the entire world.

One imagines that a Puritan reformer, catapulted forward in time from his dark decades in the eighteenth century, would rather approve of this televisual version of the village stocks. But there's something more nihilistic and sadistic going on here, an active flirting with the dark side. The presenters show us two bottles, containing a snake and a spider. Then, with their standard glee, they tell us that one bite from either of these is 'fatal'. Would the ultimate spectacle be the death of one of these loathed, pitiable celebrities? That's entertainment, 2003. We're playing God with our proxies.

Yet I like to think there is something in this extremism that indicates how powerful and frustrating the yearning is among the viewing masses for a full player's life. These shows exist to tell us that real human beings – which, in the last analysis, even a celebrity is – are always capable of redefining what they take to be reality. Paradoxically, 'reality' TV makes us relentlessly aware that even our most intimate and emotional experiences take place within contexts and frameworks – which we can always change. (The celebrities and participants can try to escape the compounds – and often do.) Much of the benefit of play, as a method of self-development, is that it helps us to make reality amenable to our will. It renders the real virtual and gives us a chance, through our games and simulations, to test out our future options. The millions watching *I'm a Celebrity* . . . know this deep down. Their self-disgust comes partly from the fact that they're allowing others to play with reality on their behalf. Will they ever do it for themselves? Will they ever engage with the world as full players?

It's the end of the day, all equipment has been switched off and I'm waiting for a call. I'm also thinking about a conversation I had this morning with the director of a Glasgow design studio. There's no point in denying that I mostly move among the creative classes: a growing minority of the total workforce, to be sure, but also a milieu which won't shut the door on any serious conversation about the values and potentialities of play.[17] So I find myself falling into these kinds of discussions all the time: everybody in this realm, all these symbol analysers and supercreatives, have something to say about the role of play in their lives, either in or out of the marketplace.

This designer is on the explicit end of the scale: her website has two separate sections, one for 'work', the other for 'play' – the former representing her client list, the latter a showcase for her staff's personal or experimental projects. But she was railing at the way people don't quite understand how play, well, works. 'Too many people out there think that when they're playing, it's fooling around, an escape from things. Yet I know that I couldn't provide a service to anyone if I didn't do a huge amount of playing – exploring, testing, putting myself in the place of something else, seeking beauty.' Lots of *mmm-nnn*s from me. I'm enjoying her company, this place.

I mentioned an idea I heard the other day about the role of the consultant in an organization – that they're like versions of what the psychologist D.W. Winnicott calls a 'transitional object'. Children's toys are transitional objects; they play with them to develop and improve their relationship with the physical world, to increase their sense of mastery.[18] So too consultants – they are toys through which companies can safely learn new things about themselves and the world. And my new friend flared up (appropriately enough, her company's symbol is a struck match).

'That's too true! And I must admit, I'm very fed up with it. We're often treated like a toy by the larger, more traditional organizations we work for – but not in a good way. We get all excited, labour furiously to get a presentation or strategy or logo done – and then they decide to do something else that day, something more "important" and "productive". The real work, so called.'

Perhaps, I mused, the problem is that organizations might want to utilize your playfulness, or even allocate a space of play within their building, but their system as a whole is never truly *in play*. It still regards play as this radioactive, fissile element: an energy source, sure, but one which – if it isn't properly contained and harnessed – could irradiate the entire place and melt down all existing boundaries. Can't we think a little more about the metaphors of play we're using? And never mind that, can't we think about the sheer scientific reality of play as a principle of natural variety, the sign that our universe is creative and dynamic, rather than a clockwork model? *Can't* we?

Not for the first time over the last few years, I've stilled the table with my rampant ludicism. 'Sorry, I'm in my own state of meltdown here . . .' As I'm smiling and wincing at the memory, the phone pipes up. At last: someone who can hear all this, and understand.

So why do we need a play ethic?

I hope that the foregoing – my own play day – provides one obvious answer. We need a play ethic because we need to become fully conscious of the players that we already are, and understand the forms of play that we already use and inhabit. I think it is time that we accepted the primary, daily reality of *homo et femina ludens*: man and woman the player. On this basis we should begin to redesign our institutions and constitutions, our marketplaces and infrastructures, even our relationships of time and space, so that we can follow this playful human nature – rather than constantly shave the blade against, across and through it. I don't think this is a revolutionary agenda, eradicating an old world and installing a new one.

It's much more like a concerted push in the right direction – an imaginative 're-form' of the basic timber of social humanity. And in order for this to take place, we need a strong play ethic: a set of principles, backed up by a confident world view, that can mobilize people to effect change.

In order to convince you that a play ethic is both possible and desirable (and hoping that, if you're already here, you're halfway there) I have used three main strategies in this book. I've identified the barriers to our perception of the playful nature of our lives; I've gathered together substantial resources and expertise to dismantle or circumvent these barriers; and I've tried to enlist as many sympathetic companies and individuals as I can to come through the gap with me, under banners that I hope many of them might recognize and identify with.[19]

The most substantial barrier is implicit in the title of this project. The work ethic has been a cornerstone of industrial modernity for over 250 years – and in many ways, is its most powerful and enduring ideology. Its essence is simply stated: that work, no matter how alienating or ill-suited to temperament, is noble in and of itself. Work is good for the soul.[20] A more appropriate metaphysic for the early to middle stages of industrial capitalism, requiring the passivity and self-discipline of its workers, could scarcely be imagined.

Yet for many people in the second half of the twentieth century – particularly after the rise of rock 'n' roll and mass consumerism in the fifties and then the counterculture of the sixties and seventies – this notion was becoming ever more anachronistic. By the early seventies, rising affluence, generated by ever-more productive technologies, began to generate visions of a post-industrial utopia amongst writers and thinkers in the developed world. How will we cope with a 'leisure' society, mused the mandarins, where automation and social reorganization will give us more play days than work days?[21]

Somehow – by a combination of oil crisis and financial deregulation, the political failures of the New Left and the triumphs of the New Right – these visions were unravelled and delegitimated, their utopian ambitions running into the day-to-day mire of 'crisis', 'strife' and 'inflation'.[22] Two decades of Conservative and Republican governance in the UK and the US connected the hazy individualism of the sixties to a hard-edged self-help ethic in the seventies and eighties, with market contractualism tearing apart the old collective mentalities of class and industry.[23]

When the exhausted populations on both sides of the Atlantic finally looked for a political change, they turned to parties – the New Democrats in 1992, and New Labour in 1997 – that promised a commitment to full employment . . . but at a cost. The old biblical injunction from Paul in the Thessalonians – 'Them that shall not work/shall not eat' – was revived by Bill Clinton and Tony Blair in their 'workfare' policies. These made welfare payments conditional upon intrusive, coercive programmes of training or low-grade job placement, with no option of non-participation. But the most remarkable and sustained tirade came from Blair's Chancellor, Gordon Brown. With a stern Presbyterian fervour, he proclaimed that the 'revitalization of the work ethic' was what the listless, demoralized, post-industrial citizens of Britain needed most.

The germ of this book began in the late nineties, as I watched New Labour prepare this new 'spirit of capitalism' for implementation.[24] **Chapter three** is my faintly disgusted examination of how this ideology could rear its censorious head again after four decades of pop-, sub- and counter-culture had progressively expanded the repertoire of human potentialities.

Yet a play ethic, by definition, must have ambitions to legitimize a certain social order – even if that order emphasizes experiment over routine, dissensus over consensus, self-realization over self-division. The joyous idealism of popular culture can provide the inspiration, and some of the content, for a more richly playful society. But in order to change the thinking behind the way our systems and structures are arranged, it is necessary to look to the sciences, both natural and social, to search for alternative accounts of reality. Possibly because I am a musician, I have always been attracted by the idea of structures both 'at play' and 'in play'. I have always loved the way that a group performance can somehow, at its best, reconcile unity and diversity – the overall coherence of the shape (a song, a genre, an occasion), enriched and developed by the dynamism and energy of its parts (this bassist, that mood, these flights of fancy . . .).[25] Could this apply to other structures – like companies, schools, families, societies, technologies?

So **Chapter two** attempts a 'General Theory of Play', one that both undermines the creaky old Newtonian/Cartesian vision of a 'machine universe' supporting the industrial work ethic, and highlights an exciting new consilience of the sciences and the humanities that can justify a vision of reality as inherently playful. I also adapt a groundbreaking study of play 'rhetorics' – meaning general themes and traditions of play – from the American play scholar Brian Sutton-Smith.[26]

What I find extraordinary and liberating about Sutton-Smith's 'seven rhetorics of play' is the way that they richly expand what we might regard as 'playful' activity, shattering the puritan prejudice forever. If the root of play is about engaging creatively with the world, then Sutton-Smith's seven-fold typology – outlining the major 'play forms' in human culture – shows us how to map and define those engagements. In this schema, play can be as productive as it is wasteful, as interested in fate as it is in progress, as communal and competitive as it is individualistic and imaginary. In the ludic world of the early twenty-first century, Sutton-Smith's rhetorics of play are a crucial 'reframing' device. They help us to see in our societies what the work ethic, with its damnable murk and gloom, has occluded from view: a possible and desirable play civilization.[27]

The seven rhetorics are divided into two groups:

The modern rhetorics

Play as progress (play in education, as healthy development).
Play as imagination (play as art, as scientific hypothesis, as culture).
Play as selfhood (play as freedom, voluntarism, personal happiness – the expression of individuality).

The ancient rhetorics

Play as power (the contest of players – in sport, markets, law, war, even philosophy).
Play as identity (the play of the carnival, the binding rituals of community).
Play as fate and chaos (the play of chance – gambling, risk, the cosmos at play).

The seventh rhetoric, the puritan stereotype of **play as frivolity,** Sutton-Smith keeps until last, thereby placing it within a much larger framework. This kind of play – laughter, subversion, inversion, tomfoolery – is both ancient and modern: a permanently available defence against all attempts at social authority and power (perhaps especially against a play ethic!). In other words: yes, you've gotta laugh. But that's not enough to realize your full playhood.[28]

So having found a way to breach the granite stonework of the work ethic, **Chapters four** to **seven** represent all the possible 'tribes of play' that might stream enthusiastically through the rubble onto these new grounds and plains. Some of them have been massing since the birth of romanticism in the eighteenth century; some of them have had to wait till the mid-1960s, when feminists made their most concerted effort to change the way the world was ordered. Some of them almost instantaneously popped into existence in the mid-nineties, and still hardly know what to do with themselves; and some of them have been sustainedly playful since the earliest daubs on a cave wall.

The 'soulitarians' of **Chapter four** represent my cheeky attempt to rally the digital generation around a flag of collective consciousness. How can digital players recognize themselves as a social and political force, with interests and an agenda?

The very productivity of our new technologies, our increasing abilities to do more with less, are the constant prize of the play ethic – a prize which becomes graspable once the conceptual poverty of the 'labour metaphysic' is overturned. If the proletarian was merely a 'meat machine', giving nothing to the authorities of power and money but his or her physical labour, then what do we call the 'immaterial labourers' – those who offer their ideas and sensibilities for hire – of the information age? The huge issue here, of course, is whether the communication networks and technologies of our times are more appropriate for play than for work. If so, is this a society of mutual collaboration between passionate and capable individuals, instead of a market economy constantly heaving and straining to commodify what is beginning to look like the uncommodifiable? The activities of digital players – whether downloaders or hackers, free software coders or new media artists – are pointing to what some writers are calling a 'new commons' (or to use an even older phrase, 'common-wealth'). What are the shared resources we need to establish in an information society, so that all its citizens get the chance to be players? And here's the cheeky bit: if members of this digital generation called themselves soulitarians, might they become more ambitious about the political implications of their playful activities? (Only a suggestion. Trying to enlist digital players is like trying to sculpt water. But run the code through, at least once.)

The 'lifestyle militants' of **Chapter five** are another group attempting to forge an activist identity out of huge societal change – in this case the rise of feminism and the consequent erosion (if not quite dethroning) of patriarchal relations. What this has done to men, women and children is an extraordinarily mixed and complex tale – a long and rumbling 'gender-quake', to use Helen Wilkinson's term – whose tremors look like continuing for decades to come.[29]

At the very least, it has had a deep impact on the gender definitions of play. Men of all ages strive to find a new ludic identity for themselves, something bigger than the testosteronal workplace. At the same time, women struggle to reconcile their traditional nurturing impulses, and the play that that usually entails, with the existing cultures of work. Even though companies are still too often marked by 'command-and-control' structures, it's historically unprecedented for women to occupy those positions and exert that kind of power. So their ambivalence about the balance between the ethics of work and play is acute. Children have also been profoundly affected by this shift in gender power. Indeed, their own cultures of play have become ever more important, as families mutate and transform themselves, trying to find the ties and connections that can maintain love and respect, in times which promise only greater fluidity and change. The 'toy stories' of the playful family are worth hearing in all their detail.

Yet out of this matrix of emotion, I believe that a new social structure can be built. Instead of our existence being defined by the necessary pains of *work* and the compensatory pleasures of *leisure*, a better arrangement might be to embrace the many dynamisms and enterprises of *play*, while accepting that our social duty is to *care* for those whose fragility, either temporary or permanent, means they must retire from the game. From *work-leisure* (and its less polarized variant, *work-life*), to *play-care*.

The 'wisdom lovers' of **Chapter six** are those enlightened souls who wish to take control of their time and space in order to pursue their most deeply held interests. In these ever more playful and fluid times, education desperately needs a new narrative of purpose. In one sense, it simply has to recover its own original play ethic – an ethic grounded in the tradition of child-centred education, intellectually kick-started by Jean-Jacques Rousseau in *Emile*, and developed by a range of outstanding figures, from Friedrich Froebel's kindergarten model to Howard Gardner's theories of 'multiple intelligence'. The confidence to incorporate these methods may be high, and the intellectual resources to back up a player's education considerable, but the playful scholars are up against the worst kind of industrial-age politics. They are faced by a modern army of clip-boarded Gradgrinds marauding across the developed world, applying tight quantitative measures called 'audits', 'outcomes' and 'performance indicators'. At the very least, this 'science of quantities' in education needs to be supplemented (and perhaps even replaced) with what some biologists and physicists call 'a science of qualities'.[30]

We need a new way to look at the complexity of the educational experience – one that regards the apparent 'messiness' and 'imprecision' of play as a deep resource for understanding, rather than something which has to be squeezed out of curricula tailored to deliver better performance statistics for short-termist politicians. I suggest that scholars might unite around a new notion of literacy – a 'multi-literacy' that ties together the deep humanism of the teaching profession with the ludic realities that face their pupils in the new century.

Artists have always been the outriders of a play civilization, reminding us with their acts of imagination what strange, transformative creatures we are. Yet since the Industrial Revolution, the esteem that romanticism conferred on the artist has also been a kind of confinement. Here, in the freedom of the studio or the gallery, in the urban bohemias and demi-mondes of the artistic community, the life of play has been lived – often at great psychological and physical cost. But if we are moving into a players' society, where the very systems of production are themselves hungry for experience, content, new ideas and new sensibilities, should artists still retreat to the high ground (or fetid depths) of romantic purity? Or could there be a 'play aesthetic' – something which could mesh the history of experience that defines artists and their communities with the powerful and open communication channels of the information age? Some, of course, are already forging such an aesthetic. **Chapter seven** puts them in context, and suggests a new direction for art and play from some surprising sources.

Chapter eight is where the progress of these tribes is temporarily impeded, by the need to negotiate terms with the management classes of modern business culture. In my experience, particularly in the private sector, these classes are an ambiguous, Janus-faced lot. One face of the Janus has to deal with the impersonal, purely formal demands of shareholders, while the other spends every day looking at communities of workers who are doubtful whether their companies will be quite as 'enabling' and 'supportive' as they say they are. When the storms come, will the organization protect them by deploying them usefully below decks? Will they lash them to the hull in order to experience its full ferocity? Or will they do both, depending on the latest merger and acquisition, or management fad? (Throwing them overboard is the other option, of course – perhaps less fashionable in these post-monetarist times.) The phrase 'cognitive dissonance' was tailor-made for most managers.

Thus some thoughtful managers, and their counsels in the class of business gurus, have been thinking about the power of play for at least two decades. Sometimes it's about liberating their own strategic imaginations, with workers as their raw materials and palettes; sometimes it's about trying to instigate a culture of creativity within the walls of an organization. Results have been mixed; nevertheless, I argue that there are some resources here – some rationales and operating models – which can connect to the new counter-cultures of play through their mutual interest in expanding human potential. (I also manage to track down Richard Neville, the author of the original ludic political tract *Playpower*, in his native Sydney, Australia. Neville is now, of course, a management consultant himself.)

Yet, as one senior multinational manager once told me, 'We only operate within the rules of the game set by politicians. If they change the rules, we play differently.' **Chapter nine,** the politics of the play ethic, is by far the most policy and theory laden – and, for that, some moderate apologies. But I like to think that out of all the games and strategies deployed here, this is the most serious play of all: to gather together a range of already-existing innovative ideas – about welfare infrastructure, the balance between market and gift economies, the need to move from social security to social autonomy – and try to justify them as the necessary grounds of play. The many 'realistic utopias'[31] of the modern and postmodern ages shouldn't be discarded, in my view, as clapped-out visions ready for the dustbin of history, from which we might be able to pick a few usable parts. The information age is far too mobile, far too liquid as a world system, to imagine that we live in the best of all possible worlds. I offer the player, rather than the worker, as the figure of social agency that might be able to braid together various strands of the future, currently tangled and badly arranged.

My last proper chapter has been, over the last three years of writing this book, thoroughly transformed by historical events. Spirituality and play are both attempts to create experiences of transcendence in the midst of our everyday lives. So I began my research by trying to imagine what kind of spiritual resources would serve a play ethic (given that Max Weber's original analysis of the work ethic was actually titled 'the Protestant ethic'). Should it be a New Age play ethic? A holistic play ethic? I was aware that in many non-Christian religions there was an explicitly ludic element – the Buddhist vision of Indra's Net, or the great god-games of Hindu mythology, or the poetry of the Sufis, all of which I explore in **Chapter ten.** Even within Christianity, I knew there was a Gnostic tradition – a belief that divinity was incarnate, a presence in the actions of creative humans – which could rehabilitate Calvin and Knox and their filth-drenched view of human potential.

Yet when twelve Islamic terrorists crashed two passenger planes into the Twin Towers of the World Trade Center in New York, 11 September 2001, I was launched into a private struggle about the ultimate ethics of play, which has marked the progress of my writing ever since. I could easily have decided to defend play against intolerance and iconoclasm – the freedom of the Western postmodern imagination to connect any sign to any other sign, to turn meanings and traditions inside out on a whim (and certainly not a prayer): Britney versus the fatwahs, MTV over the mullahs.

But what I chose to consider, in a very substantial sense, was the profound diversity of my rhetorics of play. Is communal play – the rites and rituals that confirm membership of a culture, tribe or community – a way into understanding why non-Western traditions like Islam might be enraged by the semiotic frenzy of Western consumer culture? Is cosmic play – the deep webs of existence posited by the Asian traditions of Buddhism and Hinduism – a kind of necessary corrective to the egoism of the modern Western player? Might the variety of play rhetorics available to a northern liberal – the ethical chord chart from which they performed their lives – need to be constrained, or at least weighted, in a global context of multiple truths and value systems? Might some forms of play, in a world of potentially clashing civilizations, be more ethical than others?

These are frontier issues on the horizon of what has come to be known as 'globalization', and the struggle to make it a benign and creative, rather than a malign and destructive process. And there is one thing that a richer understanding of play in cultures can bring to the struggle: that is, an appreciation of the diversity of consciousnesses that human beings can generate amongst themselves. In *Song of Myself*, the great American bard Walt Whitman once asserted his right to mental pluralism: 'Do I contradict myself? Very well then I contradict myself, (I am large, I contain multitudes).' How could anyone justifiably impose one exclusive system of power and money on a planet peopled by such capacious souls? When the anti-corporate protesters argue for their 'one no, and a million yesses', they are asserting the right of global humans to imagine their futures as a multitude of strategies and scenarios. Without that diversity, humanity's ability to think its way out of the tight corners that its own ingenuity generates will be badly constrained. And play is surely one of the universal resources for our human diversity of consciousness.

We should always remember that, for we advanced mammals, the play moment begins in a tension between experiment and safety – the need to fully test out all the possibilities of being human, yet under conditions which are themselves not fatal, violent or beset with privation and pain. Is it too idealistic to imagine an extended 'play moment' for our planet – where global sustainability and global creativity sustain and reinforce each other in a peaceful yet energetic spiral? If it is idealistic, then guilty as charged. Players are literally nothing if not congenital optimists.

Is there a particular way in which you should read this book? Well, I know how *I* read books. I hit the index for favourite concepts, names, themes; I stick in a thumb anywhere and see how far the prose will take me; I read the conclusion first, the introduction last; I fold corners, annotate indelibly. (I've even ripped chapters out when a photocopier's been too inaccessible.) I suppose my preference would be if people read the theory chapter first, and then journeyed all over the rest of the book with some kind of conceptual compass to guide them. Please don't ignore the footnotes: there's a lot of scholarship and research there which will lead you off in many fascinating ludic directions. For anyone who wants to know more directly about me, **Chapter one** tells a brief story about my own life as a player (fragments of biography are scattered throughout the book). For anyone who wants to dig deeper, the Play Ethic website (www.theplayethic.com) has comprehensive supporting material; links to most of the sources and annotations in the text; and a regular play journal updating these themes of the book to current events. It'll be great to see you there.

But this is yours to play with now: I hope you find it . . . engaging. As the Danes say: *lego*. Play well.

NEXT MOVE:

The Birth of a Player

Playing my self

The first player that I consciously knew was the son of my 'nana' (the tough and snippy woman who looked after us while my midwife mother was out on the district). Bill Devlin was the first person in my immediate world who was clearly not a 'worker', yet who seemed to have purpose and status in our community by virtue of what he did.

Bill was a professional dancer. Nana's shelf was crowded with pictures of him, inscrutable in black wraparounds and goatee, posing with some showgirl or minor seventies' celebrity at his regular gig, the ring-a-ding London club The Talk of the Town. Another picture showed him in shorts and flip-flops, wraparounds still on, looking casual on a jetty in the South of France: at the other side of the shot, clearly looking to make a quick exit, was a lean and improbably attractive Prince Charles. And whenever *Fiddler on the Roof* came on the TV, we were all enjoined to 'keep our eyes on the Cossack dancers'. Somewhere in the routine, clad in boots and furry hat, Uncle Bill (undoubtedly with goatee, though probably without shades) was high kicking furiously. Of course we all pretended we saw him, and cursed the end credits for scrolling too quickly, missing his name every time.

We all knew that Bill had 'another life' in London – the lurid and excessive tales of his experiences there occasionally made their way back to my nana's low-roofed council house in Coatbridge. That life once stretched one of its tendrils around my father. While on a railway association trip to London, my dad hit the town with Bill. Dad ended up in a Soho dive, absolutely transfixed by the most beautiful woman he'd ever seen. He used to deliver the punchline with relish: 'And just as I was beginning to worry about myself, Bill came up to me and said, "Look again, John. She may be even more amazing than you think." I did – and, b'Christ she was a man! Jesus, you couldn't get me out of there quickly enough!' I never noticed any brittleness in the laughter that this story generated – no shifty eyelines betraying some ghastly misdemeanour. So I just let it sink in: another aberrant stitch in the family tapestry, but nothing that would unravel anything else. (Another flash: my father chuckling long and loud about a famous Scottish female impersonator, Stanley Baxter, and how he had 'the best women's legs on television'.) Yet it's that openness to 'another life' – literally, being open to a degree of otherness or difference, without it threatening your own integrity – that I remember vividly from my past. Not just the predictable machineries of class and religion that made everyone react like Buckaroo toys, destructively kicking out when the load got too heavy. That happened, too. But it's not the whole story.

So I knew very early that Bill Devlin might well have begun on the same tracks as I was travelling, but had somehow jumped the rail and steered his carriage onto the open road. If he didn't work, but made money and was clearly respected, then what was he? He was an artist and a performer. He seemed to make a life out of playing around. That seemed like a life for me.

The first and last time I met Bill Devlin, he was dying. The disease was obscurely systemic ('He's just shutting down,' I was told). We all trouped down, on an endless Glasgow to Euston train journey. I was taken to his bedside, and found there a wheezing, semi-conscious cadaver in a grey-painted room. (Was this how all dancers ended up, I thought. Was this their fate?) As I sat at his side, trying to be as gloomy as everyone else, but in reality quivering with curiosity, Uncle Bill's eyes suddenly widened. His hand fluttered out, and rested on mine like a leaf. The grip was negligible, the faintest possible pressure: but his stare was powerful, pupil-less, desperate. After what seemed like an age, his fingers slipped off, and his tumerous face clouded over again. The room, full of relatives and friends, quietly erupted: that was progress, maybe he's coming out of it, well done, son. But to this day, that grasp and stare has felt to me like a deep recognition of some kind; like a transfer of something.

His death came only a few weeks later, and again we took that interminable journey down to attend the funeral. I remember nothing but the wake in Uncle Bill's Barbican flat: scuttling around adult legs, stuffing down chipolatas, a child liberated from the gloom. But at one point someone stopped me and handed me a pile of records. 'You love music, son,' said the looming relative. 'Take these home with you.' In the middle of a pile of showbizzy covers was a record by a man called Bobby Darin. The cover photo showed him to be smooth of cheek, impossibly slick-haired, and, I couldn't deny it, a bit like me. When I got home to Coatbridge and put it on, I immediately registered the utter swing of the music and the drawled confidence of the singer. Darin was like my father's anointed Sinatra, but with a measure of extra grittiness and cheekiness. That record remains one of my essential CDs and I take it along with me whenever I go away. Darin was the first elective thumbprint in my singer's clay, the man I chose to sing like.

But it was Bill Devlin's record; his taste had commingled with mine. The gift that his weak fingers and bottomless stare passed to me became a tangible, useful thing. I can't forget him, nor can I underestimate the moment, nor can I forget the curiosity that started there, and never stopped. How could Bill's kind of life commence from the cramped, grey space of my nana's council house? How could you get from here – Coatbridge-here, worker's-here – to anywhere you wanted?

Playing my class

'One singer, one song.' The phrase would rise from some dangerously smoky corner of the room, uttered by heavy uncles with glassy glints in their eyes. 'On ye go, wee man. One singer, one song.' And if it was myself who had been dragged and prodded on to the shagpile rug – actually eager for the call from my father, monitoring the party as it hit its rowdy peak, expecting his cry to sail upstairs at any minute – I would shut my eyes, hum a little melody to make sure there was nothing straining and launch into my best Frank, my finest Tony. To becalm my Uncles Desmond, Gerry and Phelm for any period of time – let alone the all-night landslide that was my gran's Hogmanay party – was no small achievement. So I knew I deserved their rebel yells and rib-bending hugs at the end of 'I Left My Heart in San Francisco'.

But the point was, no matter how good you thought you were, you had to hang around for the rest. One singer, one song: wherever the tradition comes from – the rituals of folk meet the cabaret of Tin Pan Alley – it had one iron rule: in short, that everyone had their 'turn', their party piece; and that everyone was compelled not only to perform it, but also to appreciate everyone else's turn. 'Best of order,' an uncle would slur menacingly:

and whether it was 'Solitaire', or 'The Mountains of Mourne', or 'Tiger Feet', the performance would meet a strictly policed silence.

My parents' turns were both exhilarating and surreal. Dad did his perfect melismas, uncoiled his vibrato and surfed the high Cs through the Sinatra canon; Mum seized any lull in the proceedings to perform her recitation of 'Little Rosa', an exercise her elocution teacher taught her many years ago. It was full of corn and sentiment, and enunciated with the most outrageous cod Italianisms – so out-and-out theatrical that a stunned silence was always guaranteed.

From the particular corner of the post-industrial west of Scotland I come from, we have a synonym for the idea of 'playing around with': footer. To footer around with something would be to toy idly with it, take your time over it, turn it upside down and inside out before you'd let it go.

Our family was always footering around with the categories of class and culture. Probably the most passionate debate – particularly as I began to put my life and background in the perspective of books and other students' lives – was whether we were working class or not. 'Well, we work, don't we?' was my father's brusque reply. But, as a pimply young Marxist, I would be adamant. 'Come on, Dad! We live in a bought house. You're white collar, nearly a manager now. Mum loves opera and you've got a rack of *Encyclopaedia Britannica*s against that wall. All you wanted your three sons to be was three lawyers. Now that's middle class, surely . . .'

We were always trying to juggle our passion for roots with our passion for routes. In many ways, we were as sociologically determined as could be. My parents were both from Irish immigrant stock, second generation, born in the cauldron of religious intolerance that was Lanarkshire. John and Mary Kane (née Brady) were aspirant Catholics in good public sector jobs (my mother a midwife, my father a wages clerk in British Rail). They worked furiously to hang onto their bought terrace house, the first Catholics to live in this primly Presbyterian neighbourhood. So in some way, our domestic culture was very over-determined: automatic Labour voters; fearful of Protestants ('She's as Orange as sin,' my mother would say); parents oppressively determined to see their boys put some clear water between themselves and the false stereotypes of their community. You might have expected our mood to be one of grim seriousness, involving the constant monitoring of behaviour and disportment; the rigorous self-discipline of the minority group in the face of a hostile present, but a hopeful future. If a work ethic would take grip in any domestic soil, you'd expect it to have done so in the Kane household.

Wrong, wrong, wrong.

For one thing, and something I didn't realize until the old man retired, my father almost entirely despised his job: he was almost exultant when a mainframe computer automated his clerking job out of existence. Most of his domestic dreaming was done before the television or the record player. Sport, music and comedy were his great and abiding loves, which he avidly communicated to his boys. He'd tell us, as the Sunday afternoon transmission of *An American in Paris* hummed away on the Baird for the umpteenth time, that he'd always wanted to be a dancer like Gene Kelly. 'Can you imagine the son of a miner's family being able to dance like that?' Whenever there was a family wedding, I would observe with a combination of embarrassment and pride my parents' performance on the dance floor, noting their well-oiled movements, the sharp click of both their heels. That looked like one cool way to be an adult.

My father always had a secret romance going on with his own physicality – even as his working life was taken up with wage ledgers, bolshy shop stewards, all the tedious strategizing of middle management. He was an excellent football player: the school team guys would always tell me that when they saw him in kickabout, wondering aloud why he hadn't 'passed it on to you'. For a west of Scotland white male, football can become more than just another leisure diversion. There can be so much longing involved – for community pride, for male heroism, for some temporary victory amidst the banality of working life – that it seems if not more important than life or death, then at least a credible raison d'être. I've only occasionally made that level of passionate investment in the game. Scotland stumbling out of the World Cup in 1978 still opens up a minor chasm inside me, and even now, in my thoroughly enlightened state, I can mildly exult when my tribe's team (Celtic Football Club) seems to be definitively pulling away from its rivals. Patriarchy, such as it is these days, clings onto its protected media; and when the moment comes for men to talk among themselves, unleavened by the presence of women, I know I can just about keep up with the inevitable footy discourse.

But in recent years, I've tried to admit (at least to myself) what most men rather shamefully suppress: that football is a celebration of male beauty, of our ability to joyously play. We're all aesthetes, appreciating a physical and emotional drama. The brilliant Bill Shankly put it best when he called football 'working-class ballet'. And the parallel can be reasonably drawn: the costumed specimens leaping and running across their grassy stage, expressing themselves within choreographies (or 'team tactics').

Could I play? Oh, I tried and tried, but only a little. Balls refused to be trapped properly, or they'd curve their way accurately towards another waiting foot, or fall fortuitously to mine. Yet I remember my few best passes, one save as a goalie, and a chipped goal for the school team, as some of the most intensely gratifying moments of my life – when intention, skill and body all aligned themselves in the flow of a single movement.

The working class is also the playing class – and has always been so.

Playing my dues

How did I become a musician? I seem to remember it as the only way to play with my father – listening to him sing, listening to his records, then trying to touch him with my voice: a voice undoubtedly composed from those inputs. He was at that time a harsh, impatient, vaguely angry man, dismissive of his being a parent ('All I wanted was three goldfish'). But when we sang, or I sang for him, I got to him and melted him a little. So when I sing, it's like Winnicott's version of play – a resolution of tensions, a sublimation of deeper injuries, a fantasy of mastery.

But that voice – itself an ideal version of the father's authority, and attempting to source its power in other musical patriarchs like Stevie Wonder and Frank Sinatra – has taken me to places that I never expected to go. True, at twenty-one I was perfectly set up for the world of work: a good degree, a vocational ambition and the fair wind of parental approval. My place was booked on a teacher training course at the University of London. Then those tinny songs that I'd been writing with my brother Gregory gained us a publishing deal. I gave us a name – some dualistic phrase picked out from a scan through the dictionary: 'Hue and Cry' – and within a year we were recording in New York, video making in Los Angeles and having hit singles on *Top of the Pops*. All this just for trying to project a virtual image of yourself, in body, voice and words, that reconciled the difference between father and freedom, between authority and selfhood. And to get money for it! How unalienated could a labour be?

When those strange wheels of fortune that drive the pop business started to turn for me – tipping me into a world of stylists, video makers, sniffing producers and wildly libidinal PR girls – I was surprised to find myself hanging onto a kind of puritanism, even in the midst of bacchanal. I distrusted spontaneity, regarding every move as choreography, or mask-play. I had a fetish for planning and its execution: there was no liner note unworthy of the closest attention. I was fastidious about the necessary excesses of the music biz: it was years later that I found out just how many spectacularly smoking wrecks had been left in our wake. Only when the stage or the studio mike beckoned did I allow myself to enter that state of flow and absorption that the true player feels.

Should I just have enjoyed the ride? Journeyed through the seventy-two-hour days, the pharmaceutical landscapes, the inconsequential sex, the luxury without consequence? Perhaps. But there was something about the rock 'n' roll lifestyle – that heedless pursuit of pleasure and experience – that seemed just as oppressive, just as much of a compulsory regime, as the classroom of disgruntled faces on a December morning would have been. Between 'getting out of your head' and 'keeping your head down' there had to be a different way in which you could free your mind; a richer kind of autonomy; an option beyond Eros or Apollo, sheer hedonism and sheer conformity.

For five tumultuous years, with my brother Gregory, I struggled with these polarities, while trying to write tuneful pop songs that justified the record advances. Even as the free booze was being demolished and the tour buses were hammering down arterial roads, I was musing over abstruse points of social theory. I had been in a pop band for six years by then; and Charlie Watts's famous axiom – that a rock 'n' roll career was 'five years of playing and twenty years of hanging around' – had proved true. The lifestyle meant that there was a lot of time (after the minimum duties of hedonism had been fulfilled) for serious contemplation. So I carried my utopian tracts around with me like copies of the Gideon Bible: Andre Gorz's *Farewell to the Working Class*, Theodor Adorno's *Minima Moralia*, Greil Marcus's *Lipstick Traces*. And I thumbed them furiously whenever any air from the real world (first Gulf War, fourth Tory term) entered our bubble.

Then all the air came in at once. Our manager quietly imploded and disappeared, resurfacing years later as a psychology post-grad, PhD-ing his way to a professorship. Our various record companies either dropped us or folded, our debts started to bite our ankles, our musical energies seemed to seep into the ground. Pop-jazz aesthetics were fine and noble, but they weren't holding up my end of the household budget. The dreams were getting trashed by the numbers, and something had to give.

So it was that I found myself in the bourgeois-bohemian end of Glasgow, on a cold-tea morning in mid-1993, perched in front of a wry BBC Radio Scotland talk-show producer, pitching for broadcasting scraps. The pop star – been on *Top of the Pops* five times; shared a backstage soup tureen with Madonna; knew Columbus Circle like a native New Yorker – had to learn to become a freelancer. That is, to turn up on a dreich Monday morning, say hello to the same disgruntled faces, achieve a whole lot of tiny things for not that much recognition and fight the Great Wars of the Corridor. Thus began my eight-year journey into the work ethic, pursued through a string of media corporations (BBC, Channel 4, Microsoft and latterly Scottish Media Group). It was a long, fascinating, frustrating trip – some flashbacks of which appear throughout this book.

Yet a few months after my thirty-sixth birthday, having helped to found a successful Sunday newspaper in Scotland and looking at a properly professional career path for the first time, I walked out of the office door. Much of the force behind my decision came from a little scrap of musicians' banter – a casual exchange that had been sifting through my mind for years, gathering strength and resilience. The more I thought about it, the more it seemed like a way to integrate all the disparate parts of myself – and also to answer some considerable questions about the world I was in, and the world I wanted to be in.

Playing ethically

So all this began, appropriately enough, as a play on words.

In an airless room in west London, somewhere on the curved rim of the early nineties, myself and a few other musicians were nailing down a groove: gig tomorrow, slight panic, last chance to get it right. We'd arrived at that warm, delicious time in a rehearsal when everyone's separate inspirations – from bass, electric piano, voice, drums, tenor sax – are slowly fusing together. The bare bones of a song getting some muscle, skin, a countenance.

And we could see it; we knew. The same verse and chorus had been

cycling through us for four hours now, looping round and eventually settling down, anchored deep enough for us to start letting the details matter, fine-graining it all. We agreed it was funky, smart, on the money: all
those short, sharp words that musicians use when they can barely contain
their joy.

The drummer let out a huge Welsh sigh, shook a spectacular spray of
sweat from his head and thwacked his drumsticks down on the snare.

'Don't let any fucker tell *me* I don't have a work ethic.'

He glared at the lead singer cartoonishly. I glared back. Ianto was a guy
who could make his kit rhyme like Dylan Thomas, and here he was coming on like a clock-watching journeyman. But I was paying him union scale,
and we had just shared some transcendent moments – and those are two
incommensurables, pure money and pure art, which can only ever orbit
each other, never really touch. I had only a few seconds to defuse this
social bomb, however gently and daft-laddishly delivered. I did my best.

'Ianto, you don't have a work ethic.' A beat, to allow his brows to
gather. 'You have a *play* ethic. You're a player, not a worker. You're a
bohemian, sir.' He grinned through his skunkweed smoke, an improvisor
enjoying this improvisation. I could see him filing it away to be brought
out for the next airless room, and its own crucial, fusing moment. 'That's
exactly what I've got, Mr Kane. But sincerely, I am completely fucked. Shall
we go and kiss some Jack?'

Mr Daniels was indeed embraced that evening; my fuzzy remembrance
is that the gig went well. But for months afterwards, I tossed those words
around in my head, rubbing the phrase like a pebble, trying to smooth out
the nicks and bumps on its surface. *The play ethic*. It came from banter,
the phatic burble of musos trying to get through a session. But it seemed
to resonate and connote like crazy – not just among my own community
of musicians, but also in the world beyond. In the midst of the inherent
confusion of my pop life, I felt I'd stumbled upon something much bigger.

My musings developed into the following hazy thesis, inflicted on hap-
less passing musicians for months afterwards: we all know what the work
ethic is (and a roomful of dissolute jazzers, fleeing from jobs, the state
and even daylight, into the mystery of their fingertips, will know most
acutely of all). But could a 'play ethic' ever become an equally powerful
social phenomenon? What would it mean to live your life in the modern
world – to be active and purposeful with politics and technology and
money – if you believed that play was more important to human beings
than work? That the values of playing (improvisation, fantasy, abundance)

were more integral, more ennobling – more ethical, in short – than the values of working (routine, self-denial, propriety)? Could a play ethic ever shape the mainstream of a society, rather than just caper at its margins?

My fellow musos liked the idea, but couldn't get that excited: 'I'm doing this to get away from the nine-to-fivers,' said one gently stoned tenor player. 'Why should I be bothering about whether they're getting inspired or not? As long as they leave me alone . . .' In my media years, there was a slightly more active interest. Ludic ideas weren't edited out of columns; water-cooler conversations about a more playful workplace weren't immediately closed down by managerial overlords.[1]

But when a big idea resonates with your life energies in this way, answering major private and public questions – Am I a player? Could others be players? Could it be good and generative to do what we do, rather than trivial and disregarded? – you have to make the next move, definitively and decisively. So, armed with an Internet domain name, a book deal, an adult life's worth of clippings, books and Web links, and a downshifted lifestyle, I went in search of the play ethic. What I found was, literally, a new way of looking at the world: a quantum shift in my perspective, which I'll probably be reckoning with for the rest of my life. If I've been able to turn this into a few useful tools to help enable twenty-first-century women, children and men to cope with the complexity of their lives, then the moves will have been worth making.

A GENERAL THEORY OF PLAY

'I play with my mind, my imagination – it helps me joyfully create something'
Imaginative play

'I play against others – it's a test and measure of myself'
Power play

'I play whatever I feel like doing – it confirms my freedom and autonomy'
Individual play

'I play together with others – it confirms my identity'
Social play

PLAYER
I'm engaged
I'm creative
I'm active

'I play with my body and mind – it builds strength and knowledge'
Healthy play

'I play around, for laughs or lust – it keeps all things in perspective'
Trivial play

'I play with future possiblilities – it makes me ready for the unexpected'
Cosmic play

I will not return to a universe
of objects that don't know each other,
as if islands were not the lost children
of one great continent. The world
is flux, and light becomes what it touches.
– Lisel Mueller, 'Monet Refuses The Operation', 1986

[Science] is a bricolage of experimentation . . . initial playful
activity is an essential prerequisite of the final act of
understanding . . . new scientific practice needs time to
develop its conceptual tools and its empirical data by
playing with them, that is, by constantly repeating and
combining them until they become common usage or reality.
– Paul Feyerabend, *Conquest of Abundance*, 1999

The aeon is a child at play.
– Heraclitus, 52nd fragment, 5th century BC

Let's play a mind game. Imagine an intellectual history in which play was taken as seriously as work. A history where the heavy, corrosive rain of the puritan mindset has long dispersed, leaving only a few shallow puddles and the occasional musty smell. What would such a landscape look like?

Thinking seriously about play opens out at least as broad a vista of knowledge as thinking seriously about work. The theory and practice of play – from Plato to Playstation 2, from Schiller to the situationists, from *The Decameron* to complexity theory – provide just as comprehensive an understanding of the human condition as the intellectual legacies of work have done.

But when you abandon the road map of industrial society, it's initially hard to recognize this new terrain. Even as a thought experiment, to imagine a world beyond the work ethic is to reveal all the inadequacies of our existing understanding of play. What we perceive as play has several different forms, each of which makes a strong claim to define exactly what play is, and can be. Brian Sutton-Smith describes these forms as 'rhetorics' – i.e. ways of thinking and talking about play that express a certain vision of human nature and culture, and which can be deployed by everyone from teachers to generals, hackers to CEOs.[1] By looking closely at these rhetorics we see that different kinds of play imply both a very modern and a very ancient vision of humanity:

> **The modern vision** sees players as the ultimate embodiment of human freedom. They move through the world with imagination, passion and confidence. Players are constantly dreaming of new possibilities, in the midst of constraint and routine, and they have the energy to make some of them, at least, a reality.

> **The ancient vision** sees players as determined by forces largely beyond their control. They are caught up in games of chance and contest, which they must respond to as best they can. They must play their part in collective rituals and festivities. And they must play simply for the sake of playing – whether they be shamans, fools or tricksters.

So on one side, play is a charter for the rampant egotist; on the other, an excuse for sanguine fatalists. The player is either forging the world anew, or grappling with its eternal flux and pervasive systems. How can one style of living encompass both these extremes?

To be a player is to try and live and thrive between freedom and determinism, chance and necessity. It is this seeming paradox that the player needs to embrace. It is pointless to ignore a rhetoric of play, or to promote one set of rhetorics above another, for the sake of an easier intellectual life. That's what the work ethic attempted to do for two and a half centuries, pigeonholing play as 'trivial', 'frivolous', 'silly'. Once properly investigated, there's no going back to a simple definition of play.[2]

But in terms of the stated ambition of this book, an immediate question arises. How could any ethic – a theory or system of moral values – be derived from something as mercurial and contradictory as play? Just how *do* we arrive at a play ethic?

Part of the initial answer to this question lies in a new synthesis between social and natural science. The best ethics ground their claims in an authoritative vision of what is natural about the world and ourselves: like any other ethic, the play ethic is at heart an argument about human nature. And so, for the play ethic to succeed, people will have to know that it goes with the grain of their humanity, and the social and material universe, rather than against it.

Much of the research that goes under the name of the 'third culture' – that community of scholars who disregard the divisions between 'art' and 'science' – substantiates a vision of a universe amenable to play. In many different areas of study, the same conclusions are being drawn: that play is a deep, natural and lasting resource for modern humans.[3] In a whole range of cutting-edge new sciences (from complexity studies to game theory, from mind science to network analysis) the moment of play is identified as a generator of originality, energy and new development. Wherever play is present, there are possibilities: whether in the protons that 'play dice' in quantum physics, or the irrepressible behaviours of higher mammals, or the unexpected changes of modern society. Within our existing conditions of nature and culture, technology and society, play represents the permanent potential for innovation and progress.

So the play ethic – a way of living with both the ancient and modern extremes of play, underpinned by a new scientific consensus on human nature – begins to take shape. It is a world composed of surprises and emergences, risk and enterprise, chance and imagination; a world receptive to our passionate intentions, but demanding in its own right, requiring an evolution of our characters and responses.

The core statements of the play ethic then becomes clear. **Players need to be energetic, imaginative and confident in the face of an unpredictable, contestive, emergent world. Players also accept the complex relationship between all forms of play whether ancient or modern.**

To justify these claims, we first need to fully assess the beautiful yet twisted structures of our existing rhetorics of play. Once these are fully comprehended, we can use science to construct something from their ambiguity: a general theory of play.

Play as progress

It may be the staple backing track in every karaoke machine in the world, but 'The Greatest Love of All' (immortalized by the melismatic soul singer Whitney Houston) gets the play as progress rhetoric down perfectly:

> *I believe the children are our future*
> *Teach them well and let them lead the way.*[4]

The child as resource and hope, childhood as both pupil and teacher: this is the way in which modern play presents its most virtuous face. In the context of children as bearers of 'the future', the front-line troops of social progress, play becomes useful and functional. Of course child's play comes before all its uses and metaphors: the child simply must play; at that stage they have no other option.[5]

The science is clear on this: play is good for all young, warm-blooded organisms. The consensus from biologists and psychologists, derived from over a century of observing animal and human play, is that play is a necessity, not a luxury, for advanced mammals. It is the way we test out our strategies for survival and reproduction at an early and crucial stage, in an environment relatively free from risk. By helping to make us capable organisms, play therefore ensures the progress of ourselves, our society and our species.[6]

Yet science only furthers a much earlier consideration of play, which emerged out of the intellectual revolutions of the later Renaissance and the early Enlightenment. Play could only begin to be taken seriously in the West when childhood began to be taken seriously. Most modern historians of childhood identify a series of changes, starting with the aristocracy and urban elites of the late sixteenth century, when children became visible as children – rather than as coddled adults or labourers in waiting – for the first time since classical Greece.[7]

The basic premise of the European Enlightenment – its belief that societies could advance, and that rational humans were the agents of that progress – found its ideal proof in childhood. The child's unquenchable optimism and energy embodied the hope that human society could be bettered. And play, in all its irrepressible variety of forms, was the obvious expression of the child's potential for progress.

The first recognizably modern argument for the powers of childhood play was Jean-Jacques Rousseau's *Emile* (1759). Rousseau had faith in the original goodness of human nature, at least before it met the deformations of society. *Emile* was directed specifically against the notion that the child was born with an inherently malevolent nature: an 'original sinfulness' which only punitive parenting could cure. Rousseau argued that, like the 'noble savage', the child occupied its own distinct world, whose fragilities and strengths had to be respected in their own right: a realm qualitatively separate from adulthood.

Accordingly Rousseau defended the play of children against the 'hoops of society'. The ideal child would 'run about barefoot all year round, upstairs, downstairs, and in the garden . . . [learning] to perform every exercise which encourages ability of the body'. Addressing a child of ten or twelve, he wrote, 'work or play are all one' – as long as they are both carried out with 'the charm of freedom'.[8]

Many other joyous, exuberant children ran barefoot through the imagery of the Romantic poets of England and Germany, particularly in the poems of Goethe and Wordsworth, Blake and Shelley. The child at play, freewheeling and natural, was one of the touchstones of romanticism's critique of the Industrial Revolution. Rousseau's *enfant sauvage* was held aloft as a pure essence of humanity, a precious moment of innocence and spontaneity, against which the depredations of the steam engine and the spinning jenny could be measured.[9]

But the ideal child of romanticism met the brutal reality of child labour and exploitation in the early nineteenth century. With this in mind, education was obviously the best means to narrow the gap between the Romanticists' ideal child and the harsh reality of nineteenth-century industrial childhood. Yet the early systems of mass education, aimed at making the proletariat literate, were stamped, in the language of Charles Dickens, by 'Gradgrindery' – the brutal imposing of facts and figures by authoritarian teachers on their pupils. Factory schools, producing factory minds.

A few educators, inspired by Rousseau and the idealist traditions of European Enlightenment, tried to create schools that could harness the playful passions of the child – who might themselves go on to build a better, less deforming society. The most play-oriented of these was the German Frederick Froebel, for whom child's play had an almost spiritual force. Inspired by the world of Johann Pestalozzi, a dedicated Rousseauvian who worked with disadvantaged children, Froebel wanted to add some philosophical sinew to Pestalozzi's 'loving' teaching. His first 'kindergarten' was opened in 1837 as a play-space where children 'could blossom like flowers'. Despite his persecution by the German government, Froebel's kindergartens spread all over Europe and America. The blossoming was encouraged partly through giving children paints, clay and all manner of malleable materials – what Froebel called 'play gifts' – so they could externalize concepts in their minds, rather than have 'the facts' imprinted on their brains.[10]

These educators amongst others – most notably the Rome-based slum teacher Maria Montessori – were the guiding lights for what came to be known as the 'progressive' tradition in education, which came to dominate primary- and grade-school teaching on both sides of the Atlantic in the last thirty years of the twentieth century. And 'progress', then as now, is measured by how much the playfulness and creativity of the child – their natural urge to explore and hypothesize, compare and dramatize – is both respected and utilized by educators.[11]

Education makes play functional, a key to healthy development, and thus an excuse for reform. For the Victorians, the provision of 'rational recreation' – another phrase for healthy play – became an obsession. Public parks, swimming pools and sports halls were all liberally provided by the new urban authorities in order to maintain the health (and doubtless the efficiency) of the working classes. In this moment, play first took on the character of a 'physical education', still featuring in modern curricula.[12]

Yet, while this period might be considered as the heyday of 'play as progress', the persistence of the progress rhetoric has hardly lessened. Of course, play is also an explicit theme of our hyper-consumerist society – the word is usually an indication of all kinds of excesses and hedonisms in popular culture.[13] Yet we still hold onto healthy play as a possibility. The crucial question is: where and when does it happen?

Since the middle of the nineteenth century, the invigorating powers of our playful nature have gradually extended their reach: they've become not just good for the progress of animals and children, but good for the progress of adults too. In psychology, the great struggle has been to overturn the dominance of the psychologist Jean Piaget – a stern, Genevan Calvinist who regarded child play as a necessary but primitive stage of development, literally a childish thing to be put behind us.[14] Yet a whole range of psychologists have begun to observe play as a constant possibility in our lives, something that can benefit us at any stage of adulthood.[15]

This research breaks regularly out of the labs and into the heartland of news and opinion. The July/August 1999 cover feature of the popular US magazine *Psychology Today*, for example, was 'The power of play: make it work for you!' The list of advantages that play brings for humans, children and adults is extensive. Play makes you live longer. Play helps women select a trustworthy mate (men who are playful, or who can play with children, are less likely to be rapists or murderers). Play for adults improves their memory; it can even make them happier, more elated. As Sutton-Smith says in the piece, 'The opposite of play isn't work. It's depression.'[16]

A cover feature in *Time* magazine in April 2001 reiterates most of the same points, but acknowledges that many parents still fear that play is a distraction from their child's progress – rather than being its precondition. Yet an article in *New Scientist*, based on the very latest techniques in brain imaging, suggested the opposite. The piece argued that early play in children and animals is less about practising to fight and mate (the pure imperatives of survival), and much more about improving brain power at a crucially formative moment. For many primates, the very act of playing seems to strengthen and extend the number of neural connections in the brain. To quote the evocative words of neuropsychologist Stephen Siviy, when observing brain chemistry under experimental conditions, 'play just lights everything up'.[17]

So the philosophy, psychology and biology that support play as progress are a powerful anchor for our dreams of human potential. Our childhoods are where the human motor gets assembled; and we adults can keep ourselves in peak performance if we are able to take ourselves apart, through play, and reassemble our selves in a more dynamic way.

Play as progress is the way we reinvoke the brimming energies of child-hood – the better to face the thrills, spills and challenges of the adult world.[18]

Play as imagination

Every child is an artist. The problem is how to remain an artist once he grows up. – Pablo Picasso

Modern play isn't simply about properly aligning our psychology with our biology – through better education, appropriate therapy or some other social conditioning. Sometimes play becomes a tangible process that escapes functionality and utility, literally 'transforming' human experience, casting it in new shapes and styles. This is the artist's vision of play as imaginary – the idea that art, literature, music, images, computer code, every kind of human symbolizing, is driven at its core by the values of play. Nowhere was this more prevalent than in the Romantic period.[19]

As many historians have commented, the imagination became an intel-lectual obsession in the late eighteenth and nineteenth centuries. Imagi-nation replaced the Christian 'soul' – a soul that had first been punctured by the secular rationalisms of the Enlightenment, and then shredded by the alienations of industrial society – as the guarantee of meaning in life. But more than this, it cemented the links between play and imagination.

While the power of the imagination was influencing art, literature and thought, it was also extending its reach to ethics and politics – and so, therefore, did play. When Percy Bysshe Shelley wrote that 'the great instru-ment of moral good is the imagination' (In Defence of Poetry), he was pro-moting art as our means of enlarging human sympathy, the medium which allows us to identify with 'the pains and pleasures of our species'. And when Schiller coined his timeless play aphorism – 'Man only plays when in the full meaning of the word he is a man, and he is only completely a man when he plays' – he was defining play, like Shelley's imagination, as something that could unify the divided selves of early modern society. Schiller was addressing all those for whom the word 'reason' implied the destructive science of industry, and 'sensuality' meant a numbing escapism and self-indulgence. Play, like imagination, could mend the broken soul.[20]

The lasting legacy of the Romantic period, as regards play, is twofold. Firstly, the emphasis on imagination allowed a playfulness with language and symbols, perhaps best expressed by William Wordsworth:

> Oft on the dappled turf at ease
> I sit and play with similes
> Loose type of things through all degrees

What also survives is the notion of 'the play of the imagination' as an act of creative sympathy, or as Robert Burns put it:

> O wad some power the giftie gie us
> Tae see oursels as ithers see us![21]

All the way through the modernisms of the late nineteenth and early twentieth centuries, this double meaning of imagination – as both 'just a play', and a 'just play', an act of sympathy and an act of symbolizing – animated its major artists.[22] André Breton wrote in his *Manifesto of Surrealism* that 'Imagination alone offers me some intimation of what can be.' His fellow surrealist Luis Buñuel concurred: 'Somewhere between chance and mystery lies the imagination, the only thing that protects our freedom.'[23]

Surrealism remains such an influential tradition in contemporary art and media because of its inherently playful imaginative vision. In the pathway between the conscious and the unconscious, all manner of behaviours and forms could slip out, behind the sleep of reason. From Duchamp's urinal to Isodore Isou's automatic poetry, from Magritte's visual inversions to Breton's dramatic pranksterism, the surrealists created a variety of play forms which still fuel most of contemporary art and advertising.[24]

So there is already a fascinating (and productive) tension here between the first two rhetorics of modern play. The rhetoric of play as progress encourages us to regard ourselves as being hard-wired for playful creativity, only awaiting the right education and conditioning to flower and blossom. But this does not mean imaginative play automatically follows from progressive play. Indeed, if it's done correctly, the first should subvert and overreach the second. Play as progress is always tainted by its functionalism, its tendency to put play at the service of social stability.

The 'full play' of the imagination, at the beginning of this new century, has become a huge topic for businesses, policy makers and consumers, as well as the artistic community. How much 'imagination' should the managers of large organizations, for example, allow their staff to exercise, at their own level? Can too much initiative, exercised by too many people, turn an ordered business strategy into chaos?[25] How much 'imagination' can educators allow into the teaching process – when the curriculum is geared towards a competitive jobs market and is based on test results rather than an open-ended journey towards understanding?[26] How much 'imagination' will consumers exercise (or be allowed to exercise) with their rapidly expanding range of interactive technologies – from the Web to digital broadcast, from game consoles to wireless communicators of all kinds? What is the tension between 'just imagining' – the passive reception of pre-packaged material, pumped out by media conglomerates; and 'a just imagining' – sharing material with peers, creating new material with dissenting views, 'hacking' into systems to test their robustness and accountability?[27]

The great play historian Johan Huizinga once defined play as that moment when 'an influx of mind breaks down the absolute determinism of the cosmos.'[28] And when the playing animal fuses with the playful imagination, our cosmos – whether social or material, technological or cultural – does seem amenable to transformation. But there needs to be a pilot at the helm of these powerful processes of play. Some presence, or will, needs to insert itself between biological urge and symbolic possibility. That brings us to the third modern rhetoric of play.

Play as selfhood

Emancipate yourself from mental slavery ... none but ourselves can free our minds. – Bob Marley, 'Redemption Song'

Bring together play as an essential mechanism of human development (progress) and play as the force behind our imaginative powers (the imaginary), and we arrive at play's most contemporary definition: play as selfhood. We are at play, in a sense, when we feel we are at play: our subjective experience is the crucial indicator that the ludic moment is happening. Play is an attitude before it is anything else.[29]

Play as selfhood is a vision of absolute human autonomy. For players, private will manifests itself fully in public action; players are filled with the excitement of pursuing their root desires in a disciplined, determined, self-conscious manner. Who we are, and what we do, come together in the act of free play.

This is the play definition that we are most familiar with in modernity – and it is one that has been most often presented as the polar opposite of work, and is therefore the work ethic's most enduring target. But crucially, this is also play as leisure – that unfettered but temporary realm that work permits for the recharging of batteries, for winding down, chilling out, doing what you want. Hence the consumer guides in British weekend newspapers, launched as 'Play' or 'At Play', stuffed with literally thousands of cultural options and lifestyle activities.[30]

In the furiously competitive consumer cultures of the developed West, where the boundaries between generations and classes are becoming ever more permeable and mixed up, play is clearly attracting more positive evaluations. From having faintly risible and infantile connotations, play has become a strong brand value in and of itself. The self-oriented player – able to consume and produce according to his or her whim, seeking pleasure and self-fulfilment over pain and duty, changing shape and appearance according to need and desire – is the very thing to be.[31]

But the idea of a 'playful self', of a self that plays with its boundaries and masks, was birthed long before tricksy ad campaigns and postmodern theory. The clear starting point is Renaissance literature, and that list of writers – from Rabelais, Erasmus and Machiavelli, to Shakespeare, Donne and Marvell – who used their art to imagine a self that was not validated by Church, nobility or tradition. And their most favoured strategy was the ludic self – a literary persona that toyed with the very idea of being a single, unitary consciousness.[32]

These writers gloried in their characters' contradiction, writhing deliciously on the prongs of irony or mockery, adopting contrary stances and antithetical positions as their mood saw fit. This extraordinary material has ended up almost as pop-culture cliché: Hamlet's eternal anxiety about whether he 'is' (or isn't), Machiavelli's cynical play of masks invoked by every political columnist. But the truth remains that there is more that unites a Renaissance poet like the early John Donne and the modern rapper Eminem than separates them – they are both compulsive adopters of personae in their lyrics, they both dramatize their selves through hyperbole and bathos. The poetic player of the Renaissance city square and the rhyme-bustin' 'playa' of the trailer parks and ghettos occupy the same long tradition of free, egoistic ludicism.

The eighteenth century's Enlightenment self combined with the nineteenth century's Romantic self in Freud's intense investigation into the mechanisms of the psyche. Psychoanalysis allows modern humans to know the curious structures of their selves better – their pathologies and neuroses – so that true intentions, rather than false ones, might be realized. This freedom to fashion the self, to be conscious of the operations of identity and thus to shape them, divided artistic communities down the middle. For example, it terrified some modernist writers (Eliot and Beckett) and exhilarated others (Yeats and Lawrence).[33]

This freedom to be and become – exalted by the existentialists and the Beats, by the musicians of bebop and rock 'n 'roll – prepared the way for a different, more public kind of freedom. The sixties' counterculture turned up the century's most self-consciously ludic thinkers and writers. There were the situationists of Paris and Amsterdam, like Guy Debord and Raoul Vaniegem and Constant Niederhuys, urging the rioters in May '68 to dig up the Parisian boulevards for beaches.[34] Or Richard Neville in the UK – interviewed in Chapter eight of this volume – whose *Playpower* was a ragged-loonpanted handbook for the player's lifestyle. In America, Timothy Leary, Ken Kesey and Abbie Hoffman spouted slogans – 'Steal this book!', 'Turn on, tune in, drop out' – that enshrined free play as the key principle of the hippie movement.[35]

Modern play in all three of its definitions – as progress, as imagination, as self – can become an unlimited fuel supply of human dynamism. Play is the primal force which built our early selves, and can revivify and infuse our adult selves with a craving for action and innovation. Play is also an attempt at self-mastery, whether shaped from the outside by education, or impelled by internal dreams of a better, more integrated self. As Howard Gardner, the Harvard educationalist and psychologist, says: 'We play to master our self, our anxiety and the world.'[36]

It would be relatively easy to create a play ethic from its purely modern definitions. The player as a richly potentialized individual, imaginative, energetic and freely intending, is attractive and appealing.[37] But there are other ludic voices that intrude on this shiny, happy, positive vision of play. They come from a time and a place well before the advent of the modern era and its humanist optimism.

Ancient play – the rule of the game

Play is about freedom. But it is also about the freedom *to get it wrong*; to imagine a future, and then have it tumble down around us in reality; to pursue one line of action, only to discover that the consequence is far distant from our intention. This is the other side of play's profound ambiguity. Not only do we play, but we are often played with – by others, by systems of which we are elements and by the sheer unpredictability, uncertainty and complexity of life.

This is not a modern, but an ancient understanding of play – more coercive, more violent, less voluntary, less optional. Ancient play, as it manifests itself in the present, signals a world view where we are as sport to the gods, mere counters in their celestial game. Here, individual will is subordinated to the mass celebrations of the crowd, the carnival and the festival. This is where struggle and contest, rather than collaboration and creation, are the main initiators of playful activity. And this is also where our reaction to these demanding conditions of play can be one of sheer frivolity.[38]

Any ethic must be built on an understanding of human nature which claims some kind of authority. Therefore to regard play as primarily a means to human progress is to tell only half the story. Play can be the means to self-mastery, but it can also master the self. We can choose to play – but we are often compelled to play as well. Any play ethic which did not reckon with the dark, unruly, coercive and dangerous traditions of the ludic would rest on shaky foundations.

Play as fate and chaos

The television ad was unforgettable. A huge, pulsing hand sailed over the rooftops of modern Britain, diving under bridges and over football stadiums, leaving a trail of magic dust behind it. Eventually, the hand came to rest at the window of a standard suburban semi, at which a particularly unremarkable face presented itself, in a state of rapture and wonder. Out came a massive forefinger, and pointed directly at the citizen's chest. 'IT'S YOU,' rumbled a celestial baritone.[39]

Thus was the UK's first National Lottery, sold to the masses in 1995. This most ancient tradition of play as fate – where luck and chance rule our lives, and the gods express their whims through the vicissitudes of our lives – has rarely had a more dramatic and perfect illustration in the modern era. The surrender to implacably awesome forces in these images is terrifying. If the great Greek mythologizers could view these ads, they'd recognize a culture that knows what it's like to be played by the universe.[40]

Play as fate is properly the most venerable of our traditions of play, partly because we, along with other animals, know that unpredictable things can happen. Predators may attack, hailstorms and financial disasters may strike, life may be conceived and life may be terminated – and we have to find ways to live with that existential anxiety. It's no surprise that most major religions conceive of their deities as wilful players with their lives, votaries of chance. Religions were our earliest play tales.[41]

Most of the 'creation' myths at the heart of the major religions are in some sense shots in the dark – chanced acts, cosmic gambles, *actes gratuites*. 'Let there be light,' said the God of Genesis, as arbitrarily as someone flipping a coin or placing a bet at the racetrack. The gods who birth the universe in the *Mahabarata* do so in the midst of a dice game. Indian cosmology, particularly in its Hindu version, commands that the multiple realities and living dreams of play spread out from the top downwards. 'Qualities of play are integral to the very operation of the Hindu cosmos,' says Don Handelman.[42]

The notorious superstition of gamblers – the lucky charms, the rings, the personal rituals – is a sign that this most ancient meaning of play is still thriving. We recognize that the gods are at play with us, and need somehow to be appeased. Yet the most interesting aspect of play as fate is its immediate challenge to our modern conception of play. Fateful play is a largely passive, not active practice – a truth accepted by even the most skilful poker player or adept horse fancier, waiting for their luck to change. This is also not play entered into as an imaginary realm, a pure play of the mind: real money is wagered, lost and (less often) won. And the rules are not set by the player, nor are they amenable to change – unless through nefarious means, for which there are the highest penalties.

The sheer ubiquity and economic force involved in games of chance throughout the developed world might seem like the ultimate proof of mass irrationality – a huge anomaly at the heart of societies which like to think of themselves as rationally ordered, democratic realms. Play rarely appears in a more degraded and derided form than this.[43]

We should recognize the deep human truth of fateful play, says Sutton-Smith: it might actually give a 'fairer representation of the actual chaos of both nature and humanity' than we realize. How might our purely modern player – in touch with her child-like energies, her imagination unbounded and endlessly inventive, confident about her intentions and desires – regard a world view so willing to be subverted (or promoted) by the music of chance? Faced with a universe which thrives on chaos, chance and unpredictability, our purely 'modern' player might well feel baffled or angry. Play's ability to hold the extremes of human nature in tension is well illustrated here.[44]

Play as identity

But the ambiguity of play won't allow there to be a victor. For there are other play forms which are just as pre-modern, compelling our participation and opening us up to the darker forces of our own nature. In other words: we are players because others expect us to play.

This is play as identity – the way that a sense of communality is forged through rituals of pleasure in public spaces and place. These rituals can be time honoured, or recently forged. But once acceded to, they bind the player in a series of routines and expectations to which they willingly submit, as people whose collective identity – ravers or gays, Afro-Caribbeans or Scots, villagers or New Yorkers – is forged by this particular celebration. The most obvious form of collective play is the festival. This can be as ancient and calendrical as New Year or Beltane Fire; as historic as the Mardi Gras in Rio de Janiero or the Burns supper in the Scottish diaspora, as recent as the Notting Hill carnival in London or the Love Parade in Berlin. In his classic work on festivals, *Time Out of Time*, Alessandro Falassi defines the functions of collective play as a 'periodic renewal of the life stream of the community by creating new energy . . . which gives sanction to its institutions.'[45]

It's easy to see collective play as one of those ancient and unruly traditions that work culture is forever trying to domesticate, as a 'leisure' pursuit. Consider, for example, the amount of corporate media and investment devoted to the music-dominated 'festival season' across the developed world over the last few years – from Lollapalooza and Woodstock in the US, to Glastonbury, Ibiza and Berlin in Europe.

This is clearly a recuperative exercise for big business. The 'chemical generation' that became conscious of itself in the UK in the late eighties through a fusion of drugs, dance and location was (and continues to be) an explicit challenge to a work-dominated culture, which emphasized marketplace efficiency above all other values.[46] As the social critic Jeremy Rifkin notes, the more adroit capitalists are trying to make cash from this chaos by creating an 'experience economy'. Now, entertainment spaces of all kinds – from malls to holiday resorts, bars to cinemas – aim to deliver that collective tingle beloved of two generations of festival goers.[47]

But what makes this play form truly ancient is the whiff of primordiality about it. The way we achieve genuine festivity, says Falassi, is by representing 'the primordial chaos before creation, or a historical disorder before the establishment of culture, society, or regime where the festival happens to take place'. The pre-modern excess of festive play can be seen in the blissed-out faces of the Ibiza dancers, leering out of any music magazine or lifestyle TV channel. They are literally ecstatic (both metaphysically and pharmacologically) with collective pleasure.

Play as contest

In *Homo Ludens*, Johan Huizinga rests his whole argument on the notion that all the great achievements of civilization – philosophy, law, art, politics, science – are essentially the results of playful contest and debate. When two people are pitted against each other – whether they are philosophers or warriors, artists among their peers or jurists in a court of law – their intention is to win or succeed. And their weapons are the techniques of play: imagination, simulation, the chance moment, the ironic stance. While playing to win, they raise standards and levels of achievement in human society. For Huizinga, the form which expresses this most perfectly is sport – but it can also include 'slanging matches, debates, boasts, potlaches, parading of wealth, drinking contests, abusing and deriding adversaries, beauty contests, singing, riddling.'[48]

If any realm of contemporary society could easily be seen to manifest a 'play ethic' – at least according to this specific definition – then surely it is sports culture. Even in 1938, Huizinga was gloomy about how sports had been 'appropriated for the enrichment of the owners, rather than existing as a display of virtue by the people'. Yet looking at the vast media spectacles of sport available to the Western consumer, it would be difficult to deny that the contest is, if not exactly a display of virtue, then certainly therapeutic. Figures like Tiger Woods, Venus Williams or David Beckham are exemplars of the benefits of competitive play – and this is often tied back into the modern rhetorics of play as progress, and play as selfhood, in a powerful fusion of ancient and modern traditions. Their tales are the best proof of the existence of meritocracy – a spectacle of raw talent, passionate commitment and applied skill overcoming humble beginnings; the player as winner of the finite game, whose gaming is aimed at victory above all.

It is perhaps not surprising, therefore, that sports culture has filtered through to other contestive realms. The use of 'play' as a noun in American sports – 'a play' meaning a pre-thought-out strategy that is actioned on the pitch – has now been co-opted by business. For example, in 2001, the American style magazine *Vanity Fair* reviewed the year for the top media using various categories – 'wealth', 'gossip', etc. – to rate their performance. One of these categories was 'play of the year', which referred to that particular mogul's major (and by implication, most daring) business decision of the year.

Each 'play' was characterized both by vigorous competition ('Rupert Murdoch saw Barry Diller coming up in his rear mirror, and had to block off the franchise') and the embrace of chance and risk ('Branson raised his capital in a tough bear market, and weathered the storm'). This is the world of Robert Altman's *The Player*, where paranoid media executives maintain themselves in a permanent state of readiness and suspicion, wondering who the next wunderkind will be, and how long they've got before they get turned over.

Another contemporary rendition of contestive play comes in the notion of the 'playa'. Emerging from the hip-hop cultures of the English-speaking African Diaspora, playa culture taps into the same naked market logic as the corporate players, except from a different location. Those who are part of this culture embrace luck, contingency and sudden death. They gain status through battle and taunt, rap and weaponry. Their identity is forged out of ostentatious public rituals, conducted at the club night or in the street. The gangsta rapper, the local drug dealer, the 'ghetto fabulous' superstars of the black economy: what other figures in the urban spectacle so willingly evoke all those ancient traditions of play? Yet as many commentators have pointed out, this vicious agonism comes from despair as much as power, nihilism as much as exultation – the fate of black America as a partially incarcerated nation within a nation.[49]

The complexity of play

These six main rhetorics of play – progress, imagination, selfhood as our modern traditions, fate, power and identity as our ancient ones – allow us to start reading our modern civilization as irrepressibly, inescapably ludic.[50] That they arrange themselves around a venerable philosophical divide should be a matter of some consolation to those still intellectually phobic about the word itself. We could easily map the modern and ancient traditions onto dualities like play as freedom versus play as determinism.[51]

But the more interesting question is whether there is a powerful logic to the wild diversity of play forms in our world. Or even more daringly: is there a politics, a rationality for social development, that can be derived from play's centrality to our lives?

I argue that a proper understanding of play's traditions are a powerful new way to *describe* our contemporary world. But what might play *prescribe* for us? What kind of 'good society' does it evoke or suggest? In this sense, the case for a play 'ethic' has still to be made.

Living as a player is precisely about embracing ambiguity, revelling in paradox, yet being energized by that knowledge. Moreover, an argument can be made that ethics become even more important in an endemically uncertain world. An ethic of play is, in effect, an ethic which makes a virtue, even a passion, out of uncertainty.

We have just left a twentieth century that could be characterized as the age of the machine – both as a material fact and as a dominant cultural metaphor. But underneath that surface narrative, the machine mentality has been slowly crumbling, its foundations in science becoming ever less secure. The Newtonian universe was, more often than not, cast as a clockwork mechanism, where every event could in theory be precisely reversed once the inviolate laws of nature were sufficiently understood. So many scholars have stressed the historical necessity of the scientific world view to the rise of industrial capitalism. At the very least, the sense that rationality, efficiency and planned order were values that applied to the social world, as well as the natural world, was a predominant belief in the industrialized societies until after the Second World War.[52]

As new theories and discoveries in physics and biology steadily percolated their insights through the mainstream culture of the century, this arid social rationalism eventually began to erode. And, based in the deeps of the scientific revolutions of the twentieth century, I believe one can find a powerful explanation for the gradual rise, and imminent predominance, of play values.

These are sciences in which all those tensions between play as modern freedom, and play as ancient determinism, become interflowing ends of a Moebius loop, rather than stark and irreconcilable opposites.[53] This is a knowledge that understands play as the fruitful, novelty-generating energy that sustains the vibrancy of a system – rather than the distracting interference that impedes the functioning of a precision machine.[54]

Like the work ethic, the play ethic is sustained by its own mix of scientific theories. This mix explains not just how humans relate to their technologies, their cultures and each other, but how they regard the nature of the universe in which this process takes place. Before players take on the work ethic, they need a sense of what might count as good, beautiful and true in a player's world. And to begin to construct that way of seeing and perceiving the world, we need to take a brief (and necessarily disputable) journey through the key post-Newtonian sciences of the last 100 years. When we come out at the other side, we will be ready to define a play ethic on its own terms.

Physics: God does play dice (and is malicious as well as subtle)

The image of Einstein sticking out his tongue at a Magnum photographer is probably the least threatening and most playful representation of twentieth-century science: the great thinker as wild-haired eccentric, his abstract theories generated by a carefree, convention-defying mentality. Yet it was Einstein who struggled most vigorously and eloquently with the playful implications of quantum mechanics. In his debates with fellow physicists about the spooky behaviour of sub-atomic matter – its ability to seem to be in two places at once (non-locality), or to change its status under the act of measurement from a scientist (wave-particle duality) – the great man constantly used metaphors of chance and gaming.[55]

Einstein's famous attributed quote 'God does not play dice' is more than just a glib epigram. So many of the twentieth century's great physicists have invoked playfulness to help them capture the shocking unpredictability of this 'post-quantum' universe. Erwin Schrödinger saw science itself as exactly cognate to play, in that both were practised beyond compulsion: 'Play, art and science are the spheres of human activity where the action and the aim are not rule-determined by the aims imposed by the necessities of life.'[56] While Manfred Eigen and Ruthild Winkler contend:

> Everything that happens in our world resembles a vast game in which nothing is determined in advance but the rules, and only the rules are open to objective understanding . . . Chance and necessity underlie all events. The history of play goes back to the beginnings of time . . . Once begun by the elementary particles, atoms and molecules, play is carried on by our brain cells. Man did not invent play. But it is play and only play that makes man complete.'[57]

Quantum physics places us in a post-Newtonian world. Things that were once considered predetermined in Newtonian physics are now seen to be mutable, unpredictable. It is not surprising then that so much of it can be described in ludic terms.

We used to think we understood the universe by laying bare its workings. Now we are beginning to believe that we understand it better by entering into its games, by respecting its creativity, by joining in the play of living forms.[58] This is the sensibility that arises from the true successor to quantum physics, as a scientific paradigm that resonates with our post-cold-war, post-atomic world: the sciences of chaos, complexity, systems and networks.

Nature: carnival and contest

Compared with Einstein's mugging, it's just as playful and lightsome an image: the butterfly flapping its wings in Islay, and somehow leading to a typhoon in the Ivory Coast. The 'somehow' is the mathematics of chaos theory: a growing set of formulae that chart how tiny disturbances in a system can lead to huge but unforeseeable changes in its behaviour. The mathematics that describe this had been known since the nineteenth-century. But it was only when late-twentieth-century science started really deploying the power of computers that it became visible – literally visible: those loops, fractals and attractors generated from streams of now computable data, which make up both the reality and the symbolism of chaos and complexity.

As biologist Brian Goodwin says, this realization that the overall behaviour of complex systems (like the weather, or the brain, or human society) cannot ultimately be predicted has 'enormous consequences':

> This means the end of scientific certainty, which is a property of 'simple' systems (the ones we use for most of our artefacts such as electric lights, motors, and electronic devices, including computers). Real systems, and particularly living ones such as organisms, ecological systems and societies, are radically unpredictable in their behaviour, as we all know. Long-term prediction and control, the hallmark of the science of modernity, are no longer possible in complex systems.[59]

Yet as Goodwin and so many other scientists are eager to tell us, chaos theory doesn't mean that the universe is entirely random.[60] The best we can do as observers is try to model the processes and guess at the 'limited set of possibilities'. This is where chaos theory itself mutates into complexity theory – charting the 'order' that emerges at 'the edge of the chaos', which takes place inside any active, healthy, developing system.[61]

Like chaos, complexity science is rooted in computer simulation and statistics, and requires a degree of mathematical specialism that few of us possess. But it's enough here to note just how riddled with a whole range of play rhetorics this field is. For example, when taking issue with orthodox Darwinism, complexitists stress just how unpredictably creative the evolutionary process is. Organisms aren't guaranteed to survive simply through being the fittest; nor can we put down their extinction to catastrophes like meteor impact or volcanic eruption. There is something intrinsically 'chaotic' about the way that species move through their ecosystems over time – they thrive or go extinct 'not due to their individual success or failure', says Goodwin, but through 'the interactive structure of complex processes ... The game of life, we might say, is one of creative emergence and extinction.'[62]

Indeed, Goodwin derives a very explicit and wide-ranging theory of play from complexity science itself:

Darwinism short-changes us as regards our biological natures. We are every bit as cooperative as we are competitive; as altruistic as we are selfish; as creative and playful as we are destructive and repetitive... We are biologically grounded in relationships which operate at all the different levels of our being, as the basis of our natures as agents of evolutionary emergence, a property we share with all species... These are not romantic yearnings and ideals. They arise from a rethinking of our biological natures that is emerging from the sciences of complexity.[63]

Culture: it's all in the game

There are other contenders to a new scientific 'consilience' around play. In *Non-Zero*, Robert Wright composes a history of human society from the perspective of game theory: a form of mathematics that tries to model how elements in a system interact. There are two essential kinds of game in human and non-human nature, says Wright: zero-sum games and non-zero-sum games. A zero-sum game is like tennis: it's finite, it's competitive, someone wins and someone loses. A non-zero-sum game is like economic exchange, or cultural tradition, or a vibrant community: it's open ended, accumulative and fruitfully messy, and it increases rewards for all those who commit to participation in the exchange (despite occasional glitches and bad behaviour) over a long period.[64]

What game theory does best is to show how the evolutionary psychologists' notion of 'reciprocal altruism' works: the idea that all forms of social cooperation are borne out of maxims like 'Tit for tat' or 'If you scratch my back, I'll scratch yours'. Wright's formulation is a new echo of the old idea of enlightened self-interest. As a play-driven theory, it sheds some interesting light on the kind of ethical behaviours a truly ludic society would encourage.

Wright sees a strong anticipation of game theory in the philosophy of Immanuel Kant, in particular his concept of 'unsocial sociability' – the idea that being sociable is the best means of achieving your own personal desires.[65] In this non-zero-sum game, people engage other people in their self-interested but order-generating strategies – the result being a general increase in interdependence and connectedness.

It is as if those ambiguities that so divide the modern and the ancient rhetorics of play had, at last, found a connecting logic. Modern play emphasizes egotism, imagination, self-awareness; ancient play trusts its destiny to wider forces and surrenders itself to collective rituals. Yet game theory binds them together in a fertile dynamic. As Wright says, this is 'a paradox of human nature: we are deeply gregarious, and deeply cooperative, yet deeply competitive. We instinctively play both non-zero-sum and zero-sum games.' We understand the deep ambiguities of play, its competitive and cooperative strategies, its egoism and its collectivism – yet we use them to forge an increasingly mutual world civilization.[66]

Game theory, as its name suggests, comes back time and time again to the theme of play. Invented by the Hungarian mathematician John von Neumann, one of its key conclusions is that all successful game players need to bring an element of randomness into their strategy if they are to have a chance of winning. What works for riverboat gamblers, swordsmen and lawn tennis champions also works for less developed organisms, caught up in much more urgent games of survival. The rabbit that behaves predictably while on the run from a predator – rather than jerking unpredictably this way and that, as the animal does – won't pass on many genes. In his book *The Mating Mind*, Geoffrey Miller calls this 'proteanism', after the Greek god Proteus, who evaded his captors through trickery and shape-shifting.[67]

This capacity – which is present, as Miller says, in almost all moving organisms – 'depends on the capacity for the rapid, unpredictable generation of highly variable alternatives'. Because of our huge brain size, our ability to create alternatives is enormous. But because we humans are so sensitive to the cues for reproductive fitness, we turn this basic randomness – this unpredictability-as-survival strategy – into our vast array of cultural forms and behaviours. So playfulness – that endless surge of messy innovation which begins with the infant human – becomes the most important 'fitness indicator' of our creative health and imaginative strength in later life. Our continuing playfulness indicates to potential mates that we can respond to all the risks and challenges of existence with resilience and resourcefulness.

All successful animals must be 'neophiliacs', says Miller: they must be passionate for novelty. At a basic level, most organisms need brains that can tell them when an occurrence is unpredictable and novel (like the sudden emergence of a slavering predator). So humanity's particularly glorious success comes from our runaway love of novelty, our thirst for the surprising. 'Many games demand mixed strategies,' says Miller, 'and many evolutionary situations demand unpredictable behaviour. Human creativity may be the culmination of a long trend towards ever more sophisticated brain mechanisms that produce ever less predictable behaviours.'[68]

For the play ethic, this is almost too good to be true. In Miller's evolutionary account, nature commands that humans *should* play in order to survive and thrive. This is science supporting that modernist, progressive definition of play beloved of the Enlightenment, romanticism and the psy-disciplines.

Yet what if our human creativity wasn't the very acme of natural creativity, as Miller seems to suggest, but was merely one eddy or swirl in an implicitly creative universe? What if there were other forces driving the generation of beautiful form than simply sexual selection and evolutionary fitness – perhaps mathematical or systemic ones?[69]

Just like game theorists, complexity scientists regularly invoke play in their explanations. Under complexity, our individual interactions – no matter how vigorous, singular and inventive they may seem to us – are merely part of the massive carnival, the implicate order, of the universe. The complexitists' player needs to radically temper his or her egoism – to accept that they are only a player in the 'team game' of life, co-evolving with others.

The network metaphysic

We know how to 'surf the Net', 'how to network': these are now utterly tired phrases. To be fair, this isn't entirely the fault of lazy popularizers: there is a scholarly looseness about how the term 'network' is actually used. At one extreme, it's simply a looser model of business interaction, allowing a more reciprocal relationship between the internal parts of an enterprise. At the other extreme, in the hands of some third-culturalists, it's almost a new metaphor for twenty-first-century life – the more networked our existences are, the more interesting our lives will be.[70]

But for the culture of industrialism, in which an individual's submission to routine is what is most valued, a network society is something of a disaster. The industrial mindset is too brittle to cope with the way that networks operate. Sticking duteously to the job description brings no benefits or advantages in this climate, because networks 'switch off' those who don't contribute vigorously to the overall how of energy or information.[71] However, for the player who balances the modern and ancient traditions of ludicism, the network is a place of adventure. As Kevin Kelly puts it, 'a network is a possibility factory'. The more that viable nodes are connected to it, the greater the rewards for all those who vigorously participate. 'Out of this tangle of possible links,' says Kelly, 'come myriad new niches for innovations and interaction.'[72]

So, to cast this in terms of the play ethic: if your actions are adaptive, imaginative and passionate, but if you also accept that the results of your actions won't be predictable or retractable, then you will be able to make the most of the networks of modern life, wherever they pertain. But if your actions are conservative, routine and apathetic – yet you hope that your acceptance of your role will guarantee you a certain security and status in the hierarchy – then you will eventually be switched off from your networks. And for good reason.

The play ethic is for the proliferation of networks throughout everyday life. Yet this isn't about our total submission to the marketplace – far from it. The play ethic is about counterposing a purely neoliberal, capitalist network with a whole thicket of other networks – emotional and sexual, geographical and traditional, artistic and civic. The reward for participating vigorously in them can be a rich new twenty-first-century identity, where individualization and collective duty strike an entirely new bargain, based on the unleashed activism of the subject. And this is activism almost in a purely technical sense, the opposite of 'passivism'. When we play, we are expending the energy required to thrive in a complex society.[73]

In my opinion, recognizing the richness of our play heritage is one of the best available fuels for that activism. It tells us that networks, or complex adaptive systems, or social strategies are now our reality. This is what our early twenty-first-century existence feels like: before we work ourselves into the ground, we play for ourselves, and with others. Work is parasitic upon play, the full and extensive play of civilization and production, of living creatively: it always has been.[74] By recognizing our essential ludicism, by dignifying our play with an ethical force, we can begin to create and act, rather than simply consume and spectate.

Towards the play ethic

These deeply playful and mutable sciences represent a framework (perhaps one should say a sprawling, messy web) within which the ambiguity of play matures into the complexity of play. Seen through their prism, play's contrary traditions seem less paradoxical, less contrary. In short they seem united by their difference. They have maximum individual freedom, but also have the coherence of a whole.

The modern and ancient rhetorics allow us to see the 'whole' of play in all its maddening dichotomies. When we do, it is immediately obvious how appropriate the play ethic is to our contemporary condition. For us not to be daunted, crushed or demoralized by the complexities of our world, we have to reduce its burden upon us: we have to learn to create space to dream of alternatives, try out scenarios, give ourselves room to experiment, allow ourselves to say 'maybe' or 'as if' to our dilemmas, rather than always a definitive 'yes' or 'no'. To invert the title of Milan Kundera's famous novel, we have to embrace 'the bearable lightness of being'. We have to be able to transform the uncertainties and risks that our increasingly complex twenty-first-century world presents us with – that is, we have to become *players*. And we have to believe that this activity is necessary and worthwhile – *ethical*, in other words.

The core statement of the play ethic now becomes clear. We need to be energetic, imaginative and confident in the face of a unpredictable, contestive, emergent world. We need to accept the complex relationship between all forms of play, whether ancient or modern.

The play ethic today

Play's ultimate function for humankind is to maintain our adaptability, vigour and optimism in the face of an uncertain, risky and demanding world.[75] However, we endure a political tendency in the developed countries that believes, by and large, that work is the most functional and useful mode of human existence. In the UK, it has become an explicit cultural aim of government policy: the Chancellor, Gordon Brown, takes every opportunity to trumpet a 'reinvigorated work ethic in every community of Britain.'[76]

A culture in which everyone defines themselves through their work is, by definition, a much more ordered, rational and administered society than one that guides itself by the rich traditions, world views and epistemologies of play. Yet if the new work ethic of the New Right and Third Way parties is a response to the postmodern world of the last twenty years, it is a particularly repressive and authoritarian one.[77] It sometimes seems as if industrial culture is desperately holding down the lid on a more playful civilization, bucking and bubbling underneath, hoping to turn its irrepressible energies and fecundities into some kind of useful, hydraulic, controllable power.

Armed with our general theory of play, let's turn our faces to the world; from our broad descriptions of a ludic universe, let's begin to hazard some ethical prescriptions, and tie them to specific circumstances. It has been pleasant (and quintessentially playful) to imagine a space in which a general theory of play could develop out of the looming, intimidating shadow of the work ethic. But the core function of play and simulation, as mentioned at many points before, is to give us higher mammals a chance to exert our virtual mastery over a skill or scenario, so that we are better prepared for the actual engagements of survival.

That moment has come: chapter by chapter, the job of this book from now on is to prise loose the grip of industrial society from informational society, the world of workers from the world of players, finger by finger. And with every loosening of the grip, a new tribe of already emerging players will escape: the soulitarians, lifestyle militants, the busyness class, the liberal semiocrats, the infinite gamers . . . The carnival awaits us.

First, however, we need to administer a sharp, disorienting rap to the knuckles of the work ethic, twenty-first-century style.

THREE / 65

THE ANGELS MAKE WORK:

Putting the Protestant Ethic Behind Us

Labour must be performed
as if it were an absolute end in itself,
a calling.

– Max Weber, *The Protestant Ethic and the Spirit of Capitalism*, 1904

You will never work in a place like this again.
This is brilliant. Fact!

– Ricky Gervais (David Brent), *The Office*, BBC, 2002

The Iron Chancellor made his grave way to the podium, shuffled his papers and addressed the collected corporate heads. The moment was mid-November, London, 2001. Gordon Brown, MP, had been on the stump for a good few weeks now, giving long, sonorous speeches on both sides of the Atlantic, ensuring (for whatever strategic reasons) that his political vision was firmly lodged in the Western consciousness. Sift through each of these speeches and addresses and you would see one term regularly come up, time and time again. And there, before the Institute of Directors – just as he had at the Labour Party conference, and to a *Wall Street Journal* reporter, or to anyone who asked him – he cited the same phrase: 'The work ethic – so important to success in the years of the first British industrial revolution – is being once more reinvigorated in high unemployment communities, where it had in recent decades withered . . .'[1]

The collected bosses murmured their approval. We, as civilians, should pay closer attention. Whatever Brown thinks 'the work ethic' might be, he is clear – and has been for a number of years – about its emotional and moral content. A comprehensive search through Brown's various public performances over the last few years reveals that the phrase always appears within a highly charged, highly judgemental context.[2]

For example, the work ethic is a source of *vigour* for communities, which *wither* in its absence. It is a *restoration* of older, better values, which have been silenced, *drowned out*, by some unspecified clamour. This was a time when work was *hard*, when selves strived only for *improvement*. The new work ethic brings *stability*, because it is a *regime* of opportunities and sanctions.

If, however, the work ethic is *dissipated*, a spectre appears – a spectre that clearly haunts the Chancellor's dreams. This spectre has its own medical problems, a *syndrome*, called 'Why work?' Worst of all, in a phrase repeated throughout Brown's speeches, it has own fetid lair, where one loathsome ritual rules supreme. *It sits or stays at home, on benefit, doing nothing.*

Invigorate, wither, restore, drown out, improve, stabilize, regiment, dissipate, sit, stay, benefit, depend, respond, do nothing. As a set of possible human actions, this is a familiar and grim vocabulary. The only thing a human is expected to do, in the eyes of this minister, is to act in a purely functional way, whether to serve economic efficiency or ethical norms. Only by being functional can health and progress be ensured; if this expectation is not imposed, then lassitude and corruption will surely follow. There is even a specific place and posture, a particular arrangement of a human body, which is to be prohibited most vigorously.

It is extraordinary how close Brown's Presbyterian imagination is to the classic Christian and Protestant texts of the original work ethic. St Paul, a great favourite with reformers, says to the Thessalonians, 'If any would not work, neither should he eat.' Brown's revision of welfare into workfare is no less severe. The long-term unemployed will receive 'four options – of work, work-based training, work experience including in the voluntary sector and self-employment'. But, as he reminds us in Pauline fashion, 'there will be no fifth option'. This is Brown acting in the very best of Puritan traditions. The first legislature to make idleness a 'punishable crime' was that of the state of Massachusetts in 1648, set up under the zealous Calvinism of early settlers like John Winthrop.[3]

Brown's phobia about inactivity is again echoed in the core Protestant texts of the eighteenth century. 'It is for action that God maintaineth us and our activities,' said the reformer Richard Baxter. 'Work is the moral as well as the natural end of power.'[4] (The reverberations across the centuries are sometimes deafening. New Labour's slogan in the British general election of 2001, their victory masterminded by Gordon Brown, was 'The work continues'.) And as the Chancellor imagines his ideal new Britain, where 'enterprise is open to all' – where we not only have rights to work, but the *responsibility* to work – it's interesting to recall the vision of heaven as promoted by the Puritan reformers across Europe.

Johann Kasper Lavater said, 'We cannot be blessed without having occupations. To have an occupation means to have a calling, an office, a special, particular task to do.' Heaven lies in one of the four welfare options, damnation in the fifth. Even more brutally, Baptist William Clark Ulyat imagines his paradise thus: 'Practically, [heaven] is a workshop.'[5]

Yet we should perhaps look more closely into Brown's background, as the son of a Presbyterian minister whose parish was the tough dockyards of Glasgow, to find the pulsing source of his zeal for labour. There are many brimstone-fired quotes that can be dug up from the Scottish reformers of the seventeenth and eighteenth centuries. Take Minister Abernathy, for example: 'Diligent labour in one's calling diverts the mind from filthy objects and enableth it from such vanity . . . moderate sleep and watchfulness are profitable herein.'[6] Sounds like he'd be an excellent benefit fraud officer, diligently knocking on the doors of the work shy (and play zealous), busy with their 'filthy' objects.

However, the Scottish reformer who stands directly behind Brown would seem to be Thomas Carlyle. Born in Ecclefechan, Scotland, and commanded to read the Bible every day, Carlyle was a Puritan facing the Victorian age. In Carlyle's essays *Past and Present*, written in 1843, work becomes the noblest possible calling:

> All true work is sacred; in all true work, were it but true hard-labour, there is something of the divineness . . . Labour is life. From the innermost heart of the worker rises his God-given force, the sacred celestial life essence breathed into him by Almighty God . . . in Idleness alone is there perpetual despair.[7]

'Labour is life': the phrase jumps out at you like a campaign slogan in waiting.

The debt that New Labour pays to Christian moralism has often been noted, but with Brown, the commitment to work as an expression of moral and ethical fibre runs deep. 'I don't deny that I want to make the work ethic more important to the organization of the welfare state, so to that extent you could say it has got an ethical basis,' he admitted in a 1998 interview.[8] He is the son of Knox and Calvin to the ends of his boots. Anyone who saw the television pictures of Brown's extraordinarily spartan wedding to Sarah Macaulay in 2001 – high-street suits and chainstore sandwiches, a celebration in a crowded back garden, rather than a grandiose public event – could see someone almost physically ill at ease with luxury and excess.

The conjunction of man and moment is fascinating – stern Presbyterian meets crisis of welfare state under late capitalism – and it couldn't be a more complementary match. To cement its political hegemony, New Labour required a new work ethic; Brown's microscopic interest in the good character of the poor has aimed to 'reinvigorate' exactly that. The great Puritan reformers have found their heir in one of the most powerful men in one of the most powerful countries at the beginning of the third millennium. 'For Satan finds some mischief still / For idle hands to do,' said Isaac Watts in 1865.[9] 'The soul's play-day is the devil's work day,' said another, anonymous, eighteenth-century reformer.[10] 'No fifth option,' thunders our own great reformer.

After a century of modernist art, Hollywood and Madison Avenue, exponential drug use, gender radicalism and sexual liberation, technological fluidity and spiritual diversity, why do we still tolerate the uptight severities of the work ethic? Why do we give the time of day to politicians who regard play – or at least, that free time ('idleness') in which they make their playful decisions – as devilish, degenerate, corrupt, dissolute? Why can't we assert an alternative theology of human activity? Why can't we say that the *angels* make work for idle hands?

The work ethic is a tough adversary because, as Max Weber said, it represents the 'spirit of capitalism'.[11] Because of this, it is impossible to separate New Labour's zeal for the work ethic from what old Marxists call the 'continuing crises of capitalism'; crises which, it must be said, have been as much opportunities for governments and businesses, as they have been problems. The work ethic is useful to the governing classes of early twenty-first-century market democracies because it has the time-honoured effect of imposing social order. In the face of what seems like endless fragmentation and diversity, the Anglo-American political response has been to combine the old Puritan virtues with a kind of productive patriotism. As Brown rhapsodizes in an address to the Yale Club in New York about 'the British way':

> For centuries, your land and the islands of Britain have been linked not only by history but by ideals. For while the United States was born in a revolution against a British government, it was also a revolution for an assertion of fundamental values that Britain and America hold in common and represent to all the world: a passion for liberty and opportunity for all; a belief in the work ethic and in opening enterprise to all.[12]

Not to mention a consumer culture that melts everything solid into air, puts mad and burning dreams in the minds of men, women and children, and is a force for the incitement of rampant desire and uncontrollable aspiration 'in all'. It's perhaps no surprise that a cradle Calvinist like Brown cannot comprehend what the American sociologist Daniel Bell once called 'the cultural contradictions of capitalism'. In order to function, capitalism needs both docile producers and avid consumers. The problem is that the second identity tends to subvert the values of the first.[13]

But it's these plastered-over cracks in the edifice of the modern work ethic that the play ethic wants to wrench ever wider. And if we want to overturn the work ethic, we have to start with its exuberant twin: leisure.

Doing nothing or choosing play?

Let's return to our Brownian nightmare – the work-shy, stay-at-home, do-nothing. In truth, this shapeless, evasive figure is never literally inactive. The spectres might well be having sex (sometimes procreatively, sometimes not), an event that (so far at least) usually happens outside of the surveillance and control of the state, but which has consequences for the state in terms of social support for parents and children. The spectres might also be psychonauts, intoxicating themselves, one way or another, on a spectrum of soft to hard drugs (including caffeine, nicotine and alcohol); perhaps, behind their walls, they might even be creating, refining and distributing these substances, from marijuana to heroin. Lastly, these spectres might well be deploying technology in a purposeful, determined, even passionate manner – but not in a way that has an obvious value in the labour market. This could include renting videos and watching satellite television, and using game technology and the Internet to explore virtual worlds and extend communities of interest.

At the very least, what we can discern from this – if we take an almost anthropological, Martian's-eye viewpoint – is a richly textured culture, with no shortage of opportunities for action and intention. So perhaps what Brown really means is that nothing 'good' or 'useful', from the perspective of the work ethic, is being done here. But isn't this more like leisure? The 'work shy' are indulging in practices that the work eager reserve as a treat for themselves on the weekends and on holidays.

So the problem for New Labour is that the spectres are living in a culture where leisure has broken the boundaries of work and has expanded, cancerously, to fill the void. To 'do nothing' useful or good after a hard week's alienation is permissible; to do nothing *but* do nothing useful or good is utterly impermissible. The whole New Right rhetoric of 'dependency' (enthusiastically employed by Brown and others in New Labour) is driven by the notion that those without employment are using state benefits to live 'leisurely' lives. In short, they are sampling the joys of nurturance, narcosis and narrative without the labour and pain that justifies them.

No one can deny that violence, substance abuse and low spirits are rife in areas of Britain that have been beached by the end of industrialism. But it's my argument that those pathologies are partly generated by governmental 'regimes' which regard the possession of work – no matter how shoddy or meretricious – as the only proper measure of social status. We live in a consumer culture, readily accessible to those who are the targets of Brown's discipline, which constantly programmes us with dreams of self-realization, potency and plenitude. We are urged to 'just do it', to 'search for the hero inside ourselves'.[14]

Who can blame those who understand the cultural contradictions of capitalism – the seductive power of its dreams, and the cramped nature of its society – and reject the whole work-to-consume norm as bogus and hypocritical? I would prefer them to construct a new society, rather than to simply reject the current one. But to evade the control of the work police, to defraud benefit for the sake of more spending money, to sink into the bliss of drugs and partying – all these are desperate and defensive actions that are inarticulately (but sometimes articulately) protecting a realm of physical and mental autonomy.[15]

Rather than building a system that aims, above all else, to stop people sitting at home and doing nothing, we should be valorizing that moment as a creative opportunity. This could be a space for contemplation and thought, leading to properly motivated, ethical action. Yet it might not be action about which a state, keen to make its citizens behave in an efficient, orderly, decent manner, would necessarily approve.[16] I refuse to accept that the only answer to the excesses of leisure is the predominance of work – because I refuse the duality of work and leisure completely. To think of yourself as a player is to widen the spectrum of actions that might be regarded as valuable, productive or creative in a society.

From the perspective of the play ethic, leisure and work are not only alter egos, but also evil twins. Both work and leisure create distorted, super-charged realms, in which the proper judgement of what a 'valuable' or 'creative' action might be becomes impossible. How can we live in such a schizophrenic way – when we work we are essentially slaves, and in our leisure we are potentially gods? For the player to avoid this dualism – in which all his or her passions are poured into either furious self-denial or lurid spectatorship – their very vision of the world has to change.[17]

The world isn't at work, it's in play: and as the previous chapter hopefully proved, our social and natural reality is dynamic, not static. It is far more amenable to individual intervention, and less implacable and categorizing, than the giant iron cage we call work and leisure.

Yet of the two terms, leisure was always the most labile, the most unstable, containing within it a folk memory of a pre-industrial culture of

'Happy Mondays' (the name of a famous hedonist rock band of the eighties and nineties, of course), collective festival, and non-regulated activity.[18] As the industrial process required that workers be more productive – that is, more skilled, healthier, and more highly motivated – the moral regime of puritanism and its Poor Laws became inadequate. Subtler tactics had to be deployed by the nineteenth-century ruling classes in the face of a combination of collective militancy and individual recalcitrance, to keep the workers in line and in the factories.

Education, as we have noted, slipped between a Romantic and a utilitarian model, poised on the edge between creating dutiful and skilled operatives, or energetic and imaginative souls. Leisure became just as much a target for regulation and social agonizing. So the division between 'rational' and 'irrational' recreations was born – between those that would improve spirits and restore energies (libraries, swimming pools, sports halls), and those that would deplete them (gambling, fighting, etc.).[19]

Yet when capitalism began to hit its structural crisis at the turn of the century – a crisis largely of overproduction and unsold inventories – the protean energies of play were let into the steel compound of *homo et femina laborans* once again. Irrational play, ironically, became necessary to the next stage of capitalist expansion. What Stuart Ewen calls 'channels of desire' were opened up in the previously repressed and straitened worker, through the beginnings of mass advertising and mass media (radio and films, then television).[20] Almost from the very beginnings of twentieth-century consumer culture, leisure became a battleground for conflict between rational and irrational recreations.

Weird, self-indulgent figures kept assembling themselves out of the heart of this new consumer phantasmagoria, usually around forms of music – flapper girls, reefer kings, zoot-suits, be-boppers, beats, mods, rockers, hippies, yippies, punks, grungers/gen-X'ers, ravers, crusties, riot grrls, hackers, anti-capitalist carnivaleers. Right between the bars of the iron cage of twentieth-century modernity, there was a constant party going on. What popular culture did, in that insane whirl between audience, creators/performers and producers/managers, was to keep the elemental diversity of play's myriad forms alive and thriving. It constantly slipped the regulatory reach of government and big business by virtue of its sheer and irrepressible fecundity; even when it was repressed – as, for example, when the camera refused to go below Elvis Presley's waist level on the Ed Sullivan show in 1957 – it only made pop culture's attraction stronger.[21]

Play's fruitful ambiguities, its pervasiveness and dynamism in our lives, was maintained by the sub- and countercultures of the twentieth century constantly challenging the existing boundaries of leisure for their limitedness and safety. What greater challenge to the sports stadium, as a collective mass of people gathered for a playful purpose, than the outdoor festival? If selfhoods were meant to be enriched by good education and regular exercise, could they not also be enriched by hallucinogenic drugs? If our 'lifestyles' could be composed through our intelligent consumer choices, then how about the 'lifestyles' of a seventies punk, an eighties new romantic, or a nineties raver – using music, fashion and drugs to create temporary zones of autonomy and freedom?[22]

At the end of his giant history of work, Richard Donkin quotes the line from the hit film *Trainspotting*, where its wild hero Renton faces the impoverishment of working life, and opts to 'choose something else' instead of 'choosing life'. What he chooses is a heroin habit. 'How many others have chosen this path,' muses the *Financial Times* writer, 'in preference to a fast-food counter or machine watching in a factory. Work and the prospect of work must offer hope of something better if it offers nothing else. In future, work will need to earn its place in our lives. We cannot live for work. Instead we must take control of our lives. But the choice is ours.'[23]

Yet, as Renton correctly perceives, 'life' is far too capacious and inclusive a term – it gives no critical purchase on that duality of work and leisure which turns some of us into workaholics, and some of us into leisureholics.[24] The point about Renton throughout *Trainspotting* is that he is a fascinating blend of both extremes. At various stages in his life story he is both utterly at the mercy of his drugs, and completely in command of a property business; he is often reduced to the merely physical, yet is also able to articulate his experiences brilliantly. The film opens with his desperate flight from the police while shoplifting, the beginning of a rollercoaster existential ride. It does not end with his death but with his departing for Europe – a large stash of stolen money in his satchel, old enemies left behind and a new self to construct.

The enormous popularity of Irvine Welsh's novel amongst the youth and young adults of the nineties – what I call in Chapter four the soulitarians – stems from the way his narratives provide one answer to Gordon Brown's biblical accusation: that the only alternative to the work ethic is doing nothing. What Renton would say – his nose in a Herman Hesse book, his body coursing with chemical and erotic pleasures, his business increasing in prosperity – is that the opposite of the work ethic is this: *being ready and feeling capable.* Renton doesn't say it, but I'd suggest it's what he really meant. 'I choose something else. I choose *play.*'

Work will make you behave

Where the whole man is involved
there is no work. Work begins
with the division of labour.
– Marshall McLuhan, *Understanding Media*

Why, are so many Western politicians and thinkers still holding so tightly to the work ethic?

One answer is obvious: to maintain power. Third Way governments across Europe and America in the late nineties sought to manage one basic contradiction: the tension between 'social cohesion' and 'economic dynamism'.[25] New politics was about reconciling the stabilities of community and lifestyle that made for a happy society, with the instabilities that global markets and new technology generates in those same lives. The New Labour answer was to come up with a new kind of social hierarchy – a new order of work in which everyone has their contented place. This is the presumption behind all of New Labour's welfare reforms: an almost cosmic system of labour, the great socializer in an age of structural inequality. And the explicit presumption, articulated in many of the key Blairite texts, is that humans enjoy work more than play.

This is the implication of many of the disciplines that feed into New Labour – Christian socialism/communitarianism, with its distrust of 'rights talk'; evolutionary psychology, with its tragic pessimism about human motives; and the anti-humanist writings of Foucault, which see mentalities as perpetually susceptible to being shaped by power.[26]

The nub of this complex of ideas is to assert a limit on the progressive possibilities of human nature. 'The soul's play day is the devil's work day' means, in practice, that single mothers have to be patrolled, young unemployed men are put into a form of environmental/voluntary sector National

Service and the rest of us endure a regime that is more and more suspicious of freely choosing adults.[27] We cannot expect that politicians (except in the rarest circumstances) will deploy ideas in any other way than to sustain their own power. Yet as evidenced by their titanic efforts to 'rethink' or 'reimagine' work over the last decade or so, public intellectuals also seem to take a lot of psychological compensation from the concept. The most eloquent lament for the old stabilities of the industrial era has come from the American sociologist Richard Sennett, articulated in his beautifully written essay *The Corrosion of Character: the Personal Consequences of Work in the New Capitalism.*[28]

He begins with the standard wisdom about how work operates in the new economy. The companies we labour for take it as a principle that their existence is unstable. Our workplaces assemble as teams, realizing their 'projects' – which then unravel when the job's done, retaining only the most cursory of ties. No one with intelligence, talent and self-discipline regards 'loyalty' to a company, or to any entity, as anything other than a temporary measure. In the age of downsizing, re-engineering, and the 'virtual' organization, how much can a company be loyal to you, anyway? So, as Sennett says, we face an implacable modern paradox, a crisis of adult experience. 'How do we decide what is of lasting value in ourselves, in a society which is impatient, which focuses on the immediate moment?' he asks. 'How can long-term goals be pursued in an economy devoted to the short term?'[29]

Sennett's words are evocative, and unlock a cellar-full of familiar alienations. We *are* overworked, stressed out, debt ridden, disaffected. We have less time for our families than we feel we should have; we take less pleasure from our entertainments and consumptions than we expected to take; we feel less connected to our communities and localities than we ever did. In our workplaces, we subject ourselves to routines and duties which at best seem pointless, at worst unethical or immoral. Yet we also feel like hollow citizens, too weary to respond to any political entreaty with anything other than shrugs, sighs or cynicism.

The constant watch words of the new capitalism are flexibility, creativity and self-improvement. Workers are urged to 'get up to speed' with a runaway, globalized world: we must become mobile and tensile, enterprising and capable. We must harness our chariots to the sun of intense competition. Yet these injunctions come from companies that hire you for a year, or maybe even less; companies that might be taken over at any time in some City of London or Wall Street manoeuvre; that try to shirk long-term entanglements like pensions, and wage and holiday agreements, and that shed labour whenever their global positions show the slightest competitive disadvantage. Trying to excel for companies that are themselves transient, provisional and unforgiving might come to seem like the grandest folly. Why believe in work, when it doesn't believe in you?

Sennett's thesis is that our sense of character has become corroded by the instability of our working lives. He illustrates this with an appropriate anecdote. For twenty-five years, the academic has known a man called Enrico, an office janitor in New York. Enrico, along with a working wife, has brought up a family and sent his children to college under the most traditional labour conditions imaginable. Enrico's hours were fixed by collective bargaining, his wage and pension defended by the same union, his entitlements made clear and defined over the 'long term'. Having secured a modest but reliable economic niche, Enrico built the story of his life out of the bricks of time – slowly improving the house, slowly saving for the future. He made sure that his well-motivated and strongly nurtured children did their homework every night, easing them towards career heights he had no conception of himself ('I don't understand a word he says,' he would boast, as his son Rico did his maths exercises). Enrico's social status might have been modest but, as Sennett says, he was 'the author of his life' – however constrained, modest and rule bound that life might have been.

Then, by chance, Sennett meets Rico, the son, on a long-haul business flight. It's clear that the son – earning in the top 5 per cent, a programmer with the most covetable skills, married to an accountant and the proud father of two children – is not the author of his life in the same way that his father was. Rico has moved four times in fourteen years since graduating, has bumped from start-up to managerial job to small consultancy. However, though he's earning well, he gets home at seven, works the odd long weekend, and is patently struggling to find the time to be a parent and, what's more, a role model. How can he teach his kids about constancy, commitment, loyalty – give them, in short, a sense of character – when his own adult life, in their eyes, is so profoundly unstable?

Sennett, who is proud of his own parents' radical past as left-wing organizers, makes a manful attempt to update their Marxist faith for the present. Given that the 'flexibility' endured by Rico is now almost an unquestioned work ethic for the majority in Western developed societies, the question has to be asked: can we 'all' live like that, without something collectively giving way? If the essential foundation of character, as the classicists had it, is 'Who needs me?', then can our characters survive the reply of the new capitalism – not that much, not for too long, and only in these specific ways?

Sennett asserts, with a romantic flourish, that 'a regime which provides human beings with no deep reasons to care about each other cannot long preserve its legitimacy.' In effect, the 'inner needs' of the people will loosen the hold of the new flexible capitalism.[30] Well, maybe. But I have my own personal experience to bring to this argument. I have a father who worked for most of his adult life in the most bureaucratic, rule-bound, 'long-term' job imaginable – as a clerical worker for British Rail – and who, in retrospect, hated almost all of his time there.

Why hated it, rather than just endured it? Because he could sing like a Hoboken angel, out-Frank anyone on a party floor but never felt he could take it further. Because he had a footballing left foot to die for, and once had trials for a big English side during his National Service, but couldn't get the life space to pursue his talent. My father's 'inner need' – based on the teeming talents and dreams inside him – was to be a star. Or, at the very least, to feed his core energies into his waking hours. I think (and he might admit) that it was the very 'long-termism' of his traditional job that made sure those potentials were unrealized: he couldn't 'author' his life in the way he wanted. The consequent frustration, I am sure, was what drove him to drive me onwards.

I'm glad he did. But, sometimes, ordinary people do care about themselves, as well as about each other – and not just in a selfish way, but also in self-realizing way. They ask: What can I be? as well as: Who am I? Yes, the new economy needs to be regulated at its globalized heights; similarly, its productive powers should be used to expand time in our lives, rather than compress it. But how we value work indicates what we value about humanity. Sennett poses the question very beautifully in his chapter comparing Diderot and Adam Smith: do humans thrive by routine and order, or by flexibility and spontaneity? Are we trees that bend with inner strength, or trees that can eventually break in the wind?[31] If inflexibility results in your dreams never getting close to realization, your innovations and creativities never really meeting the world, then it's too stiff and regimented a life for me – and for my children. In the long run, as Keynes nearly said, we're all dead. And life before death is slightly more interesting than life after death.

From workers' play time to players' work time?

The play ethic, like the work ethic, is intended to be a kind of social mythology – a constellation of meanings, a set of values and sensibilities, an inclusive rhetoric – which can help us draw energy and purpose from the irreconcilable tensions of our dynamic age. If the more conservative and controlling leaders in politics and business could begin to at least acknowledge the playful ferment all around them – rather than raise their fiery cross against it – then it's not inconceivable that reform could take place, with policies and strategies forged around a play-based rather than work-based agenda.

Much recent social science lends support to the rise of a play ethos. As many have noted, there has been an inexorable rise of 'post-materialist' values in the affluent West over the last three decades.[32] As wages, education levels and gender flexibility all rise, men and women are constantly trying to balance this genuinely new sphere of personal freedom and lifestyle choice with the compulsions of work and employment. The problem now for most executives in large organizations is that the balance is tipping ever further away from 'work' to 'life' – from the pursuit of pay and conditions to the pursuit of meaning and well-being.[33]

Could a 'play ethic' be the conceptual bridge that links the needs of organizations to function and develop in a market democracy, with the needs of individuals to make their 'labour' as 'un-alienated' as possible? If the bridge isn't built, involving serious reform and change of practice on the part of employers and organizations, then twenty-first-century capitalism may be facing a mass opt out from its pace and demands. Attempts to reinvigorate the work ethic in the UK have only accelerated disillusionment amongst the wide majority of British white-collar workers – something that manifests itself in escalating sick leave[34] and underperformance even in standard working hours.[35]

There are subtler reinvigorations of the work ethic, of course, than those dreamed of by Chancellor Brown. In a British situation where, according to the Work Foundation, '80 per cent of professionals would shun employment in organizations solely answerable to the bottom line', questions about 'meaningful work' are being raised with great regularity.[36]

An adviser to the Chartered Institute of Personnel and Development suggests that 'well-managed work is meaningful work – because the individual's time is well used, there is a degree of autonomy in how they do tasks, they are adequately supported and there is the relationship with colleagues.'[37]

So the machine metaphor, *pace* our general theory of play, can be improved – but only slightly. Instead of being a cog in the corporate mechanism, you can become something more meaningful. Like those magical little gadgets that automatically keep your room at a constant temperature, you can become a self-regulating mechanism – a 'homeostat', if you like – that can strike a balance between what you want, and what the company requires, in your working environment.[38]

University of California philosophy professor Mike Martin identifies three types of motive that need to be kept in equilibrium by the worker seeking meaning in their labour. These are 'authority motives' (money and status), 'craft motives' (satisfaction and success) and 'moral motives' (job content, belief, calling), all of them secondary to our 'personal, non-mandatory motivation to work'. Using a ludic metaphor, Martin says meaningful work is 'a question of self-fulfilment and self-betrayal... the *interplay* of private and professional life'.[39]

Yet surely the problem is that this 'interplay of private and professional life' is becoming hugely energetic and unpredictable, given the levels of openness and mutability that pervade every area of our lives. Rather than 'meaningful work', 'meaningful existence' or 'meaningful becoming' might be a better term to conjure with. We cannot be little homeostats, maintaining our even-temperedness and equanimity within a spectrum of changing conditions: the information age is far too topsy-turvy for that.[40]

If employers of all kinds now depend on the emotional intelligence and increased capacities of their employees – the best ideas and the best relationships becoming the ultimate business advantage – then they will have to cope with those potentialized employees raising serious questions about the purposes of their actions. The point is: can ethical questions about the purpose of one's conscious and productive activities really be kept in check by any organization, in order to serve its goals? Aren't human beings just too capacious to accept that kind of disciplining these days? When does the unleashed spirit of 'decision making' get reined in?

Another American attempt at defining a better ethic for work comes from Mihaly Csikszentmihalyi, William Damon and Howard Gardner, who try to establish the psychological predictors of a sense of 'good work'. 'Is it possible to understand that happy circumstance,' they ask, 'in which "good" in the technical sense converges with "good" in the moral sense?'[41] The problem is that the examples they give illustrate the need for the strength and autonomy of the player, rather than the steady equilibrium of the worker.

The first example is of a television journalist who was assigned to report on the possible health dangers of video games – specifically, their link with epilepsy. After extensive research, he found that there was no real link, but was still forced to file a story that took these findings as verified. Horrified by this contractual censorship, he switched careers to national public radio – a move that has made him actually proud of his work. They conclude by saying: 'Our studies show that the goal of carrying out good work is harder to reach when conditions are unstable and market forces are allowed to run unchecked.'[42]

What is fascinating is that both stories (the other concerns a whistleblowing geneticist) involve workers leaving their private sector employers and finding refuge in the public sector, or in more scholarly contexts. At the very least, this indicates that people value the notion of there being some ground for their passionate activities beyond a purely market realm – a diversity of enterprises allowing a full diversity of ethical positions to be pursued beyond the cramped strictures of a work ethic. When our nonwork lives become more significant than our work lives, we become less tolerant of our office pathologies – the power games, the sharp practices, the empty values. The challenge this already presents to standard cultures of work is enormous. And perhaps we should start to accept, politically, that we need a newly conceived public realm (or commons) to support our aspirations to play well and expansively.[43] Private enterprise can only be expected to go so far.

Valiantly, Csikszentmihalyi, Damon and Gardner suggest the three Ms that can lead professionals to their idea of good work: 'mission' asks us to compare our current mentality about our jobs with our original ideals; 'mentors' urges us to identify very good (or very bad) individual examples of the job or profession we do; and 'mirror' proposes that 'ultimately, individuals need to be able to look at themselves objectively and see whether they are the kind of person they wish to be.'[44] These are tough tests: and one might imagine the more nervy of employers and managers hoping that their employees never apply them.

How might a player function within an organization? Not necessarily with difficulty, but certainly with complexity. The company has to try to reproduce within itself the kinds of condition that the player will always seek – no pointless presenteeism, no coercive hierarchies, no presumption that work is the primary definer of a human being. At a minimal level of reform, this means an active sabbaticals culture (for both sexes), embracing ever shorter working time directives; and a company culture that is more like a campus than a barracks, a playground than a bureaucracy.

The player at work is a fully 'potentialized' worker who can bring a vast range of talents and sensibilities to the task at hand. But that worker will always, in the last analysis, be a player, defining him or herself in an ultimately voluntary and self-realizing way. The companies that will deploy these people best will be those that can make their work time feel as much like play time as possible.

Appropriately enough, the most serious thought given to the notion of a playful workplace has been by a toy company. Denmark's Lego have set up a business consultancy and training arm called Serious Play. The website describes this as:

> An innovative, experiential process designed to enhance business performance. Based on research that shows that this kind of hands-on, minds-on learning produces a deeper, more meaningful understanding of the world and its possibilities, Lego Serious Play is an efficient, practical and effective process that works for everyone within an organization.[45]

So far, so utilitarian. Here play is firmly placed in the sphere of what has come to be called 'staff development' and 'human relations'. The website lists a catechism which might convert the sceptical managers to the virtues of more play in the workplace:

Why does work need play?

- Play helps release thoughts that are locked in the head and the heart.

- You see things differently. Ideas come to life with more concrete detail than ideas expressed through just talking.

- Discussion during play happens on a more level playing field.

- The group at play thrives only when everybody participates, so frustrations are reduced, and team coherence and direction is more solid.

- Play lets you experiment, explore and take risks with ideas without fearing consequences that might happen in 'real life'.

- You generate a wider and more imaginative range of possibilities during play than you would during a traditional business meeting.

- People at play are more present, more engaged, more passionate and better performers.

Why does play work?

- Play is special: if it's routine it's not play.

- Play is voluntary: it can't be coerced or mandated.

- Play is imaginative: you can suspend the rules of the real world.

- Play isn't explicitly productive: direct consequences don't matter.

- Play is unlimited and delimited: play exists for its own sake and is different from work.

- Play happens at an agreed-upon location: but it can be anywhere.

- Play has its own rules: it is not constrained by the rules of work.[46]

Much of this is unarguable as a checklist of the many virtues of play, and displays an admirable sensitivity to its many rhetorics and forms. But can all these diverse functionalities and potentialities of play really be kept within the boundaries of 'improving business performance'? The business press has shown a degree of scepticism about the Serious Play initiative, regarding it as a higher form of juvenilia (the headline 'Give me back my ball: can making staff play with Lego really be worthwhile?' is typical).[47] In a sense, their suspicions are correct. This isn't so much about defending childishness from the grown-up world of money and power, but about a 'childness' that preserves play as a latent resource of potentiality and freedom.[48] There is something in a player – particularly *this* player – that rises up against the tight corralling of a classic piece of ludic culture (Lego, in all its nubbly glory) to the narrow ends of business operation:

> [With Serious Play] people see things they couldn't see before. They can look at a 3-D metaphorical model of their business and its landscape and visualize strategies that were formerly opaque and closed off to them. They

can see their business enterprise in a more holistic sense. They can manipulate it, play with it and ask all sorts of 'what if?' questions by physically manipulating their business model. 'What if our key supplier goes bankrupt?' 'What if we relocated our marketing team to Asia?' 'What if our sales suddenly doubled?'[49]

What if, indeed? The rise of 'scenario planning' in business and organization life – the immediate context for Serious Play – has regularly been invoked as the ultimate performance enhancer for major companies. As the Lego consultants promise, play understood 'not as a leisure pursuit but as a serious activity . . . can unleash creative energies so sorely needed in the business world today'.[50] But some working papers from their own research arm, Imagilab in Lausanne, raise the issue of exactly how 'unleashed' these creative energies can be. 'Might play activities inherently carry risks to the strategic success of an enterprise?' wonder Johan Loos, Bart Victor and Matt Stadtler.[51] They concede that playful strategies – challenging limits, virtualizing and simulating realities, placing oneself in the position of the other – can put all identities, individual and collective, into a state of crisis and fluidity.

For organizations, this can be dangerous. Play asks you to imagine yourself, those around you, your position, differently. What effect that has on each person depends on the individual concerned and therefore has unpredictable outcomes. The authors conclude that: 'Practically speaking, we suggest that organizations might begin to engage in processes of strategic innovation by playfully entertaining the question: "Who are we?"'

Yet the answer to that question might be far less functional, far more subversive, than the play instigators can cope with. 'If this is who we are, then do I really belong here? If I can't change this collective identity, should I go find a better, more congruent one?' What if the alternative criteria for the workplace, constructed through play, become too alternative for the players' comfort? 'The cultural stakes of play are quite high, ' admit the authors. 'It remains a highly unsettled question whether such striving can be proven to be adaptively effective, or valuable on the whole by any measure.'

The question posed by Serious Play's consultancy manifesto – 'Why does work need play?' – now seems to have a most curious answer: to destabilize work so much that it radically questions its very purpose. In later chapters, we'll investigate some workplaces that explicitly claim to be able to put their very business 'into play' like this.

So the player-friendly workplace is conceivable. The question is whether it would be recognizable as a business in the standard sense. A proper 'play audit' wouldn't just result in the introduction of masseurs at lunchtime, or a Playstation in the coffee room. It would involve looking at the entire behaviour of a company, which would perhaps result in a revaluation of that company's final product or service.

Some business thinkers are beginning to recognize that a civilization at play, and in play, requires an entirely different set of power relationships in our economies and businesses.[52] But the political space that the play ethic precisely mediates is between those in business and government, who recognize that our rituals and games of production and communication have to change – and those idealists and activists who are forcing that to happen by their own social and technological creativity.[53] Between the protest ethic and the work ethic, the play ethic might play an important mediating role.

In general, we have to revisit the idea of 'active humanity': how can modern human beings maintain their passion, enthusiasm and energy in every area of their lives? My argument is that the values of the work ethic, rooted in a love of routine, duty and repression, are actually a heavy cloak (to use Max Weber's metaphor) that inhibits people from realizing their potential.

For most of us, musing on how we feel at our most free and purposeful will involve looking at financial dependencies and patterns of spending, at family demands and imperatives – what Americans have for years been calling 'downshifting'.[54] But the play ethic is about voluntary complexity, not voluntary simplicity. It's more about 'shape shifting' – creating a much wider zone in your life, beyond earning and spending, that can truly replenish your energies and sensibilities for the demands of the modern age.

So, how should politicians and business leaders respond when faced with these 'lifestyle militants'? By refusing their lifestyle demands and forcing them to leave or conform?

Again, if we refer back to our general theory of play, we can see that such change goes with the cultural grain. Robert Wright deploys game theory to show that there is an inevitable rise in social complexity – civilization is a non-zero-sum game, where interacting social players inevitably move towards cooperative strategies.[55] Francis Fukuyama sees a new social dynamic which is ordered through networks: our agonistic participation in these, as individualized modern adults, is increasing our sense of civic interconnection, rather than reducing it.[56] The point about play is that it is indeed much more appropriate, in its values, motivations and traditions, to the operations of the networked world of informational capitalism.

Yet just as the work ethic resulted in human solidarities that wrested some humanity and comfort out of the industrial system, so the play ethic will generate human *multiplicities* – a great diversity of passionate activists, trying to reap the full potential of the communicational infrastructures they live within. The educated, potentialized info-worker should be part of a growing movement towards popular autonomy – of people deciding their life priorities as strong, self-determined characters, and fitting their working and organizational duties around that self-determination.

There is a popular and democratic struggle to use the productivity and efficiency gains of the information age to better, more humane ends. The original (and much misunderstood) Luddites were not anti technology per se: as Kirkpatrick Sale quotes them from 1812, they were specifically against 'all Machinery which hurt the commonality' – implying at least an open mind towards machinery that enhanced it.[57]

And this is where my interest in play moves beyond workplaces and organizations and into the realms of civil society – the hackers, downloaders and Linux-heads who are slowly evolving their 'open-source' constitution through the rich games of their coding; the protestors who integrate carnival and pranksterism into their otherwise deadly serious manoeuvres; the refugees from the patriarchal workplace who want to 'play' a role in their community, or just 'play' with their children more. And of course, the huge semiocracy of the cultural industries, presenting us with endless landscapes of imaginative possibility.

Where we get the resources for that struggle should be an open question – they might be spiritual as much as ideological, emotional as much as financial. Evolving a play ethic addresses the essential question of meaningful human activity in an informational age – that is, the question of *poiesis*, to use the Greek word. How might I make a mark on my world, a mark that might add value to that world?[58] The ambivalent and fluid nature of information technologies – the way the same digital systems can be used to administer and control large groups of people, or to liberate those individuals into new worlds of creativity and collaboration – is the radical moment of this new age.

We must look amongst the hackers, artists, imagineers, image-makers, musicians, loving parents and civic entrepreneurs who are trying to realize this radical potential. We must recognize their unalienated pleasure in their activities, and use that as the measure against which we find our workplaces and organizations wanting. The first of these new tribes of play come, appropriately enough, with joysticks in their hands: the soulitarians.

FOUR / 91
RISE OF THE
SOULITARIANS:
The Net,
Digitality and
Play

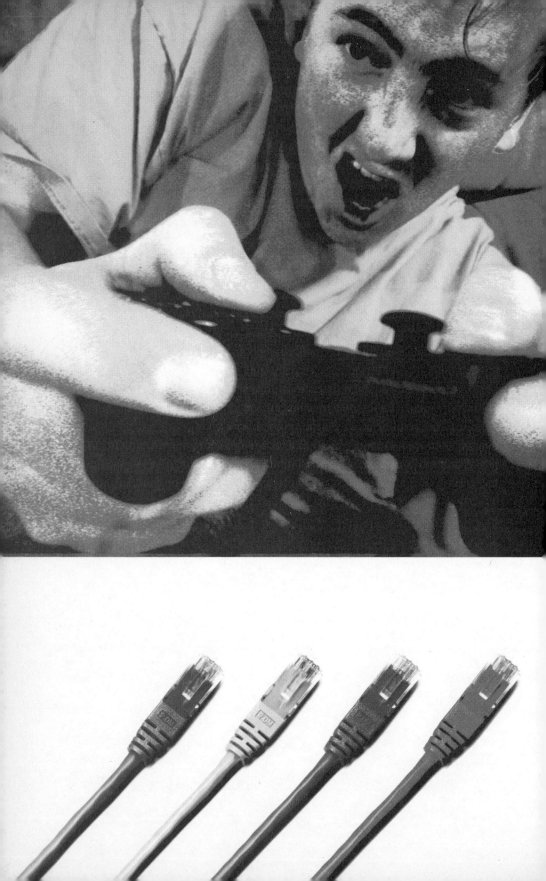

I come from the Playstation generation . . . I love creating it, creating beats, messing about with flows.
– Dizzee Rascal, *Evening Standard*, 10 September 2003

All that is solid melts into air.
– Karl Marx and Friedrich Engels, *The Communist Manifesto*, 1848

You never forget the moment when it all went digital. I suppose my first experience of the information age – that realm where all things of value can be copied and pasted, compressed and reshaped, edited and supplemented with ease – was the first time I held a three-inch Amstrad floppy disc in my hand. I knew that here was a powerful little sliver of pure existence. Between these fingers were pages of song lyrics, unpublishable interviews for unreadable fanzines, twilight notes and musings, financial records, at least one desperate plea for forgiveness and God knows what else. The text of my life, as a struggling writer, musician and lover, Glasgow-London, 1986–7.

I'd downloaded everything because a new portable PC was only a few days away and the old green-screened groaner was going into storage, but the experience of seeing my tumultuous, struggling year – or at least its textual residue – crunched down into a thin black wafer was almost worth the replacement cost itself. I portentously dropped it into a sealed envelope, entertaining fantasies of revisiting my earlier self in some modernist, glass-walled techno-palace, suspended from the side of a mist-wreathed European mountain, twenty prosperous years on. The envelope was, of course, lost within six months. (Don't even *mention* the techno-palace.) But the absurdity of the moment stayed with me. There was something unsettlingly, well, *playful* about information technology. How could all my passions and outpourings be so bathetically reduced? How could it all be so portable, so trivially encased?

The next digital epiphany came about two years later, in Sigma Sound Studios, just above the Ed Sullivan Studios on Broadway, New York. I was in the middle of recording what was to become a moderately successful pop album with my brother Gregory. One morning I trudged in, not looking forward to the day's labours. We'd had a bad session with a horn section a few days before: our inexperience had met their apathy, and the results were undistinguished to say the least. Under pressure of budget and time, the decision would have to be made: keep the horns as they were, messy and slipshod, or remove them altogether. Any decision either way would feel like a mistake, a pratfall, a hitch by the hicks from Scotland.

I pushed open the heavy door of the control room, and found my brother and our Colombian engineer grinning broadly. Between them lay a big grey box with a blue LCD screen, blinking sedately. 'Check this out, bruv,' said Gregory. As the tape played, I heard a beautifully arranged horn-track – less fussily arranged than I remembered, but certainly bang in time, and in tune. Had they brought the section back in that morning? 'Nah,' said Fernando, tapping the box. 'We just picked the riffs they played right, sampled them into this baby, and then punched them into the track in the right places.' I looked at the box and laughed: somewhere in there, the professional reputation of a supposedly crack NY session team had been salvaged. But more importantly, we could now arrange them, even re-use them as we wished, without having to call them up for another expensive gig. Their breaths and exertions, spit and technique, had become zeros and ones, bytes on a hard drive. Ours to play with.

The last time I got the genuine whiff of pure digitality was when I finally wrestled my Compaq 386 laptop to the ground in 1994, overcame my initial modem phobia and figured out how to get onto CompuServe from my home office fax line. Until then, cyberspace had been nothing more than an unconvincing purple passage in a William Gibson novel (something about 'consensual hallucinations') and a mildly diverting Disney movie called *Tron*. That is, just another science-fiction trope to divert the squared-eyed boys. I'd even written a song on that New York album about 'a new computer religion', which realized that electronic networks were 'the only thing more powerful than the boss'. A realm where insurrectionary office workers 'caressed the keys like lovers', and discovered the secret of their own collective power – their ability to 'rock the system together'. Welcome to my robot wisdom, circa 1987.[1]

Years later, I sat in my study in my Glasgow home – trolling through newspaper databases, reading financial tickers, sending emails to the three people I knew could receive them – and began to feel that familiar techno thrill. All this information and interactivity, from this digestive-encrusted chair, with these boring old Glaswegian trees swaying outside? But the feature that really compelled me was something called Mosaic: this 'browser' took you to long grey slabs, punctuated with blue text, that the manual called a 'website'. I remember typing in the Web address of a US political magazine I used to love, but couldn't find anywhere on the shelves over here. Suddenly there it was: *Mother Jones Online*. The graphic downloads were interminable, but the text came through speedily, and just as pithily as the print version. So once again, a personal matrix of time, space and memory was being compacted by info-tech. I had been missing terribly the deeply eclectic pleasure of browsing the Coliseum bookstore off Columbus Circle, pulling out every sliver of lifestyle and mentality that the cosmopolis had to offer. Now I could get that feeling via screen, mouse and phone line. Not as tactile, and nothing to (literally) write home about. But better, way better, than provincial, rainy-Glasgow nothing.

Did it feel like 'surfing', as those early cyber articles described? No: too sun-kissed a metaphor for a slouching, tea-slurping media chancer in Partick. It felt more immediate and graspable than that: as if the globe and its extremities had flattened out into a great board game. With this machine, you could jump from square to square with no more energy expended than the movement of your hands and the payment of a few domestic bills. It felt as though you were playing with the world itself: and for me at least, it hasn't stopped feeling like that ever since.

We're all so digitally self-conscious these days, as we approach a decade of proper cyber culture, that it's almost embarrassing to recall those early moments of wonder, when the alchemy of information puffed its little creations into life before our eyes. Compared to mine other people's early cyber experiences will no doubt be either much more excit-ing (traversing newsgroups in a variety of mad personae, unravelling secu-rity systems with the hackers and crackers); or much more frustrating (expecting a new universe of meaning with your first Internet account, and getting an intermittently functional hunk of domestic junk instead).

I wanted to recall my story because I think it reveals something about information technology that often gets lost in all the official, business-and-government hoopla. Firstly, there is something (in the Catholic liturgical sense) *transubstantial* about the digital world. Water to wine, wine to blood: a musician's breath becomes an immortal signal, a New York urban experience translates into a morning's surf in Glasgow. Some might claim that the transubstantiation goes the other way – from the blood-richness of real experience to the watery simulations of a virtual reality. Yet for me, it never feels like a diminishing of experience, only an extension of it, to paraphrase Marshall McLuhan.[2] On the Web I feel tentacular, as though I'm spreading my cilia, my sensibilities, as far as I can imagine across this planet – touching other worlds of meaning that enrich where I am, and what I can do next. I've always loved the phrase coined by Stewart Brand, the hippie technovisionary who founded the *Whole Earth Review* in 1972:

'We are as gods and we might as well get good at it.' Our god-like powers to shape our cultural experiences through our technological extensions is what informational culture is all about.[3]

One way to get used to feeling like a god is to become self-conscious about being a 'creator'. When faced with digitality, officialdom tries to place its inherent power and transgressiveness within useful contexts. We need information and communications technology (ICT) in schools because it will allow teachers and pupils to access knowledge and expertise; we need ICT in business because it will make companies more responsive to the marketplace, more efficient within their own boundaries.[4] But these institutions are only trying to channel the torrential flow of digitality through their own dams and floodgates: to turn a vast tidal wave of popular techno-creativity into the steady current of better educated citizens, more competitive producers, higher levels of social integration.

Yet the people – whenever they get the chance to freely align their passions to their technologies – head somewhere else. This is towards digitality as a means of playing better and more freely, and not as a means of working harder and consuming appropriately.

I know this to be true, because it once put me out of a job.

In the late nineties I was employed by Microsoft to devise editorial content for their own Internet service – content that would be so compelling, so media rich, that the user would be happy to stay in our portal space (or cybermall). But no matter how attractive or star-studded I made each edition of my music show (titled *Blizzard*, appropriately enough), the MSN users mostly ignored it and went straight for the search engine, wending their own curious way across the Web. Mr Gates spent hundreds of millions of dollars on specialized Web content in those first few brave years of the mass Internet and, in a phrase beloved by my programmer colleagues, almost entirely pissed it away against a wall. Thus I ended up as a wet trickle down the brick face of corporate retrenchment; like many others around me, I seeped away into more interesting places.

Yet in the last decade of digital culture, I have seen the same move repeated hundreds of times: the dot-commons of the Web, its interactivity and mutuality, asserting itself over the hucksters and the corporations and the marketeers.[5] From around 1998 onwards, the whole idea of property relations and profit margins started to dissolve into the thin air of digitality. Internet service providers in the UK battled amongst each other to give you a free Web service. Music fans in America started to download music from the Web in the MP3 format, then distributed it among their peers through software like Napster, in both instances bypassing the usual retail outlets of the major record companies. Almost out of nowhere – or to be more precise, Finland – a whole new computer-operating system called Linux (invented by the Finnish über-nerd Linus Torvalds) began to threaten Microsoft's dominance in the corporate and government marketplace. And did so while being free to use, and open to improvement by hackers.[6]

And at this point in the new decade, the rise of the dot-commons seems inexorable, yet certainly not uncontested. Though Napster was closed, a brace of other file-sharing services (Morpheus, Kazaa, Freenet and many others) have sprung up, covering both music and films, and ingeniously evading the technical and legal restrictions of state and business.[7] The attack on the Twin Towers in New York on 11 September 2001, with its clear evidence of the terrorists' use of electronic networks to coordinate their activities, has made information space even more of a site of struggle.[8] Competing with the calls for more state surveillance on online activity are anxieties about whether the Net only really works when it is a truly public space; whether there must be limits to the way that money and power interests try to shape its development.[9]

It's mostly a feeling on my part (although it's partly a stream of emails, invitations and serendipities along my various networks), but there are some transforming moments yet to come on the playful and open side of ICT. Somewhere, in the space created by some facility of the next generation of mobile and wireless devices, there will be a need for people to organize their random societal paths into some useful, effective flows (represented at the moment by the blogging movement), waiting for some general crisis of meaning or purpose to bring it all together in a flash. Somewhere in that nexus will be another disruptive, Napster-like or Linux-like moment.[10] This is no prediction of course, just some healthy anticipation – which is, of course, the player's paradox: strong agency and vigorous imagination in the face of radical uncertainty.

I'm getting that same tingle I've had before when I've seen the alchemy of the digital age beginning to morph my world, its boundaries and potentials. Every day I feel less alone in my digital dreaming than I have ever felt. I look around me – in the streets, in the airports, in the schools, in the supermarkets, in the clubs – and I feel the web of digitality around us all getting thicker and thicker, the filaments of connection getting stronger, with every bleep of a phone or glow of a terminal. There are statistics pouring out of media portals about the growing density and ubiquity of ICT that confirm what we already know at the micro-level of our lives.[11]

Yet a play ethic (any ethic, for that matter) must have ambitions towards proposing a kind of public activism; that is, it must be in the game of advocating guidelines for behaviour that – whether they are dutifully followed, radically interpreted or violently mutated – might bring about the 'good life' for individuals and collectives. What is the ethical player implied by digital culture? One way to do that, in a spirit of serious play, of course, would be to imagine a social type that could be both descriptive and prescriptive. Some image of a civic actor with whom digital players could positively identify.

Players of the world, unite!

Let's risk a term that tries to express their playful balancing of employment, environment and experience. The bearers of the play ethic, right at the heart of the new economy, are a different kind of worker: not proletarians, but *soulitarians*. And they are beginning to realize their collective power. These soulitarians don't just shape their identities through their uses of technology, but through their offline cultures of play as well – a whole range of self-chosen activities that have anchored them in a different orientation towards a meaningful life. These are the backpackers of Alex Garland's *The Beach*, using cheap flights and travel literature to make the world their playground. These are the ravers who grew up, but who can't (and won't) forget those blissed-out moments of transcendence, when drugs and beats blurred the boundaries of their selves.[12]

Great experiences matter to soulitarians as much as cool commodities. In the late fifties, the radical historian E.P. Thompson anticipated this in his famous essay 'Time, work discipline and industrial capitalism'. Musing on what a post-work society might be like, Thompson suggested that its rhythms might rely 'neither upon the seasons, nor upon the market, but upon human occasions'.[13] The soulitarian is above all a connoisseur of 'human occasions', from festival to tourist trail, from anti-corporate carnival to urban hangout. What can any employer give these soulful players that their own values and experiences haven't already validated?

The soulitarians happily flit between start up and corporation, self-employment and job sharing, being paid in cash and being paid in kind. If and when they work, they work for the good of their soul. Whatever they're making, and for whom, the production of character comes first for all soulitarians. For them, play is naturally what you do with your world: there's no angst or self-loathing about it. The technology that hovers like an axe over the neck of the traditional worker is more like a toy for them – something to express yourself with, not a machine to be subjected to; a means of empowerment, not exploitation. They've left for the Playstation, these screenagers and cybernauts, and they're never coming home.

This is also the generation that was allowed to download its lives for free: browsers for nothing, Web mail for nothing, bootlegged software for nothing and now everything from free operating systems (Linux) to Eminem's latest opus for – you guessed it – nothing. So they've already got a weird, almost dot-communist sense of property rights, which subverts the work ethic at its core. How much do you have to labour for stuff, when the stuff often comes as a gift anyway? How much do you have to grab for yourself, when sharing what you already have (the basis of open source software and file sharing) generates so much more?[14]

When the soulitarians graduate from college and go to the job market, the first thing they do is play around with the idea of a career itself. As a Work Foundation report says, these 'free workers' also want to find an emotional content in the work they're doing. They wish to cut deals with employers that maximize their control of their time, their environment, their personal commitments. They don't believe that fun and pleasure should be confined to after hours – they want it when they draw a wage as well. They are not the acquisitive yuppies of the eighties, nor are they the 'downshifters' and 'voluntary simpletons' of the nineties, but a class beyond both positions. They are eager to take all the opportunities that the new network society can offer, but wise enough to realize that wage labour is only one strand in their life stories.[15]

Theoretically, it remains the case that almost everybody can be a soulitarian. The work ethic was essentially mind-control: industry had to find a way to exploit the worker's body so it had to tether his and her mind with a whole weight of guilt, shame and status. But now that the worker's body is useless, replaced by ever smarter machines, industry is left with the worker's mind to exploit – and that's proving extremely difficult. For every time you ask a mind to reskill and upgrade, you make that mind more aware of its singular talents, subtler in its workings, and therefore more demanding about the life it wants to lead. The 'smart' workers are getting too smart for their own good.[16]

Soulitarian journeys

London 1: the alternative Ulsterman

'I'd quite like to be the Peter Mandelson of the Ulster Unionists,' said the Miyake-clad young man from the Shankill Road, as we inhaled bowls of French fries in a Soho bar. 'I think their communications machine needs a little educatin'. East Belfast and North Down in shock, loved-up rebirth of unionist radicalism . . . why not?'

I had wanted my soulitarians to bring their ethical and emotional hinterlands to bear on their information-age skills, but I hadn't expected (or hoped) for someone as curious and idiosyncratic as Thomas. He was small, with blond highlights and cartoon trainers, and had a wary, lowered expression; add the rutted, unmistakable Ulster accent, and he seemed like a very handy example of the regional media chancer (well, it takes one to know one). Thomas had first turned up in my London hotel room with a video camera, a photocopy of an article I'd written on play and a cheque in an envelope. He was working as a researcher for a major ad agency, pitching for a product (*sumt'in' t'do with compu'tr games*, he told me, in that stop-start brogue), and he wanted me to hold forth on matters ludic.

It was a late plane home to Glasgow, I had a bruising mobile-phone bill waiting for me and in any case I was flattered. Is this what it means to 'make money from your ideas'? How could a freelance intellectual refuse the offer? So Thomas switched his machine on, and I downloaded on him furiously for two hours. The next day, I got a flustered call from an assistant: 'Um, can we do that again? Thomas mucked up the recording.'

A mid-twenties metropolitan advertising boy who couldn't work his video camera: having spent far too many hours in the company of tech heads who small-talked like instruction manuals – and who were snooty about it into the bargain – I warmed to Thomas immediately. He'd mentioned sidelines about DJ'ing in Japan, and *that whole Prattest'nt mint'ality*. I noted him in my 'possible soulitarian' register. When we met up again a month later, Thomas picked the venue. 'It's a downstairs bar in Soho called The Player. I'm sure you'll like it.' I didn't, but I liked his slightly jejune obviousness in choosing it.

After about four hours, Thomas turned out to be the very model of a twenty-first-century soulitarian. He was well aware that his mental labour, the resource of his soul, was being exploited by info-capitalism. But he was determined that he'd use these capacities for other purposes than simply making a living. Quite what those purposes would turn out to be, I could never have predicted.

I could, however, easily imagine why he was holding down a good job in a global ad agency. His CV was almost a postmodern caricature, like something from a late-night satire show trying just a little too hard. Lower-middle-class son of Belfast teachers gets to Oxford to read English, majoring in Joyce and Wilde. Wins a scholarship to Japan, and lives there for eighteen months, becoming a fluent speaker, a model for Issey Miyake and a celebrity DJ. Returns to a country overrun by Pokemon, Tamagotchis, Playstation and Japanese-style extreme game shows. Not surprisingly, Thomas had worked ever since.

'I do what they call "qualitative research",' he said wryly. 'Which means I can dander out and see stuff, hold focus groups, surf the Net. I provide my perspectives on markets and brands, which then gets taken away and written up statistically. I even get the chance to use all my literary theory . . . So yeah, it's a life.'

But not that fulfilling. Thomas had a major problem with the mentality of most creative people in advertising: not the corruption of their sensibilities, but their pointless self-loathing. 'They all need to get over themselves. The holy truth doesn't lie in some holy world of literature or religion or whatever it is . . . Too many of these creatives are living a kind of schizophrenia – they're trying to make beautiful ads, which they secretly hope will match up to the real art, books, films, whatever, that they love. But they believe in their heart of hearts that the system they're in is so evil that no matter what they do, it's never going to solve anything.'

He paused for breath. 'That's why you get incredibly plastic brands. The people who are forging them think that what they're doing is fundamentally evil. They're creating glossy shit which perpetuates the status quo. I think you can do ads that are informative, enlightening acts of communication.'

I wondered whether Thomas was protesting a little too much here. But he clarified beautifully. 'All the time I spent in Japan, I was struck by one thing. They are remarkably free of a lot of the anxiety, that Western Christian anxiety that burns out so many people here. The Japanese play with their brands and products – in some ways, it's a very enlightened consumerism, all about performance and display, very visual over verbal. But here, it's all about "brand personality". There has to be a person in there. They talk about "a Jesus Christ in every brand – a brand without a Jesus isn't a brand at all" . . . Absolute bollocks, at the end of the day.'

He rattled out the points in his clipped Ulsterese. Ad agencies have 'contempt for the Net, contempt for digital culture, because they hate the idea of interactivity, of people becoming too unpredictable'. Naomi Klein, author of the anti-brand best-seller No Logo, was 'the Princess Di of the marketing industry – she destroys marketing, so that marketing can become even stronger after she leaves the scene'.

By this point, Thomas was beginning to remind me of those bright young men that I'd consistently met over the last fifteen years on my visits to the metropolis – all those logic crunchers and paradigm makers on legs. Aim them in the direction of a social phenomenon and they'd process it into usable chunks of data, like hay bales dropping from a combine harvester. I'd met every stripe and variety: political researcher, TV producer, think-tank commander, steely corporate adjutant. The technical term for them, in Robert Reich's words, is 'symbolic analysts'. Their job is to analyse symbols – words, numbers, signs, combinations of all three – so that capitalism can work faster, smarter, harder.[17]

I was beginning to fear that Thomas was more of a symbolic analyst than a soulitarian. Symbolic analysts use their skills to break down the wild chaos of the information age into shapes – brands, trends, angles – that their employers can use in the marketplace. And then they think no more about it: let's go clubbing! Hit the snows (or the snow)! One of the play phrases that turns up a huge search result on the Net is 'Work hard, play hard'. It's a phrase beloved by sports jocks, sales people and computer coders alike; and the 'hardness' undoubtedly comes from their awareness of being at the cutting edge of the information age, carving usable commodities out of the compacted mass of modern symbols.

The pioneer of virtual reality Jaron Lanier once said that information was 'alienated experience'.[18] The symbolic analyst is an alienated experiencer, and tries very hard to be happy in his or her alienation. The soulitarian realizes his or her alienation, and decides to do something about it. So was Thomas just exploiting the 'play' – the looseness and malleability – of cultural forms, twisting them into new and appropriate shapes? Nothing inherently wrong with that. But nothing world-transform-ing, or play-ethical, about it either.

But Thomas came through for me, and in doing so, made things even more subtle again. While he was a fresh prince in Tokyo's style scene – 'living in the empire of the signs, just like old Barthes said' – it seems Thomas got an attack of the Protestant ethic. 'It was ethics that drove me back. I was just afloat. DJ'ing for Commes Des Garçons, Miyake . . . But you never felt you were really implementing or influencing anything you believed in.'

So what did he want to do with his semiotic skills? I'd been prodding him a little (forgive the pun) about his personal relationship to the Protes-tant work ethic. He responded at a tangent, and with some emotion. 'The typecasting of Protestantism you're giving is so wrong – young Protestants could be educated into a different world about all this.'

Thomas had begun to put his own culture in context through his expe-rience of the Japanese. 'The way the world looks at them is not that dis-similar to the way the world looks at the Ulster Protestants. Here are these emotionally constipated little automatons, who work like bastards and who can't do anything else. I identified with that, and the contradiction between that and the incredible visual culture.'

The Player was filling up with braying voices and mobile phone trills, and we were running out of time together. What did he want to do with this fascinating arc of experience? Where did he want it to take him, other than to the next big media gig? 'Well, my next frontier for me would have to be about contributing back to Northern Ireland. I was deeply frustrated with the cultural status quo when I was growing up, but I knew that within that structure, there could be openness and liberalism. The way I conceive it, I actually got a hell of a lot of investment put in me from that culture – and just to bugger off round the world with that investment, and not to contribute anything back, is tantamount to a little death for me.

'I don't want to go back and become a revolutionary, fighting people to the bitter end. But it's certainly about bringing up your kids, contributing in the micro politics and day-to-day democracy of it all. Sending your kids to school packed with different ideas, so they can impact on the status quo.'

Consider his skills, experiences and employment in the abstract: Thomas would seem like the classic example of the banal professional 'player' surfing his way through the lush lands of London media. Excavate his full and complex humanity, however, and he becomes a bearer of the play ethic, and specifically, a *soulitarian*: that is, a knowledge worker who is acutely aware of his dynamic and creative potential, but who wants to point it in other directions than simply shareholder value or personal profit. His response was to follow his routes back to his roots – and thereby transform them in a literally 'radical' way.

'Yes, I'd love to do a Mandelson for the Unionist Party – to try and educate the communication mechanism of one of the most backward-looking political organizations in the West. Unionism has always fascinated me because, if you scraped all the crap away, it could be a positive movement – about the periphery against the centre, Ireland, Wales and Scotland against London. Unionism should be about respecting separate identities but blending them together to create a broader based people, with a broader background of ideas behind them. That would be hopeful for the future.'

He'd been discussing this with his family, and had realized for a while that he didn't share the standard liberal vision – essentially pro-Nationalist – on his homeland. 'To attack Unionism is to batter the second victim of colonialism. You cannot compare the old situation with apartheid in South Africa, that astounds me. Yes, the Protestants were an obstinate, ignorant ruling class – but that was never apartheid. Northern Ireland has actually had the world's leading equal opportunities legislation in place for about thirty years. How can we get away from casting these stones?'

Thomas took a sip from his Coke. 'I don't know if I could say this from within the situation. But, you know, as someone coming back from the Mecca of the communications industry . . . I could hopefully get in the door at least.'

And when he gets in there, Thomas's richly developed play ethics will have their effect. 'There are so many young people, both in Northern Ireland and Japan, who are rejecting the work ethic, but there's no structure or group or authority telling them they can do what they want to do, that it should in fact be lauded. They just become passive people, essentially. I know one guy particularly, from home, who's been washed out of the system: as the years go by, he becomes more and more stuck to the wallpaper. He doesn't have the apparatus that I have to buoy myself up, to make choices, yes or no. So his reaction is to be the ying to the Protestant work ethic's yang – a bohemian, hedonistic response. That's what the hegemony can happily cope with – people burned out and blitzed out by partying at thirty-five, no qualifications, just trickling along on social security.'

Somewhere beyond work and leisure, routine and hedonism, Thomas was interested in a new 'Unionism', with a small 'u' – if not quite *at* play, then at least *in* play, its dominant terms being questioned. And the one thing that got Thomas most exercised – a few minutes before his louche pals from the agency descended on him and dried him up – was the institution of the family. 'That's why Thatcher's politics was so wicked: simply about these little feudal family units, battling amongst each other, getting ever tighter and more defensive. She said "There is no society, only individuals and families". But it's individualism that gets you beyond the family, that displaces it as the overriding facet of your identity. That's what's so appalling about the Protestant ethic in general as it applies in Northern Ireland – it makes the place into two families, two tribes, to which you can only be expected to be loyal.

'But that's changing all over – there will be an identity crisis at the end of the work ethic, no doubt. When I research British youth culture, I see a great engine for change powering through here. Young people are picking and mixing their elements to create an identity. That's my hope for the future.'

I mused happily on how well Thomas exemplified my idea of complex playfulness: he knew play in its most ancient, and most modern, manifestations. An Ulster unionist background – with its Orange marches, its house murals, its love of partisan football clubs like Rangers – is almost wholly constituted through forms of play as power, and play as collective identity. Indeed, to opt out of these noisy, public carnivals – refusing to wear the colours, shutting your ears to the music – would be to resist a strong degree of coercion on the part of the community. One might easily imagine fleeing eastwards and southwards, as Thomas did, into cultures where anything – and any self – was possible: and this might well be a one-way journey for a bright, capacious boy. Who wouldn't want to stretch out in such a modernist playworld where the rules of the game could always change, and there was always a number of games available to enter?

But something nagged away at Thomas, some connection between the two arenas in which he might conceive of himself as a player. I met him almost at the forging moment when the connection was taking place. And it was a moment of ethics: what can I do to make all these elements in myself hang together? How can all this capability, all these experiences – all these routes and roots – enrich my soul?

I wished him luck as we parted on the Soho pavements. Then he turned around, having remembered to tell me something: 'We've done it, you know.' Done what? Turns out that the pitch his agency was going for was the new Microsoft account – their X-Box computer game, the company's multi-billion-dollar attempt to break Sony's Playstation 2 stranglehold. I had gone on and on about the computer game as the modern player's key articulacy: a medium which could simulate all kinds of personal and social scenarios, not just slash 'n' dice, and become as important to the information age as pen and paper were to the industrial age. 'And they accepted all your lines – that play is a legitimate social aspiration, that it's a way to shape your modern life . . . We did it. Well done.'

I must confess that I stood stunned and breathless; the courier bikes hurtling past my elbows in the gloom, my mind whirling around my own polarities. Thought number one: I can't believe I charged him so little. (Thus speaks the modern player, keen to resource his own life narrative, more resources meaning more choices.) Thought number two: have I just been involved in a potential moment of capitalist reform? Has my soaring vision of play shaped the public meaning of a powerful new medium? (Thus speaks the ancient player, who trusts that all sufficiently creative and passionate actions will add their energy to the general network of his life, and the effect will come back to him somehow – indirectly, unpredictably, generally.)

In March 2002, Bartle Bogle Hegarty's X-Box ads were finally shown on British television and caused no small degree of fuss. In 'Champagne', a mother strains on the birthing table, her solicitous husband at her side. With a great roar and a spurt of blood, her baby comes into the world. But frighteningly, it's moving like a rocket from a launcher – smashing through the hospital window, streaking over the dull road signs and tedious office blocks of the south-east. As the baby flies, it gradually ages, letting out a primal howl at each stage: adolescence, manhood, middle age, senescence. At the end of its arc, the now-aged human slams straight into his appointed slot in the graveyard. The credits roll: 'Life is short. Play more'. The ad takes the anti-work-ethic spirit to a shocking extreme – this product is being marketed at pustular male adolescents, after all.

But the second ad, 'Mosquito' made a more mature play-ethical statement. A soothing Caribbean voice tells us that we've lost our ability to 'make life a melody' in the face of our social expectation to 'get a job': the images shift from a natural world grooving along beautifully, to anxious adults swatting parasites with rolled-up newspapers. 'Humans, you have a natural gift for play – don't lose it,' says the narrator, as a baby looks attentively at the viewer. 'Work less, play more.'[19]

Well, I was flattered. Yet what interests me now is the gap between the ideals and the reality of play, particularly when it comes to computer games. There's no doubt that the new generation of consoles – which also include Playstation 2 and Nintendo's Gamecube – are hugely powerful bits of machinery: 'a supercomputer in every home', as the play scholar Marc Pesce has said.[20] There are two targets for all these manufacturers: firstly, that their byte-crunching machines provide either the most realistic, or the most startling, experiences; secondly, that when everyone has a broadband connection in their home, the whole world will start playing computer games with each other. Rather than rely on the fantasy whims of violence-obsessed males, Microsoft and Sony are hoping that their products might even replace the PC or TV as the main 'information portal' for the average home.

Yet in the meantime – as X-Box's first set of available games showed – it's mostly the pizza-and-beer paradigm. That is, killer cyborgs (*Halo*), snowboarding warriors (*Dark Summit*) or cars with an alarming tendency to crash spectacularly (*Wreckless: the Yakuza Missions*). Games for PCs seem to be different, being both more cerebral and emotional (e.g. *The Sims, Black & White*). Perhaps it's difficult to get sweaty and tense clicking a humble mouse, rather than juddering on a motion-sensitive joystick.

The most interesting tendency is to join the two experiences together – that of big ideas and hard action. The Scottish company Rockstar/Viz Interactive has been causing some controversy with its *State of Emergency* game for Playstation 2. This basically does for anti-capitalist activists what Lara Croft does for adventure trails. The version I saw in 2002 gave rioters points for blowing away policemen, and took points off for killing civilians. The evil totalitarian masters have had a name change as well: from 'American Trade Organization' to 'The Corporation' (some post 9/11 pragmatism, no doubt). An article in Salon.com describes the game's basic narrative: 'Joining the Freedom Movement means accomplishing a series of tasks – blowing up security stations here, killing an executive there, and so on – as the resistance gains ground across Capitol City in a march to Corporation Central, to confront the company's overlords.'[21] Naomi Klein, doyen of the anti-globalizers, has condemned the game as a 'corporate co-optation' of the protest movement.[22] Frankly, that dignifies it. *State of Emergency* is just another example of how the entertainment-industrial complex can make money out of any kind of social excitement – as long as it can be use to hit the basic consumer buttons of the target audience. Which is, at the moment, crash and slash, dice and burn.

In short, none of these games will truly embody the play ethic until they start to take some genuine risks with the medium. When do we get the *Ulysses* of the computer game, rather than always the penny dreadful or the genre pot-boiler? When do we get Radiohead rather than Black Sabbath?[23] The X-Box ads evoke some of the deeper meanings of play: I should know. But like most adverts since time immemorial, they're essentially selling you a pup. Work less, sure. But play well, rather than just play more.

London 2: the cellular flâneuse

'Are you the play-man?' She was a tall, chin-forward woman in her early thirties: and for all the hipness of her gel-flipped hair, she sounded like summer hat and Pimms on the lawn would be just as appropriate. We were all downstairs at the Commonwealth Club, sweltering in one of those ideas salons that only London can pull off regularly – great big pulsing London, magnet for all manner of concept merchants and theoretical sharks. As I sweatily tried to answer her questions between the coffee and the deserts, she lifted her chin and squinted impatiently down at me: a woman clearly used to bullet points and speed delivery. It transpired that Sarah was consulting for Vodafone, had been a conceptual artist and had founded a Web design company 'devoted to trying out new forms of play'.

By chance, I'd actually visited that company barely a week ago, in the half-finished streets of Hoxton, an area that was London's digital bohemia in the early noughties. Sarah had been out of the company for a year: and I wondered whether that explained the excessively drab and listless collection of individuals that had slumped before me in a Thai restaurant, mumbling inertly for ninety minutes. Apart from the monkish geek who'd built their most famous application (a little online kit that allowed you to make stick animals and then animate them) they were the least spontaneous, most guarded bunch of twenty-five to thirty-five-year-olds you'd ever wish to avoid. (The dot-com bust, I later realized, had bitten badly: they didn't want to say anything publicly that might be investor-threatening. And they succeeded.)

Sarah was in no way desiccated or bloodless. But there was an element of steel about her. She arranged that we drink cocktails one afternoon in a book shop cafe above Piccadilly Circus; we tapped the date into our electronic diaries, and I steadied myself for a bruising session of conceptual and professional boxing.

But when she sallied in on the day, she was immediately warmer – 'I'm feeling very *teenage*,' she told me with a big smile. The reasons? One charmingly immediate ('Just spent the morning with my Italian boyfriend'), and one slightly more substantial: 'I've just been fired.' The consultancy she'd been with – something to do with 'mobile networks' – had reduced itself from a staff of over forty to about two (the co-founders) in about a week.

Immediately, Sarah started passing one of my essential soulitarian tests: don't measure your employability by the judgements of your last employer – measure it by your own confidence, your own achievements and the richness of your networks. 'Of course,' she announced, cigarette already aloft, 'you have a slightly wobbly moment about whether you'll get the next gig – whoops, hold on . . .' Her mobile phone rang: it was a London product designer, who had met her/seen her work/chatted to her old boss, and wanted to get her in for some 'skunk-working'. She slapped the phone shut, and smiled pertly. 'Next gig! Or, well, it might be, it *could* be. But that's the cellular network for you, eh? You're never alone, or unavailable for slavery. Now, cocktails!'

Like Thomas's career profile, Sarah's seemed impeccably fin-de-siècle. She started out as a BBC journalist ('When my mum heard me reading a news report, she knew I had a proper job'). Then, while on assignment in Eastern Europe, she began to let go of the career ladder, and founded an independent news agency in Prague in the early nineties. She came home to do an 'arts and appropriate technology' degree; then, as the digital fever began to build in London over 1998, she set up her new-media company with some student pals.

Sarah found that business excited her – not as an alternative to her ambitions as a conceptual artist, but as an extension of them. 'The further up you go, the more that people like to talk in abstractions – if you talk to the senior management of Vodafone or Orange about cultural theory, they get it straightaway. It's very seductive to be in with the power people. You suggest things to them and they go and do it. So it's like cultural intervention – but you're doing it with many thousands of employees . . .'

This reminded me of my X-Box experience, about which I started to moan piteously. But Sarah cut me short. 'No, you have, you *are* making a difference.' With not a little pride, she said that there were aspects of the operations in the next generation of mobile phones that she knew she had shaped through her consultancy. 'The people in there know that they can trace lots of functionality to a conversation they had with me. But I don't need a public signature myself: I know they're in there. What I've done is to fashion tools for the corporate world that they can play with – but which then shapes their businesses. My ideas are part of that language . . . and that's big.'

To a certain extent, I believed her disdain for celebrity (or at least authorship). Sarah's advice to anyone who would listen in the mobile sector was to 'Forget about the brand, the sexy object in your hand – concentrate on the network, how you build it for openness or innovation, the applications that live in that environment.' In terms of complex play, she was stating a core ethical principle. To be a player is to give your energies to the pulsing network of life. You make your mark there, you strengthen your presence there – but you shouldn't presume that your distinctive contribution will lead to distinctive rewards.

'My mum says, "You're indulging your creativity, you're not making sure you get your due,"' said Sarah as she gulped down the remains of her sea breeze. 'But things don't just have to possess social and economic value – they can just have value in themselves. I happen to be like this: so I have a responsibility to try and explore some things. These things could be an essay, an event, an application, a beautiful space.'

If soulitarians have a sense of their collective condition, they get it through networking, or through cultivating their own networks. And part of Sarah's breezy sanguinity about losing her job – in which, as she constantly reminded me, she was handling 'million-pound contracts in multimillion-pound projects' – was due to her strength as a node in her creative network. Indeed, as the subsequent months proved, Sarah was quite the *salonière:* she invited me to a number of conferences and events that she'd either organized or was participating in as part of her general emailout.

Over the months, as a recognizable cast list of faces appeared and disappeared and reappeared through the talks culture in London, I began to see that players need to create their shared playgrounds to confirm themselves, just as much as workers used the shop floor to recognize their mutual power. Workers fought to wrest control of their bodies away from the routines of the factory system. Players, on the other hand, need a new space – as the Playstation 2 ads would have it, a 'third space' – in order to exert control over their minds again, to build up spiritual strength and mental autonomy. Whether it's the conference or public talk, or the coffee house on the corner, or the chance street encounter in a buzzing neighbourhood, players need their open-ended, unspecific places, even if only to rehearse their ethic of unpredictability and spontaneity. You can only have a next move if there's room to make the move. To be confident in your play, you have to find a way to display as well.

Sarah, in the end, was as richly ambiguous in her responses to the world as any complex player should be. At one extreme, she had just performed the ultimate act of the soulitarian player, in its most modernist guise – that is, dot-commed her name, turned her identity into a domain in cyberspace. (It's a curriculum vitae, suffused with her tone and chutzpah.) In the words of the business guru Tom Peters, she had asserted the value of 'the Brand Called Me'.[24] So many of her art projects were about the fine line between monetary and non-monetary value, our contractual and our passionate lives. What if a mobile phone could be configured as a vibrating sex toy? What if artists could measure their worth in terms of what economists would call their 'book' value? What if people could be tricked into applying for imaginary jobs, which would then shock them into realizing the limitations of their current work?

But at the end of our cocktail session, Sarah confessed that her ambition could just as easily be satisfied by creating 'a beautiful art-meets-food space ... nothing naff, just an ambience in which people could be profound and sensual'. Her last two emails to me were a breathless announcement of a business class flight to Boston ('all expenses paid! This is the life'), and news of a post-WTC site called www.stopthewar.org.uk. Just another day in the outbox of a soulitarian.

London 3: the digital son

There was one more London dot-com player I knew I had to track down, someone who would throw some salt in the dessert bowl of soulitarian values, but who also couldn't be more committed to the passionate use of technology.

I'd first worked with Ed around the end of 1997. He'd got to me through my rickety old CompuServe home page, linking me up with a whole new world again as the embers of my music career cooled around me. Ed had noted my by-line in the national newspapers that year: I had taken to writing splenetic, unforgiving reviews of any rock musician who dared to tour

Glasgow, safe from harm in my regional fastness. His Web company had been asked by Microsoft to produce some content for their new Internet service: would I like to edit the music magazine? And could I come down a couple of days a month to do so?

I immediately said yes. The notion of working with nerds rather than musicians in London was attractive: both of them were sets of boys struggling to express themselves with their technology. So it seemed like an appropriate leap sideways, for a while. I also wondered what it would feel like to take the Microsoft shilling. If you're going to squeeze competitive rates out of any company for your services, why not the biggest one of all?

At the end of the year, our product had been a resounding commercial failure (it didn't get Microsoft any more customers), an equally resounding creative success (well, we all thought so) and a lot of sociable (and reasonably well-paid) fun. Yet it had introduced me to a cast of characters, what would later be called the Net generation, the like of whom I'd never encountered before.

The Canadian writer Douglas Coupland had written *Microserfs* the year before, a novelized account of his eight months observing the lifestyles of workers in Microsoft's Richmond headquarters. The pun of the title captured the dizzy powerlessness of these coders and designers: their delicate, gaseous selves flowing this way and that, shaped by the whims of their equally amorphous colleagues, and by the latest readings of the Microsoft stock tickers in the bottom corner of their screens.[25]

The Londoners at Noho certainly weren't Microserfs, evasive and insubstantial under the feudal rule of Bill Gates. To continue the medieval metaphor, they were more like cynical guild members or merchants producing appropriate commodities for a local tyrant, but hardly buying into the mystique of his monarchy. (A visit from 'the client' was the cue for a three-hour session of mild sneering in front of a money man.) Yet they weren't Microsubversives, either. The point was 'to produce good, creative work, in spite of all their corporate bullshit', as Ed once put it to me.

And emerging from the interactions of coders, graphic designers, researchers, journalists, in-house musicians, managers and visionaries, some great work was done. I was ashamed that no one got to see it, that it barely worked on the Microsoft network itself, and that when you demonstrated it to anyone on a laptop, it invariably froze. But on our screens (and our CD-rom CVs), the idea of an interactive, multimedia music magazine worked terribly well.

Noho's room — a dark one-flight-up office in an alleyway across from Centre Point — was filled with a static cloud of permanent irony, combined with a titanic work rate. Shadow-eyed programmers would turn my duff interviews into hip — graphical worlds; and when you praised them for it, they would shift uncomfortably, as if the very act of approval meant that it was already yesterday's innovation. 'Old shit', one paler-than-white grub would say to me. 'Happy you're happy.' The presumption being that, as one of the non-coding damned, I wouldn't know any better. But they were all too much the cyborg to deliver that arrogance with any kind of aggression; too close to their machines to get that angry about a pseudo-nerd who didn't know his Active X from his Java-Jini. And I liked that low level of testosterone: indeed, part of the wisdom of my mid-life is the realization that I always have. One of the things I know about the informational economy is that, in general, it gentles the men who labour in it.

When Microsoft pulled the plug, we all had a final dinner, threw white wine around wantonly, and raised the irony to such a pitch that we parted almost in mid-comedy routine, relieved of the burden of saying 'goodbye' or 'keep in touch'. I retreated back to Glasgow, to other projects and different dreams. But I had enjoyed my first sustained encounter with the digital generation. I knew we'd hook up again.

This time, via the usual Google search, I'd found Ed in yet another builder-strewn street yet again in Hoxton. Ed is tall, dome headed, with too-large glasses and a deep Estuary voice — and as soon as I met him again, we were laughing readily. There is something about a background in music journalism that puts cynicism and idealism on the same sheet of card, bent precisely in the middle: very early on, Ed and I both realized that digital culture was rock 'n' roll for very patient, meticulous people. So we knew what there was to love in it, and shove in it, almost minute by minute.

Ed's current gig was selling interactive Web stories to cable TV people, major portals, corporate clients — indeed, in the barren dot-com-bust climate of the early noughties, to anyone who was vaguely interested. 'We're paddling in the shallows at the moment, waiting for the next big wave to swell. Will these next generation mobile phones work? Will the masses get big data cables into their homes — and even want to use them? Usual industry anxiety, clouded crystal ball, etc. We're just trying to do good games here.'

Well, if not good, then certainly symptomatic of their creator. I'd always found there to be a fascinating disconnection between Ed the media insider, and Ed the content creator: the first was effortlessly cynical and wised up, but the second was almost too cosy and eager to please. On the current state of commercial digital culture, he could be eviscerating.

'Companies who pay for adverts just don't know how much people don't really watch television. If they did the game would be completely up ... Kids love e-tech when it's really complex – we thirty-somethings and upwards don't, by and large. That's why we're so history! ... Some people like to play around with their identity on the Web – they're not sad, they're just repressed. Why shouldn't I sell them services that relieve their repression?' It was easy, and entertaining, to let him play the towering inferno of tech scepticism.

At that moment, the content Ed was selling was a series of camp 'n' cheesy online narratives – involving a gamine, Lara-Croftesque girl and an owner of a Mediterranean holiday island – into which people could intervene, adopt a character and play with other members. Ever sensitive to the rising wave, he was planning to have the game's main characters pop up on people's mobile phones as they trundled down supermarket shopping aisles ('It'd say on a text message, "Don't turn round – she's in aisle six!"'). I wondered whether people would find that intrusive, or even creepy – the idea that a game you might sign up for could escape its boundaries (the Playstation, the PC terminal), and start to bug you in your everyday life? Or might it actually trigger obsessive and paranoid personalities – the digital equivalent of someone muttering to their imaginary friend at a bus stop?

Ed responded with as neat a definition of the protean player as I'd come across. 'You don't just get out of the real world in these games, adopt a new self – you escape *with* yourself into a new world, and you test that out. It's like drawing the chalk circle. You stand inside it, you're in the game; you stand outside it, you're safe. And look: it can't be the case that the only people who might want to play with their identity online are either the despairing unemployed, or the mentally ill. We are all grazers these days – we dip into a book for a few pages, or we take a bite of this food and not the whole meal, or we download one track and not the whole album. I think people in the mainstream will want to dip into these fantasy interactions as well, as part of their daily menu. I think we're a bit more capacious and flexible these days.'

Although I couldn't bring myself to say it, I seriously doubted that Ed was appealing to the protean player in quite the right way. There was something way too populist about it all – a presumption that kitsch and camp and big laffs were quite enough to motivate people to join this club. This populism had always puzzled me about Ed: an Oxford grad, a contemporary of Radiohead ('I know those guys – they're about as radical and streetwise as choir practice.'), and never without a work of classic world lit on his desk. Today, it was Andrew Marvell's collected poems, and something by William Carlos Williams.

Sitting beside that, almost as incongruous amid the humming Macs and forests of wires, were a few plastic-gold photo frames, filled with a very conventional series of family photographs – soft-focus wedding shots, even softer-focus pics of his kids. I didn't doubt that Ed was self-consciously an adult playing games (he'd even railed at me earlier about his distrust of a particular kind of play ethic – 'all these men-children, cavorting around with scooters, pretending that things are easy when they're bloody complex. I think it's anti-intellectualism'). But there was a powerful pulse here that I wanted to lay my finger on.

I found it when he told me about his dream project, the one he was trying to raise capital for. Again, it was kitschy in the extreme – a kind of James Bond figure, 'based on a very dodgy middle-aged character, who reports back to you from wherever the hell he is, in the middle of some tight scrape: one day on a raft in the Pacific, next day in a Tokyo bar. He'll message you saying "who are you with, tell me now? What drink are you drinking?" Then he'll ask you to sign his expenses. You'll have a close relationship with him, but you'll never know what he'll do next, he won't always offer an explanation.'

There was a kind of quiet surge from Ed, some faraway shift that coloured his cheek a little. 'I know exactly where all of this comes from. This game is about my dad, who's dead. So I can bring him back to life in it, which is quite funny.' Did he die recently? 'No, ten, twelve years ago.' And is this what your dad was like?

'No, he wasn't. He was an alcoholic, my dad. He lived in a sad flat next to a cliff, actually. But this guy is what I would have loved my dad to have been – except he was, in fact, rubbish. So I want this agent to be as rubbish as my real dad, but as glamorous as my imaginary dad. As we all want our dads to be. So that hits my buttons – and also thinking about my son, and what he thinks of me. That would be good to play around with, all these male role models.'

I can't get a silence in edgeways now: he's on a long, deep roll. 'There are another two things from my youth in this game. One, I used to spend a lot of time being Steve McQueen in *The Great Escape*. But I was doing it on one of those inflatable bouncing animals on the lawn – the rose garden was the prison camp, the French windows were Switzerland. The other thing was that I used to be the fifth member of the Monkees when I was at boarding school. I used to lock myself in the lavatory and be him, and have all these discussions about what we would do together. It seemed to involve a lot of swimming and high diving. I don't know why I thought all the Monkees would be good at that. Anyway, it didn't interrupt my social interaction with my friends in any way at all, didn't interfere with my studies. But it did help me get through the day. So it's the idea of having an alter ego, a virtual person who has their own life – but this thing isn't spoiling your life, it isn't taking over, you're just dipping into it. I think about these things in almost every story I tell.'

If Ed was aware that he'd revealed the entire psychohistory of his involvement in gaming and storytelling – all these unreal, artificial figures who demand your attention, and are just as easily rejected; all these distant yet active virtual patriarchs, being coded up amid the good son's glowing family albums, and mounds of timeless literature . . . well, he wasn't showing it. And I wasn't going to make a grandstand of it, like some shrink with an a-ha! analysis. We actually allowed ourselves a few minutes of British reserve (national character pops up in the strangest of places). Yet Ed was undoubtedly soulitarian in his impulses – allowing ICT to express his interiority, rather than regulate and shape it; making the projects serve his sensibility, rather than the other way around.

By way of closing (and maybe closure, too) Ed told me a story about his meeting with Will Wright, American creator of *The Sims* – a computer game that does for soap opera what *SimCity* did for urban planning: that is, make it a manipulable, testable virtual reality. 'Will created this game which can, if you use it a certain way, utterly subvert American suburban values – but actually, deep down, he really believes in suburbia, he's deeply conservative. I told him about taking my boy to his first football game in London: by chance, we found ourselves in the visiting supporters' end of the stand. My little kid was standing there, proudly, wrapped in his team colours. But then our side started to go one-down, then two-down . . . and after the third ball hit the net, the entire terrace turned on my boy. Seven hundred adults gave it to my son. *"You're not laughing a-nee-more . . ."* So he bursts into tears, and after the fifth goal goes in, he says, "I think I want to go home now, daddy."'

'I'm telling Will Wright this – he'd been talking about how you simulate a sports event – and he's absolutely appalled. "How could you put your son through that situation! What a terrible place England is . . ." After that he couldn't bring himself to speak to me.'[26]

The last sprinkle of necessary salt from Ed came when I told him about my forthcoming trip to Finland to visit the hackers and the philosophers, the Nokia-heads and Linux rebels, in chilly Helsinki. What did he think of the whole Finnish idea of 'open-source' software – published free on the Web, updatable by anyone, a collective resource for the dot-commons? 'It's decadent, if you ask me. All that barter economy nonsense. "You can spend a few weeks with my supercomputer in the University of Colorado, if I can spend a few weeks playing with mobile phones in Helsinki." We're not going get to rid of the suits and money, to become cultural anarchists who just swap code, and somehow magically food appears on the table from our exchanges. That's fall of the Roman Empire stuff. Lying about eating grapes all day, sharing them with your mates and not worrying where the grapes actually come from. Sorry, mate. That doesn't sound *British* to me.'

Helsinki: the Finnish model

Jyri Engestrom is twenty-three, shockingly blond, American accented, and the hippest young brand consultant in Helsinki. But when I ask him to define the Finnish attitude to new technology, the story he tells seems like something out of rural folklore. 'There's this British guy sitting at Helsinki Airport, talking in English in a very loud voice on his mobile phone, about how he's just screwed this Finnish company, completely ripped it off. "These Finns just don't know how to do business."

'So as I'm watching this, I see a man sitting behind him who calmly takes out his mobile phone and dials a number. This guy's local, employed by the company – and he's phoning straight through to the boss, telling him in Finnish to cancel the deal. Meanwhile, totally unaware, this Brit is carrying on, telling them to literally break out the champagne corks . . . Now that's the Finnish attitude to new technology!'

There's much laughter around the table at Cafe Espresso, just off Vuorikatu, in central Helsinki. It's the confident laughter of a group of smart, successful twenty-somethings, at home in their own country, but also willing to take on the world – and more than capable of doing so. Around me are a conceptual artist (who's planning a virtual village), the head of a telecoms company (who's starting up a creative collective), and the irrepressibly funky Jyri. They call themselves 'Aula' – which is either a new kind of urban living space, or a commercial consultancy, or an avant-garde charity – 'Or whatever we wanna make it,' says Jyri. 'Anything's possible here.'[27]

After five, furious, head-spinning days in Helsinki, I wouldn't disagree with him. Unlike most visitors to Finland, I hadn't come here to worship at the altar of Nokia. Just before I left, a senior UK executive at the company even suggested to me that I should 'rub a little salt in our wounds . . . we've perhaps had too good a press. Sniff around, get some other perspectives.'

And indeed, there is an obvious alternative perspective to take on the Finnish miracle – one which puts the commercial power of Nokia (generating half the country's GDP, employing most of its graduates, and still the world leader in mobile handset production) in a much broader context. For Finland is also famous for a tradition of new technology that simply bypasses the market and sends its bounty out on to the networks, for the free usage of all. To understand the triumphs of Finnish dot.commerce, you also have to understand the profundity of its dot.communism.

The best-known example of this is the Linux operating system. Its source code was invented by a twenty-one-year-old Finnish student called Linus Torvalds. Torvalds published it freely on the Web in 1996, inviting anyone to come along and participate in its development. Improbably, Linux is now the supreme challenger to Microsoft's business operating systems throughout the world. IBM relaunched itself in 2001 as a Linux brand, with the system's little penguin mascot dancing all over a multi-million-pound software campaign. Linux has been so successful because it is, to use the technical term, 'open source': the kernel of its program is made freely available to anyone who wants to tinker with it, or improve it. Microsoft, on the other hand, keeps its kernel under a tight proprietary lock and key.

Linux has been rendered by the new-economy press as the 'triumph of the hackers' over money-grabbing corporations. Yet Torvalds was only paying respect to a long tradition of open-source software in Finland – including IRC (Internet relay chat), anonymous remailing and a host of other freely given gifts to the infrastructure of the Net.[28]

Of course, the US also produces both software giants and subversive hackers – Napster being the most obvious recent example. Yet both sides are almost always at war, whether in the intellectual property courts or even at the end of a police gun (remember hacker Kevin Mitnick's celebrated arrest a few years ago). A Microsoft head recently described the whole idea of the free software movement as 'un-American' in the way that it flaunts intellectual property rights. [29]

In Finland, however, it seems that open-source radicals and corporate execs can happily co-exist. Is this the inevitable camaraderie among smart people in a small country? Helsinki itself, with its elegant thoroughfares and profusion of 'third spaces', seems like a city where nobody could avoid meeting everyone after too long. Or is there something deeper than that? Something that allows Finns to maintain a creative tension between the two great opposing forces of the new economy: information wants to be free – but information also needs to make money? Somewhere between Nokia and Linux, I thought I would find the truth about the Finnish miracle.

Placed perfectly between Nokia and Linux is yet another translucently blond twenty-something called Pekka Himanen. In late 2001 his book, *The Hacker Ethic*, topped the best-seller lists in the *San Francisco Chronicle*, the local paper for Silicon Valley. With an introduction from Linus Torvalds himself (a personal friend of Himanen from their Helsinki University days), it is a short but powerful manifesto for the hacker movement.[30] For Himanen, 'open source' isn't just about downloading free software. It's about a whole new paradigm for education, democracy and how we produce and work, based on free access to knowledge, a better use of technology, and a return to the classical virtues of participation and self-government.

Breaking bread in yet another cafe it becomes clear that Pekka is the Finnish equivalent of our own 'telly dons'. I'm squeezed into a busy media schedule that includes breakfast TV, major chat shows and high-level seminars. 'Oh, you're talking to the philosopher,' people said throughout the week: it turned out that Himanen had recently hosted a popular TV series about technology and philosophy, and had also chaired a government commission on the 'Net university'. So when Pekka told me that senior Nokia executives are happy with the hacker ethic ('they can't say it publicly, of course, but they are with me on this'), he sounded more than credible. But I still needed to know how these two tech cultures – hacker and commercial, free and priced – could co-exist so easily in Finland? 'The fundamental ethical value in Finland is egalitarianism,' says Himanen. 'That shapes how we approach things like the information society in a very deep way. It's something we are always conscious of. And it informs everyone – from the highest boss to the lowest worker. Hackerism is about empowerment of the individual, which is a very Finnish notion.'

In that light, the mobile phone is the most Finnish notion of all. It is evidenced in one of the most annoying habits in everyday Helsinki life: nobody, absolutely nobody, ignores their mobile phone – no matter how crucial the conversational turning point. But it's only annoying when you don't understand the deep cultural force behind it. 'Finns never regard anyone, not any boss or politician, as any more esteemed or worthwhile than themselves,' says Risto Linturi, once the head of the country's public telecom service, and now a futurist and venture capitalist. 'That means that when the phone rings, nobody feels they are too important to ignore it. But it also means that you don't abuse it: you don't ring anyone without something substantial to communicate. For that, you text.'

Finland seems to be riding an extraordinary stroke of historical luck. The egalitarian grain of their national culture has met the cutting blade of the network society – and they're speedily carving out a new information society from the collision. Linturi reminds me that, even before the post-cold war recession of the early 1990s, the Finnish government was establishing bodies such as Sitra (their infamous Ministry of the Future), which made the potentials and pitfalls of a network society a matter of heated public debate. So Nokia's famous corporate turn – from boots and colour TVs, to software and mobiles – took place within a rich culture of theorizing about the future. Go to Risto Linturi's own website, and you will see his own detailed sci-fi chronology for the next fifty Finnish years.[31] 'This is a cold, hard country, so we have always been interested in technologies, and the knowledge to use and extend them,' he continues. 'Otherwise, we'd all have frozen and starved to death.'

Linturi, wiry and sockless, is holding forth in the basement of his beautiful modernist house, just beside the frozen shore of Kallioniementie. He pushes over an article about an American inventor who is about to put the first flying car into production. 'My venture fund has invested in that,' says Risto proudly. 'Finland had one of the first ever commercial airlines. Finns have always been interested in mobility.'

Perhaps one can understand that interest, given the immobility that has conditioned Finland's recent history – namely having to co-exist with the Soviet Union on its borders for most of the twentieth century. Yet, as many of my interviewees uneasily acknowledged, the legacy of communism – of being in bed with the Soviet elephant – is to be found in Finland's inescapably strong sense of society.

At the Cafe Engel in Aleksanterinkatu, which faces the city's triad of national institutions (university, church and parliament building), I talked to the head of research for Sitra. Antii Haukamati taught philosophy to a whole generation of Nokia-heads and Finnish hackers. Over some green tea, Haukamati easily slips into the language of the old neighbours. 'It used to be, as the Marxists once said, that capitalists owned the tools of production. Now the people can own those tools – and the most powerful tools in the world: a phone, a computer and a network connection.' Yet, ever resourceful, the Finns are even turning this communal instinct – or what they have now learned to call 'social capital' – into a competitive advantage.

My last stop was a visit to the site of the Helsinki Virtual Village (HVV), in Arabianranta, just on the outskirts of Helsinki. Its aim, by 2010, is to become an entirely interactive urban space, where the latest examples of wired and wireless living will be test-bedded. A joint project between Helsinki City Council, some local telcos and big players like IBM, it is aiming to be a test bed for the new mobile lifestyle – a place for Finnish (and other) companies to try out their latest applications. But these applications will be driven and shaped by the lifestyle and mores of ordinary Finns. So expect openness, access and inclusiveness to be deeply programmed in.[32]

One of the local companies already involved in the info-structure of HVV has its expertise in Net democracy. When I visited, Decretum's office overlooked the main site. On its wall is projected its own rewriting of Descartes: *decerno ergo sum*; I decide, therefore I am. 'We know that what people want most from their technology in Finland is to participate, to feel as if they matter, to make themselves heard,' says Marja Anttonen, one of Decretum's directors. 'The new mobile networks will allow people to do that – you can decide on something while waiting for a bus, during your meal, anywhere. We are building that society here in Helsinki Virtual Village. And then,' she paused coyly, 'perhaps we can sell those networks to you.'

Himanen sees the ethical challenge of the hackers as part of a global critique of technology. What is the true purpose of innovation? How much should creativity be at the service of profit? Is this a politics of 'social hackerism'? But there is no doubt that the hacker ethic is the Finnish ethic too. The cascade of free-software applications that have come out of Finland over the past two decades emerges from a specific social context. To explain it, you need to look at how the Finns deploy their power and money in public services.[33]

For example, Finland has an almost utopian education system – not just free of charge at all levels, but free of deadlines as well. The average length it takes for a Finn to finish their MA is about six to seven years (ten years is not unknown). And in that time, they are playing around with knowledge and technology, feeling their way into their life's vocation. That is what Torvalds did, tinkering with his operating system kernel at home and in the university's computer labs in the long spaces between exams. The mighty Linux began as the compulsive hobby of a dawdling student.

Ever the classicist (Finns are entrancingly proud of their 'humanistic' tradition), Himanen reminded me of the Greek roots of the word scholar – *shkole*, meaning 'the ability to organize your own time, and not learn like a slave'. Himanen's thinking helps us to connect the furious key tapping of pallid geeks to a much wider multitude of social 'players' who refuse to accept that their passions, talents and creativity should be corralled within the compound of 'work'. These players could also be radical parents reforming the workplace, the irrepressible hedonists of pop culture or those involved in the steady increase in spiritual lifestyles.

How depressing it was to step off the Finn-Air plane, still enthused by the experience of a prosperous society of mass scholars, inventing the future at their leisure, and walk into the brutalities of New Labour. Everyone to work, says Chancellor Gordon Brown, no matter what the job entails, no matter how pointless it is. Yet it's the soulful, playful, scholarly 'idleness' of hackers that has partly helped to swell Brown's pre-election coffers. All those world-changing, freely gifted innovations produced – HTTP, TCP/IP, Perl, Apache, Sendmail and Linux – have provided the very backbone for the network economy.

Rather than coercing the poor into their brain-destroying McJobs, perhaps the chancellor should be thinking about how to make them all ethical hackers. True, you might be time-rich and cash-poor if you're not in the labour market. But if you're knowledge-rich and facilities-rich as well then experimentation and creative play become your vocation. Look at pop music, fuelled by passion, technology and a lot of unspecific fiddling around. Hackers and rockers are spun from the same ethical DNA. So it's possible that some unemployable, disaffected kid, glommed onto a PC for days, nights and months on end, supported by free education and decent social support, could come up with the next geek miracle for Britain. But as long as the Protestant work ethic dominates government thinking, targeting resources to shape a nation of dutiful workers instead of a nation of unruly players and creators, that's an unlikely scenario.

In a recent book co-authored with Manuel Castells, Himanen describes what he calls 'the Finnish model' of the information society. If America's

'Silicon Valley model' describes 'a market-driven, open information society', and if Singapore's model implies an 'authoritarian information-society', then Finland's is an 'open, welfare information society'. Himanen gives a breathless compression of his country's advantage:

> Finland's special strengths include the competitive mobile Internet companies; the state-led system of dynamic institutions advancing Finnish technology innovation; creative computer hackerism; imaginative citizen-initiated social hackerism; the combination of the information society and the welfare state from education, health to social services; local information-society initiatives; and a national identity that is technology positive and favours networking.[34]

In short, there is a 'virtuous feedback loop' between state, business and a free and creative civil society: more innovation means more competitive companies, means more investment in 'information welfare', means more innovation. There is an extraordinary model in the book, purporting to show this 'Finnish innovation system'.[35] At the bottom right-hand corner, connecting universities and business (but with no connections to government – at least none they'd admit to) is a sphere identified as 'HACKERS: TORVALDS, HELSINGIUS, ETC'. Code subversives, and digital play ethicists, at the heart of a national social model. What a country!

None of the Finns I talked to could tell me what the next world-transforming code to come out of the country would be, but they seemed quietly confident that, in the geek trenches of Finland's information society, something would emerge. 'We don't pick winners,' a government futurist told me. 'We give people the competence to exercise their freedom.' A hacker ethic for a hacker nation. Would that the bracing winds from Helsinki's streets occasionally blew in this direction, too.

Soulitarian, cybertarian or (still) proletarian?

E-society gives us the chance to live in abstract communities, where an idea or an attitude is what expresses you, as much as a skin colour or a language, a history or a territory. The soulitarian generation understands this very well. One can wander up and down the aisles of the Glasgow branch of EasyEverything any day and see scores of people playing their roles in one virtual community or another. Giggling girls flirting with lusty boys in AOL chatrooms. Shell-suited scheme kids in computer-game combat with gold-chained ghetto kids halfway across the world. Smart business ladies flowing their typing skills into hotter than usual Hotmails.[36]

This is a house of proteans, shape-shifters, manifesting themselves in cyberspace exactly according to their wishes. I look around this space, and I can't help feeling that I'm in the midst of a liberation movement – a liberation of capacities. If the play ethic is about allowing people to develop the strength and skills of their imagination – to say 'as if', or 'imagine that', or 'try this' every moment of their waking day – then the soulitarians are seizing that human possibility by the passionate performances they conduct through their info-tech. For them, the virtual is real, and the real is virtual, the two mingling in a blur of possibilities. The soulitarians live that paradox without anxiety, in fact with evident joy.

Yet there is one deliberate omission in the argument of this chapter so far. How can you define a soulitariat without dwelling, at least momentarily, on the proletariat it supersedes? You are a proletarian if, according to one contemporary definition, you are one of those 'whose labour is directly or indirectly exploited by and subjected to capitalist norms of production and reproduction'.[37] Untangled, that means if you work for a wage – if you do what they tell you do to for money (or even if you like what you do, but you have to do it anyway) – you are a proletarian. If that's the case, then almost all of us with any relationship to the labour market are proles.

But isn't a proletarian someone from the industrial working class, blocking factory gates and stoning company limousines to create a new society? Used to be. Yet as any half-decent sociologist will tell you, the industrial working class (particularly in the first world) has become about as powerful as the women's institute, or lorry drivers, or lesbian mums. That is, they're now an interest group, pressuring for change amid an almighty clamour of other social interests. The reasons for their dethronement, in the age of globalization, are obvious and harsh. When your factory can be switched off and turned on somewhere else on the planet in less than six months, or when automation steadily advances on the skills and competencies of human labour, you're in no position to start demanding a 'workers' republic' from the shop floor.[38]

Ursula Huws, in her essay 'The making of a cybertariat?', cuts through the usual waffle about employment in the new economy, and leaves five general categories of job standing: 'goods' workers, 'service' workers, 'data' workers, 'management' workers and 'knowledge' workers. From a range of transatlantic surveys, it turns out that those who get to use their computers most are the 'data' workers, whose job is to 'manipulate and use the information developed by the knowledge workers'.[39]

So for Huws, the cybertariat aren't those who sit doodling in Philippe Starck-lined offices, envisioning new corporate cultures as they toss the softball against the chairman's oil portrait. No, it's those who have to execute their plans, face to face (or voice to voice) with the customer: rattling through the calls in a call centre, pounding in statistics with every keystroke being measured on some manager's database. No matter what they're doing, says Huws, they are characterized by a common pose: 'Sitting with one hand poised over a keyboard and the other dancing back and forth from keys to mouse . . . from telesales staff to typesetters, from indexers to insurance underwriters, from librarians to ledger clerks, from planning inspectors to pattern-cutters.' No longer the proud owner of a skill, they all own a general skill – typing, reading, cutting and pasting – and thus can flit from job to job. If the current one melts down, the new one will probably require those reprogrammable mouse and keyboard talents.[40]

It's these particular workers who might develop 'a common class consciousness', says Huws – particularly if they perceive that there's no career path that rises up from the phone farm to the strategy suite. Or if they see that outside threats – the next developing country to get properly wired up, the next wave of automation ('Hello, I am your virtual operator . . .') – will either underprice or wipe out their jobs. Then the best way to better one's income 'may well seem to lie with making common cause with one's fellow workers'.[41]

As Huws says, there have been sporadic moments of classic militancy in the e-economy over the last few years: some of them have been genuinely global in reach. But she's bemused, as is most of the thinking Left, about exactly why these particular means of production haven't exactly forged a mighty new collectivity, red banners unfurling. Why won't the cybertariat rise up?

One is tempted to answer: because they don't want to be *seen* as a cybertariat. That's the thing about information technology – it's *soft*ware more than it's *hard*ware. It's a sponge for human sensibility, with a greater or lesser degree of porousness. You can hate your computer at work, but you might love it in your non-work; the same typing fingers in one day can process claims forms until they ache, and textually seduce a lover, sometimes (if your employer lets you surf) with the same machine. How can you maintain a worker's resentment against the tools of your oppression, when the same tool (in another context) allows you to be a joyful player?

Leftist writers like Huws and the sociologist Richard Sennett wring their hands mightily about the way their analytical concepts don't function properly any more. You can't strike against your employer because they're somewhere at the end of a deep thicket of deals and contracts: there's no 'there' there (as Gertrude Stein once said) for the traditional militant to rail against. You can't defend your unique craft or skill because everyone, from executive to bill chaser, is perched before the same screens, flitting their hands from mouse to keys. The difference between them is based on what you bring, mentally and emotionally, to the technology. You also can't stop the rise of the pettit bourgeoisie and self-employed – because the one thing that info-tech undoubtedly enables is a career beyond the corporate walls, built from bandwidth, a room, a PC and a fistful of contacts.[42]

Is there inequality, instability and insecurity riddled all the way through these new social facts? Yes, undoubtedly. If you want to mitigate these conditions, do you argue for a return to a pre-informational world when life was slower, job demarcations were crystal clear and piping-hot dinners were always on the table at the right time? No way. The dream of a cybertariat is a forlorn one, simply because, as Huws has to concede, to 'be cyber' is not the same as 'being prole'. The Roman prole was clearly the lowest of the low: he could bring no property to the state, simply his body, whether it was to labour or to procreate. The twenty-first-century cyberwoman and man bring the properties of their minds to the state, and those minds can produce more than just a friendly phone conversation, or a timely marketing strategy, or a commercially effective product design.

Huws's cybertarians, who only rouse themselves when their mental labour demands better pay and conditions, are still *homo et femina laborans* in disguise. *Homo et femina ludens* require some new political language. If Henry Ford was still around, I'm sure he'd be more than happy to do business with the Global Union of Cybertarian Workers. He'd be updating his classic lines, though. In 1934, Ford used to say, 'Why do I get a human being, when all I want is a pair of hands?' Nowadays, as the CEO of an information age company, he'd be saying, 'Why do I get a heart, when I only want a mind?'

The gloomier minds on the Left would happily go along with that. New York University's Andrew Ross spent a year in the offices of two of the hottest dot-com companies of the early noughties, observing the soulitarian workplace at its most saturnalian and ostensibly playful – in-house masseurs and graffiti artists, regular trips to the art gallery and memorable office parties, not to mention the obligatory 'foosball' table in the basement.[43] After recording the inevitable trauma of company takeover and collapse, with thousands of dot-commers watching their stock options and utopian work conditions evaporate before their eyes, Ross's conclusion was that they needed to recover some old workers' wisdom. After hanging out for endless fun-filled hours with their fellow neo-bohemian employees, doing the kind of 'bleeding-edge' Web design work for large companies they would have wanted to do for themselves anyway, in conditions where authority structures and workplace formality were obliterated, the dot-commers got a taste of what a 'humane' job might be like – at least in terms of creative self-fulfilment. 'Workers behaving as if they are truly free and human are a big threat to corporations,' says one of Ross's subjects. Yet the professor warns:

> Be careful what you wish for. When work becomes sufficiently humane, we are likely to do far too much of it, and it usurps an unacceptable portion of our lives. For decades, labour advocates have been asking for less alienation on the job, and for a humane work environment that offers personal gratification. Corporate America has been more willing to grant this, while taking away much of the job security and benefit blanket that came along with a corporate job in the cold war period. We shouldn't have to choose between a humane and just workplace.[44]

'Emancipate yourselves from mental slavery,' advises Ross, after Bob Marley's 'Redemption Song', and his main tool for the emancipation of the digital generation is that they begin to establish a decent price for what he calls 'mental labour'. Can the soulitarians, in short, stop pouring their souls into their work – or if they do, can they start to demand a decent rate for it? This is not an easy issue: 'economists have yet to figure out what mental labour is, and what it really costs. The one thing we do know is that the cheaper it comes, the more brutal the New Economy will be'.[45]

In one sense, Ross wishes to recast the division of work and leisure for the informational era. He hopes that chastened dot-commers will start to value the idea of a workplace that trades off alienation against security – doing a job that doesn't allow you to express yourself in full, but which does provide vacation time and health benefits in the meantime. Yet it's worth remembering that his analysis does emerge from a US context, in which – by comparison to Europe – the notion of workers' conditions is a much less collective and regulated affair, whether it's in the 'new economy' or the old one.[46] But in another sense, he also wants the dot-commers to retain some of their idealism – the urgent belief that productivity and subjectivity could be in perfect alignment – because it can undoubtedly improve the objective conditions of the soulitarian: as Ross says, 'The widespread persistence of these ideals has made it more difficult for corporations to stop employees from taking their knowledge with them or to "enclose" ideas and technologies as their own property.'[47] People can be free agents with their skills and capacities, deploying their wisdoms across market and non-market arenas. Pekka Himanen's vision of open-source welfare, or what he calls the 'open-resource' model, is being taken up by many different activisms and organizations – using the enthusiasm and expertise of post-dot-com professionals.[48]

Yet Ross seems unwilling to allow that the 'soulfulness' of a soulitarian might extend beyond some formal recognition of the costs of mental labour. Isn't that vision of realized human capacity, which surfaced even in the deepest trenches of the dot-com boom, more than just a bargaining tool in the 'talent markets' of the future? Should the digital player just give up on his or her sense that informationalism hints at an entirely new social, economic and cultural order – one just a few steps closer to a utopia that the original theorists of the proletariat would have readily recognized?[49]

A remarkable philosopher has been trying to build a radical new politics out of the digital condition. Yet his conceptual vocabulary is studded with words like 'love', 'spirit', 'joy' and 'creativity' as much as it is with 'militancy' or 'resistance'. If a young soulitarian wanted to find his or her twenty-first-century Marx, they could do no worse than to immerse themselves in the work of Antonio Negri.

In their widely acclaimed volume *Empire*, Antonio Negri and Michael Hardt argue that our dominant activity these days is 'immaterial labour' – where we are involved in 'communication, cooperation, and the productions and reproduction of affects'.[50] The first two are obvious: all businesses these days, in the cheesy term, are 'people' businesses. Even if they're selling a useable widget, it's the cultural performance around it – marketing, retail design – that gets you to part with your cash. But the third element, the production and reproduction of affects, is where the new proletarianism becomes really interesting. What they mean is emotional work – 'affecting' people for fun and profit. Which covers everything from jobbing Hollywood actors striking for better rates in commercials, and the team of nice ladies at Past Times who help you get a present for your mother, to the pushiness of the charity professional with her clipboard in the street.[51]

As Negri and Hardt put it, what most Western businesses and organizations are 'parasitic' upon these days is the 'multitude' of communicating humans, driven by the forces of 'love' and 'creativity'.[52] Though it can seem like a softening and humanizing of working life – that 'informality' so beloved of T-shirted tycoons in the dot-com era – it's actually a dangerous frontier for capitalists. Why dangerous? Because in order for the new proles to do their 'immaterial labour', they have to be more communicative, collaborative and empathetic amongst themselves than workers have ever been before. The old proles had their unity forced upon them from the outside: corralled together into the factory gates, they found they had a common interest in forcing those machines to slow down, compelling their owners to distribute their wealth and improve their conditions. But that unity was a violent, self-loathing construction, only forged in opposition to the machines and their owners.

The new unity of the communicational 'multitude' is at a very deep or 'constitutive' level, as Negri and Hardt like to put it. This unity comes from the fact that, in an informational society, we have all the tools we need to produce in our heads; we don't depend on capitalists to provide the factory or the tools of production. 'Capitalism today needs to make free men [*sic*] work. Free men who, one day or another, might think in a different way, because the raw material of production is thought. This means that emotional and ethical values enter work in a fundamental way.'[53]

The Oxford English Dictionary gives the root of proletarian as the Latin *proletarius*, 'a Roman citizen of the lowest class under the Servian constitution, one who served the state not with his property but only with his offspring'. Perhaps there is something in this original definition for our new proletarians. Like their Roman forebears, they are serving the state not with their property, but with their creative offspring – a new source code, or a new shop dressing, or a new turn of a chicken breast. Yet where the old proletariat was forced only to think of itself as a unit, the new proletariat is *already* a collectivity – made up from communication, interaction and emotion. At what point will it realize its power? How lightly does the cloak of social conformism lie on its shoulders? And how easily might it be thrown off?[54]

It is the motivation to throw off the cloak that interests me. There is an old word, capacious and imprecise, which captures all the language that Negri and Hardt use to evoke their new militants, these joyous members of the creative multitude, and that is *soul*. Although old materialists would shy away from the term – though perhaps not Negri, entirely[55] – a ludicist would want the concept of soul to act like a conduit, a processing point, translating a whole new range of resources for the active, passionate, creative self. In these translations, the major spiritual traditions and practices – that is qualitative as well as quantitative knowledge – would be central.[56]

So after Negri and Hardt's 'new proletarian', I would still propose the 'soulitarian' – the ethical player, not worker – at the front line of the new economy. The soulitariat, from hackers to creatives, from performers to reformers, from bored students emailing in the university library to office workers surfing in the local cyber cafe for escape routes, take their communicative, affective and symbolic skills and use them to connect up to their interior and exterior lives. The soulitarian has a clear notion about – indeed an ethical and spiritual commitment towards – a more satisfying, meaning-driven life within the new economy. Soulitarians are active dreamers with concrete tools: they are inspired by the alchemical potential of digitization to live creatively in the new century.

Yet along with the rise of information technology, there are other enormous trends in our world system that put more than our understanding about technology into play.

To put it simply, some players – the generations that overlap with, but stand mostly ahead of, the soulitarians – are also parents. Some of them, also, are explicitly childless. Some of them are mothers; now striding through the marketplace and the organizations, exhilarated about wielding power for the first time ever, removed from the triviality and marginality of received womanhood – and with an ambivalent attitude to play. But some of them are also fathers – whose faces are beginning to turn away from the idols of industrial patriarchy, the presenteeism and the authoritarianism, and beginning to see their children and loved ones almost for the first time: willing to play with them, rather than chafe at their ties. And some of them are the children of these parents: born clicking, as one study has it, and with a new competence about shaping the world that can leave their parents gasping to keep up.[57] But still yearning, in all the ways that children have always yearned, for the good-enough mother and father to help them through their early stages.

Yes, we are players because we have the technology. But we are also players because we can be bigger selves, bigger souls, than we ever were: because, in the wake of feminism and individualization, our sexual and familial roles are loosening and morphing. We are able to play with our identities, and not just in a virtual, simulatory way but with the bodies and minds that surround us in our daily lives. The *Harry Potter* books, and the all-encompassing theme parks, and the action (or in-action) toys are as much the material manifestations of this field of play as the mouse or the mobile phone – although, of course, both technologies (and many others) are being used to help people dance through the genderquake. And in the proper spirit of play, this is both an exhilarating freedom *and* a thick web of consequences and challenges. The need to be ethical about one's play, to give it dignity and meaning and effect, pulses strongly here.

So, who's next? The lifestyle militants.

FIVE / 135

LIFESTYLE MILITANTS:

Women, children and men at play

'You know what *ohana* means . . .'
'I know . . . It means, "nobody gets left behind . . .
or forgotten."'
– *Lilo & Stitch*, Disney film, 2002

Someday, after mastering the winds, the waves, the tides
and gravity, we shall harness for God the energies of love,
and then, for a second time in the history of the world,
man will have discovered fire.
– Pierre Teilhard de Chardin, *The Phenomenon of Man*, 1955

We are family
I've got all my sisters with me
We are family
Get up ev'rybody and sing
– Sister Sledge, 'We Are Family', 1984

Before (and alongside) the soulitarian generation, there is a huge majority of people – the children of the sixties and seventies – who have their own memories and dreams of personal liberation, and are trying to reconcile them with the responsibilities of work and family in the early years of this century. We need to explore that vast spectrum of thirty-to-fifty-somethings, whether singletons or parents, identifying themselves as post-hippies, post-punks (and now post-ravers). For them, the play ethic should be a tool to shake up the structures of their existing lifestyle stasis – whether in organizations, relationships or communities. Radical parents are obviously in the forefront of this – men and women who are beginning, jointly, to demand an end to the overwork culture in the Anglo-American economy. For modern men in particular, the values of play imply prioritizing their personal relationships – with their children, their partners, their communities – over their working time.

And for women, the play ethic opens out a new front for gender politics. Can the full rhetorics of play help liberate women into a new creative space by means of the new commitment of male players to nurturance and emotional articulacy? We know that all work and no play makes Jack a dull boy: a play ethic would want to establish a woman's right to play, as well as her right to work.

The new space of playfulness that's opened up between adults and children – from the 'tweenies' stretching upwards to adulthood, to the 'middle youth' reaching downwards to stay in touch with their childhoods; from the 'Graystation' generation to the Disneyfication of family life – is also worth exploring. Is this just a temporary trend that sharp cultural enterprises will exploit, or is this a brand new space of civility and reciprocity between the generations, a genuine advance on the past?

We R Family

To begin, allow me to recall a scene from my sojourn into the work ethic, a few months into the new millennium. So far I have bravely embraced my new condition. But in this particular instance, my commitment is beginning to fail, and badly.

I sit down with my daughter at the rainy end of a miserable day, and try my best. My jacket's been thrown into the corner, my hair is trickling wet, my shoes are leaving commuter marks on the toy-room carpet. But there she is, a blink under three years, bearing her Duplo bricks with solemnity and purpose.

'Castles, Daddy.'

'Castles, dearest.'

The irony is not lost on me, as I squat down among the primary colours. Hasn't it been castles, castles, for the last twelve hours? Colleagues, so-called – nothing collegiate about them today – clawing and scheming for advantage, only a week into the rationalization: boiling oil pouring down over everyone on the lower ramparts. And yes, I'd tipped my saucepan's worth. The smell of sizzling reputations is in my nostrils. The horror, the horror.

The daughter. My daughter is getting annoyed at the distinct absence of the usual home-time scenario: adult abasement before tyrannical toddler. So I wriggle even further down, and get my head below her eye line as I lie lengthways and slightly propped up, surrendering to her flow. She wants an audience (don't we all?). Her Duplo tower is very intricate, madly colourful and teetering in a direction that surely even she knows means imminent collapse. As I reach out to fix it – *you know that's never going to work, honey* – she flicks my hand away with all the certitude of the recently sentient.

'It's my tower, Dad. You make *your* tower.'

Of course, I think shamefully. She doesn't want the 'one best way' for a Duplo tower. She doesn't worry about excess, or asymmetry, or redundancy. She has no fixed plan, other than that which might emerge from the methodical snapping of plastic to plastic, blue to yellow to red, the long infrastructural one hanging by just one nubble from the transparent decorative brick – but that's all right, even as the whole thing inevitably falls, helped on its way by some gleeful bashing from her. And from those pieces, irreducible and always usable, you make something new. Create, destroy, create.

I start building, slowly, very satisfyingly: something involving Tigger, a cot, a set of wheels and a Lego wall of semi-clear plastic bricks. My daughter looks up through her tresses, sees her father settle and uncoil, and returns to her own thing.

Where does play begin? Literally, with 'the family' (however we wish to define those primary carers and nurturers), or not at all. Although there is debate around the edges, the scholarly consensus is that an early experience of vibrant play – supported both intimately and at a distance by active carers – is crucial to the future development of the child.[1]

The development and progress of our children is an urgent matter for parents these days. Many social commentators have noted that Western parents are investing hugely in their children's prospects. Cartwheeling through our individualized lives, with no real faith in any collective movement towards social betterment, we regard our children as our only secure purchase on the future. So for the more angst-ridden parents – usually those working the hardest – making children capable for the future is paramount. Under these conditions, the rhetoric of play as progress – play as the initial (and hopefully lasting) constructor of human vitality – comes under detailed scrutiny, and often bears the most intense hopes.[2]

Yet play, as this book is at pains to stress, is a multi-faceted phenomenon; prioritize one of its modalities, and you're only suppressing many others. And however much we try to story our lives as a narrative of upward progress, the sheer surprise and energy of play can subvert and undercut that in a variety of ways. As I've said, play starts with the family, flexibly conceived. So might there be some untapped resources in the ludicism of the family that could support our wider thinking about the public impact of play? This vital matrix of love, care and communication might not just be the 'haven in a heartless world', as Christopher Lasch once put it, but the launch pad into an exciting world – or at least a resource for our resilience, when we arrive there.

Yet the cruelties of the work ethic, and the work-obsessed society it legitimates, are acutely felt here. For what is the point of investing in the full development of your child if the world that he or she steps into immediately denies or represses most of the capacities that you have so assiduously cultivated? What happens when your flexible, empathetic, inventive, bold and optimistic child – your child as full player – meets the petty reductions, controlling specialisms and arbitrary hierarchies of the working world?

The urgency of how families play together comes from the fact that parental adults themselves are searching for a new identity – one that gets beyond the stressful wobble of 'work-life balance' and strikes out for a different social grounding altogether. And one of the resources for that altered consciousness is the new culture of mutual enjoyment opening up between parent and child. It's mostly filled with toys, stories and toy stories.

Just toying

Ce n'est pas une image juste, c'est juste une image?
(It's not a just image, it's just an image?)
– Jean-Luc Godard, *Vent d'Est* (film), 1970

Toy tale 1: Hamley's, London

They've put ET back under the plastic, and it's mewling horribly: *hold mee* . . . *hold mee* . . . The robot dog staggers blindly towards the end of the table, red crosses in its eyes: the little boy waits for the sickening smash. The little girl frowns as Amazing Ally, the flaxen-haired cyborg, tries out another of her 4,000-odd emotional programs, her lips levering eerily up and down. 'Come on, girl! You know it's right! Oh, way cool . . .'

The occasion is toy-testing hour at Hamley's, with the store's prime toy testers – George (five) and Fiona (eight). But it feels like Pinocchio does Silicon Valley. The very patient young Hamley's representative has been telling me in hushed tones about the day the man from Sony came to demonstrate the Cibo cyberdog. 'You know, it recognized him in a crowded room, and brought him his ball back . . . I agree, that was a bit creepy.' We overhear the familiar keening cry of a Furby Baby, rousing from its AA-batteried slumber. 'The £30 toys aren't that good yet,' says Mr Hamley, languorously stretching out a palm to catch another pink, twitching automaton, 'but they soon will be.' George, meanwhile, is hauling at Teksta's ear, to test whether it's 'fixable'. Snap! Ah: it isn't.

If Toys R Us, as those famous American philosopher-retailers put it, then Who R We? In the centre of the Christmas madness – where parents hammer through lunchtime shopping centres, emails to Santa crumpled in their hands, where lovers and partners quietly freak in gadget shops, trying to remember hints dropped in August – the question might invite a less than philosophical answer. We R consumer junkies, guilt-ridden nurturers, planet-despoiling spendthrifts. We R infantilized kidults, taking refuge from the world's difficulties in a Disney universe (or maybe even a plutopia) of happy endings, gentle humour and endless plenitude. To conclude this Grinch's discourse: toys are us, because we are toys ourselves – boneless, manipulable playthings, tossed around in a world of hidden persuaders, mendacious politicians, implacable markets. End of toy story.[3]

So why is it that, a few hours later, I'm standing drop-jawed before a demonstration screen in Sony Interactive's head offices, thinking the world will never be the same again? A twenty-eight-year-old marketing manager called Lee, who queued up all night to become the UK's first Playstation 2 owner, is putting the corporation's latest crystal-clear widescreen through its paces. Cars lumber around corners, people idly adjust their clothing, lips pucker and hair cascades, litter tumbles across a street as fluidly as that plastic bag in *American Beauty*. Of course, there's a pumping powerhouse of a shoot-out going on at the heart of all this, alarmingly raw chunks of cyborg warrior flying everywhere – but that's not the real shocker. What truly disconcerts, what sucks you in like a bad sci-fi moment, is the absolute verisimilitude of everything on that screen.

'Supercomputer vector circuits in that box,' says the gamine play-girl from Sony, proudly and incomprehensibly. 'It'll be able to produce anything you ever want to imagine.' At the moment, under Lee's capable thumbs, it's producing urban carnage with a cinematic, almost Tarantinoesque urgency. But I know what she means. Already, in a lurid flash, I'm dreaming of my new adult toy: PS2's *It's Sinatra's World (And You Can Live In It!)*. Don't just read about the Rat Pack, those heroes of swingin' hedonism: put on your trilby, seize your thumb pad, and actually join Frank, Sammy, Dino and the gang as they burn their way through casinos, croupier girls and Cadillacs driven recklessly in the Nevada desert. All this at such a level of mind-wrenching virtuality that you could pick out the stitching on Davis Jr's monogrammed golf sweater. Your own fantasy may involve placing Jeanette Winterson in a Bloomsbury salon with Strachey and the Webbs, while occupying the seat of the second viola in a Britten symphonia. Or perhaps you'd like Vinnie Jones, a packed Wembley Stadium, and an endlessly repeated, bone-splintering grudge tackle. Whatever. But watching this thing do its stuff (and Microsoft's X-Box is no less powerful), you know that such absolute wish-fulfilment is now entirely practical.

If this particular toy is 'us', then we are about to assume the status of meddlesome minor deities – gods in our daily worlds, exerting the power of life and death (or at least comedy and tragedy) over a population of artificial, log-offable mortals. The year 2001 proved to be an appropriately millennial Christmas: the shops full of black-boxed 'emotion engines' that turn Aldous Huxley's 'feelies' into a reality. We have shaped these advanced, silicon-rich, semi-sentient toys, and now these toys are shaping us, as adults and children. But into what?

A new kind of human self, say American academics – and they're not sure whether it's cause for celebration or panic. On one side is a Gnostic nerd called Marc Pesce, inventor of VRML (the code that enables virtual reality on the Web) and author of *The Playful World: How Technology is Transforming Our Imagination.*[4] For him, a 'miracle moving baby', or a train set that responds to voice commands, or a box of Lego that can be programmed like the Borg – all of this is just preparation for a dazzling, Star-Trek-like near future.

'Kids playing with these toys will have a strong innate sense that the world is programmable, that the inorganic is in some sense alive, that reality can be simulated almost to perfection,' expounds Pesce. 'They'll grow up regarding the material world, literally, as their plaything.' His hope is that these 'playbabies' (a toy retail marketing term for five to ten year olds who love their interactive toys) will be much better adapted to the wild science of the twenty-first century than their TV-age parents might be. When the geneticists, computer scientists and nanotechnicians nowadays talk about manipulating matter and information at very tiny levels, says Pesce, 'then it's these kids who'll know how to live in such a world – where our power to change our bodies and our environments will be so great. We'll have much to learn from them.'[5]

If we can even recognize who they are, that is. On the other side of America, in Boston's MIT, psychologist Sherry Turkle has long been sounding a cautionary note about the 'cyberization of everything'. She's been watching how children play with hi-tech for over twenty years – and she claims that this Christmas's batch of 'smart' toys could well be a step too far.

How have children always played with toys? As inert objects, brought to life by the child's imagination. 'This allows the child to explore their own inner life, to test out their emotional responses, by literally throwing the doll around. They can do this safely, in a free zone called play, and thus skill themselves for maturity. By mastering the toy, they master themselves.' But you need the rag doll to be, literally, made of rags for this process to work properly. What happens to the child when, as the toy is dropped to the floor, it whines for attention? When a cuddly toy offers empathy when treated well, and sullenness when treated badly? What Turkle sees these cybertoys producing is 'the first generation of children who think that artefacts need real, demanding emotional nurturance – rather than just being the screen, or the props, through which they project themselves'.[6]

In a few years' time, will we be surrounded by flaxen-haired Children of the Damned, who talk about 'Furby-kind-of-alive' (as opposed to 'human-kind-of-alive', or even just 'stupid toys')? Turkle remembers a boy from her researches in the eighties, saying that 'when robots are as smart as people, I guess we'll be the only ones who go to church'. In other words, Turkle says, he thought that people would still retain a monopoly on emotion, sensuality and spirituality. But with these new toys, the children's attitudes are changing, says Turkle. 'They are beginning to talk about a "computer" kind of love, as well as a human kind of love. What kinds of relationship are appropriate to have with a machine? The question isn't whether our children will come to love their toy robots more than their parents, but what loving itself comes to mean.'[7]

Perhaps it will mean less than before: perhaps differently than before. The news that major gadget manufacturers like Matsushita and Panasonic are devising robot toys to give to elderly people – both to keep them company, and to monitor their health signs – brings out the sceptic in Turkle.[8] 'Does the fact these smart toys are first being marketed to the young and the elderly mean that we're reinforcing their marginality to our busy lives? Are we tacitly acknowledging that we do not have enough "human" time to spend with them?'[9]

Pesce agrees that this is a strange new territory. 'All these toys and games are muddying up a child's perception of the world. Whether that's good or bad remains to be seen.' The cover story for *Time* magazine ('Tech comes to toyland') rounds up a largely negative crew of academics and commentators, who make predictable points in defence of 'traditional' toys. 'In the past,' says Dr Polly Carmichael, clinical psychologist at London's Great Ormond Street Hospital, 'children had richer individual fantasies. Now there are fewer opportunities for that.' Another critical quote comes from Caroline Goodfellow, curator of the Bethnal Green Museum of Childhood in London. For her, these 'gizmo' toys are 'basically designed to sell and make money, [and] not with the child's best interests at heart'.[10]

One British academic interviewed for the *Time* piece who didn't make the final version is psychologist Mark Griffiths of Nottingham Trent University. His own extensively researched position about the effects of smart toys – whether they be bleeping Tamagotchis or pulsing Playstation 2s – is 'everything in moderation'. It's true, he says over the phone, that 'a small minority of children get too wrapped up in their hi-tech toys. But the vast majority of young game players say that it's an excellent way of building up self-esteem and technological adeptness. You set your own skill levels, and excel at your own pace.'

Griffiths sees a continuum between games like chess and Monopoly, and computer games: 'You learn basic rules, and then you embark on a course of mastery that can take years, and requires a lot of practical scholarship.' As for smart toys, he observes his own eighteen-month-old daughter playing with his five-year-old son – prodding away at their pocket games and bleeping dolls – and actually hails it as the correction of a long-standing gender imbalance. 'I think it's progressive for girls to be so intimate with new technology. My mum can't programme the video, but her four-year-old granddaughter does it in seconds.'

Even the most committed gamesters have more perspective on their cybertoys than you'd imagine. Editor of Playstation 2's official magazine Mike Goldsmith has a boy in the early years of primary school who thumbs his Gameboy and his Pokemon with a passion. 'But I always make sure he has a mix of things to do – that he gets out there, takes the skin off his knees, comes back covered in mud. I remember when I was a boy, my dad would sit down with me in the woods, and we'd make little buildings and boats out of bits of kindling. I love those memories and I'm going to make sure my kids have those experiences as well. But interactivity in our daily technology – from the Internet to toy dolls – isn't just going to be wished away. I think I'd be a bad parent if I didn't acquaint my children with this world.'

There is no stronger parable about the intelligence we project onto – and into – modern toys than Pixar's *Toy Story* films. The filmmakers' own vision, generated from the heart of Silicon Valley, is decidedly nostalgic. These slinkys, cowboys and potato-heads – mostly taken from America's post-war 'golden age' of toys – follow an iron law of toyhood: when the kid comes in, drop to the floor. It's almost a perfect illustration of Sherry Turkle's worries: the 'good toy' must protect the freedom of the child's imagination at all costs.

But the very magic of these films derives from the same massive processes – the digitalization and virtualization of everything – that Mark Pesce sees as inevitable and unavoidable, and particularly so for twenty-first-century children. The miraculous life in these pixellated toys – the seeming humanity that courses through Woody and Buzz, Hamm and Jessie – is a prophecy of the life (or at least the applied intelligence) that will inhabit most objects in the adult world of the twenty-first century. And for all the melting humanity in these toy stories, there is cautionary darkness too. When the brutalized toys in Sid's yard started moving of their own volition in the first film – warning the spiky-haired torturer, in Woody's words, to 'play nice' – it was a faintly queasy, but superbly rendered moment, worthy of the Grimm Brothers at their most Gothic. Now, watching this little girl in Hamley's distractedly return to her Amazing Ally – wheedling in her best mall-rat tones that she needs some 'funtime, girl!' – I find I can't get this image of revolting, insurrectionary toys out of my head.

Let us, however, praise the perpetual subversiveness of the tyke and the scamp: in their sticky hands, the triumph of the cyberdolls is far from assured. Toy tester George is constructing a ragged mountain of robot dogs, silicon dolls and various bits of packaging. Rather pathetically, their arms and tails wave from the middle of the pyre, accompanied by some worried 'yelps' and 'hi there's'. George's mum, Sharon, tells me about the time that the house hamster merrily crapped all over Teksta's back, temporarily shorting this future master of the tweenie verse. 'I think the little thing was terrified,' she confesses. 'Well, both of them, I mean.' As far as these mothers have observed, life with smart toys is much like life with dumb toys: they just generate a different kind of mischief. 'No matter whether it's an infra-red ET, or a talking dolly, or a whatever, the first thing they want to do is to take all its clothes off,' says Elaine Davidson, Fiona's mum. 'Or play fights with it,' adds Sharon, as her beloved George sets Teksta and Poo-Chi to war.

Were they worried about their kids getting too emotionally wrapped up in these whining, wheedling toys? 'Well, the Furby comes out for a few weeks every other couple of months, and they get absorbed in it again,' muses Sharon. 'But it's back up on the shelf when a new board game comes along. It snores a bit on the top shelf, and then it's forgotten about.' Elaine laughs. 'Actually, these robot-dolls would do a lot better if they had better hair. Fiona can't see past her Barbies for that. Straight into the plaiting as soon as she gets a new one.'

So boys and girls still like the toys they've always liked ('Action Man, Lego, Playmobil – George still can't see by them,' says Sharon). And it turns out that even the most intensively researched products get it wrong on the simplest things. One of George's first toy tests, observing how the dogs just kept crashing into things, came up with a blindingly obvious improvement that went straight up to head office. As George told me, with some impatience, 'Why don't they have a lead?' And Fiona's mum came up with the most practical point of all: 'The thing I like about these cybertoys is that they're not real pets. Think about all the abandoned animals you get at Christmas every year. All you need to keep these ones going is a few batteries every week.'

As the Hamley's man calls an audibly shrill halt to the proceedings, the toy testers are to be found waving spring-loaded wands at demons in the air, or fiddling around with the cardboard and cellophane scraps of a magic set. 'Can't sell enough of these magic toys,' he says, wistfully, as ET's arms thunk repeatedly against the transparent surface of his box.

Over at Sony's headquarters, Lee Bottomley, a perfectly pleasant, if somewhat dishevelled, son of the Estuary, is telling me how his three-year engagement broke up because of all 'the gaming' he was doing. 'She just couldn't take it no more,' says Lee, half-absorbed in the pectoral diversions of *Tekken Tag*. 'If I ever have another relationship, I'll make sure she knows what all this means to me.' Nudging thirty, Lee is easily part of the 'Greystation' generation – the great demographic hope for those commentators on the industry wearied by the constant moral panics raised by shoot-em-ups. Will older users want more mature, more conceptual content?[11] But Lee knows exactly what he wants from his 'emotion machine'. 'I can switch it on, and straightaway I can be driving a Ferrari, scoring a goal, fighting with some gorgeous babe or killing people. Isn't that what it's all about? I can just disappear into it, for days even.'

The Sony play-girl is beginning to hem-hem a little, so we quickly get onto Lee's hinterland. In which there is, not surprisingly, a dearth of compelling landscape – save for one fact. He still plays Tetris 'for relaxation', because it reminds him 'of those little math'matical computer games you used to get at school. You know, get the square to fit on these other ones without piling up too high . . . Gawd, we loved those. Everybody wanted to play with those.' He tells me there's a Playstation version of this most basic of computer games – the coloured blocks falling from the sky, sometimes predictable, sometimes not, and all of them having to fit together like Lego, or wooden blocks, or pebbles that a child might arrange on a sun-kissed beach. All the massive computing power of late capitalism at his fingertips, and it's still about one brick on another brick.

And if toys are us, this is the philosophical bottom line: *homo et femina ludens*, man and woman the player, are compelled to be gamesters. As the American theorist Daniel Bell once said, there are those games with nature that we must perform to ensure that we survive; and there are those games between persons that give that brute survival some point, some meaningfulness.[12] If (or more likely, when) our machines become our companions, we will play games with machines, too. The mainstream of twenty-first-century life is going to be ludic, virtual and artificially intelligent, whether we celebrate or regret that fact: and as we watch these toys strut confidently off their table edges, or weary at the repetitive clunkiness of an avatar in a computer game, we may be forgiven our deep relief at their cognitive stupidity. But we've been dreaming of this moment for millennia – the golems and mannikins of pre-modern times; the beautiful automatons and singing birds of the Chinese empire; the runaway toys of middle-European fairy tale.[13]

And most germane, from the late nineteenth century, was Carlo Collodi's Pinocchio – Frankenstein's less cautionary, more hopeful cousin. Remember the test that the good fairy sets Gepetto's beloved creation (in Uncle Walt's version, at least) before it can shrug off toyhood for boyhood? He has to prove himself 'brave, truthful and unselfish'. Not a bad ethic for any entity, organic or mechanical: maybe we should let our consciences be our guide. Not Prometheus, but Pinocchio Unbound – which sounds a more manageable future, at least. Technology as our child, rather than as our master. Before I leave Hamley's toy-testing room, I resist the urge to let ET out of his box. At least, thank God, it's stopped mewling.

Toy tale 2: Legoland, Windsor

In Legoland UK, just across the dale from Windsor Castle in Berkshire, a standard issue wee boy is hurtling his complicated Lego car down a steep incline. 'Rrrumm! Crash!' Again and again he chucks it down the slope, until he gets his desired result: the car shatters in a hail of nubbly blue spars and grey cogs. 'Yesss!' But this boy is a true Lego-head. He ambles over to the wreck, picks through the debris, and begins to snap a few pieces back together again. Construct, destroy, reconstruct – or just generally fiddle around with bits of indestructible plastic. That's been the Lego way since time immemorial.

Except it's not any more, really. Above his head, a high-tech display has been telling the boy exactly how fast and how far his car has travelled down the slope, while in another room, some groups of school kids are manipulating 3-D Lego bricks on a computer screen, programming their own virtual worlds. Down the hill, another class is starting up its Lego robotics kit, with iMacs beaming instructions to weird, staggering bipeds. We seem to be a long way from that wooden box under the bed, full of red bricks with bite marks all over them; that simple, practical place where the idle dreams of this century's post-war generations were stored. What's happened to our Lego?

'Nothing except success', would be the line from the seventy-one-year-old, privately owned company from Denmark. Recently Lego – the word is a Danish composite for 'play well' and the Latin for 'connect' – was commended by *Forbes*, a leading American business magazine, in its issue dedicated to the most influential products of the last one hundred years. Lego was dubbed toy of the century, equal to the paperclip, the paperback and the vacuum cleaner in its impact. Forbes cited its 'educational value, universal appeal and enduring popularity'.[14] With a new theme park opened up in the US – Legoland California – Lego's corporate hucksters are building the brand like there's no tomorrow. By 2005, they want the name to be 'the most powerful in the world among families with children', a company memo said in 1997. A 'Danish Disney' is clearly their long-term ambition.

In our heart of hearts, who could possibly deny them a fair wind for success? Any baby-boomer who says they do not have their primal Lego memories is a complete and utter liar. Tummy downwards on a deep-pile carpet, surrounded by enough plastic fragments to model a nuclear meltdown, cursing Santa for not putting enough of those transparent quarter-circle ones in the stocking this year. Of course you've been there.

It wouldn't be too difficult to say that, from just after the war until the early 1970s oil crisis, we have lived through the Age of Lego. This was a time when progress was a matter of patient construction, of comprehensive planning: a societal settlement getting more stable with every brick snapped into place. This was a time when the houses most of us inhabited, the streets we navigated, the factories and offices we poured into – well, they all looked like Lego bricks, from totteringly high towers to low sprawling suburbs, spread neatly across expanses of green or grey. Lego was the modern(ist) toy for modern(ist) times. It shaped us in order that we might shape the world. No wonder America's leading business magazine loves it.

Compared to the mess of plasticene and paints, the hormones surging through Action Man and Barbie, the endless fiddliness of Meccano, Lego was pure reason and logic, placed in the soft hands of a child. Whenever you saw those little nubbles on a brick, with the tiny raised letters, you'd know – like a physicist knows his atoms, like a fundamentalist knows his god – that the world basically made sense. Because the next bit would always fit. And the next bit. No matter what passions and storms raged around the household, or inside yourself, Lego never let you down.[15]

Then the world started to go out of control, and our characters with it. Free markets, green scares, soaring divorce rates, hyper-consumerism, privatization, the end of the cold war, the digital revolution: we all know the litany. The world ceased to fit together like a Lego wall; the pieces lost their quality control, started to buckle and twist. So as a way for children to begin to make sense of a changing world, Lego had to change too.

Just how much change has occurred is evident when you stroll around the merchandise shop at the Windsor Legoland. Lego is trying to cover every angle in the current kids' marketplace – and for purists like myself, it's become a little weird. There are now straightforward cheesy product tie-ins, with Lego versions of Winnie-the-Pooh, *Star Wars: The Phantom Menace* and *Harry Potter*, which seem almost indistinguishable from the give-aways you get at McDonald's. Then there's the modern sex war, battled out between some rather ham-fisted designs. One new, very girly line has Lucinda and Cressida and Harriet going to the Dolphin Show, and Christian and Olivia playing with Thomas the Baby. All at their Sunshine Home, no less.

At the other end of the shop is a creepy new Christmas line called Slizer (say 'slicer' with a zed). The promo video shows Slizers emerging from pods, flinging ammunition discs all over the place, about as playful as the killer aliens in *Starship Troopers*. 'Destroy enemies – protect sector,' rasps a deliberately dehumanized voice. 'We are Slizer. Join us.' So little Lego girls just want to cavort cutely with dolphins, and little Lego boys just want to lose themselves in a faceless robot collective? Not much post-feminist subtlety here.

To be frank, it just doesn't feel like Lego; but like any other leisure giant, Lego is all about narrative these days, weaving scripts and stories around its products to trigger core emotions. The oldies are still the goodies: Lego System Cowboys and Indians, I am delighted to see, is still a big seller. But as you cast your eye over the Rock Raiders and the Aqua Sharks and Marie's Creative Corner, you begin to notice something odd. It's as if there's a rash breaking out across these perfectly moulded surfaces; a disfiguration that stops these toys from smoothly seducing their intended consumers.

It's those pesky Lego bits. Creative Marie has one nubble at the bottom of her white mule shoes. Bizarrely, the CD boxes for the computer games have them studded down their sides. Why? They're beginning to seem like mere decorative icons, rather than the essential point of the toy. In trying to become more of a world brand, Lego is also trying to become less about bricks. The company is quite honest about this. 'Our mission is to produce creative play material, not to make bricks,' says Michael Moore, head of communications for Lego in the UK. 'I couldn't imagine not producing them, but there is nothing in our philosophy which says that couldn't happen.' Yet as you wander around Legoland Windsor on a crystal-clear winter's morning, you doubt just how far Lego can stray from the click-and-snap of its heritage. This is such a fun place precisely because almost everything you see, at whatever scale, is made out of your standard sizes of Lego unit.

And anybody who's once tried to make a Thunderbirds' carrier out of his remaining green bricks – or a Millennium Falcon out of his white – will not fail to love these models. You can find Big Ben, an Arctic Polar Bear, a Triumph Superbike (86,320 bricks), Edinburgh Castle or the entire area of London Docklands. A forty-foot-high T-Rex turns out, on closer inspection, to be made entirely of those tiny little black numbers that used to disappear down the back of your couch. The mosaics on an Egyptian ghost-ride are made from all those speciality bricks your mother never got around to buying you. And no matter what the display, you are desperate to run your fingers across each surface. The memories come back, almost physically: so that's how everything fits together.

In the Duplo Workshop, a mother sits with her two flaxen-haired pre-school girls (there's barely been a kid here over the age of five all morning). They've been building fairy towers with the fat bricks and now their

mum is answering their anxious enquiries about the Lego toy train passing overhead on a rail. Why doesn't it fall down? Who's driving it? What
makes it go? She patiently takes them through the basic Newtonian laws,
moving Duplo bricks around as she does. You realize that if Lego stretches
too far away from this material, tactile root, it becomes just another mega-
brand in the infotainment marketplace. In short, if it goes entirely from
bricks to clicks, it'll lose its very identity.

They say it won't, of course. The new technologies it's embracing will
allow it to retain its old values, but in more relevant forms. New Lego, new
century. 'Our message to parents is that children are our vital concern,'
says Petra Bedford, marketing director of Lego Media, who make the Virtual Lego software. 'We are a reliable and dependable partner that will
stimulate a child's imagination and creativity.' However, there does seem
something slightly perverse about a child building her virtual Lego toy
town on a PC screen, when they could be down on the floor grappling with
the real nubbly stuff. And how can Lego really hope to compete with
Playstations and X-Boxes, offering a world where almost anything can be
simulated with perfect photorealism?

The much-heralded Mindstorms (robotic Lego) seems more promising at
first. As you watch the kids program behaviours into their creations, they
seem to master quite difficult strings of logic with ease. This natural apti-
tude for maths is exactly what Mindstorms' inventor, Seymour Papert of
the MIT Media Lab in Boston, argues will come when children creatively
interact with computers.[16] Or computers as kid-friendly as Lego's. Yet the
jury on smart toys, in terms of the research, is still out. Many researchers
say it's not the smartness of the toy that really develops your kid for the
future. 'We already know as a society how to raise highly verbal, curious
and intelligent children,' says David Shenk, an American critic of high-tech,
in a recent *Atlantic* magazine article. 'The ingredients for doing this turn
out to be surprisingly low-tech. Parents and their surrogates spending lots
of time with individual kids, speaking to them very early on, playing music
for them, proving a measure of security while allowing a measure of independence.' With, one is tempted to say, a bog-standard bucket of Lego sitting between them.[17]

Most of us can easily become sentimental about Lego – and after a
gentle and innocent day at Windsor, as a big kid watching little kids have
a great time, it's hard not to be. But we might just have to face reality.
We might have to let go of 'our' Lego, except for the very young, and
hope that its values survive in the digital world. And although it was born

in the industrial age, the shock troops of the information age appear to think very kindly of the brand. Go to the nerd's global water cooler – www.slashdot.com – and there are strings of comments, already numbering in the hundreds, about how fabulous Lego is.[18]

One poster, Anonymous Coward, compares Lego with the hot new software program challenging Microsoft's supremacy. 'Linux is like the ultimate Lego set. No wonder so many Slashdot readers played with Lego when they were younger. We're all still tinkering with a bunch of tiny, interchangeable parts.'[19] That sounds like a powerful consumer constituency who'd readily come to the aid of a confused toy giant, one way or another. Yet you're only one click away from bathos on the Web. Another site alleges the original idea for Lego was stolen from a schoolboy called Iver Carsten Iversen, in Kolding, Denmark. Iversen's son claims Lego's founder, Ole Kirk Christiansen, then a school carpenter, saw a wooden giraffe the boy had made in class. Held together by wire, the giraffe, it is alleged, was composed from 'interlocking wooden pieces'.

True or not, this sends a deep message to Lego's founders: whatever you do, don't forget the bricks. And by chance or design (guilt?) there are two enormous yellow giraffes at the heart of Legoland in Windsor. As I left the park, they were nodding their nubbly heads at knots of delighted children below. Begging forgiveness, perhaps.

The kidult: two cheers

These toy tales are an idiosyncratic attempt to describe a new space of connection between children and adults: a mutual interest in play, its technologies, rituals and materials. As we'll see later, this is partly a result of the long fall of patriarchal work culture. Men are casting around for a new social role after their status as primary worker has been dethroned, and finding it in various cultures of play, whether it's 'gadget dad' playing materially and enthusiastically with his children, or the 'new lad' committing himself to a life of leisure and hedonism. It's also undoubtedly the result of a change in the respective realms of childhood and adulthood/ parenthood, brought about by the general 'loosening up' of social structures in the West since the Second World War. Individualism and informationalism – a strong sense of personal choice and customization of lifestyle, accompanied by an increased ability to inform those choices – have affected both adults and children over the last thirty years.

The phenomenon of the 'kidult' illuminates the issues well. Media reports slip easily between definitions: is it about children acting like adults before their time, or about adults acting like kids well after their youth? Similarly graceless terms are 'middlescent' or 'adultescent' (for middle-aged adolescent), and the identification of the 'tweenager' – the child between eight and ten who aspires to teenage behaviours and purchasing patterns.[20] So while the age range of kidultery is wide, it seems to be that teenagedom – that historical result of post-war affluence – is the generally desired condition for large numbers of children *and* adults. And play of whatever kind – performative, imaginative, sociable, competitive, sheerly trivial – is the expected behaviour in this shared zone.

Yet if we take our play seriously, then it's important to try and separate out different play forms in this realm of the kidult. For each will make a different and subtle claim on its players. The parents who go to see a digital-effects blockbuster with their children – The *Lord of the Rings* is a classic example, but the same goes for films like *Toy Story*, or *Shrek*, or *Stuart Little* – are allowing themselves to share a mythic moment with their loved ones. Adults are availing themselves of a moral and ethical opportunity here, arising from this joint experience with their child. It's not just an 'excuse' for enjoyment, but for the kind of deep questioning about the true ends of existence that the adult's working life rarely affords. G.K. Chesterton once wrote that 'fairy tales are more than true – not because they tell us that dragons exist, but because they tell us that dragons can be beaten'.[21]

Yet *are* these the same adults who, according to many UK press reports at the end of 2002, were seen purchasing the branded icons of their pre-teen past (old cartoon and kid show characters like Bagpuss and Zippy) for their children's Christmas, or for themselves if childless?[22] Not necessarily. The rise in quality children's fiction – like Philip Pullman's *His Dark Materials*, Neil Gaiman's *Coraline* and scores of others – reinforces the idea that adults' embrace of child culture is more than just a retreat from the demands and pragmatisms of the grown-up world, but a kind of embracing of the roots (and routes) of human wisdom and understanding.[23] The film adaptations of classic twentieth-century kids' comic strips – from *Batman* to *Spiderman*, *X-Men* to *Daredevil*, and films inspired by strip culture, like *The Matrix* – never relinquish the complex entanglements of power, money, sexuality, biology and technology featured in their original stories.

Watching your young ones play with the toys and figures of your own infancy establishes a basic continuity with the formative experiences of your past. Indeed, with cult Web phenomena like SchoolDisco.com (where adults organize fancy-dress reunions, wearing their old school uniforms in nightclubs), and FriendsReunited.com (where adults can trace their school-friends and compare notes on progress or regress), the desire to measure our adulthood by our childhood has become a commercial opportunity.[24]

The much-maligned 'scooter' phenomenon of the early noughties, where pedestrians were terrorized by the onrush of fully grown commuter adults whizzing about on silver push-plate collapsible scooters, was another creative response to this more compensatory and therapeutic form of kidultism. The scooters were partly a solution to the need for speed in the morning rush hour, partly a reconciliation with one's treasured skate-board memories of the past.[25]

But, as this book constantly maintains, to mistake a few forms of play for the whole presence of play – in this case, play as self-expression and freedom, and play as triviality – is deeply unsophisticated. For kidultism can also open up realms of imaginative, carnival and even cosmic play (i.e. play that asks us to ponder on our place in an unpredictable universe). The generation of parents whose imaginations were excited by *Star Wars*, or the hyper-realities of video culture and early MTV, will be 'kidult' in these richer senses of play. As our cultural narratives, whether in words or digital images, get ever more phantasmagorical and compelling, parents will share with their children what Freud called the classic children's virtue of 'epistemophilia': that is, a love of figuring out what might count as 'truth', in any particular circumstance.[26]

So, whether it's the kidult using juvenile spontaneity as a mixture of therapy and anti-depressant, or the kidult exploring alternative states of consciousness and ethics, kidultery allows a full spectrum of play forms to be explored. And that's always a sign of the 'adaptive potentiation', in Sutton-Smith's words, that makes for healthy humans – the need to test out realities through a range of capacities.[27] The new child-adult/adult-child, seen from this evolutionary vantage point, is a positive trend: it sug-gests that we are keeping ourselves open, in our mammalian complexity, to all possibilities for adaptation and development.

It's worth considering some of the more detailed and rigorous critiques of kidultism, particularly from the child's side of the equation. Are there elements of the distinct experience of childhood that should not be appro-priated or simulated by adults, whether for therapy or profit?

The Demos report *Other People's Children,* by Gillian Thomas and Gina Hocking, summarizes much of these critiques, and essentially comes up with the charge that adults are guilty of 'colonizing' and 'commercializing' childhood.[28] The commercial question is perhaps more easily dealt with. We are indeed seeing a huge general expansion, matching the expansion of the media in general, of markets and niches devoted to child consumers. Cartoon and youth channels proliferate on cable and satellite channels; and though the cartoons are often witty, post-ironic productions, they are interspersed with a range of children's adverts that, in their dumbness and obviousness, make the intent to exploit all too obvious.[29] There is already a broad range of European national prohibitions on the question of children's advertising: the increasingly vigorous debate within the UK and US portends some change in this area.[30] But what kind of change? And in its zeal to defend a certain notion of childhood experience, what might be lost in the process?

The Demos authors line up the usual list of suspects and statistics about the new youth markets. The increase in personal expenditure in US and UK kids is matched by targeted channels like the US's *Fox Boys* and *Fox Girls*, or UK bands like S Club 8 and Atomic Kitten, and buttressed by young versions of adult mags like *Cosmopolitan* and *Elle*. The moral scares around these media circulate obsessively around the topics of sexuality and obesity, the latter topic becoming (in the UK at least) a major item on the political agenda.[31]

Yet the authors' qualifications of this gloomy scenario are interesting. These new markets for children are also 'partly a reflection of greater democracy in the family' – that is, children being able to speak up and articulate their demands, expecting to be heard. Nevertheless, the authors conclude that the overall effect of commercialization 'seems to be a diminished space – culturally, psychologically and physically – for children to occupy with confidence'. Commercialization also 'generates greater confusion about what, if anything, the distinctive character of childhood is or should be'.[32]

One way in which Thomas and Hocking seek to get at that distinctive character of childhood is through a concept taken from sociologist Frank Furedi, 'colonization'.[33] Parents colonize their children's lives when they set children's agendas and intensively supervise their activities, mostly through regulating their forms of play, both public and private. Children are discouraged from exploring their immediate social environment, and steered instead towards tightly monitored 'play zones'. Their private, free-wheeling, noisy and messy play is subjected to various 'cognitively improving' schemes – the authors mention the 'Baby Einstein' pack that gives children a soundtrack of Mozart, poetry and foreign languages.[34]

There are many other examples of 'controlled play' – they can involve, for instance, curtailing school playtimes (and physically or verbally exuberant behaviour in them), or surveillance cameras overlooking school yards and parks. There's even a particularly renegade professor, Kevin Warwick of Salford University, who suggests that children should be implanted with a tracking chip so that they can be always be 'kept safe'.[35]

Colonization implies a territory – with distinct resources and cultures – waiting to be colonized. To their credit, in an attempt to break out of the usually negative discourses around children that emphasize their vulnerability to risk and danger, Thomas and Hocking propose a 'positive vision for quality of life for children'. It gives a sense of what they think the authentic territory of childhood should be, as a guide to better policy and mindset among all adults, from parents to marketeers to politicians.

Yet what is so remarkable about their three-part framework is how readily it combines our rhetorics of play; and what is so disheartening is that the authors feel these admirable human capacities should be reserved purely for children. Thomas and Hocking regard these skills as something that all adults have had to master to develop themselves, and which they must identify and encourage in their children. But they must be 'left behind', like scaffolding falling from a building, as work, markets and bureaucracies take over their lives.[36]

The first competence – 'climbing trees: establishing independence' – is about play as it expresses freedom and selfhood. It articulates 'children's own understanding of what enables them to feel good about their childhood ... it incorporates ideas of competency, resilience, self-esteem and independence'. Yet the authors' description of this theme is riddled with barely suppressed adult longing for exactly that sense of 'control over our own lives'. Adults curtail the climbing of trees, metaphorical or actual, 'because they have forgotten how to climb trees [themselves]':

> As a result, when they interpret how children develop their growing sense of self, they tend to focus on the rational, tangible aspects of becoming a person, such as gradually earning and inheriting the various aspects of status: the permission to do various things, the ability to earn money, the presence of one's own place and space, etc. In the institutions of society, children's autonomy is most likely to be encouraged when it is conducted on pseudo-adult terms – for example, in school councils, peer research schemes or youth parliaments ... We need to create time and space –

physical, emotional, virtual, psychological – where children can be children in the ways they want to be.[37]

Replace 'children' with 'adults' in the last sentence, and the play-ethical critique is made: don't adults deserve that exquisite zone of autonomy too? Most of the social types described in this book – soulitarians, new busyness people, play aesthetes, liberal semiocrats, infinite gamesters and all – are bidding for exactly that space, or a strong version of it, in their adult lives. Third agers (or 'older people') are now seeking the same sense of agency and self-determination, by exploring their own creativity or embarking on 'independent journeys' of meaning.

Thomas and Hocking suggest that children's selfhood should not be expressed just through the 'purchase of favourite toys, characters and brands', but also through 'control of their own time'. Yet this is also the defining quality of an ethical adult player. If adults gain 'control of their own time' through a limitation on working hours, or a radical regime of sabbaticals and annualization, or a model of cultural activism that makes them less slavishly consumerist, does that make them 'childish', by the Demos authors' terms? Or are they just being fully and responsibly human?

The second skill of contemporary childhood proposed by Thomas and Hocking is 'running races: learning to perform and grow up'. Again this maps perfectly to the rhetoric of play as contest, power and agonism – and also to the sense of play as a means of development and personal evolution. It's healthy for a child to have 'a sense of moving forward', through whatever means and measures: the simple marking of height, or telling the time, or making friends, or ever-neater handwriting. Agonistic play answers a need to feel some measure of 'success': and as the authors correctly point out, 'the problem is that our current definitions of "success", and "competition" are too narrow . . . We know that, beyond a certain level, IQ and economic success are not indicators of fulfilling relationships or fruitful lives, so why do we sort and direct children by these rules?'[38] The child's growing sense of performance should be a richly sociable affair – compared, contrasted and confirmed by many different people, not just educators or employers.

Yet again, the question has to be put to the authors: why should these values be confined to the realm of childhood? Shouldn't adults' sense of performance and capability *also* be measured by such progressive values? 'We need to broaden our definition of success and increase the range of people who are involved in securing it for children,' say the Demos writers. We need to do the same for adults, too, says the play ethic.

The third skill is called 'the dressing-up box: social networks, imagination and play'. As before, the authors unwittingly reference many of the play rhetorics and forms explored in this book. Yet they still seem to regard them as confined to childhood rather than as an attainable social condition for all humans, old and young. Children need, they say, a 'gift economy' – that is, they need to live in rich networks of relationships and materials (primarily carers bearing toys and resources), all motivated by values of trust and support. This is an 'invaluable web' of sociability, something that the authors want children to recognize and value at an early age. The dressing-up box becomes a metaphor for 'the communal resources, tangible and intangible, that communities provide for children'. What might our equivalents be, muse the authors, for those 'hand-me downs, ancient relics, jumble-sale items and gifts', used by the pre-school, the drama group, the private home? Its 'shared contents are continually raided for innumerable fantastical purposes, and then returned. The more people who use the box the richer it becomes'.[39]

Soulitarians (particularly the hacker contingent) would instantly recognize that picture. Their version of the 'dressing-up box' is the free software and cultural content left in a common place on the Net – available to anyone who wants to use it (as the Demos writers' children do) for 'innumerable fantastical purposes', and to leave their own improvements or innovations as a return gift. And as would be the case among kids, no cash transaction is involved.

The 'display' and 'experiment' that the dressing-up box encourages will be about creating a 'sense of belonging' – trying out roles with others who are as willing to experiment as you are, building a complex sense of connectedness to the social world. For children, say the authors, this 'may be more about fancy-dress parties than about citizenship education'.

But again, from a players' perspective, one might resist the notion that this is only a kid's game. Much of our adult behaviour in the information age is a kind of 'dressing-up-meets-citizenship' – the desire to try out roles (whether sexual, productive, emotional or artistic) in our multi-choice lives.[40] We wilfully inhabit the paradox of 'real virtuality' – testing the power of our imaginations, seeking possibility in the midst of specificity. If this is a child's urge, then all postmodern people are children.

Throughout their report, the Demos writers stress that children lack one key social resource. To escape from their current constraints, they need a 'commons' of resources and trust throughout society: a sustained mutuality that will help us welcome 'other people's children'. Yet this is a lack that underlies much of adult life, too. For adults to play fully they also need a playground – or more technically, they need to establish the 'grounds of play'. The material and infrastructural conditions which could maintain and sustain our sense of independence, our confidence to perform and self-develop, and our imaginative energy should be available to us throughout our lives – not just in childhood.[41]

To see adults as 'colonizing' children's lives is an extraordinarily crude representation of what is in fact a complex, unpredictable yet hopeful process. It's true that contemporary parents are expressing their general fears about an uncertain future through over-protectiveness with their children. As Laurie and Matthew Taylor say, these are times where all ideologies and world views seem insufficient or broken, and our political imaginations are at a low ebb. Children can seem like the last remaining credible narrative of progress we have.[42]

Yet grown-ups' yearning to share an imaginative and creative space with their children – predominantly through all the many forms of play – offers a way to enrich that imagination. To make an 'ethic' of play is to try to claim some kind of authority about human nature from this particular area of human practice. This can be used, as the work ethic was, to shift structures and political systems. An alliance of adults and children around the necessity for more profoundly playful lives, from birth to death, is long overdue. The challenge is to find a political language that can articulate that alliance. For this reason, the 'kidult' gets at least two cheers – for being the right cultural phenomenon, initially headed in the wrong direction, and with infantilized overtones that are now hard to shrug off.[43] But the search for a truly cross-generational politics is on.

People carrier: the playful family

Yet we should always be on our guard in terms of 'family politics'. If the Demos report has any residual bias, it is towards the family as the most efficient (or least worst) reproducer of social order we have, despite its pre-eminence as the main location of abuse and violence towards children

and women.[44] 'Family-friendly' policies forever run the risk of social con-
servatism and repression: which particular image of the family are these
policies friendly towards? 'Family-creative' or 'family-dynamic' policies
might be a better general direction. The family could be seen as a 'people
carrier', a subtle and extending structure that takes in marriage and separation, kinship and friendship, nurturance and creative stimulation.

The recent book from Al and Tipper Gore, *Joined at the Heart: the Transformation of the American Family*, was clearly written as a semi-manifesto
for ex-vice-president Gore's second assault on the White House, a contest
from which he ultimately withdrew. Its general endorsement of the family
as the core institution of American life – above market and community –
would undoubtedly have been electorally effective. However, there is a surprising emphasis on the diversity and flexibility of emotional relations in
the American family – summed up by the explicit devotion of one chapter
to play.[45]

In the Gores' book, play has a kind of galumphing charm about it. Big
Al comes back from a hard week's legislating in Washington and is immediately embroiled in playing monsters with the kids on the family bed. Tipper makes sure that she and Mr Gore get the chance to 'play around' while
the kids are away at sleepovers (all specifics thankfully occluded). Play is
therefore very much regarded as functional to family harmony, a repairer
of the stresses and strains caused by work culture (about which the Gores
are more than critical). 'Play is to work as dreaming is to waking,' they
assert: 'that is, play is restorative.'[46] Play as identity is also explicitly
invoked, in terms of the way that 'family rituals' both bind its members
together and connect them to other families: the way we do Christmas or
Kwanzaa, Halloween or a christening, 'creates a pool of good feelings that
families can draw on in tougher times'.[47]

The Gores are implicitly endorsing their own version of a play ethic. In
the preceding chapter on work, they remind you that 'ethics is a plural
word', but '*work ethic* is singular; it needs to be seen along with our other
ethics, and not as the single dominant purpose of our lives'.[48] Their vision
of play – sociable, physical, fanciful, kidult-ish – ties in with the notion
that play is at its best when it is purposeless, a kind of refresher course
for coping with the all-too-purposeful world of work and civics. Yet the
Gores are also forced to concede (from their assiduous reading of the
available scholarship) that play might have its own productivity and purposefulness. Play can be, in their words, 'an aerobic workout for the

human capacity to change'. Perhaps, they suggest, a 'sustained immaturity is an advantage in a constant world of change'. The end of play can be read as the end of personal development: 'when one is mature, the implication is that growth is over'. The Gores hint at a play-adult who will be 'partly child-like – but in a good way'.[49]

So playfulness keeps the American working family held together in stressful times; it also fuels those working parents to keep their minds imaginatively open, ready for the next challenge that the American economy might bring. Yet while this notion of a play-driven family unit is attractive – both adaptable and nurturing through its sense of carnival and creativity – there is more to play than just making families function better.

The Gores propose the interesting thesis that America's various addiction crises – whether in drugs, drinking, eating, shopping, Web surfing, working or whatever – are caused by the relative absence of play (or at least, its restorative and aerobic version) in modern lives. Perhaps we seek to 'lose ourselves' in thrills and pills because we don't have the opportunity to 'find ourselves' through play. If we don't regularly experience the 'containable release' of the best play moments – with our hobbies and pastimes, or in joint creation with others, or with our children – than a part of us becomes pent up. The sick business culture of 24/7 schedules, intensified competition and presenteeism keeps us away from the best kind of play. To get some sense of transcendence in between the grey appointment blocks of our screen calendars, we go for our drugs. The buzz of addiction is similar, say the Gores, to holding your breath for so long that you have to gasp for air – and that gasp takes in as much oxygen as you can get, as quickly as possible. Play is the air we breathe but when we're mostly starved of it, we take our hits as intensely as we can.[50]

Yet will our desires for transcendence – the intense experiences that put our ordinary lives into perspective – be entirely satisfied by the Gores' hearty play? The rhetorics of play as imagination, and play as selfhood, suggests otherwise. Any vision of the family at play which doesn't expect that play forms will be about excess as well as health – the experimentations of the teenager with sex and narcotics, for example – has an essentially unrealistic image of play. Yes, the family that plays together has a better chance of staying together: but 'playing around' in the family – whether through parental infidelity or the experimentations of youth – must be an accepted instability in the family unit, caused by individualization on a historic scale.[51]

The Gores level a similar attack on the screenager – that spectre of the child becoming paranoid, obese, even post-human: entranced, immobile grubs, glommed onto computer or television screens, while parents look on anxiously. But to say that virtual culture means passivity, and that true play is always by definition a physical or sociable activity, is simply inaccurate. The mental and imaginative activism that young people display in cyber culture is well evidenced; and the bias against the dot-com generation is partly an attempt by print-literate elites to defend the cultural basis of their authority against rising new literacies.[52] Indeed, as Michael Wilmott shows in his researches on the 'networked family', new media could actually enable a more active family than ever before, spreading out across distances of space and time, using smart mobile appliances that can keep members in touch with each other, aware of each other's needs and agendas, able to participate in much more complex family events.[53]

How do you keep a family together in the slippery, mutable world of the player? You *are* a family because you *do* family – that is, you constantly perform and refresh your ties, responsibilities and emotional investments in those that are close to you, not just through blood, but through shared experience. Family is a performance and an emergence, not a given, defensible entity.[54] Childminders become family; lollipop ladies become family; your child's friends become family. The 2002 Disney film *Lilo & Stitch* gets it tear-jerkingly right when it defines the family as *ohana*, in the Hawaiian language. 'That means nobody gets left behind, or forgotten,' says the miscreant Lilo. Not even a blue-skinned, pathologically criminal, genetically engineered alien (Stitch), who regards his new welfare-hounded family as 'little, and broken, but still good . . . yes, still good'.[55]

The networked family expands and contracts; it finds its essence stretched by time and space. Like the amoebic blobs that host the CBeebies kids channel on BBC digital television, it constantly changes shape, all parts joyfully colliding with each other. So if nobody wants to be left behind in the playful family, then nobody *has* to be left behind. The ever-expanding bandwidth of our societies promises an almost constant and almost fully present connection with others through our devices – the Evernet, as George Gilder calls it.[56] Under these re-enchanted conditions, everyone that we deem family can be taken with us wherever we go, wherever we have to go.

Should we lament that brief societal idyll where school locked into home and thus into the workplace, and parents were expected to be present (in their own ways) to shepherd the children into a functionally adult existence? Or do we recognize the new reality of the networked, mobile family, and try to build structures of love through these webs of connection?

The husband and wife who end a marriage but re-establish a genuine friendship; the life-literate tweenagers (never mind teenagers) who exult in their lifestyle choices; the youngest ones who start out with a lust for life and are encouraged never to lose it; the grandparents and friends who discover that they are neo-parents, flavours in a rich nurturing mix. Is there actually the opportunity for *more* loving and constant relationships in a fully informational (and informal) family? Are all the many mediated ways that we can express our connection with someone – texting and instant messaging are only the start of it – actually generating a new version of the truly happy life? Might our full-spectrum play make our families more resilient and responsive, rather than weaker and more fragmented?

Of course, the fields of play extend wider than the family. The early noughties' backlash against parents' rights, originating in the US, came with a startling new vocabulary for children, from the now-militant child-less: 'anklebiters', 'crib lizards', 'crotch fruit', 'fartlings', 'germ mongers', 'semen demons', 'vomit comets', 'spawn' and 'sprogs'.[57] Singletons in the workplace were beginning to complain about having to 'cover' for their parental colleagues, posing very uncomfortable questions for their employers. If John and Mary can get time for their children – whether they're sick, running in the school races, or grappling with their Lego for the first time – why can't I get an equal amount of time for my life-enhancing activities, whether it's snowboarding or gardening, a garage massive or a t'ai chi class, visiting a grandparent or campaigning on an issue?[58]

Proponents of the play ethic would answer: well, why not indeed? If we understand play as the exercise of human freedom and self-fulfilment, from birth to death, then of course the play time of the childless and the single should be equally rated. Rather than set themselves against radical parents, the 'child-free' advocates should join with them. Together, they could make a powerful common front for more humane employment conditions in the mainstream of the new capitalism. The idea of 'downshifting' always had the faint implication of stepping back from an active life. The play ethic isn't for 'voluntary simplicity', but for voluntary complexity. That famous 'juggling act' – between work and non-work, individual and community, money and altruism, pleasure and duty – should be something which we enjoy, rather than rue.[59]

Yet we need to take a further journey into those child-free cultures, of egoistic play, which intersect with gender in a most explosive way. We might glimpse a vision of a playful social politics, where men, women and children find a way to march forward together to transform their conditions and resources. But we will not get anywhere near it if the feminist critique of 'men at play' is not fully reckoned with. The childhood rhyme, added to by feminist writer Rebecca Abrams, captures the problem well. All work and no play does make Jack a dull boy. But what about Jill?

The ballad of Jack and Jill: men and women at/in play

The statistics rattled through the media outlets to a chorus of disbelief. UK working fathers in 2002 were spending two hours a day looking after their children, compared to only fifteeen minutes per day only thirty years ago, said the Equal Opportunities Commission ('revolutionary behaviour', in the words of the pamphlet). The New Dad, much trumpeted through hopeful columnists (and doubted by hardened feminists), seemed to have arrived.

There were also some wearily familiar numbers: 86 per cent of fathers still worked full time (compared to 31 per cent of mothers) and 6 per cent worked part-time (compared to 58 per cent of mothers); only 2 per cent of mothers worked over sixty hours a week, compared to over 12 per cent of fathers (with two-thirds of fathers working over forty-eight hours a week). In addition, considerably more men than women seemed to be worried that asserting their childcare and caring obligations at work would affect their career prospects. The headline in the piece even placed the blame on men: fathers were 'too scared' to ask their employers for flexible hours. 'Young fathers need to feel very secure in their careers, and they believe that asking for flexibility is seen as a lack of commitment – which makes them more vulnerable,' said Jack O'Sullivan, the spokesman for pressure group Fathers Direct. 'There's a different culture around work/life benefits for women. It's more legitimized for female workers to work part-time, for instance. But men are scared to ask for this.'[60]

Yet at the very least, here are the first signs of a 'masculinism' that begins to take male responsibility for nurturance, maintenance and caring. Though it doesn't seem to be about pushing back that infernal combination of patriarchy and the work ethic that keeps men at offices, factories and shops way beyond the necessary completion of tasks. Fathers are presumably swapping one form of play in their non-work time (their recreational hours at sport, carousing with pals, etc.) with another – time spent with children and families. Yet as Dave Hill notes, the question of the 'playful father' is not a simple one:

> It's a good thing that fathers are doing more stuff with their kids, but the manner of their involvement is what matters. There are dads and there are dads, and their engagements with their children vary, not only in quantity but in quality as well . . . The man whose lunatic working hours prohibit him from seeing his children awake from Monday to Friday – unless, of course, he and his partner wish to be relieved of their house – may compensate richly for this absence at weekends, while the daily involvement of the sort of father who is always on hand to entertain his brood by showing them how a tomato will explode in a microwave then leaves mum to clear up the mess is not quite being the male role model most of us would applaud.[61]

There's much to ruefully recognize here. But at least what comes out of this is a variety of male parenting styles, rather than the usual patriarchal monolith. And most of them indicate a male commitment to the domestic, nurturing and affective realm that's unprecedented in history. Men are now playing with the components of fatherhood in new and enthusiastic ways.

So will a particularly male contribution to parenting evolve within the family of the future? The Irish psychiatrist Anthony Clare suggests that the male style might involve qualities like 'consistency; detailed involvement in projects; awareness of space, time and context; a direct, physical caring'.[62] If these qualities pertain (Clare amasses an impressive amount of psychological and biological data in support of them), it would be easy to see why the rhetorics of play – particularly those involving imagination, healthiness and free will – would dominate the culture of the New Dad. Men might be willing to commit themselves to an equality of domestic and community care if the medium through which they could express this commitment was largely creative, participative and energetic in nature – i.e. if they regarded it as 'houseplay' as well as 'housework'.

Indeed, if male attentions were directed fully towards the question of domestic reproduction and maintenance, it seems almost inevitable that there would be a burst of 'labour-saving' innovation in response. Marketing categories like 'gadget dad' are already presuming a confluence between male familial identity and technology.[63] It's always possible that the multimedia centre or MP3 library will become the new 'garden shed' for the domesticity-averse male. But it's equally likely that fathers will begin to take an interest in the networks and systems that sustain the modern family – and find ways to develop those enthusiastically and imaginatively. Might not a 'networked family' need a network enthusiast – and aren't men, by their evident enthusiasm for new technology, able and ready to step into that role?

The father delightedly and intensively playing with his children, while intelligent machines labour tirelessly in the background to reproduce the family's living conditions, might seem like a laugh-out-loud fantasy to some feminists. (They shouldn't laugh too loudly: the world's first commercial robot vacuum cleaner, the Roomba, went on sale at the end of 2002.[64]) But beyond the jokes, the question is worth posing: what distinctive contribution to domestic care and maintenance will men bring, once their commitment is fully equal? What activities will go with the grain of masculinity freed from patriarchy? Is it possible that a new male domesticity would bring a richer playfulness to the family sphere – one that tried to strike a different balance between pleasure and maintenance, creativity and routine? Perhaps the hardest to convince on this issue might be 'working' women themselves.

So what about Jill?

There's one striking irony to note in the midst of all this: some of the most avid defenders of the value of the work ethic will come from the ranks of women, not men. For many women, particularly the mothers and daughters of the feminist era, the notion of a play ethic might easily be interpreted as a mixture of 'back to the hearth' and 'stay with the soft toys'. Most mothers know, instinctively, that it is good to play with their children. Yet few in the early twenty-first-century developed world believe that the child's right to play must necessarily trump the woman's right to work.

Having escaped from the sphere of domesticity, the domain of the carpet and the kitchen table, how might the post-feminist woman in the labour market regard the call – from men, at least – to re-evaluate the virtues of play?

Going by the comments of Rebecca Abrams, author of *The Playful Self: Why Women Should Let More Play Into Their Lives*, they will regard it with considerable scepticism.[65] 'Play is every bit as gendered as work in our society,' Abrams has written. 'The old industrial work ethic was a man-made product, and there's a real risk that the newly hatched play ethic will be, too.'[66]

The soulitarians, in her view, will merely be different boys with different toys, still excluding women from the game. And if technology could be deployed in order to reduce working hours, the reality may well be an expansion of housework, rather than the elysian fields imagined by play ethicists. Will male 'players' participate in all that? Abrams believes that the rise of interest in play among the 'policy boys' is due to the squeeze between the rise in working hours and men's desire to spend more time with their families – which leaves them less time for their traditional playgrounds of pub, club and sports hall. Given that an entry into the marketplace means that women's total labouring hours – both public and private – has increased, Abrams wants feminism to re-examine its emphasis on women's right to work, and try to articulate a 'woman's right to play'.

Abrams makes some telling points here – but we need to redefine her terms in the light of the framework developed in this book. She conceives of men's 'play rights' purely in terms of sport and conviviality – that is, of play as leisure and recreation, something that is pursued in spite of their 'involvement' in their families and workplaces. Yet as we have seen on several occasions already, play is a much more powerful social logic than this. It gathers up men from the soulitarians to the family players in its whirlwind: a playful fatherhood offers the taste of an unalienated life spent among the swing parks and Lego bricks, the swimming run and the family day out.

Women are brought up to exercise responsibility all their lives, says Abrams: from a very early age they are expected to care and pay attention to the detailed needs of others, and particularly men. The 'service ethic' is what women have, for centuries, been subtly (and not so subtly) manoeuvred into.

Feminism defends women's right to play as, in some sense, a retreat from this long-term sense of duty. To be a free female player means to have the willpower to leave a bad marriage, or strike out for sexual pleasure, or to employ domestic help rather than slog away at chores. Women's self-consciousness about their appearance – again, encouraged from an early age through fashion and dolls, says Abrams – is another inhibitor to free, self-realizing female play.[67]

In the same section, Abrams praises play for its 'ability to reconcile dissonant parts of ourselves'. One part is a woman's right to assert her 'selfness' (neither selfishness nor selflessness, says Abrams) through play; the other part is a woman's sense of responsibility to others.[68]

So could there be a caring play, or a playful caring? Abrams is doubtful. The 'maintenance of conditions' that care implies (whether the basic security and needs of children or elders, the infirm or the disabled) is 'motivated by caution, and rooted in stasis'.[69] Women's need for more free play has to be asserted against the weighty complexities of their early-twenty-first-century lives. They are readily welcomed into the labour market, often occupying new positions of authority in organizations. Yet few women would want to entirely abandon that emotional connection to nurturance and community. So Abrams sees play as a kind of restorative activity for the inevitably over-burdened modern woman.

Yet her fascinating analysis suggests something more than simply a balancing of play possibilities between Jack and Jill – something aerobic to stop them becoming dull boys and girls in the endless task list of the information-age workplace. The ethics of care – requiring a different investment of emotion and self than that of play, but still plumbing depths of reciprocity and meaning – are worth thinking about.

Of course, play should be understood better, and much more broadly: it pervades much more of our productive and sociable lives than is perceivable from the work-leisure division (or even the work – life division – but more of that later). But can we play *all* the time?

Leisure and home were the zones where the alienations of work were meant to cease, temporarily: the work ethic affords us these 'havens in a heartless world'. But the play ethic has the problem from the other end. If play is a tidal wave of opportunities to live creatively, demanding energy and capacity from the players surfing its wake, then what about those who can't maintain their balance, who injure themselves in the effort, who literally go under the surface?

'Care', which Abrams identifies ambiguously as both the lot and the glory of the female condition, is exactly what these resting or injured players need. But the context for that care, in a world where scarcity is potentially banishable for all, is different from work society where much of the 'care' (physical and emotional) was exercised to patch up the injuries, stresses and strains of industrial life.

A play society, which puts the emphasis on living creatively and arranges its socio-economics to support that, will be an exciting place to be. But there *will* be those who – either through exhaustion, or infirmity, or inability, or just through choice – won't be able to keep up with the pace of the players' mainstream. Any aspirant social ethos needs to find ways to recuperate those who fall out with its boundaries, or repair those who find its strictures demanding. The gambit of this book is that there can be an attempt at a societal ethos for play (while absolutely accepting that there may be other versions of a play ethic available, as well as a diversity of work ethics other than the Puritan/Protestant one).[70] The aim is to seize a historical moment with a strong vision of the future – and faint hearts never won fair prize.

So here goes. While the work ethic reproduces its labourers through the dualism of *work – leisure*, I propose that the play ethic reproduces its 'living creators' through the continuum of *play – care*.

From work – leisure to play – care

We only earn the compensations of leisure when we submit ourselves to the alienations of work: that is the ethical deal that the work society offers us. The play society proposes a different ethical contract: we can only explore all the wondrous creative possibilities of play if we also make space and time for care and understanding.

The first deal traps us within a model of working-to-consume which is, as many have pointed out, essentially schizophrenic: the values of constancy and discipline that the work environment always ultimately demands – no matter how soft and understanding the workplace culture – are eternally subverted by the extremism (either utopian or dystopian, exultant or nihilistic) of leisure consumption. Rationalist patriarchs thrive in this duality: love it or shove it, hump and dump, on top or not.

Indeed, when Abrams talks of male play as being eternally competitive and testing, it's curious that she doesn't imagine that this might be an exploitation of male psyches also. Cultural capitalists of all kinds make a lot of money out of men adopting a 'work hard, play hard' mentality, whether they're locking them into the sports zone, or encouraging them to upgrade their cars, or selling them neo-pornographic lads' mags in the high street. Believe in the myth, and from the inside it feels like self-empowerment; looked at from the outside, it seems like a mostly mechanical existence – either fully on, or fully off.

There is no doubt that masculinity and femininity can variously emphasize certain play rhetorics over others – and that under patriarchy, males conducted their lives in the public realm through rhetorics of power and freedom. For much of human history, '*homo ludens*' was an apposite description. Yet in the age of feminism, it should be possible for both sexes to be fully aware of their playful selves and societies: it rests on a kind of emotional democracy, where men and women decide together on their rights to fulfilment and self-creation, each respecting the full agency and intention of the other. When this emotional democracy becomes the norm, men and women may begin to build a common ground on the necessary conditions to sustain creative living.

A play ethic starts from the premise that we can arrange our productive and social relations to support everyone's active passion: that a particular dispensation of technology, economic regulation and democratic structures can remove the need for most, if not all, alienated labours.[71] The productivity of a playful society rests upon individuals pursuing their creative agendas in unity and tension with others. The realized designs, the specific products, the array of services that twenty-first-century human beings need will be realized through a freewheeling mix of public and private activity, gift economies and money economies, a diversity of reciprocations and exchange.[72] But crucially, this does not mean some kind of bucolic, peaceful equilibrium. People will still be committing themselves to exacting, demanding tasks and labour, as well as pursuing various forms of bliss, self-transcendence and boundary crossing. But they will be *consciously choosing* those extremes (and all other subtleties in between) rather than being chosen by them.

Yet the ability for full conscious choice requires a particular kind of wisdom, which Abrams's feminist-inspired reading of play points us towards. If players, men and women alike, are to be full players, then they must have a kind of interior grounding – a sense of connection with their universe, rather than disconnection – that enables them to make the most of the paradoxes and complexities of a players' life. At one level this is a spiritual question, or at least a philosophical one; at another, it is about political economy. But it is also about gender, and about accelerating that dissolution of power structures that feminism has begun. The struggles of the female player in a post-feminist world – between her autonomy and freedom, and her deep calls to the maintenance and cares of others – should become the male player's struggles too. For play to become the right of Jack *and* Jill, care also has to become the responsibility of both sexes – Jill *and* Jack.

In her chapter on play rights, while listing a whole range of strategies to increase women's opportunities to play, Abrams notes that 'sharing the caring' is key. 'While most women would not want to relinquish altogether the role of carer, the quality of their lives would be greatly improved if they were more able to share the care – with partners, with employers, with the state. We need to stand up for our right to hand over at least some of the caring we do, so that we can take and enjoy opportunities in our lives for playing.'[73]

What's interesting here is the sense that care of others – whether child-care, or looking after the elderly, or 'making a home' – is not something that the new female player wants to give up entirely. What Abrams hints at is the deep continuum between care and play. Care, as Zygmunt Bauman has often argued, should be its own reward; it needs no external justification or rationalization – even more so in these liberated times, where individualized people are not forced into social duties.[74] Care stems from the same ethical plenitude as play: now that we are freed from necessity, how should we behave towards others? In a way, both care and play are coping mechanisms for the human propensity to excess and abundance. Play articulates our infinite capacity to virtualize and imagine our world. Care articulates our infinite capacity to wrap ourselves up in the emotions and sensitivities of others.[75]

Abrams talks of the 'otheration' that women are subjected to from early childhood: the conditioning that compels women to always find their meaning in their relationships with others, compared to the inviolate ego-ism of masculinity. She's right to say this 'other-orientedness' is an ob-stacle to women's selfish (perhaps the world should be 'selfist') play.[76] Yet what if *both* sexes accepted that 'otheration' was the price to pay for a truly playful existence? What would a new domestic sphere be like, occu-pied by families and friends, men and women in full equality, who were balancing their playful liberties with their caring responsibilities? Or even more radically: what if the fall of patriarchy revealed a humanity that wanted nothing better to do than balance its urges to play and care, to be played with and cared for?

And how might that balance be struck? With work/leisure, the emotional and mental reckoning is obvious. 'Pain/pleasure' maps the dualism directly: it makes us a machine, to keep us subjected to the machines. But with play/care, perhaps the relationship is more non-dual than dualistic.[77] 'Openness/boundedness' might be more appropriate language: or 'diffuse/ concentrated'. The full possibilities of play become tempered when one's co-player, actual or potential, cannot reciprocate on the same level of performance as oneself. We realize how fragile we all are, how contingent our performance is upon health, capacity, luck. Yet in an environment beyond scarcity, we don't fear those who fail as symbols of our own possible failure – the 'lunch is for losers' culture of ultra-work values. Instead, we move towards them to learn how we can inadvertently fall out of the game, or deliberately decide to step out: and in that moment of care, much knowledge and understanding about how to sustain creative living is exchanged.

Instead of pity for the weakness of the cared for, a desire to bring them up to our functional norm – the work ethic as welfare – the complete player can recognize that there is a huge variety of ways to be an agent in life: not just labour and duty, but imagination, humour, games, celebration, reminiscence, exploring and developing the self. This is the play ethic as well-being, or more accurately, *well-becoming*.[78] The player can bring an eclectic knowledge of human strategies to the situation of the person in need: and rather than being dependent on the strength of the carer, the cared-for is empowered by the picture of complexity and possibility that the carer presents. The player-carer is also empowered, to the extent that an appreciation of the blockages and twists that occur in human agency also sheds light on how they can chart a more profound path for themselves. Care informs the player about the marvellous patterns and braids that could be made in the space between self and action, between who we are and what we do by means of apprehending and untangling the knots of a person in need.

To sum this up as axiomatically as I can:

- Leisure makes us compliant workers; care makes us wise players.

- Just as 'man' didn't live by work alone, fully conscious women and men will not be able to live by play alone.

- With the right to play comes the responsibility to care.

This last line might sound very like the communitarian verities of Third Way politics. But there is an ultimate difference. The 'responsibility' end of the Third Way vision implies a certain disdain and constraint of liberal culture, by politicians who shakily mount various high horses about moral reform and self-discipline. Yet the role of care values in the play ethic is to show how responding to the needs of others is a means of self-development – the development of our 'response abilities', as it were. The liberalism of play is taken seriously, and embraced: but the wisdom of a play ethic comes from our acceptance of paradox and ambiguity. Players know that strength and weakness, dependence and independence, success and failure accompany them throughout their lives.

As social workers know all too well, caring properly for others is a mixture of empathy and critique. That means recognizing a client's needs in all their complexity, but also having the confidence to suggest pathways out of the mess. Care is at its best when it recognizes each extreme, and tries to apply the right method for the right person at the right time. Social workers, in fact, have much to teach us about a play ethic.

Social work – or social play?

As part of the creative consultancy New Integrity, I have explored what it might mean to 're-imagine' social work.[79] In Britain, at least, social workers occupy a fascinating but demanding space in the continuum between play and care. At one extreme, they have the statutory power to *enforce* care – particularly in cases of suspected child abuse, or in potential adoptions, or in terms of protecting those with mental health problems either from themselves or from their community. Yet the dilemma these professionals were struggling with was that their wider community – and particularly the media – saw them as incapable of exercising this power. As one participant put it, 'We're damned if we do intervene in someone's life or family – we're regarded as "interfering busybodies" who take children away. Or we're damned if we don't intervene – then we're described as "unprofessional and negligent", people who let children die or be abused. Social workers just can't win!'

The desire of social workers was for the wider public to accept that, in these difficult situations – where human pathology might end up in the worst forms of destructiveness of self and others – the social worker was the only professional capable of generating 'the least unhappy result'. The tendency in recent years in the UK has been to either medicalize or criminalize the moment of human crisis that social workers tend to deal with.

Social workers' responses to these strictures have been mixed. Some are happy that their often overwhelming jobs were becoming more limited and professionally defined. Some are anxious that the more interpretive, communicative and preventative aspects of their jobs are being 'managed' and 'professionalized' out of existence. They should be building people up into fuller lives through interpreting and responding to needs, rather than compelling them to be 'normalized' (or worse, work-ethical) according to central government diktat.[80]

This divide almost too neatly breaks down into a division between 'social work' and 'social play' – the former being shaped by government regimes into an agency of social control, the latter being an open-ended tradition of experiment, empathy and diversity as a response to crisis or deprivation. Indeed, there is even a new school of social work theory – called 'constructivist social work' – whose intellectual traditions sit happily within the general theory of play. Its supporters take our sense of reality to be always a construction of language and signs. They see the job of the social worker as an act of 'restorying' their clients' lives, helping them to build better narratives of progress and capability for themselves, with the professional carer becoming skilled in forging these new stories.[81]

Yet out of all the 'caring' sectors – including teaching, health care, counselling, etc. – social work indicates exactly at what point play must shift and change, and become the act of care. Is the bruising on a child's back, or a woman's face, a matter of 'real virtuality'? Do we 'take this reality lightly'? Two experts in constructivist social work answer the point directly: 'The debate is not about whether things like injuries to children are real – of course they are real – but about what kinds of device we use to make sense of how they occurred, to determine future risk and to decide what action to take.'[82]

Social workers need to be masters and mistresses of a most demanding and paradoxical situation. They must deploy the widest range of human sensitivities in order to fully understand a situation in which bodies, minds and lives might be damaging others and themselves. And yet they must also be empowered to intervene in those situations – to remove a child from its parents, or section a disturbed individual – in order to prevent greater harm occurring.

In a sense, social work is the only kind of 'ethical work' to which a profoundly playful society could give credibility. The 'play of society' is what we have a right to in a post-scarcity, post-patriarchal, highly productive and technologized world – the right to compose a life from many materials, the right to define how we bring value and creativity and utility into the world, the right to develop our 'response abilities'. Yet the 'work of society' is what we are 'responsible' to, in the direct sense: the inevitable fragility and varying capacities of human beings, as they stretch for goals, or toil under injuries, or are distorted by the strains of socio-economic inequality, either past or present.

On this last point, there is a fascinating overlap between advanced social work thinking, and one of the keynote policies of the politics of the play ethic: the citizen's wage or guaranteed income.[83] One of constructivist social work's most esteemed advocates, Bill Jordan, has written that a harmonization of welfare benefit schemes into a 'citizens' income' would generate the kind of culture of care, responsibility and reciprocity that Third Way governments are keen to encourage in their populace – but from bottom up, not top down. 'It allows all citizens to participate [in care] through chosen combinations of paid and unpaid work, under divisions of labour and shares of the burdens and benefits of cooperation that are negotiated between them – in groups, associations and households.'[84]

A citizens' income would allow local and informal groupings to develop services for those in need – a 'caring activism' that would be all the stronger for not having been coerced by punitive discipline from central government through 'workfare' schemes. Social workers could then meet social carers, and even social players, in a new zone of collective security. Their rich cultures of care would give us all the confidence to 'play our lives' in a whole variety of valuable ways. Sometimes in the market, sometimes in the community; always guided by a sense of creative self-fulfilment in the presence of others; always reassured that our play can happen at a variety of levels, with a variety of values.

And if we fall, we can easily find our foothold again in an ethical universe that validates *both* the initial risk *and* the process of recovery. One might say this is not just a social net, but also a social trampoline – a broad and generously sprung support on which players and carers both operate, skilfully coordinating their acrobatics and aspiration according to strength and skill.[85]

The great sociologist of modern ethics Zygmunt Bauman has grappled gravely with the legacy of social work in a world where the 'player' – in Bauman's sense only an agonistic and narcissistic player, defined by the 'market game' – is dominant. 'The tacit, rarely spelled out assumption is that for not-independent people, such people as do not join the game of selling or buying, there is no room in the society of players. "Dependence" has become a dirty word: it refers to something which decent people should be ashamed of.'[86]

Yet even though Bauman's notion of play is limited, his desire to assert the value of care entirely on its own terms actually supports the play-care social contract. In a world where the welfare state and its social services are now no longer needed to maintain the health of a reserve army of labour (as in the industrial age), their justification falls back upon elementally moral and ethical grounds: as the title of Bauman's essay puts it, 'Am I my brother's keeper?' Yes, we are, says Bauman,

> Social work, whatever else it may be, is the ethical gesture of taking responsibility for our ineradicable responsibility for the wellbeing and fate of the Other: and the weaker and less able to demand, to litigate and to sue the Other is, the greater our responsibility ... the uncertainty which haunts social work is nothing more or less than the uncertainty endemic to moral responsibility. It is there to stay forever: it may be neutralized only together with the ethical conscience.[87]

So the ambivalent yet powerful caring of the social worker, requiring full response ability, but with the power to control and coerce always implicit, is the very problematic of ethics itself. 'When we presume in advance that we know how to deal with clients in all their difficulties', said a social worker in my session, 'we're riding for a fall. Every situation is different, and requires all your skills.' In that sense, the carer is as open to contingency and unpredictability as the player.

The point of transition between the two should be clear by now. The carer's response, however imaginative and skilful, arrests the *virtuality* of human experience, and tries to respond to the *actuality* of human need and weakness. Yet for most social workers, the point is not just to repair the weakness, but to build up and strengthen frailties in order that clients can enter the 'game of life' again – that is, to fully exercise their right to play. Players are responsible to the frail and weak because we wish them to become 'response able' again, to become part of the general reciprocation in informational society. We wish them to become our brothers and sisters again, whether we are their 'keepers' or not.

Lifestyle militancy
– after 'work–life' balance

Is the play–care balance just a different version of the work-life balance – an overused phrase which nevertheless points towards a genuine struggle for a more humane society? Like 'work-leisure', 'work-life' presumes a schizophrenic existence – the notion that we need to accept the alienations of our social and economic function (work) in order that we can generate the resources to pursue 'life' (which is presumably recreation plus parenting plus voluntary service, etc.). The imbalance comes from the uxorious demands of the former distorting the rich satisfactions of the latter (which are regarded as somewhat more elevated than leisure per se). Again the image is of a fundamentally distorted lifestyle. Here are two cultures of coercion and freedom, heteronomy and autonomy, caught in an endless relay race, with a bitterly resented hand-over.

Much of the current debate about work–life balance, in the UK at least, is being led by employers and politicians, both worried about skyrocketing degrees of sick leave in general, and the competition for talent at the higher levels in particular.[88] The columnist Madeleine Bunting has noted that the amount of time taken off for sick leave by British employees now outstrips the amount of days lost to industrial action at the height of seventies' militancy.

Flexi-time – the ability of the employee to manage his or her work hours in ways and patterns beyond the regular nine to five, Monday to Friday routine – has come up as a possible solution.[89] The chief executive of the banking giant Lloyds TSB, Peter Ellwood, puts it authoritatively:

> When an employee leaves a company, the average cost to the business is more than £3,000. Stress-related sick leave costs UK industry £370m a year, yet employers are more likely to offer counselling than flexible work options that might prevent the stress in the first place. Of the employers surveyed

by the DTI [Department of Trade and Industry], 56 per cent had never considered flexible working locations, such as working from home, and 57 per cent had never considered offering job-sharing schemes – two common ways to reduce workplace stress.[90]

Implicit behind all this is the sense that work must ultimately be separate from 'life'. Ellwood allows that 'people have the right to a life outside work', and expects them to increasingly make their employment decisions based on how much they can exercise that right. This might be partly an adroit withdrawal from the corporate-culture extremes of the eighties and nineties, when various 'company ways' tried to engage the hearts and minds of employees through a variety of propagandist means.[91] The most savage satire of this 'touchy-feely' culture is the BBC TV series *The Office*, which subjected the rhetoric of 'company as community' to the roughest of treatment.

David Brent, the office manager, is an excruciatingly recognizable figure to most information workers in Britain: the ingratiating, I-hear-your-pain aspirant leader, who uses empowering language to shroud the pettiest kind of workplace power struggles and hierarchies. Madeleine Bunting noted that when Brent lost his job in the last episode of the series, it topped a popular chart for the best TV moment of 2002 because, in her view, 'it was a moment of pure triumphant revenge for millions of viewers who dream of just such punishment meted out to their own bosses'.[92] In the work–life balance equation, this almost seems like an insurrectionary attack from the forces of life. Bunting's story was also pegged to a government-backed survey, which noted that UK citizens looking for a new job would prefer flexible working hours to a £1,000 pay increase, and rated that flexibility as much more important than the prospect of a company car.[93]

There is no shortage of well-planned and feasible schemes, either on the drawing board or put into practice by governments and companies, around the notion of flexible working hours. All of them aim to maintain employees' loyalty by allowing them to increase control over their working time, by decreasing the overall amount of working time or sometimes both at the same time.[94] Yet the question raised (and most appropriately so in the realm of the arts, through TV programmes like *The Office*) is this: will an appropriate work–life balance lead to an equilibrium? Or will it lead to a new and even more unstable dynamic, where the values of 'life' begin to seriously question the intrinsic structures, goals and strategies of most organizational 'work' itself?

This is where the play–care continuum is an attempt to address the limitations of work–life balance. The latter divides our lives into Manichean realms, the compulsory and the truly meaningful, conducted within a fear-driven atmosphere of competition and market relevance. Instead, play-care presumes a plateau of value-creating human actors and activities (from the donatory to the monetary, the duteous to the freely creative). Play and care is supported by interlocking systems of economic and social security, and recognizes fragility and dependency as the moral test of our creative living. We cannot be *response able* (able to partake of all the marvellous reciprocations of play) if we are not *responsible* (sensitive to those who cannot join the fray, or who need time away from it for repair and sustenance). And vice versa: we cannot exercise our caring responsibilities properly and humanely without a keen sense of response ability to the widest variations of human motivation and experience.

So in a sense, work–life balance is only a way-station to a much deeper process of reform – a politics not just of time, but also of resource and autonomy, which the notion of the 'player' over the 'worker' is an attempt to articulate. Time spent away from work should not just be an occasion for more leisure, or even more care, but for a rethinking of human purposefulness. As Charles Leadbeater has suggested, it could mean the revival of an 'amateur' spirit, of doing things for love and passion, which may fuel social experimentation as well as mere re-creation for the grind.[95] The 'lifestyle militancy' of the player deliberately unbalances the 'work–life balance' in favour of life. This is a search for an existence where making meaning contends equally with making money, and where each might even support each other. Yet rather than seeking to escape from the thick tangle of relationships of postmodern life, the player wants to dive deeper and more energetically into the melee – making new connections, building new structures, proposing better games and strategies. It's social and civilizational enterprise, rather than just private enterprise.

The question of where that energy comes from has partly been answered in this chapter. There is an enormous resource in the new open relations between parents and children. To use Rebecca Abrams's clever phrase, it's not about childishness in adults, but 'childness', a joyful readiness for anything, which dissolves much of the patriarchal (and dare it be said, matriarchal) fixities of the work-and-leisure culture. As the soulitarian chapter has shown, it also comes from the sheer interactivity and openness of the new communication technologies themselves – allowing more voices and cultural production into the public realm.[96]

Yet even given these enabling conditions, the energy of the full player needs further resourcing. One obvious resource is the arts – that realm of 'making a mark upon the world' which presumes the least possible distance between intention and action, and the maximal possible conditions of creativity and agency. Play as imagination is the strongest rhetoric here. But in an age where the power of the idea and the image, of sensibility and experience, becomes an explicit concern of politics and business, how important is the notion of 'mental emancipation' implied by much artistic practice? Will a play ethic be the best prospect for a revived legitimation of 'the power of the arts'? Or is this yet another attempt to corral art's anarchic power for socially functional ends?

Another resource is education: and out of all the institutions of the industrial age, public education (and its primary institution, the school) has always been the most ambivalent about work. It was born both out of a Romantic and Enlightenment commitment to the child as a symbol of human perfectibility, and as a form of social and behavioural control.

Between education and art, we can now examine two ways of 'socializing the player'. A play-ethical education will attempt to make its 'top-down' institutions genuinely enabling, skilling children and adults for autonomy rather than conformism. A play-ethical arts and media will try to connect the endless possibilities of creativity with the audiences and public that might take art beyond egoism or social utility. And of course, education and the arts must have their own mutual dialogues too, around the merits and demerits of a play ethic.

But teachers, for once, first.

SIX / 183

WISDOM LOVERS

An Education for Players

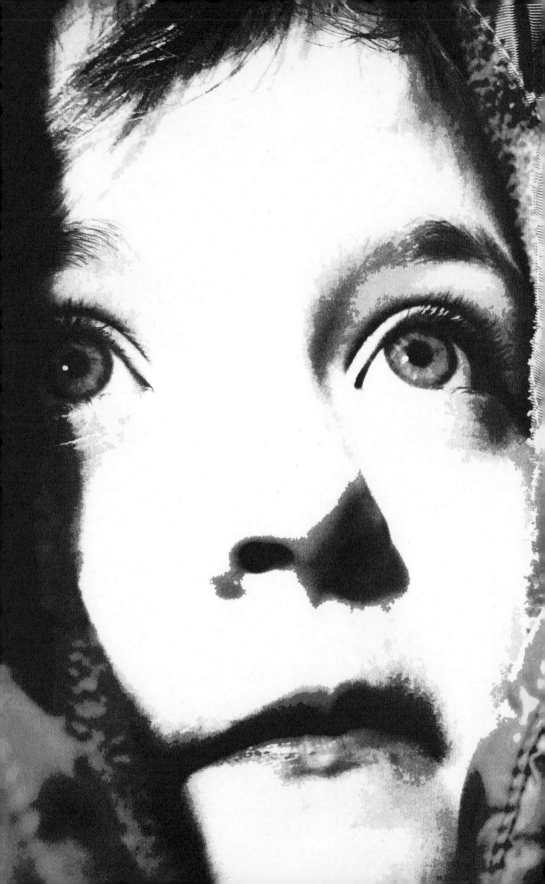

What of the individual child at a historical juncture where there is clear evidence that the intellectual, labouring and signifying capacities of the culture are in transition and flux?

– Allen and Carmen Luke, *Journal of Childhood Literacy*, 2000

To be prepared against surprise is to be trained. To be prepared for surprise is to be educated.

– James Carse, *Finite and Infinite Games*, 1986

Over about six months, scattered throughout 2002, I bought the UK's main weekly paper for teachers, the *Times Educational Supplement* (Scottish edition). As a product, it's as huge and supplement-stuffed as any market-leading Sunday newspaper, often wrapped in clear plastic to keep all the bits in. Once you rip it open, it's no exaggeration to say that an entire culture spills out onto the table – with its own heroes and villains, rituals and phobias, truths and fictions, radicals and conservatives, shibboleths and iconoclasms.

It may seem strange to say this about a trade publication, but I found the *TES* inspiring. So many experts straining to translate their findings into useable tools for pressured teachers; so many teachers trying to raise their sights above their daily labours, and remind themselves of why they wanted to walk into a classroom in the first place. And so much prose with a pulse – mixing experience and theory, practical common sense and starry-eyed idealism. If only the media servicing other sectors of society – like business, or science, or politics, or even the arts – had the same humane capaciousness about it.

Perhaps this is because educators deal with the unfolding of human potential at its most delicate stage. And a teacher who does not avail him or herself of the full range of available skills and responses as they face their meaning-hungry children – whether it's the latest multimedia presentation technology, or the quiet conversation in a corridor after class – is surely less than a teacher can be. The figures that mill through the pages of the *TES* are a bunch of hurried, straight-talking generalists: easily moved to passion about their jobs, but acutely aware that a whole society is examining their daily performance. Principles and pragmatism jostle each other vigorously like hungry kids in a dinner queue.

In terms of play, it sometimes seems as if the deepest conundrums about the purpose of education have remained unresolved since the nineteenth century, when the Rousseavians faced off against the Gradgrinders. 'Education as a cradling of the soul as much as a feeding of the mind', writes the bearded executive member for education on Edinburgh City Council in the *TES*'s main op-ed column.

> The really powerful education experience is the chance to discover who we are and how we see the world. And the really life-changing moments are the realization that we do matter to others and that others matter to us. Sadly, a curriculum obsessed with exams, targets and results means that this kind of thinking rarely gets the time to blossom . . . The task of education isn't simply to provide fodder for the jobs market: it's to nurture young people and their potential . . . [educational success] is as much about the emotional as it is the examinable.[1]

Yet elsewhere in the same issue, a news page covers the resignation of a UK education minister over accusations that exam results were allegedly 'rigged' (specifically, they were downgrading a perceived trend to mark 'too highly' in previous years). The incoming male minister is described as a 'bruiser'; the outgoing female minister has become notorious for her remarkable public confession that she was 'good, but not good enough' to do her job.[2]

Rarely in any area of public life are contending ethics of human potential so dramatically opposed – and by figures occupying the same authority structure, albeit at different levels. For one set of leaders, education is a system that generates the non-systemic, the emotionally literate, the deeply soulful and the profoundly sociable. For another set, education is an exam machine – yet a machine so hyper-rationalist that it is driven to subvert its own standards of objectivity, and discards those executives who can't cope with (or ignore) the contradictions. One could go through any copy of the *TES* and restage this opposition, within and between articles and sections.

So it would seem all too easy to counterpose the values of play against the values of work in modern education. Teachers should aim to develop full-spectrum, multi-active, deeply inquisitive humans – rather than grades-obsessed drones ready to slot into their place in the labour market, where their worth is measured by statistical results alone. A viable play ethic in education could simply be the assertion of what Sutton-Smith calls the 'modern' discourses of play. From this essentially Romantic perspective, education becomes the creator of authentic and imaginative agents, who defy the strictures of a bureaucratic, overly administered world.

But educational Romanticism isn't enough – because our early-twenty-first-century societies are, indeed, more complex than the Dickensian stereotype implied by Romantic play. We live in a world that is deeply, constitutively playful – and we need a play ethic to make the best of these new conditions. But there is toughness, danger and power in this new ludic world as well. Whatever an education for players might mean, it will not be an easy option.

Education and the rhetorics of play

We need a bit of 'virtual reality' when it comes to thinking anew about education. Can any institution in our lives be as over-determined by conventional wisdom as this? As we did at the beginning of our theory chapter, let's imagine a school that exists in a society where play values are the mainstream, and work values have become a carefully managed minority interest. Our framework of the rhetorics of play are useful here again, as a kind of 'play audit'. They can give us some sense of how our existing structures – whether they be the traditional subject disciplines, or school timetables, or the boundaries between school and society – would change and mutate in a genuinely post-work world.

Trial, error and health: play as development and progress

This is the easiest rhetoric of play to accommodate to current educational wisdom, as held in most countries in the developed world. In terms of the basic neurological and physiological health of children, a strong pervasion of play in school life has much to commend it. In Finland – which regularly tops the OECD world tables on educational performance – formal schooling isn't commenced until the age of seven because of a deep-seated belief that the basics of early learning skills are forged through play. When actually in school, Finnish children are allowed to play for an hour a day, with their self-determined activities using both the expected disciplines – music, art, sport – and any other modes of expression that might appeal to the child.[3]

In *The Excellence of Play*, a range of educators makes an impressive case for play activities – whether truly 'free play', or with a minimal level of direction and context – as the crucial factor in early child development. Much of the research here backs up the notion of play as 'adaptive potentiation' – our mammalian need to rehearse our responses to a complex world.[4]

The question for most of the writers, who come out of a largely English educational scene, is how to defend play against the increasing prescriptions of a 'national curriculum' and its accompanying audit culture – which obsessively monitors and measures performance of children in 'essential' skills against national standards. This regime regards the sprawl and indeterminacy of play as a nightmare of imprecision, and more generally a distraction from the imperatives of the labour market. That this culture has only intensified under a New Labour government, for whom (as their election slogan has it) 'the work continues', is surely no surprise.

Yet might a curriculum scoured of play be *the very opposite* of what children really need in the network society? As the editor of the collection says:

> Perhaps one of the greatest attributes of play is the opportunities it affords for learning to live with *not knowing*, for it is readily recognized that we all learn more effectively through trial and error, and play is a non-threatening way to cope with new learning and still retain self-esteem and self-image [her emphasis].[5]

'Learning to live with *not knowing*', in a complex, unpredictable twenty-first-century world, begins to seem like a master skill. If the knowledge demands facing children increase as exponentially as they have done over the last twenty years, then an ability to hypothesize and imagine scenarios within which new information can be subjected to a strong and confident sensibility is going to be essential.

Swarmers, nomads and virtualists: play as power and contest

So play activities might well need to be reasserted in the 'factory' school climate of the moment – but not as a kind of Romantic counterculture to a world of technologies, systems and markets. Indeed, without a proper typology of play, that kind of purely modernist emphasis on play as selfhood and authenticity would be insufficient. The *agonism* of play – play as the inevitability of contest, comparison and negotiation with the interests of others – also has to be recognized in education.

But this goes beyond the usual kinds of dispute about the role of competitive sports in a curriculum,[6] or even the more sophisticated debates about the introduction of citizenship classes into UK state schools – where the anxieties about a depoliticized generation are addressed through lessons in civics and activism.[7] Our children already live in a world of networks: and in themselves, networks demand a level of participation and commitment, energy and skill, that outstrips the duty-and-routine ideals of industrial-age education. To be blunt, our children know that they will have to be 'players in the Net'. How will their time at school be of use to them in this respect?

The thorny question of how we use information and communications technology (ICT) in schools can perhaps be newly addressed from a play perspective. In *Deschooling Society* (1970), Ivan Illich advocated that schools dissolve themselves, and that the educative moment should disperse itself into a 'learning web'.

This would be a network which took the entire urban space as its classroom – from bank to restaurant, from laboratory to hospital, from sports ground to market district. It would use computers, telephones and television to facilitate the creating of self-directed communities of interest, forged from teachers, pupils and the community. And it would encourage a mobility and situatedness about learning that would, in Illich's modest terms, 'blur the distinctions between economics, education and politics on which the stability of the present world order and the stability of nations now rest'.[8]

It doesn't take much effort to note the prophetic power of Illich's vision. For isn't the 'learning web' up and running – in this wired and wireless, surfed and webcasted, simulatory and game-consoled, text-messaged and videophoning society? Except that it is much more explicitly and self-consciously a 'playing' web at the moment. I've already described the adult 'soulitarians', who deploy their digital and communicational articulacy to shape their world as they wish – whether to make their money, make their escape or even make another 'virtuality' to live in.

Yet among the school populations of the developed world, there exists a shadow world of the techno player. They use mobile phones to swarm together in public places. They use Google search engines to find material that might impress a teacher, or instant messaging to share gossip and practise for adulthood. They join online multiplayer games (like Habbo Hotel, Everquest or the Sims Online) where a rich community experience can be had with hundreds of thousands of other players.

At the very least, formal education should recognize that children are becoming self-conscious about being players in networks. Their concrete sense of community is becoming more an abstract sense of connectedness, disembedded from space and flexible about time. The Romantic definers of play in schools might recoil from this world regarding it as non-tactile, non-organic, non-sensual. Those who would wish schools to become more friendly to the values of the marketplace might find a justification in these individualized swarmers, nomads and virtualists. Their capacity for abstraction, and their thirst for the evanescent, surely makes them eminently suitable for day-trader jobs in the City.

Yet if we look at these debates from the perspective of our rich model of play, we can see a rather traditional role for education in the face of the natural agonism of our networked children. Never was a 'play ethic' more necessary than in this world – a world where disconnection from your networks can result in the most extreme kind of social exclusion; where pathological and destructive behaviour (like computer viruses) can reduce the effectiveness of the whole system; and where the intensities of 'virtual' consciousness can distort and degrade the continuity of 'actual' consciousness – that is, our day-to-day relationships with real people.

Educators should work with the grain of these times, and find ways to teach humane values within these new flows and spaces of the virtual and the networked. A 'net ethic', as the Finnish philosopher Pekka Himanen calls it, already exists in the hacker cultures of the West where sharing of common resources (mostly digital, but increasingly non-digital too) is a social norm. In hacker cultures, collaborative projects are driven from the bottom up and involve thousands of people; and in this collective creation, individuals' urges towards creativity and inventiveness are encouraged.[9]

The moment of learning could be about forging a fully humane, yet fully contemporary student out of these broad values – joyful soulitarians rather than alienated technoproles. That is, children who are encouraged to express their moral, ethical and reciprocal selves through the channels of the information age rather than use these media for actively destructive ends, or passively submit themselves to the external programming of others.

So a 'play ethic' would ask educators to transmit some sense of collective existence to the young soulitarians: if we are all to live well together, in all our diversity, then how should we behave? We are used to questioning the legitimacy of the old and familiar collectivities: class, nation, region, ethnicity, gender. Yet we are not sure about what kind of sociality to put in their places. What visions of human togetherness might survive in the network society? And what could a teacher say to his or her pupils about it?

Posses and crews: play as identity

From the perspective of those interested in maintaining social order, industrial-era schooling had no problem about the kind of social bond that the majority of its pupils would need to internalize. Children would have to accept their position in the division of labour and professions, get used to their status in a workplace hierarchy and educate themselves to function within those organizations.

The 'solidarity' that socialists (and perhaps some socialist teachers) invoked was a unity based on alienation and objectification: a coming together of those who shared the pain and discomfort of their experiences as human cogs in the machinery of industry. Yet both sides of industrial culture, business/state and worker, accepted their identities as given, defined by the structures of capitalism.

It's fascinating to note that the rise of the 'comprehensive' ideal for education came in the sixties, which represented the first wave of what has come to be called the 'post-scarcity' society,[10] a society where automation and improved production techniques began both to raise the intellectual demands placed upon workers, and sometimes even replace those workers altogether. The division between grammar and secondary schools – or between intellectual and technical – became increasingly untenable in an economy where 'immaterial' production (services, entertainments, finance) was just as important as material production (cars, goods, processed minerals).

The relationship between a more comprehensive education, and the wider social and cultural changes of the sixties, is complex. The countercultures of the sixties were the first expressions of what has become a regular pattern in developed societies – that is, between grass-roots assertions of new identities (whether aesthetic, sexual, ecological, globalist), and then a period of repressions and reactions, grudgingly followed by institutional reform.[11]

There is no doubt that the seeds of this thirty-year 'revolt of the sensibilities' were deeply planted in the new institutions of comprehensive education throughout Europe and the US. The regular conservative assaults on 'progressive education' after the advent of the New Right were motivated by a sense that the school was becoming a 'scholarium', as Spinoza might have put it[12] – a place where individuals could be brought to the fullest development of their capacities, and then be able to define their life narratives (and times).

The assault was largely successful in its attempt to reindustrialize the philosophy of education, arguing for quantitative, exam-led assessment, for schools to be allowed again to select on the basis of ability, for the divisions between intellectual/creative and operational/technical to be re-established.[13] Yet this is causing much distress to the generation of teachers who came into the profession with a different social vision entirely. These teachers presumed that their efforts would create a general intellectual majority, using their learning to practise the arts of living in a society where productive labour was automated to a minimum.[14]

Yet the challenge for educators is that their pupils are living as if a culture 'liberated from labour' already existed, as evidenced by their technological, cultural and emotional choices. Many are what new media consultant David Docherty has called the 'cookie monsters' – those who expect technology, as an open and interactive medium, to give them access to all kinds of art and experience without any respect for property rights or payment.[15] Are these young people 'stealing' their songs and movies – or are they taking the logic of interactive media more seriously than anyone, as a challenge to economic models based on scarcity and property?

What is obvious, in terms of identity, is that the free use of technology is generating a kind of emergent, unstable collectivity amongst the screenagers. This means asserting the dignity of the player, rather than the dignity of the worker; defending the rights of the 'soulitarian', instead of the proletarian. This new techno-identity both enables and is enabled by the power of relationships: the incessant activity of mobile messaging, Net chatrooms, mail correspondence, online multiplayer gaming. And by the power of arts and culture: the constant redefinition and extension of selves and others that an immersion in our entertainment culture implies: the pop-star competitions and reality shows of TV, the labyrinthine DVDs of fantasy blockbusters like *Star Wars* or *The Lord of the Rings*.

A historical understanding of play as identity can give educators a context within which to deal with this new sensibility – which has, in truth, very ancient roots indeed. For carnival and other collective forms of celebration, ritual and performance have been a powerful means of confirming social identity for thousands of years. Collective play is a deep human constant that puts the cramped solidarity-through-alienation of the industrial age into its proper perspective.

If this tendency of humans to come together through play is becoming resurgent again as the labour metaphysic increasingly unravels, then the job of the school is an acutely play-ethical one. How can school be a place where the notion of carnival – the coming together of talents and passions – is richly and meaningfully experienced? This is a way of addressing one of the deficits in the case for progressive education. It may be thrilling to sweep away the existing structures and rituals of school life – the classrooms, the surveillance, the regulation of movement and sound – in a tornado of romanticized idealism about the sovereign rights of 'free play'.[16]

But as this book constantly stresses should be obvious by now, free play is only one tradition of play – which has its place (see below). Other forms of play can be deployed to guide and structure that passionate individualism. Nothing depends more on structure than, say, a theatrical performance, whether the script is generated by the players themselves or taken off the shelf. For decades, the ideal of the 'school play' was the means whereby all the various talents of a school – from performers to artisans – could be celebrated in an annual performance.

Yet the question is whether 'school play' isn't a much deeper concept than simply a boisterous year-end musical. What might educators think of regular waves of collective creativity in their schools, overlapping the boundaries between the disciplines and occasionally subsuming the curriculum? If you're teaching evolution, how about a Darwin festival? If you're teaching the Holocaust, how about some collective ritual to embody its significance?[17]

This would prepare children to make the best of a world in which they have to be more inventive in their social relationships than ever before – sophisticating their techniques and strategies for sociality, experimenting with their lifestyles alongside other, equally complex and demanding humans. Should these new skills of association simply be discovered in the rough and tumble of interactive play in the digital realm? Or can school become a place where the many ways of being social are first experimented with, perhaps even developed as a literacy, in a place of safety and care?

One might imagine two distinct modules in the civics class of a young player. 'My Networks' (dealing with power strategies, both one's own and others') and 'My Carnivals' (finding ways and means to share energies and purposes with others). Yet if these are the social frameworks into which a young player would be 'socialized', it's worth reminding ourselves of the frameworks they replace which could easily be rendered as 'My Duties' (accepting a given position in the division of labour and the status structures of society) and 'My Community' (accepting collective norms and constraints as a necessary social bond). Neither of these options requires very much energy or creativity on the part of the young worker – just a routine completion of the necessary training, and then a steady adherence to the societal rules. But young players, faced with the necessity of networking or the carnivalesque as the context for their socialization, need to be a lot stronger and more capacious than young workers. An education for players would then build on the play traditions that focus precisely on the surpassing capacities of the individual.

The dream seeker's allowance: play as imagination

No aspect of play excites the idealism of teachers more than its capacity for stimulating the imaginations of children. Yet there is a fascinating tension between this rhetoric and the rhetoric of progress. Much of the research of the last twenty years on the role of play in early-years education, for example, has been at pains to stress its benefits to the general development of literacy and numeracy in children. The role of play in the grand theorists of educational psychology – Piaget and Vygotsky – was to act as a 'practice venue', a place and time where children could ready themselves for more organized kinds of representing and symbolizing (reading, writing and arithmetic). And much recent research has proceeded on these lines, outlining the myriad ways in which the 'play moment' in early schooling could 'serve' the attainment of traditional literacy.[18]

We have to note the historical and political context of this research – a time when, as mentioned above, there has been a backlash against the evils of 'progressive' education by a succession of New Right and Third Way governments. Even a title like *The Excellence of Play* has a defensive tone about it. Play has to be justified to a managerial regime, with its own strict standard-setting metrics (core curriculum, basic skills and closely monitored results), which usually regards play as suspiciously fuzzy, inefficient and immeasurable. The mixing, morphing and semiotic freedom implied by play as imagination sits uncomfortably with a 'back-to-basics' educational orthodoxy which needs to see rising literacy and numeracy levels. Or else, heads (and head teachers) roll.

Yet this is another instance where the struggle between eras – the modernist industrial age and the postmodernist informational age – sometimes involves moving backwards, even in the face of evident waves of progress and development. The Australian educational thinkers Allen and Carmen Luke have proposed an extraordinary and counter-intuitive thesis.[19] In their view, the strong emphasis on print literacy in early-years education, right across the northern and Western world, is actually a kind of institutional backlash. And it is directed against new forms of *techno-literacy*, mastered by children yet mostly baffling to their adult teachers. It often takes the form of a 'moral crusade', where 'the unruly techno-subject is the symptom, and an earlier and more prescriptive print literacy training is the purgative'. The hope is that early literacy might 'inoculate' children against the virus of digitality – particularly when it's used in all the different modalities of play: gaming, interaction, simulation and immersion (texting, online and offline games, Web surfing, etc.).[20]

There is a fascinating reversal here. Since the very beginning of the Calvinist era, literacy and morality have been intertwined.[21] With the arrival of the media of film and television, that moral anxiety was heightened, the passivity and spectatorship of most film and TV causing most of the worries. Audio-visual media produced an 'articulacy deficit' in children, which it was the job of schools and parents to redeem through the early and determined inculcation of print literacy. Yet the paradox in the current parental/teacher anxiety about 'screenagers', 'video-game addicts', 'texters' and 'vid-kids' is that the articulacy deficit *is all on the adult side*.

'Kids are the experts, adults are the novices,' say the Lukes, in regard to 'computer mediated play entertainment and communication'. This is 'a new youth competence and practice' which, looked at closely, refutes any charge of illiteracy. It is adults (teachers and parents) who are 'struggling with, and in instances, actively resisting the integration of online communications into their working and leisure time'.[22]

There is also a gathering body of research that tries to assess what the real cognitive effects of new media and interactive technologies might be on children. So far, the results largely favour the new technologies. A UK government-funded study of computer games made two benefits clear: learning new skills, such as problem solving, concentration, improving memory and collaborating with others; and acquiring knowledge related to the school curriculum.[23] MIT's Seymour Papert, who was once a colleague of the child psychologist Jean Piaget in Geneva, says the Playstation generation is being profoundly developed by its 'entertainments':

> Game designers depend on millions of people being prepared to undertake the serious amount of learning needed to master a complex game. If their public failed to learn, they'd go out of business. Kids who talk about 'hard fun' don't mean it's fun in spite of being hard. It's fun *because* it's hard. Learning happens best when one is deeply engaged in hard and challenging activities.[24]

Yet the wider sociological context to this is important. This new techno-literacy – which kids are assembling by themselves in their own largely unregulated time and space – is an honest response to a fundamental shift in the structures of post-modern life: the life of flows and networks, mobility and the power of culture and ideas, summed up by the 'information age'. Children are using play to make themselves imaginatively capable for this new world while their schools are, by and large, still preparing them for an industrial era.[25]

Yet these flexible, mentally playful 'soulitarians' *could* be much better served by their schools. We may need to go all the way back to Hegel for an answer. What does the state – and by association, its education sector – do for its citizens? One answer is that it can use its resources to create places and times that help the child recognize the society they're in, through describing a 'life narrative' that recapitulates the development of the society itself. How can education write a credible life-story for the new techno-kids? How can the skills of teachers both pedagogically and emotionally help the transition from childhood to adolescence to 'personhood' in millennial cyber-capitalism? The Lukes hazard their suggestions: 'We want all educational interventions – even and especially those in early childhood – to begin from an analysis of the new material stratifications of labour and forms of life generated through new technologies, and globalized forms of information and capital.'[26]

In terms of the rhetoric of play as imagination as it applies to schools, this obviously means a kind of literacy teaching that is technically multimedia, and semiotic in its method. The 'free play' of the mind – that mental capacity which unites the Romantic poets with the pure scientists, the twentieth-century surrealists with twenty-first-century advocates of 'neural plasticity' – becomes a powerful ethical basis for a new kind of 'communication studies'.

This is not to deny traditional literacy as a necessary skill – but it is to reduce its overbearing emphasis in early education. We must decouple early literacy from the neo-Calvinist morality that currently grips it – casting it as a vital 'inoculation' against the seductive world of images, dialogue, simulations and all other kinds of semiotic promiscuity. The Lukes note that we have elaborate and useful diagnostic tools for assessing if children are succeeding or failing in their reading, whether in terms of comprehension or critical judgement. But why don't we similarly 'identify "failure" at watching films, "poor" or "uncritical" television viewing, deficiency at Web surfing and emailing'?[27] Of course, this is exactly the role that media and cultural studies has tried to play in the Western education system over the last twenty-odd years – and never has a subject been more vilified, mostly by the remaining representatives of an industrial-age mindset.[28]

All schools must teach a story of increasing mastery. But can twenty-first-century schools continue to downgrade, or shy away from, the very tools that will give children mastery over a dynamic, informational world? And of course, though there is much fevered research into the application of ICT to education,[29] it mostly takes place in the context of equipping children for a labour market. The post-modern labour market isn't just constantly producing new and unexpected kinds of job, it also allows children to think about creating their own kind of productive life, one that blurs or morphs all existing categories. The 'play, unpredictability and performativity' of these life journeys, in the Lukes' words, should be inspiring for teachers. How can they develop children's capacities, energies and resilience to thrive in this much more open, risky world? Yet there is no possibility of being able to think towards the kind of pedagogy required if teachers are fettered by a mindset defined by industrial modernity.

One further tradition of play, properly recognized and identified, could begin to dissolve those fetters. In the process, we could begin to comprehend the kinds of destructive (and self-destructive) alienation from education that growing numbers of young people exhibit. For the one value of play not yet mentioned is that of play as selfhood and freedom – the protean spark, as it were, that animates our embrace and participation in all the other forms of play. Just as those who must play, cannot play, can we adapt this for education: those who must learn, cannot learn?

Howard Gardner notes approvingly Plato's line about the purpose of education being 'to get children to *want* to know what they *have* to know'. That is, education as a kind of subtle mind-disciplining, instilling habits that would support the functioning – and maintain the dynamism and health – of a modern, democratic, science- and markets-driven society.[30]

Yet there is still something in Plato's contending idea of the *shkole* – the person who has control of their free time – which can point education beyond this predictably functional role, as the grand socializer and competence giver. Can an education for players also be an education for freedom? Or must that take place elsewhere?

How to be me: play as freedom

Any parent who has bought into the delights of multi-channel television knows exactly the status that myths and narratives of playful freedom have in their children's lives. It's the end of the school run, and as soon as the adult's back is turned away to some household chore or other, the babble and squeak of MTV or Cartoon Network rise out of the TV room.

Peer carefully around the door and the sight is a child (uniformed or not) in a sprawled slump on the couch or floor, school bag upside down and spilling out, with images and noises of r 'n 'b rebellion, or animated anarchy and abandon, stilling their features and widening their eyes. It's a classic work-leisure moment: let out of the disciplinary institution at the end of the day, these inmates make a bee-line for fantasy and wish-fulfilment, for hyperbolic versions of complete human autonomy.

It's a realm where boys and girls are beautiful and self-directed; where technology is at the beck and call of its users; where cartoon characters show an extraordinary resilience, an irrepressible ability to bounce back. Parents – probably themselves buckling under heavy workloads, perhaps even exacerbated by this school run – shrug their shoulders. Who can blame them for wanting to chill out or veg out after a hard day at the chalkface? Don't grown-ups take their own opportunities for respite from the grind too?

Free play thrives in the leisure zone – that time and space for escape and repair from the institutions of work culture (which include the school). But the richer perspective of a play ethic can situate free play as one element in a multi-dimensional vision. Free play becomes more than a compensation for unfree tedium, but a necessary element in a complex environment.

There is no doubt that information-age schools need to 'reproduce creativity' in the way that industrial-age schools 'reproduced labour'. The rhetorics of play are certainly one way to articulate that need. An education for players is respectful of the intensive and open-ended nature of children's development through long periods of social and individual play. It is clear-eyed about the power relationships and societal networks that they will have to engage in, and the strategic nous required to thrive in them. It also understands that new kinds of sociability and togetherness – physical and virtual, emotional and informational – are being tested out by their pupils, and that schools need to find a way to support children's strivings in this area.

And a player's education presumes that such a fluid and recombinant society needs expanded capacities, and expanded competences, among its members. So it proposes a pedagogy that places old literacies (text and numbers) in a strong continuum with new literacies (interactivity, coding, simulation and imagology), not discontinuous or in opposition. A full play of the mind and heart.

Yet all this capacity-building and strengthening, all this re-imagining of one's social universe as unpredictable and opportunity-strewn, is pointless without the *will* to dive into the resulting melee. Children who sit before their media spectacles – passively consuming narratives of action, adventure and autonomy – are not to be blamed for seeking out this kind of mental escape route. Yet can a circle be closed (or at least some feedback loops established) between a popular culture constantly dreaming of unfettered liberation, and an educational culture of duty, constraint and regimentation? Can the school become a place where children gain the strength to be free and creative, rather than receive the training to be productive and functional?

Reggio Emilia: the player's education system?

No discussion about freedom, play and education would be complete without a reference to the forty-year experiment in progressive schooling known as the 'Reggio Emilia' approach. Begun after the end of the Second World War in northern Italy, this attempt to create an education that 'did nothing without joy'[31] has been celebrated throughout the world as a paradigm of what 'progressive' or 'child-centred' education could be.

Considered purely as a set of teaching techniques, the Reggio approach fits almost perfectly with a play-ethical approach:

• *Play as development* For Reggio Emilia, children are 'full of life, power and confidence, not need' – and thus their desire to experiment, make errors and self-correct them, try and fail and try again, must be deeply respected as a fundamental learning process. Before this image of the child, the teacher's role becomes much less about being the source of all knowledge, filling empty heads, and more about facilitating understanding (asking questions, helping the topics of projects become clearer, providing resources) and co-learning with the children (recording their activity, presenting it back to them, discussing the results).[32] The presumption is that play progresses human development, and that this must shape the function of teaching and the role of the teacher.

• *Play as power and contest* Groups are kept small and homogenous in terms of age group, because the Reggio thinkers believe that they encourage 'cognitive conflict' between children – a kind of conceptual and emotional agonism that is 'necessary and desirable for learning and development'.[33]

• *Play as identity and carnival* Reggio's prime theorist, Loris Malaguzzi, used to describe the space of a school as 'the third teacher'. One aspect of each school is the careful construction of 'piazza' spaces, both for the whole school and within each classroom. In these, children and adults can find the opportunity to display their projects, mount dramas, performances and concerts, and otherwise express and affirm the collective identity of the school through creative activity. 'We value space because of its power to organize, promote pleasant relationships between people of different ages, create a handsome environment, provide changes, promote choices and activity, and its potential for sparking all kinds of social, affective, and cognitive learning,' wrote Malaguzzi. 'All of this contributes to a sense of wellbeing and security in children. We also think that the space has to be a sort of aquarium, which mirrors the ideas, values, attitudes and cultures of the people who live within it.'[34] Though a carnival or festival isn't exactly like an aquarium, what the metaphors share is the idea of the space of learning as an expression of the full and diverse sensibilities of the learners.

• *Play as imagination* Reggio schools are 'more like excellent experiential children's museums' than traditional line-them-up institutions. As the schools' learning takes place almost entirely through project work, the buildings are like a permanent installation space. Each project is served by an *aterlieristi*, a trained art teacher, who turns all the material generated by the children into beautifully finished boards and artworks. And the deep conceptual underpinning of the Reggio approach is called 'The Hundred Languages of Children' – which presumes that children develop through expressing themselves in many more symbolic languages than just linguistic. A project will involve visual, dramatic, computational and musical expressions of the topic, as well as the traditional linguistic forms: there is even emphasis on synaesthesia – expressing one medium in the form of another (music as words), and then returning to the original medium. Music plays constantly throughout the school day. The digital media are one of these 'hundred languages', given as much legitimacy as any other.[35]

• *Play as freedom* It is this dimension of in the Reggio approach that provides the most telling point. The system was born out of the profoundest moment of freedom – the end of the fascist dictatorship in Italy and the restoration of a regional identity which had a long tradition of democracy and cooperation throughout its society and economy. 'It was a moment when the desire to bring change and create a new, more just world, free from oppression, was urging men and women to gather their strength, and build with their own hands schools for their children,' writes Leila Gandini.[36] Loris Malaguzzi's stated ambition was to 'change the culture of childhood' – the implicit assumption being that education's job was to produce a new generation of fulfilled and potentialized children, for whom the simplistic, power-laden attractions of fascism would not be remotely attractive. This post-war idealism interleaves with the diverse and self-confident economy and society of the wider Emilia-Romagna region, to create an almost perfect general context for Reggio's vision of education. A vision which puts the sustained unfolding of children's potential at the centre of its activities.

So there is a strong historical meshing here – between an education that aims to maximize human potential, and a society ready and eager to receive and deploy it. This makes the idea of play as freedom a natural assumption in the Reggio experience. The will of an individual, if fully nourished and multilaterally expressed within a community, is regarded as a positive and creative force. With the folk memory of totalitarianism lingering in the Reggio consciousness, this makes the 'right to play' more than just a fashionable assertion.

The Net Academy: shkolars rule?

Out of that strange techno-cultural connection between Helsinki and San Francisco comes another model of how education can accommodate the creative energies of the free player. The hacker cultures are identifiable with some of the very oldest traditions of education – that of the Greek academy. Pekka Himanen, author of *The Hacker Ethic*, says that a key principle of hacker culture is a use of technology to 'optimize time to have more space for playfulness' – to use machines to make life less machine-like. He compares this 'freedom to self-organize time' with Plato's idea that 'no free person should learn anything like a slave'.[37]

Himanen goes on to talk about the way that hackers improve the programs they work on. Programmers present their own improvements to a community of peers and co-learners, respect their judgements and integrate their collective wisdom into their next piece of code. Could this be the model for a 'Net Academy, in which all study materials would be free for use, critique and development by everyone', wonders Himanen?

> In the Net Academy, every learning event would permanently enrich all other learners. Alone or in the company of others, the learner would add something to the shared material. This differs from our present mode of disposable learning, in which every student starts from the beginning, passes the same exams isolated from everyone else, and never gets to benefit from the insights of others. Worse, after the exam the examiner basically tosses all those individual insights into the wastebasket. This is as absurd a procedure as would be the decision of each generation of researchers to finally toss all their results away ('I see, $E = MC^2$; so what – toss!') and let the next generation start over.[38]

Hard-bitten teachers might be asking exactly what they have to learn from a group of already qualified and cognitively sharp computer programmers, who have an untoward enthusiasm for improving software. Is the free-learning model of the hackers simply a kind of barter club of ideas for people whose professional job in the IT industry has slipped over into a hobby?

Yet anyone who sees any schoolchild (from around nine years old and upwards) left alone with a networked computer – able to use one of the more powerful search engines, savvy enough to have her own instant messaging handle – immediately understands that a new culture of learning is emerging, of which the hackers have been merely the advance pioneers.

As usual, most of the existing reaction to spontaneously organized 'Net academies' have been phobic and scaremongering – i.e. students downloading from 'pass' essay sites, in the hopes of getting a shortcut to a good grade.[39]

But it's easy to see how the same technology could generate a fertile culture of supportive mutual learning between students driven by their passions – able to find sources, share insights about them instantly and then move up to a new level of understanding. (I saw exactly that in the Helsinki Media Lab in early 2001 – classrooms full of self-directed secondary-school students, using their electronic networks to enrich their projects through collective support and exchange, with the teacher as more of a multimedia librarian and head researcher than a top-down pedagogue.)

What is most frightening about these trends, at least to educational establishments and orthodoxies, is their sheer *speed*. Can we trust a learning curve that would seem to ascend so high, so quickly? Yet this is what so much research into the info-generation is struggling with – that cognitive capacities are actually being *increased* by the playful use of ICT.[40] The existence of hacker culture – where applied amateurism has generated one of the world's major software platforms, Linux, challenging the business models of all existing computer corporations in both its openness and its robustness – is startling evidence of this.[41]

From these examples, we can discern some new educational models, covering primary and secondary-school stages, which could be identified with a play-ethical approach: models which aim, as the Finnish Information Minister phrased it, to build 'the competence for freedom' in people. The Reggio approach is successful in unfolding the full cognitive, emotional and expressive potentials of young children, through the richest kind of multiform play. Moreover, as many of its advocates say, the 'Reggio revolution' is already extending throughout much of the policy and practice of early years education.[42] Might not the Net academies of the hackers be the second stage of a player's education – one way to relate these 'Reggio' children to a challenging world of technologies, geopolitics, multicultures and networks?

This second stage would imply a major deconstruction of the exam- and results-driven culture of most developed-world market democracies. Older children would be presumed to have retained that 'life, power and confidence' of their early years. We would expect that they make their interests and passions central to their learning paths; that they increase their knowledge and understanding through peer collaboration and creative projects; and that their teachers continue their early years' role as ever more adroit recorders, facilitators and thought starters.

There is a thorny political reality hiding behind these blooms. Both Finland and Emilia-Romagna are among the most notably egalitarian and productive, wealthy and self-confident places on the planet.[43] Neither has massive income disparities or long-term dispiritedness among post-industrial communities or implosion of traditional identities, leading to explosions of stress and fear. They have none of the systemic inequalities that so disfigure the essentially neo-liberal economies of Anglo-America (and for that matter Australia), fearfully warded against by the social-democrat and Christian-democrat mainstream of Europe.[44] So the educators of Emilia-Romagna and Finland have a much-reduced proportion of 'at-risk' schoolchildren – those who arrive in the morning requiring not just cognitive enhancement, but societal rehabilitation, whose anger and alienation needs to be addressed and reduced first, before anything else can happen in their minds and hearts.

'Freedom's just another word for nothing left to lose,' sang Janis Joplin three decades ago. Yet when the model of self implied by work culture is an incomprehensible state of being for some children (and a distant memory for their parents), then something must occupy the vacuum. And this is where a play ethic can help, in re-evaluating certain kinds of human activity that would otherwise seem destructive and certainly unproductive. For it's a fact that the sense of freedom of the delinquent child – that is, the child so damaged by systemic inequality that he or she rejects the legitimacy of all institutions, school in particular – is often expressed through a militant embrace of all the rhetorics of play.

Sweet Sixteen, a recent film by the British political filmmaker Ken Loach, is clearly intended to be a straightforward socialist critique. Its aim is to outline the corrosions of character, the violence and betrayal, unleashed by the collapse of the heavy industries that once provided solidarity and cohesion. But what is displayed on screen, through the exhilarating vigour of its local performers, is actually a carnival of the play forms.

The lead character Liam, a delinquent turned drug dealer, is a player in the most challenging sense. He is able to manage his social networks (getting his pals to help in his drug dealing). He is confirmed in his identity through carnivalesque forms of sociality (his partying, his chilling out with pals). He uses technology as tools for conviviality and fun (binoculars to mobile phones, tape recorders to air guns). He pursues his own intellectual passions (astronomy and music), and is, to put it provocatively, something of a 'consciousness entrepreneur' (selling coke and smack to local users and friends). Above all, he exults in a spatial and temporal freedom: Liam is master of the streets and high rises, running all over his decaying territory with his equally lithe pals, defying the *askholia* of any institution bounded in time and space.

Yet he is, in the local parlance, a 'ned' – the Scottish acronym for 'non-educated delinquent'. Education, if mentioned at all in the film, is something that is quickly left behind by these young players: their only reaction is a frown of irrelevance, no more. In itself, the drugs economy that the film's action revolves around is a perverse mirror of the kind of 'multi-active' society implied by many of these play-centric educational models. As a local dealer, Liam uses a variety and combination of intelligences (kinetic, musical, interpersonal, etc.); he deploys many of the 'hundred languages of children', manifested through a variety of symbolic forms.[45]

It is an irony often noted among educational commentators that the most advanced forms of teaching – the full Reggio and Net Academy, in our terms – are used on the most deprived and 'special needs' pupils.[46] In a society that still believes in the educational ideal of childhood – i.e. in the possibility that there might be a universal stage of human development, from which all might progress equally – it is right that our most damaged children bring out the best in our education. But the sense of futility that most teachers feel, particularly in Britain and America, comes from the sense that systemic inequality has stacked the cards against some children before they even enter the playground on the first day of school.

A play-ethical approach – similar in effect to Howard Gardner's multiple intelligences – could begin to discern different kinds of competence and capacity between children from varied social backgrounds, validating and combining their powers in new ways. Yet the marks of inequality and poverty still stand, as roadblocks or inhibitors in the educational pathways of children.

Before pro-play teachers decide to devote themselves vigorously to the rectification of social inequality (and this writer will hardly discourage them), it might be worth considering a few, less reputable, less 'positive' rhetorics of play, to complete our play audit. They might give us a clue as to how an education for players might be justifiable in a much wider and grander context than that defined by government.

How can an 'education for all human beings' genuinely match our children to the demands of their profoundly global world – perhaps even help them to imagine it differently? How can the need to 'get up to speed with the twenty-first century' produce not a stratification of understanding – the divisions between clever classes, practical classes and troublesome classes implied by much 'Third Way' reform – but a truly 'democratic intellect' or 'intellectual democracy', to use Scottish philosopher George Davie's phrase?[47]

Paradoxically, this might not come from pursuing an ideal of supreme stability and equilibrium, to which we all bend our efforts, but from a vision of the universe which presumes an essential creativity, and thus unpredictability, to matter and mind. We all need to be capacious players, because the world is open, not closed – a series of inescapable choices, mingled with startling surprises. How do we educate children to exult in the unexpected? Or more accurately: how do we ensure that they retain that exultation?

Cosmic rough riders: play, unpredictability and learning

Uncertainty is wondrous, and certainty, were it to be real, would be moral death. If we were certain of the future, there would be no moral compunction to do anything ... If everything is uncertain, then the future is open to creativity, not merely human creativity but the creativity of all nature.[48]
– Immanuel Wallerstein, 'Uncertainty and Creativity', 1997

Let's return momentarily to the young ned in *Sweet Sixteen*. The sheer inventiveness and energy of his lifestyle shows all the indefatigable optimism of the true player. But it is a response to a context that is shot through, to say the least, with uncertainty and chaos. As an example of those areas that the network society 'switches on and switches off' (in the words of Manuel Castells), Greenock is exemplary.[49] The River Clyde that flows past the town has, on one side of its banks, a literal graveyard to the shipbuilding industry; and in the hills and estates behind, a range of screwdriver assembly plants and hastily introduced call centres are besieged by locals looking for work.

Liam's response to this is to improvise a lifestyle, and a skill set, out of these post-industrial and informational fragments. Suspend the moral issues about drugs and theft, and his behaviour looks exactly like an application of the flexible, semiotically skilled, experience-rich educational pathways mentioned above. He is, indeed, an enterprising young Scot – but not in ways that any educational modules on 'youth enterprise' could easily endorse.

The picture becomes even more subtle when we look behind the character to the young actor who plays Liam in the film. Drawn from the local community (Loach's usual method of casting), the sixteen-year-old Martin Compston clearly knows, in his skin and in his reflexes, what the post-work culture of young men in Greenock is like. It's the authenticity of his performance that has been the decisive factor in the film's international acclaim by critics and audiences.[50]

Yet Compston himself was a promising young footballer for the local league side, Morton, before this part came along. Now, after his gentle induction into the acting profession, he shows all the signs of eagerly looking forward to his thespian future. At the film's Scottish premiere in Edinburgh, I asked him whether he felt that a return to the industrial past was even desirable for young Grenockians: would he ever want to work in a factory? 'No way,' was his answer. 'But there's lots of people who could be in the same position as me, if they were given the chance. They're no less talented than I am.'

Yet the fictional character (a resourceful young criminal) and the real-life actor (an ebullient young performer in two media, drama and sports) are different only in degree, not in kind. In the words of the Lukes, both their 'pathways' are marked by 'unpredictability, play and local performativity through discourse'. Both the actor and the criminal face uncertain futures – full of options that appear and disappear, are realized or wasted, are fortunately or unfortunately timed.

Yet to maintain their progress in each sphere, they have to accept the flux and chaos of their realms, for better or worse. Both actor and criminal have to adopt some of the core values of play. In particular, it's that sense of 'real virtuality', or simulating your self, which is involved in performing an acting role, whether it's on a stage, or by being a 'face' in the community.[51] And their medium for effecting change is, for both actor and wide-boy criminal, about language and discourse: the actor's script, the criminal's patter, both of them only as good as their last gig.

In terms of an education for players, you might easily imagine some alarm at these comparisons. In order for our children to survive and thrive in an endemically risk-laden world, should they be taking their inspiration from the asocial instincts of the criminal, or the permanent optimism and flexibility of the performer? The fact is, however, that young players *are increasingly taking on both identities*. This means an attitude to property and consciousness (theft and drugs) which does not respect the capitalist and Puritan norms, and which ranges from almost unconscious protest to fully conscious counter-capitalist activism. But it also means a belief in their right to personal expression and self-determination – which presents a huge challenge to any company or institution that might expect their collective loyalty in exchange for wages or benefits.

We are educating children at a time when the major frameworks for understanding and guiding our societies are in meltdown, or at least are undergoing radical restructuring. Their own accelerated culture is bearing all the stresses and strains – but also the possibilities – of this meltdown. Yet the question for teachers is still acute: how do they use their pedagogical moment to support children in their struggles to surf and channel this ever-ramifying reality? There are two reframings that might focus educators on the needs of what Douglas Rushkoff calls the 'children of chaos'.[52]

Teaching to a new reality

Before anything else, perhaps a different understanding by educators of what we take to be 'reality' at the beginning of this century is in order. The historian Immanuel Wallerstein (the author of the quote at the beginning of this section) uses the scientific disciplines of chaos and complexity theory to make it clear that we are living in momentous times. Yet rather than be bewildered by the great clash of forces, and by the huge increases in data and knowledge that such clashes generate, Wallerstein advocates that we brew up a new determination for action, rather than just analysis. We need, in short, to educate for social *creativity*, not just social cohesion:

> It is precisely in periods of transition from one historical system to another (whose nature we cannot know in advance) that human struggle takes on the most meaning. Or to put it another way, it is only in such times of transition that what we call free will outweighs the pressures of the existing system to return to equilibria. Thus, fundamental change is possible, albeit never certain, and this fact makes claims on our moral responsibility to act rationally, in good faith, and with strength to seek a better historical system. This offers a great opportunity for creative action.[53]

The implication for curricula should be obvious: children should be 'taught the complexity' of their societies, networks and cultures, both local and global in order that their sense of agency, when they leave their educational moments, is adequate to the openness and possibility of the times. What the Scottish-based global think tank the International Futures Forum (IFF) calls the four areas of complexity – consciousness, the economy, sustainability and governance – are all up for grabs in the minds of policy makers and protestors, environmentalists and artists.[54] Why should these debates about the fundamental driving processes of our twenty-first-century world not be brought into the centre of our curricula? To be sure, it would slow up the mechanical procession towards exam results and certification. But it would surely be a better use of teachers' enthusiasm, skills and idealism, in order to genuinely 'bring out' (*edu-care*) in children the capacities needed for this unstable but exciting new world.[55]

The implications of how education fully embraces the new sciences, which posit a material universe that is in itself creative and playful, rather than grim and determinist, can only be hinted at here.[56] But the essential point – which is essentially epistemological and ontological, about our ideas of what counts as truth or reality – could easily be taken on board by most teachers and presented to their pupils openly. 'Even we grown-ups,' they might say, 'aren't sure about what the right course of action is for our future, in any aspect of our lives: and it seems as if science, whether social or nature, cannot guarantee us a desired result. So . . . shall we explore our confusions together?'

A less authoritarian framework about what counts as truth and reality in a changing world will certainly resonate better with young players whose very experience of the real, through networks and culture and stimulants, is already much more fluid and malleable than that of their educators and parents. Yet there are other resources that can be marshalled by educators in their efforts to fit pedagogy to the player – and these can come from teachers' deepest ethical sense of their role and function.

Teaching for the cosmic rough riders[57]

James Carse, in his *Finite and Infinite Games*, has some characteristically brilliant comments to make about education and the player:

> To be prepared against surprise is to be *trained*. To be prepared for surprise is to be *educated*. Education discovers an increasing richness in the past, because it sees what is unfinished there. Training regards the past as finished and the future as to be finished. Education leads to a continuing self-discovery; training leads towards a final self-definition. Training repeats a completed past in the future. Education continues an unfinished past into the future.[58]

So a work ethic requires its subjects to be 'trained', in Carse's sense. Education must make children useful for an economy whose divisions of labour are a means of maintaining social order and equilibrium – and does so by presuming that professions and functions remain continuous, through a defined past, present and future. Vocational studies, the 'training' medium par excellence, consign a large proportion of children to a 'final self-definition' in the labour market.

Yet in these mutable times, the jobs for which a child might be 'trained' could well be on their way out by the time the 'trainee' gets anywhere near the interview room. The sense of education being 'fuckin' pointless' – which films like *Sweet Sixteen* articulate – comes from the inevitable failure of a 'training' approach, in its poor equipping of children for their unstable new realities.

A play ethic, with all due modesty, claims that its subjects should be *truly* 'educated' – that is, prepared for surprise, regarding everything as unfinished, aiming at 'continuing self-discovery'. Education, says Carse, is about the 'strength' to respond to the unexpected; training is about the 'power' to minimize the unexpected. To regard education as a means to attaining a level of power, suggests Carse, is to cramp children's imaginations towards attaining social positions validated by the past – doctor, nurse, tradesman, teacher. Education as the strengthening of the child means an entirely different orientation to their context. Carse makes a polemical distinction between society and culture, regarding the former as 'a culture which has forgotten that its rules were once chosen, and now prefers to think of them as being imposed'. Workers belong to society – and players to culture:

> Culture is an enterprise of mortals, disdaining to protect themselves against surprise. Living in the strength of their vision, they eschew power and make joyous play of boundaries. Society is a manifestation of power. It is theatrical, having an established script. Deviations from the script are evident at once. Deviation is antisocietal and therefore forbidden by society under a variety of sanctions. It is a highly valued function of society to prevent changes in the rules of the many games it embraces. Deviancy, however, is the very essence of culture. Whoever merely follows the script, merely repeating the past, is culturally impoverished.[59]

So a play ethic asks teachers to attend to the inner strengths of children, the subtle development of their characters and personal resilience, in order that they can (to quote Carse) 'live in the strength of their vision'.

But beyond that, a players' education has to begin to open children up to a variety of post- and non-Judaeo-Christian world views, as much for the way they can help them understand a world of complexity, as for multicultural tolerance. What can Buddhism, Hinduism, Islam, Confucianism, Jainism teach children about living in a universe that evades complete control and precise prediction – the faith that underlies both the Protestant ethic and Newtonian science? What are the parallels between the spiritual, emotional and cultural 'webs' that the non-Western religions see humans as embedded within, and the technological webs and networks that children are gleefully surfing and negotiating in their daily lives?

Carse's thoughts also point us towards the next chapter, on the relationship between the arts and a play ethic. The culture of twenty-first-century children in the developed West, in all its interactivity and creativity, is beautifully defined by Carse's notion of 'an enterprise of mortals, disdaining to protect themselves against surprise . . . making joyous play of boundaries'. This is the message that children are giving their educators and their parents – in their gaming, their immersion in narratives and images, their mobile and networked sense of the social (and sociable). They already know that their world is going to be a cosmic rough ride, and they are preparing for it as best they can, in their own times and spaces. Culture is the preferred medium for these players – that perpetual communication which plays with the boundaries.[60] Not 'society' – or, to be precise, those specified hierarchies and fixed functions of a socio-economic regime, which try to forget their origin in creative and contingent human activity, and present themselves as the natural order of human behaviour.

The players' republic

Education has always prepared children for 'society'. Yet 'society' has never been prepared for truly educated children. The great divisions that still rend the teaching profession throughout the developed world – between the Romantics and utilitarians – are caused by this fundamental misalignment. If an 'education for all human beings', in the words of Howard Gardner, is the ideal aim of twenty-first-century systems of learning, then a society, economy and media 'for all human beings' must also be our collective target.

Is a society dominated by the values of work truly 'for all human beings'? Going by the soulitarians and the lifestyle militants already described (and the artists and entrepreneurs, activists and non-dualists to come), it would seem not. The 'slave mentality' implied by the work ethic is being refused by ever-increasing numbers of people in the developed West. Part of that rejection is driven by the success of mass education – not as the social indoctrination of the malleable, but as the enrichment of minds, hearts and bodies. Educated individuals have an increased sense of potential – whether emotionally, cognitively or physically – which makes them ever more difficult to manage, order around, administrate. There has always been a *shkole* hidden inside the school, sustained by the idealism of teachers and the desires of pupils; a realm where being 'in charge of one's own time and efforts', being a true scholar, has glimmered as a possibility.

The 'general intellect' of the Italian autonomists,[61] or the 'democratic intellect' of George Davie, is only conceivable on the back of the achievements of generations of teachers. The best of them actively pursued the open-ended development of their pupils – making the most of that set-apart space between home and work, filling minds with imagining and wonder. The great tensions of our contemporary societies – our dissatisfactions in the midst of affluence, our drive to individuality in the face of great systems and infrastructures – can be laid, unfairly and gloriously, at the doors of our educators. They have raised the game of the human subject. We are not returning to an age of conformity and ignorance.

But if we continue to gird our ever more protean children with the bonds of a limited functionality – whether they be the demands of a 'new' or an 'old' economy – these tensions will only get worse, and our general unhappiness and disgruntlement will only deepen. The 'learning society' is an attempt at the kind of alignment that is necessary: a vision of a world of self-educators seeking out new knowledge at every stage and place of their lives. Yet if all that is being learned in such a society are the skills and competences needed to satisfy the momentary demands of a labour market – however hi-tech, experience-driven or varied – then it seems more like a nightmarish scenario. The 'learning society' could too easily generate a lifelong anxiety about one's fitness and readiness for entry into the kingdom of work.

What would a 'playing society' be like? Well, for one thing, it would be a society prepared for truly educated children. The time-sovereign 'shkolars' would require a degree of social security and collective resource similar to that provided in school – a 'ground of play' which would give them the opportunity to freely create their lives and direct their passions and talents. The welfare implications of this are obvious: we need to devote resources to a space of social autonomy. This is often called a 'social wage' or 'citizen's income', though I prefer 'creative support': the general limitation of working hours is the complementary policy.[62] There needs to be a recognition that the capacious, dynamic creatures that might emerge from a players' education system cannot simply be expected to develop their vocations under the existing regime of jobs, functions and professions. Rather than close down all experiment and self-exploration once the moment of school is over, we need to find a social architecture that can sustain that kind of activity throughout a life.

Much of that architecture – in terms of ICT and networks – is already in place, or is about to be established. Illich's notion of the 'learning web' was before its time in many ways: one of its prophecies was the vision of learning occurring throughout a city or urban area – at street corners or at office desks, in parks or in zoos, among crowds and in flows of transport. Of course (and this was Illich's main point) this could happen right now. One might easily imagine a kind of urban regulation which could make an entire town or city a resource for learning, where doors would be open for those who wished to understand a particular process or specialism.

Technology isn't the only solution here: deinstitutionalized minds might be more helpful.

Yet the rise of ubiquitous computing and wireless networks does seem to fuel the idea of the city as school to even greater heights. An information environment that allowed learning humans – children and adults – to extract the maximum meaning from any time, space and location (through everything from the 'wireless newspaper' to the mobile videophone),[63] becomes much more fluid and alive than one in which 'work' values dominate. Where doors are closed, property is defended, surveillance is paramount and control is presumed.[64]

This is already one of the great tensions of our interactive age – the extent to which ICT allows for self-expression and self-determination, and the way that conflicts with the strategic management of organizations and companies. The Internet was partly born out of scholarly sharing and the values of the gift, not of monetary exchange. But the point of a play ethic is to try and find a new accommodation between such tensions. Our children need to align their increasingly playful education (and self-education) with the world beyond youth and school. What this presumes – a kind of 'communicational commons', within which children can explore their knowledge interests freely and powerfully – has implications way beyond the educational sector.

In later chapters, I'll explore the growing sense that current technologies profoundly challenge our economic and social models – and that the values of play are the best response to that challenge. But in the meantime, the need for a players' education establishes a beachhead in that debate. If 'shkolars' are to maintain their sense of experiment, freedom and sovereignty throughout their lives, not just within the ideal school, they must have common resources to support those values. The construction of a players' republic may begin with the opening of the school gates. But it certainly won't end there.

SEVEN / 217

THE PLAY AESTHETIC

Arts, Media and Play Values

It was modern poetry for the last 100 years that had led us to this place. We were a handful who thought that it was necessary to carry out its programme in reality and to do nothing else.

– Guy Debord, *The Society of the Spectacle,* 1967

We have art only because we do not have the life it promises.

– J.M. Bernstein, *The Fate of Art,* 1992

I wanna get up and do my thang.

– James Brown, 'Sex Machine', 1970

It's a moment I know all too well, from the soles of my feet upwards, through my chest, along my buzzing teeth. The band's starting up.

I've been in this situation in the grandest circumstances, and the most gruelling. I once looked out at 85,000 faces in Wembley Stadium, as an opening act for Madonna in 1987: we managed to get them to recognize our one chart hit, and to perform a Mexican wave to our cover version of Prince's 'Kiss'. I've also stood on a sticky carpeted floor in a Leeds pub, seven years later, and tried to quell a beery crowd with a few piano and vocal songs. I've floated sublimely over a jazz orchestra, opened for soul titans like Ray Charles, Van Morrison and James Brown, thrown it to the rafters in beautifully resonant big-city concert halls – and each time, felt that nothing else in my conscious life would ever be as pleasurable. I've also stormed off stage, swearing, at a shitty jazz venue in Birmingham, disabled and broken by rage and insecurity.

So when the band starts up, I will admit that it's no small thing for me. Even this particular occasion – doing a favour gig for charity in a poky club with a pick-up group on a Tuesday night in suburban Glasgow – isn't different, in essence, from any of the others. What we have here, what we always have here, are two irreducible, yet intertwined elements: passion and technology. Every musician who's here – from the virtuoso who can almost do too many things with her talent, to the chugger who can do the minimum required to get his mojo over the footlights – has forged their skill from those initial two elements. At some point, they've heard some music, some particular organization of sound, which has popped open a kind of chasm inside them, a new space filling up with a surfeit of presence that itches the skin and pushes at the ribcage. Call that something 'passion'.

Maybe at the same point, or moments after, they've wondered – while gazing at a sleeve, or at a video – exactly how that person makes those noises with these particular machines: microphone, guitar, turntable, Rhodes piano, sampler, conga, Yanigasawa alto, whatever. The listener's body is twitching at its extremities, or wriggling its trunk around a groove, or walking and talking a different way than before – and it needs to start holding onto something, explore and test something, that can amplify and materialize this passion. Call that something 'technology'.

Between passion and technology, there is a continuum of what we can call 'skill' or 'technique'. But there's no point in being purist about this. You learn what you need to learn, to say what you need to say – and that goes for the gap-toothed ghetto kid taking the mike with his blustering MC skills, as well as the digital perfectionist who can't let a track leave her Mac until it's as perfect as a sculpture. Although musicians will bitch, and sneer, and defend their genres if they feel defensive, they all know deep down that steady tolerance of all musics is the win-win strategy. You never know when someone's new move will get under your plates and stroke you unexpectedly; you also never know when something strange or unexpected will flow through you, when you'll surprise yourself by what you just did.[1]

The only significant order in this chaos, at least at this particular charity gig, is the pecking order – who gets to go on first. Once that little bout of savannah Darwinism is settled, I sit and wait my turn. The backing band can do most things well – they are punks and rockers, jazzers and mods, early twenties to early forties – and so they hazard interpretations of a diverse procession of songs and styles: Lou Reed, Aretha Franklin, Radiohead, Moby and the Beatles. The archive is theirs, ours, everybody's. There are no police in the room to stop us from playing something; nobody fucks up badly, and some move the air in a particularly memorable way. I'm surging when I hit the little stage – Stevie Wonder's 'You Haven't Done Nothing' has been building up inside me all day, like steam – and I'm trembling when I come off it. But instead of my usual screw-eyed microphone benediction, and because I can't remember the words, I take my little 2002 PDA on stage with me (I downloaded the Stevie lyrics from the Net onto it earlier today). All the way through the funk, I hold its glowing white screen to the side of me, like some T-shirted, twilight-era Sinatra muttering through his auto-cue, flipping the wheel to get the next verse.

So tonight, I feel something I never felt before: I'm mixing my head-tech and my heart-tech; the tech I do my business with and the tech I express my inexpressible with. That's new: never did that before. Am I falser now, or realer? I'm unsure. But that's good.

Art, play and society

My own experience as an artist has also been, by and large, my most tangible experience of what a fully mature play ethic would feel like. For me, the artistic moment has always been defined by a mental attitude towards a specific situation. Out of these musicians, technologies, predilections and resources, what would be the most beautiful, moving and meaningful result? This is not to say that the result was always achieved.[2] But the aspiration was there: to put my own finite capacities and opportunities at the service of an infinite dream of great art – in this case, the perfect popular song.

However, I wouldn't want to imply that the player's life and the artist's life are interchangeable, or that all players should aspire to being artists if they are truly serious about a play ethic. Our own seven play rhetorics are a strenuous attempt to spread the value of play across a whole range of social practices and institutions, not just the arts.

Yet there is no doubt that the arts occupy a primary place within a play-centred society. A work culture might regard the arts as *recreating the good worker* – a kind of entertainment, perhaps even a mild enlightenment, that compensates for the alienated, routinized grind. But a play culture regards the arts as *creating the good player*. It promotes the arts as a means of developing one's subjective agency, emotional literacy and aliveness to forms of expression. By producing or consuming culture, individuals face the information age with renewed vitality and imagination. For players, art is not a private pleasure, but an input into the daily practices of creative living: keeping organizations healthy, networks flexible, relationships vibrant and life-options multiplying.[3]

For the play ethic, artists are those committed to keeping society literally *in play*, through their practice and performance. Plato's apportioned role for artists was that of propagandist: their job was to 'lead people unawares from childhood to love of the beauty of reason'. Anything else would subvert the authority of the Guardians through their imaginings.

James Carse argues against this and proposes a different role for the artist, in a life of play and possibility: 'True poets lead no one unawares. It is nothing other than awareness that poets – that is, creators of all sorts – seek. They do not display their art so as to make it appear real: they display the real in a way that reveals it to be art . . . [True poets] make war impossible because they have the irresistible ability to show the guardians that what seems necessary is only possible.'[4]

It's a subtle and shifting affair, the distinction between art and play. From the turn of the century, when artists like Picasso, Matisse, Kandinsky and Klee aspired to draw like children – because children 'draw what they imagine, not what they see'[5] – there has been a strong identification of play with art. Both are assumed to share the values of originality, autonomy and innocence. This understanding goes further back to the rise of the 'imagination' in Romantic thought, which poets and philosophers invoked as a resistance to the depredations of the industrial age. The 'play of the mind' is readily seen as the shared root of play and art.[6]

But they should not be automatically conflated. In psychology and biology, for example, there has been a century of attempts to make a viable distinction between the two. Karl Groos, the first serious scientist of play, held that 'play is biology, and art is culture'. We actively choose to make art, but we are compelled by our natures to play – play develops the core capacities that makes the artist possible.[7] Daniel Berlyne usefully identified play as 'diversive exploration', and art as 'specific exploration'. Howard Gardner confirms this distinction by describing play as serving our 'mastery of anxiety, self and world' – with art being about the 'mastery of symbolic systems'.[8] In relation to our general theory of play this holds up well. The arts clearly emerge from the human tendency to explore, experiment and 'play with' reality, yet they use a specific form or technique, craft or practice in order to discern (or defend) a pattern or shape in the flux of life.

We reach for art, as both audience and maker, when we wish to articulate our playful mastery through specific arrangements of signs and symbols which have their own connection to art histories, traditions and genres. The classic idea of an 'art work' explicitly captures this distinction between play and art. The 'work of art' is about a construction of meaning that usually has some kind of boundary in time, space and materials – a painting, a film, a song, an experience captured on video – and is tied to some kind of author or creator, someone responsible for the 'work' itself.[9] Yet without play's diverse explorations, the art work's specific explorations could not happen. The deeply rooted drive to imagine and simulate realities, so that an organism might be ready for whatever might threaten its survival, is the basic condition which enables us to turn images this way and that, to seek out compelling patterns, to compose new forms from existing elements – in essence, to do art.

Yet if, as this book argues, we are in transition to a society where play values (rather than work values) become dominant, then art's relationship to play needs to be radically rethought. If art arises in a context that sees humans as essentially creative and transformative – rather than routine bound and duteous – then much of the antagonism of romanticism, its need to break the 'mind-forg'd manacles' of industrial society, must necessarily fade away.

In the early seventies, the German conceptualist Joseph Beuys claimed that 'every human being is an artist, a freedom being'. By this he meant that the creative principles of art, its ambition to transform and reshape its immediate conditions, defined the human condition (rather than that all humans should necessarily dance or sculpt).[10] Part of the positive story of the arts at the moment, in an information society becoming conscious of its playful potential, is that Beuys's 'universal artist' is almost upon us.[11]

From the 'karaoke' culture of the TV talent shows to the digital underground of dance music makers; from the grassroots upsurge in reading and writing groups to the new great halls of visual art in the UK's major cities; from the manic invention of advertising culture to the street-level use of mobile communications to staged radical public art experiences – there is no shortage of evidence that Carse's player-poets are out there, at all levels of the society, trying to make reality seem like an art form itself. Later on we shall look at the way that self-proclaimed artists are grappling with the deeply sign-laden nature of twenty-first-century everyday experience.[12] They are consciously seeking a fusion between playful and artistic responses – meshing play's perpetual openness to change and possibility, with art's need to interpret and express meaning.

But as well as Beuys's wisdom, we must also consider Andy Warhol's insight: 'in the future, everyone will be world famous for fifteen minutes'. The original Roman definition of *fama* meant 'the public display of character'. In that word 'display', we see another threat to the traditional domain of art, presented by a mass society of players who are beginning to self-consciously make an art of their own lives and experiences.

Every surface, screen and built structure of our lives is now deliberately layered and shaped by signs, designs and symbols – what the American critic Virginia Postrel calls 'the age of look and feel'.[13] Can art – defined as an individual's mastery of symbolic form – survive in a world where *everyone* is a 'symbolic analyst', from the head office to the Playstation terminal?

We need to think about a 'play aesthetic' that can respond to this relentlessly 'symbolizing' society, rather than try to cordon off some pure realm of the 'artistic' in order to defend its essence. But this isn't going to be an easy task. If society itself is 'in play', what does art bring to this incessant process? Fixity or fluidity? A compass, or more swirls to the blizzard?

Putting your spectacles on

One function of art in a play-ethical society might be as the place, or occasion, when players can experience a moment of 'being together', despite their innate diversity and differences. Whether the crowds are beating their paths to the latest big film, or the rock concert or festival, or a giant new art gallery like London's Tate Modern or Bilbao's Guggenheim, there is no doubt that such giant entertainments satisfy the contradictory psychic needs of living in the information age.

We truly enjoy our new powers of individualism, and resist the idea that they might be curtailed by some over-zealous assertion of community. But these powers go sour without the occasional experience that others might also feel this way. To fill a hall, or a tent, or a field, or a terrace with devotees to one beautiful spectacle or other, is to accept that 'being together' these days is only fitfully achievable. But when it is achieved, it runs a current through the assembled crowd. The art spectacle can be a powerful sensorial experience, to store away in the safebox of the self. But its power resides in the fact that it is not your experience alone.

The great ambiguities of play – that tension between the anarchism of the modern player and the boundedness of the ancient player – are operating fully here. For the player, the arts are an energizing paradox, a complex experience. They nourish both the *roots* of our soul and our *routes* to other souls, without presuming that both pathways are similar or coincident.[14]

The pop theorist Simon Frith puts these paradoxes well in his musing on the value of popular music:

> What makes music special – what makes it special for identity – is that it defines a space without boundaries ... Music both takes us out of ourselves and puts us in place, by music being both a fantasy of community and an

enactment of it, by music dissolving difference even as it expresses it . . .
At the same time [pop music is] rootless, cut free from any originating time
and place – and rooted, in the needs, movement and imagination of the
listener.[15]

We are still capable of being together, and enjoying it, while exulting
with our favourite band, or film, or conceptual artist. But this is a togetherness of the strangest, most unsociably sociable kind.

The major social thinkers tell us that this might be the last and noblest
function for art: to be the place where our players' ability to construct,
deconstruct and reconstruct our view of the world is temporarily arrested
in the face of great beauty or irony. Manuel Castells, whose ideas about
the deeply unstable nature of information societies have profoundly
informed this book, takes an almost transcendent view of the power of
the arts. Great art might be the only thing that stops us being trapped in
our 'personal hypertext', the 'broken mirrors' of our cultural preferences,
and gets us to face each other's raw humanity:

Art has always been a communication protocol to restore the unity of human
experience beyond oppression, difference and conflict. The paintings of the
powerful in their human misery, the sculpting of the oppressed in their
human dignity, the bridges between the beauty of our environment and the
inner hells of our psyche . . . [these] are all media to go beyond the
inescapable labours of life, to find the expression of joy, of pain, of feeling
that reunites us, and makes this planet livable after all.[16]

So great art could temporarily becalm our incessant desires to link and
surf, connect and disconnect, and leave us collectively (if temporarily) rapt.
The religious overtones of this view of the powers of art are obvious. –
The enormous Turbine Hall exhibitions of the Tate Modern in London – the
space itself as cavernous as a cathedral – are clearly intended to still the
chattering opinions of their clued-up visitors, as in the giant red shell of
Anish Kapoor's *Marsyas*, or the orange pseudo-sun of Olafur Eliasson's *The
Weather Project*.

Yet what of art as critique, intervention and cut-up, wilfully recombining elements to attack complacency or false harmony – a militant playing
with materials? The British artists Jake and Dinos Chapman recently purchased and then defaced some authentic prints from Goya, that great witness to human suffering, by sticking on cut-out clown heads. A darker,
more irreverent art play one could not imagine. But their work still stays
within the gallery system – our place of reverence before the altar of
meaning.[17]

The interesting question is how art might function in a network society where there are many glowing surfaces and spaces on which to display – not just inside the white walls of an institution. An art that attempts to provide a unifying experience across all these outlets could easily be regarded as sentimental, or at least presumptuously inclusive. Whose humanity is being unified here? *Is* my pain and joy *yours*, exactly? Maybe the classical techniques of the avant garde, as some younger critics imagine, will finally come into their own, in a mediascape where an intervention of symbols can flash across the world, hitting screens located at every level of society – from the palm of one's hand, to the electronic billboard in the city square.[18]

Yet though the techniques may be avant garde, the question is whether they need an actual 'avant garde' to prosecute them – that is, a group or cadre who regard their vision as ahead of the mainstream. When hunger artists like David Blaine are sponsored by major television channels and become spectator spectacles,[19] when the techniques of situationism and surrealism (the overturning of everyday routines, the deployment of limit experiences) are used by direct marketers and conceptual artists alike[20] – then it's difficult to imagine just how 'out in front' of 'the people' an artistic cadre could be.

In this ever-present Now of the early twenty-first century, it's difficult to measure just how radical our emergent play society actually is, particularly in the way it makes our artistic and cultural lives a permanent revolution. But there is a most surprising prophecy of this kind of society – a 'play aesthetic' which sees artfulness in the full range of human capacities and intelligences, and not just in its accepted zones and institutions.

Trotsky at Saatchi's

It was a line that once caught my eye as a student, something that leapt out of an otherwise crashingly dull piece of academese. 'Trotsky once predicted that, after socialism, political parties would be formed around schools of architecture, or trends in music, or scientific paradigms.' All the way through the great (con)fusions of the eighties and nineties, when most of our social and personal frameworks went molten and rehardened into ever stranger shapes, this idea stuck to me like a burr on a jacket: I just couldn't brush it off.

One day, in the middle of this book, I did the usual magic shuffle towards Google and typed in 'Trotsky', 'parties', 'architecture', 'future'. A few seconds later, top of the list came a page with the following paragraphs from Leon Trotsky's *Literature and Revolution* (1924), Chapter seven, 'Communist Policy Towards Art'.

> Under socialism ... all forms of life, such as the cultivation of land, the planning of human habitations, the building of theatres, the methods of socially educating children, the solution of scientific problems, the creation of new styles, will vitally engross all and everybody. People will divide into 'parties' over the question of a new gigantic canal, or the distribution of oases in the Sahara (such a question will exist too), over the regulation of the weather and the climate, over a new theatre, over chemical hypotheses, over two competing tendencies in music, and over a best system of sports. Such parties will not be poisoned by the greed of class or caste. All will be equally interested in the success of the whole. The struggle will have a purely ideological character. It will have no running after profits, it will have nothing mean, no betrayals, no bribery, none of the things that form the soul of 'competition' in a society divided into classes. But this will in no way hinder the struggle from being absorbing, dramatic and passionate.[21]

In the midst of a bloody national revolution, writing a text which always has one eye on the lethal corridor battles in the Comintern, Trotsky seems to have anticipated almost precisely the aestheticized, media-dominated public sphere of the West at the beginning of this century. What else are we doing, other than 'dividing into parties' about 'forms of life' which 'vitally engross all and everybody'?

It might be environmental issues (substitute GM foods for Trotsky's 'gigantic canal'); or the latest cultural edifice (substitute Bilbao or Tate Modern or Liebeskind's 9/11 memorial for the 'new theatre'); or global warming ('the regulation of the weather or climate'); or the continuing disruptions of bio-science and info-tech ('chemical hypothesis'); or Britney versus Radiohead, Stockhausen versus Glass ('two competing tendencies in music'); or golf's relative sexiness vis-à-vis football ('a best system of sports'); or the question of what kind of schools we need for an information age ('methods of socially educating children'); or the question of edge cities and suburban sprawl ('the planning of human habitations'); or whether black is the new brown ('the creation of new styles') ... With trend-spotting antennae like that, it's clear that the young Leon Trotsky would easily walk into any advertising agency or think-tank job with supreme ease: Saatchi's would have him in a minute.

Of course, it wouldn't be the first time that a Marxist became transfixed by a vision of society and culture as being in a permanent upheaval of forms and styles, driven by an irrepressible passion to communicate. Marx himself, in *The Communist Manifesto*, was notoriously in love with capitalist culture. 'Constant revolutionizing of production, uninterrupted disturbance of all social conditions, everlasting uncertainty and agitation distinguish the bourgeois epoch from all earlier ones. All fixed, fast-frozen relations, with their train of ancient and venerable prejudices and opinions, are swept away, all new-formed ones become antiquated before they can ossify. All that is solid melts into air . . .'[22]

So the fact that two of the great anti-capitalists seemed to be able to predict the cultural contours of actually existing twenty-first-century capitalism (much better than they predicted the fate of socialism or communism) tells us a few interesting things. One is about the real power of the arts – that is, its potential to release us from the policed compound of 'recreation' and 'leisure'. Trotsky imagines an art beyond 'prettiness', more than mere decoration. The condition of this move is, of course, 'the elimination of political struggles . . . in a society where there will be no classes, there will be no such struggles'. Trotsky puts his multi-channel, wildly eclectic, deeply aesthetic society in the context of 'a culture whose [economic] foundations are steadily rising'. Only in a society beyond scarcity, he says, will the really important struggles begin – 'the struggle for one's opinion, for one's project, for one's taste'.

Again, these hoary old communists seem to have got their socialist predictions wrong, but have anticipated the capitalist present with uncanny accuracy. We do indeed live in a society where art has become the property of all people. Under postmodernism, no more high-low cultural hierarchies; under informationalism, every opportunity to dialogue, montage and sabotage, with email, text, interactivity of all kinds. And whereas we do not live in a classless society in the developed West – far from it – we do live under conditions which are moving ever further from scarcity, and which allow more and more people to define themselves by their individual aspirations and skills, rather than their economic disadvantage.

Within that society, Trotsky goes on to confidently assert that 'we have no reason to fear that there will be a decline of individuality or an impoverishment of art in a socialist society'.[23] In truth, of course, Trotsky had every reason to fear precisely these declines, and precisely this impoverishment. Ask Alexandr Solzhenitsyn, or Václav Havel, or any artist or intel-lectual who has been repressed, imprisoned or otherwise persecuted – never mind being forced to do 'ideological' schlock – in the blacker books of twentieth-century, actually existing socialism.[24] Yet when he describes art as 'the most perfect method of the progressive building of life in every field', the revolutionary stands up for the play ethic, not the work ethic. Trotsky's instincts for the player's condition rather than the worker's are evident – an energetic readiness for risk and opportunity, rather than an accommodation with routine. I'm sure he would have looked upon the expressive techno-cultures of the early twenty-first century – the code-sharing hackers, the byte-transforming (and copyright-flouting) remixers, the garrulous bloggers and texters and 'smart mobs' – and nodded approvingly. 'Liberated passions will be channelled into technique, into construction, which also includes art,' he wrote, a formulation which encompasses Beck and Linus Torvalds, Bjork and Damien Hurst, just fine.[25]

It is precisely the question of how we 'liberate the passions' of twenty-first-century humans that I've been worrying away at in this book. We need the chaos, the surprise, the dystopianism and utopianism of art more than ever, to propel us towards a play-dominant rather than work-dominant world. We need a vibrant art and culture in the information age because it points us to the necessary space in a system, network or field where movement and change can always happen.[26]

Trotsky's vision of socialism might not be shimmering before anyone these days, but the exhilarating aesthetic society he imagined in 'Litera-ture and revolution' has partially been realized by the same forces – that is, by the massive productivity of the information age – which he thought would mature the political revolution. 'I think, therefore I produce' could be the new philosophy of the information age. One could easily imagine the Russian revolutionary very much at home in the early twenty-first cen-tury, thrilled by the incessant 'struggle for one's opinion, one's project, one's taste'. Yet so many contemporary thinkers yearn for an art that might (temporarily at least) arrest this dissensus, and bind us players together in a moment of irony or beauty. The problem is that, in an interactive and playful society, almost any kind of aesthetic experience is available to any-one, at any time.

A brief but instructive tale of media, art and bedtime

What strikes me is the fact that, in our society, art has become something that is related only to objects and not to individuals or to life. That art is something which is specialized or done by experts who are artists. But couldn't everyone's life become a work of art? Why should the lamp or the house be an art object but not our life?
– Michel Foucault[27]

It's March 2003: kids in bed, all is quiet. Hiding from a phalanx of implacable deadlines, I slump onto the couch and punch my way through the video interface on the cable television. I'm surfing the available bandwidth for something that I know will be worth my attention span: with my finger on the 'search' button of the remote, I blip through what must be scores of differently themed channels. I stop at a few to marvel at their utter consistency. The cartoon channel is showing some pop-art-esque funny with three super-heroic little girls, which cuts easily into a chokingly gendered toy ad for dolls. The home improvements channel is showing a bunch of homely looking people (among them a Titianesque woman, braless, in a T-shirt) pulling concrete slabs onto a brutally degrassed garden. The American financial channel is an insane palimpsest of figures and symbols, inside which a besuited figure is enunciating crisply. The historical channel thuds with sepia footage of warship gun barrels, retracting backwards like salutes, while a Very Posh Actor rumbles sonorously on. The music channel greets me with a finger-splayed and gold-encrusted fist in my face, as some bulky-looking hip-hoppers bounce around in their low-riding cars. And as for the reality TV channel . . .

In short, Trotsky's dream of an art society is visualized here, in the thousand channels provided by the cable operator: all forms of life, vitally engrossing everybody. It's rare for me not to find something that is closer to what I exactly want to see – whether as drama, ideas, performance, news and information – than I've ever been able to get before from a television set. I know it's not perfect yet: why, for example, can't I surf an archive of television and get even closer to what I want, in the way that a powerful search engine renders up the riches of the Web?[28] But in the meantime, even in these straitened circumstances that only sample the available televisual richness, I know where I'm heading.

The channel is called BBC4 – the so-called arts and ideas channel set up by the BBC on the new digital spectrums in the UK. And though I'm just as often disappointed with it (which is what one would expect from a single channel catering to all of Britain's intellectuals and aesthetes) sometimes I have watched programmes there that I feel I've waited all my life to see. Recently, I chanced upon Werner Herzog's documentary of Buddhism, *Wheel of Life*, and sat literally transfixed for an hour, wrapped up in beautiful otherness. Now, I'm watching a videoed documentary (the budgets aren't too grandiose for BBC4), and for the first few minutes I'm struggling to figure out exactly what's going on.

A tiny little mummified figure is lying on a floor, vibrating slightly and moaning pitifully. Around it are remarkably ugly examples of chain-store pottery, whose lids have been removed and replaced with material that crudely imitates the original product, and cast in the shapes of animals. Their creator is telling us about the albino python that she stuffed 'really badly'. The entire collection of objects sits in a damp basement under a bare light bulb, casting pinched little shadows.

I seem to be in the presence of 'arts television' (of which I've done my fair share), surely one of the least satisfying television genres. Unlike most other forms of television, which encourage you to immerse yourself in their realistic worlds, arts television – defined by those deadening words 'profile' and 'coverage' – is doing its best when it makes you feel you have to see the art in the raw: to lift yourself from this slumped entrancement, and dive physically into the city to witness the object or process itself. It's self-defeating, really, which is no doubt why the BBC have lifted most of it out of the mainstream schedules and created a plush gallery space for it on the bandwidth.

But I soon realize that this is less like arts television, and more like *art* television. Indeed, it turns out that the programme is a profile of the current batch of Becks Futures contestants, Britain's most lucrative prize for young artists.[29] What I'm finding extraordinary, as the programme passes, is that these artists have almost entirely defined themselves in relation to the television I've just surfed past, in a variety of ways – from positive embrace, to militant negation. They're almost taking this 'hypertext' in the same way as industrial-age artists would regard the landscape or city-scape: it's simply the terrain that a young artist in 2003 must occupy, the second nature now become first nature. And they all explore that condition which Castells has called 'real virtuality' – constantly testing what our notion of reality and experience might mean, in a profoundly semiotic and mediated world.

In terms of my previous channel-surf, most of the exhibits could easily fall under the category of 'reality TV' – situations captured on video, slices of non-mainstream experience: performed or found, observational or con-fessional. Alan Currall stands before his parents' hearth in their Stoke family home, all of their heads cropped by the camera, asking them what they would do if a nuclear war started. 'They don't know much about the subject,' says Currall (that much is evident), 'but I thought it would be powerful to ask them about it, as their main job in life is to protect me, keep me alive.' Another film, *Now I'm in Heaven*, is Currall reading through his will, detailing his worldly possessions in thirty-two minutes. Rosalind Nashashibi's films show women at a jumble sale in Glasgow, set to an Egyptian love song on the soundtrack; she also captures a group of Ameri-can glider enthusiasts quietly going about their obsession. David Sherry records himself carrying a bucket of water through the streets, and appar-ently sewing blocks of wood to his feet. Bernd Behr's videos record the artist compulsively throwing himself off a column in a Parisian street (the site of a famous surrealist stunt): he also sets up a camera to observe the demolition of a south London council estate, debris emerging mysteriously from behind a wall.

Every time the BBC4 documentary shows little clips of their work, the effect is genuinely subversive. The evenly managed image world of televi-sion, where the harsh luminescence of video filming usually captures the least demanding and most consensual of human relations – chat show, game show, reality doc – has been invaded by obsessives, bores, hobby-ists and fetishists. The video artists are showing us the way that televi-sion could be, if we had the freedom, imagination and power to make it entirely our own way.

But there's another connotation of the videos that's becoming obvious: they are all celebrations of the power of action, not just mediation. Many of the artists give the impression that it's not just the means of represen-tation that they want to play with, but the very fabric of material and social reality: they are trying to take seriously Foucault's injunction to treat their lives – their bodies and emotions, their histories and habits, their egos and others – as art objects. What is extraordinary, in terms of play, is the way that many of them return to the oldest play rhetoric of all: play as frivolity, play as subversion, the play of the trickster and prankster, the antics of the holy fool.[30]

The most hilarious and profound prank is performed by Carey Young, an IT consultant and artist, who convinces the sponsors to sign a legal disclosure form banning them from speaking about the artwork that she will show them only once (we see her opening a suitcase to show the object to a faintly bemused sponsor on the BBC4 documentary, reminiscent of the glowing suitcase scene in the noir classic *Kiss Me Deadly*). 'I wanted to play with the idea that Becks sponsor art so that they can seem more liberal. Indeed, the more extreme it is, the better it is for their reputation. So this is a piece of art which challenges their very right to do that.'[31] More so than most of the items in this show, filming is part of the artwork itself: Young's ice-cool demeanour, her evident ease in the world of business, representing the most artful stylization of a life experience.

The most militantly and explicitly playful artists are Inventory, a mysterious London collective who appear on screen with their faces pixellated out. Of all the artists, they evoke the decade between the late sixties and the late seventies, when Western avant-garde art saw itself as a form of politics and power.[32] Yet they are also obviously inspired by the 'carnivals against capitalism' that took place in the late nineties and early noughties. The two items shown are examples of 'reclaiming the streets', but in a way that resonates perfectly with the play rhetorics. In one piece, *Coagulum*, the artists huddle in a scrum, forming a 'human blood clot' that whirls up and down Oxford Street in London, with Dixieland music playing in the background; in another, they stage a football match on the Mall in London, using the gates of Buckingham Palace and the arch of Admiralty Arch as the goalposts. Their earnest, theory-laden spokesman makes their ludic intentions clear: 'This is about a more playful vision of living, one which occupies space in a free way.'[33]

And just to recall: all this comes from sitting here, cup of tea in hand, finger resting lazily on remote, cosily settled in the domestic scene of couch, television and quietly sleeping children – but with my mind being expanded and tested by a documentary narrative of unforgiving avant gardists, not quite believing what I'm seeing. And once it finishes . . . the ten o'clock news. Thunderous pictures of metal statues of Saddam Hussein falling in a Baghdad public square. Where, and who, am I now?

The tantalizing thought about all these artists is that they might well be conducting these strange, obsessive activities anyway, outwith the authorizing and legitimizing stare of the video camera (indeed, Inventory force anonymity upon themselves in order that their artwork can have maximum impact). In a sense, this is a move on from the first appearance of conceptual art in the UK which tried to take the multi-channel, multi-choice, hyper-textual society on board: the 1997 Sensation exhibition at the RCA in London. Yet the shift feels like the last gasp of postmodernism, towards something more active and engaged: a play aesthetic, perhaps.

It might be worth reminding ourselves what 'postmodern' art means, if only to distinguish it from its modernist predecessors and the playful art of the Becks futurists. When Manet, Courbet and Gericault presented their shocking and difficult images at the very beginning of the modernist era, they did so in order to grapple with the emptiness of their times – not to surrender to it, or simply mime its pointlessness. Whether through Picasso's *Guernica*, or Duchamp with his toilet seat, the twentieth-century modernists wanted to resist the world politically, or highlight its kitschi-ness and trashiness – but always with the goal of a happier world as a buried, utopian core. Yet the only way this goal could be fought for, believed the modernists, was through violent technique, difficult forms to make objects so brazenly useless that they challenged the rules and con-ventions of the workaday world.

If that struggle to dig out precious signs of a beautiful new world from the ugliness of the current one defines modernism, then the Sensation artists were almost precisely postmodernist. In fact, 'sensation' sums it up perfectly. This was art which was mostly about sampling the blitz of con-temporary experience, recombining it in startling ways. But it barely hoped that its insights might anticipate a radically different world. Indeed, the world view that overarched most of these artists was thoroughly settled. Fittingly, in an exhibition drawn entirely from the Saatchi collection, the presumption was that the commodity rules, that the media spectacle is all-inclusive. All the edges that separate gallery art, advertising, film, graphics, fashion and digitality, media had melted away; and like the best commercial images, each artwork was designed for instant impact. Young British art re-embodies the everyday pleasures which an overly academic modernism suppressed. It speaks to those who are guiltless about the thrills their bodies enjoy.

You could see the new British art as a counterpart to the chemical gen-eration in popular music – a search for bliss through intense, rapid signs and symbols. But as you can't separate rave from Thatcherism, neither can you separate the new British art from the era its artists grew up in (their average age was thirty-five). As Peter Wollen has noted,[34] their art strangely paralleled the New Right era – high-Thatcherite in its global ambition and entrepreneurial acumen, low-Thatcherite in the 'domestic cruelty and militant ordinariness' of its topics. He perceived a struggle at the heart of this exhibition with some artists pining after the modernism that's now lost, and others content to succeed in the shiny new order of the commercialized spectacle.

But the Beck's artists almost seem to want to evade this struggle altogether – this furious battle over whose signs are more powerful in a mediascape, artists or advertisers, film makers or conceptualists. That particular nineties power play, which reached its sickly climax with Brit-Art figures like Damian Hurst becoming pop-chart populists, seems not to concern them. As ethical players, they regard the signs of their art as an index of some tangible experience, some real shaping of space and time and consciousness. This is what the media of 'real virtuality' can allow: creative living, captured on a tape or hard disk.

The liberal semiocrats

Let's return to the moment where I first apprehended these artists. A standard scene of domestic consumption – but one which exploded my consciousness out of this space, and has sent me roaming across the informational networks to find out more about these extraordinary figures. We can no more call this merely a 'leisure' or 'entertainment' moment – some fantasy of community, or sexuality, or potency, to compensate for our profound containment in work culture. Even in their currently underdeveloped state, the media portals of the twenty-first-century household encourage us to be more like active 'researchers' and 'aesthetes', exercisers of sensibility and taste, than simply couch potatoes or passive viewers.

And of course, receptive organizations and businesses are alive to the possibility that one might be able to 'brand' this new sort of activism. Who will build the spaces and portals where players might at least begin their journeys into the 'semiocracy', into our social order of information and signs? Who are the 'liberal semiocrats' who will keep the bandwidth open for creativity and play?[35]

The BBC has been especially adroit in turning itself, across all of its available media channels, into a kind of semiotic commons. Auntie Beeb is now a carnival of communities of sensibility, a nest of overlapping networks, each of which defines itself by a taste, an idea, a stance in the world. I know that BBC4 speaks to my particular formation but I'm also aware that other channels (the youth channel BBC3, the news channel BBC News24) are targeting different sensibilities. I also know that all these shows now have an Internet back-up, where varying degrees of supporting material, links to sources or cognate areas of interest, are available.

Discovering an item like the Becks Futures documentary in a branded digital channel like BBC4 is only the beginning of the kind of experience a fully play-oriented media would provide in the age of potentially infinite bandwidth. The bewildering eclecticism of the average Web surfer's bookmark list is a clue to just how customizable we wish our media to be: how much we wish the cultural archive to serve our sensibilities and interests in a very intimate and detailed way.

It's been apparent for a number of years that the biggest obstacle facing the development of a televisual archive comparable with the Internet – indeed, crossing over with it – is that of copyright: media interests want to hold onto the distribution of their material to develop as much syndication revenue as they can. The defence of 'fair usage' has come to a crisis point in America where the rights of artists to morph, copy, transform or even cite artistic and creative works (whether audio-visual or textual) are under attack. Yet the same corporate powers that wish to prevent a radical artist from subverting the eighty-year-old image of Mickey Mouse are also inhibiting much more diffuse forms of media appreciation by their rigorous policing of the content that occupies the bandwidth. Why can't a generation of 'teleastes' (similar to cineastes) be allowed to compose their own schedules of viewing, develop their own connoisseurship of northern soap-operas, the performances of Leonard Rossiter . . . or documentaries on conceptual artists? As Chapter nine shows in more detail, projects like the BBC's Creative Archive and Lawrence Lessig's Creative Commons are first steps towards providing those resources for a play aesthetic.[36]

The existence of a critical and festive culture around films – its film journals and theorists, its specialist movie houses and festivals – eventually fed back into the kinds of films made, enriching the aesthetic strategies of directors and writers. What cine culture did was to ensure that films were accessible to enthusiasts, practitioners and scholars: they could build up a sense of tradition, precedent, successes and failures from comparing works in the canon.

I want more opportunities to be genuinely decentred, or challenged, or thrilled, as I sit before my television set. The Beck artists, for the brief hour they were allotted on a marginal digital channel, gave me a glimmer of what that players' television might look like. Yet the essential question is this: how should we arrange our institutions and infrastructures to support full imaginative expression (and reception) for all in an information age? Should we just rely on the systemic nous of clever, informed bureaucrats in a public broadcasting corporation? Or do they themselves need a countervailing force from below, something unpredictable that ensures their own responsiveness?

Indeed, all cultural capitalists – from advertisers to publishers, record companies to film studios – need some sense that, out there beyond the screen, bohemian cultures are whirling and sparking away, feeding the existing procession of forms and genres with necessary jolts of innovation. So the collective structures of play (those rules which bind us, or rituals which bond us, or networks which wrap us in possibility, around which organizations are built) need the individual dynamisms of play (those crazy experiments, or whim-driven purchases, or boundary-crossing activities, that creative individuals perpetrate) to maintain the integrity of a playful civilization.

The point is that this is a necessarily unstable, fissile, often conflictual face-off: no one can vote for a play society and expect anything other than a noisy life. The question of how one can devise policy for the play ethic is never more acute than in the cultural and artistic realm. How should one legislate to lose control? How can one sustain, resource and manage the essentially unpredictable, and possibly unproductive? I address this in more general terms in the politics of play chapter. But the issue of how one makes 'cash from chaos' is an acute one for those who manage and steer systems of power and money.[37] The problems might be made even more acute if the artists and creators come to be conscious of their own power – that capacity to generate novelty and difference which always has its sources before, and beyond, the marketplace.[38]

The three Ts

Not surprisingly, there have been a few recent attempts to specify what the collective interest of artists and creators might be in the information age; and from a play-ethical perspective, their limitations are instructive. American urbanist Richard Florida believes he has identified what he calls the 'creative classes' – identified functionally as people who 'engage in work whose function is to create meaningful new forms'.[39] Firstly, he describes a 'supercreative' core: not only artists and performers, media people, fiction and non-fiction writers, designers and architects, but also academics, scientists and engineers: all those who 'produce new forms or designs that are reality transferable and broadly useful ... Such as designing a product that can be widely made, sold or used; coming up with a theorem or strategy that can be applied in many cases; or composing music that can be performed again and again.'

Beyond that there are 'creative professionals' who engage in 'creative problem solving'. They work in jobs (law, medicine, high-tech, management) that require a nimble intelligence, a specialist education and the ability to act and think on your own – that is, they 'add creative value'. On Florida's own statistics, the creative classes constitute roughly 30 per cent of the American workforce – up from 10 per cent at the beginning of the twentieth century, and 10 per cent up as recently as 1980. As one sceptical reviewer has noted, this is hardly news in social thinking: Daniel Bell was pointing out in the sixties that societies and economies were shifting from a 'game with objects' (the industrial age) to a 'game between persons' (the post-industrial age).[40]

Where Florida strikes a new note is in his sense of the creative classes being bound by 'a common ethos that values creativity, individuality, difference and merit'. His work has excited city governments throughout the world by suggesting that prosperity rests on the ability to provide these creative classes with a congenial environment, to which they will flock with their skills and enthusiasms. What characterizes this environment is the quality of their bohemian cultures – not just in terms of artistic vitality (live music, alternative galleries), but also in terms of lifestyle (gay scenes, characterful neighbourhoods).[41]

Indeed, he has created both a 'bohemian index' and a 'gay index', which correlates precisely the strength of gay/bohemian scenes and the strong economic development of American cities or regions. The 'three Ts' – technology, talent and tolerance – are the elements, in Florida's view, that indicate whether a locality will ascend the prosperity ladder. 'You cannot get a technologically innovative place unless it's open to weirdness, eccentricity and difference.' Boom towns like Austin, Texas and longer term powerhouses like Silicon Valley are places 'where the geeky engineer with hair down to his waist walks into a bar and no one blinks'.[42]

When it comes to policy prescriptions for enticing and nurturing the creative classes, in the main Florida sticks with the obvious points – the need to maintain low rents in developing neighbourhoods; refraining from building malls or super-stadiums, and maintaining the carnivalesque, street-funky nature of the area. Florida seems to be sanguine about the 'beggar thy neighbour' element of his thinking – where all regions are in a race to attract this talent, and the winners and losers will be increasingly locked into their fates.

But in recent comments, he has noted some core obstacles to the rise of the creative classes. For one thing, there is the need for a 'service class' to reproduce the domestic conditions of their lives, as work and projects consume all their working hours: this deep structural inequality, as Florida delicately puts it, might have 'dire political implications'.[43] How many people, even if presented with 'a real chance to join the game' through education and proper regulation, will truly be encouraged to do so?

Yet the real embarrassment in Florida's notion of the creative classes is its erasure of the political elements of bohemia. He makes a strange and disconnected recommendation that the 'non-profit sector' (represented exactly by the magazine he's writing in) might be able to play an expanded role in the creative economy – giving people the chance to be creative 'free from the market's pressure to maximize investor returns'. Why would a creative-class member wish to do this, given his or her intense commitment to self, experience and career? Florida clearly senses that there is an intrinsically critical element to the artistic culture of an area. The 'creative classes' might also be overlapping with the 'cultural creatives', that other fashionable spectre of American social statistics (roughly coincident with New Agers) who try to maintain a critical distance from consumerist hedonism – the practices which seem to typify the creative-class lifestyle.[44]

Perhaps that need for bohemians to get a distance from the mainstream commercial imperatives of their locality indicates a wider problem with the concept of the creative classes. In short: can their commitment to pluralism, dissent and diversity survive growing domestic intolerance, generated by an America 'at war with terror'? 'We must remain an open society, in every sense,' says Florida, relating this to the way that social intolerance will scare off non-American creative workers from immigrating their talents to the US. But his anxiety is clearly closer to home: the Bush administration may be hurting the diversity, and thus the innovative energies, of America with immigration restrictions, control over flows of information, pre-emptive wars and unilateral diplomacy being 'carried too far'.

In short, America may well be in a good position to survive and prosper in the new creative environment – but not if its violent geopolitical actions, and the tightening up of its domestic culture, make it seem just as fundamentalist as the fundamentalists themselves. Florida is silent on much of the content produced by the bohemians and creative communities he so proudly invokes. Yet part of that cognitive freedom sought by the creative classes must also be the freedom to imagine differently – not just in the mosh pit or on the ski slopes or in front of a new computer game, but in terms of social options and futures.

One of my own networks, Sense Worldwide, is composed of about a thousand 'super-creatives'.[45] Working in many of the occupations cited by Florida, they occasionally allow their sensibilities to be tapped for market research – a kind of bohemian focus group that can be invited to test out a new mobile phone or chat about a new retail service and feed their responses back to a client. This sounds exactly like the 'new kind of capitalism that is powerful and full of promise, but far from fully formed' that Florida invokes.

Yet it was one of Sense's 'sensers' – the graphics design house Karmarama – that produced the defining placard image of the great anti-war-against-Iraq march in London, March 2003; an image reproduced on the front page of newspapers and in lead television bulletins across the world, and distributed as a downloadable data file by Sense itself. It was a picture of Prime Minister Tony Blair, his photo manipulated to show him holding a gun, with a flower sprouting from its barrel in a timeless sixties reference. But instead of a helmet on his head, Blair was wearing a teacup: and with a classic shoeless-nerd-walks-into-bar wackiness, the slogan shouted 'Make tea not war'. This was pure play in the service of a deeply ethical agenda – and one which captured the multitudinous humanity of that afternoon's millions of protesters.

The difference between Florida's notion of the creative classes and the active agents suggested by a play ethic rests precisely on the notion that the spirit of creativity does not confine itself purely to the marketplace, whether producing or consuming. The super-creatives, by virtue of the very imaginative and empathetic capacities they develop in their information-age jobs, have every possibility of becoming 'super-citizens'. And as our digital soulitarians have shown, it's possible that thinking intensely about the 'creative' life might raise some rather too 'creative' notions about our socio-economic priorities.

Semiocrats and iconoclasts

So there is something about art as a practice of transcendence and inter-connection – a realm within which, as Salman Rushdie once said about literature, 'any thought can be connected to any other'[46] – which means that attempts to make it useful for any particular political or economic agenda will ultimately fail. Certainly within the developed West, a thinned-out version of a 'play ethic' has been gradually forming itself – asserting a positive value in the cut, mix and paste qualities of our digital cultures, in the excesses and marginalities that come bursting into the mainstream in pop music, computer games and reality TV. An intellectual bridging between 'postmodern', 'well-being' and 'ethical play' has already begun. There are signs, for example, that governments throughout the world are beginning to recognize that promoting and sustaining the arts have a massively beneficial effect on populations, way out of proportion to the size of the initial investment.[47]

After the attack on the Twin Towers in New York, we cannot be so sanguine about the attractiveness of the 'liberalism' that liberal semiocrats might promote. Our seven-fold model of play warns us not to take some rhetorics of play for the whole spectrum: and at the very least, the critiques of Western image culture raised in the aftermath of 9/11 remind us that play also has its ancient elements. To close this part of the argument, let's look at two books which deal with some of our most pervasive Western cultures of institutionalized play – celebrity and advertising – and let's try to examine them in the light of that most illiberal of global acts.

If a 'play aesthetic' is about recombination, free action, morphing of forms and experiences, must we assume that it will eventually triumph over other mindsets and sensibilities in the world? What if other cultures decide to be, in the words of Ashis Nandy, 'non-players' in the West's cultural games – or at least attempt to play a different game altogether?[48]

The abstract desire: Rojek on celebrity

There's an old Blur album title that sums up a lot of the reaction to the world after 9/11: 'Modern Life Is Rubbish'. Away with irony, postmodernism, triviality! Away with blockbusters and reality docs, the libido of politicians, the politics of libidos! Away with the flotsam and jetsam of our soft, squashy, blithely irresponsible lifestyle culture! All hail the real New Puritans! Yet if it is democracy that's being defended here, we cannot dump celebrity culture like a bad habit – something that weakens our civilizing resolve. According to the British sociologist Chris Rojek, democracy (or capitalism) simply cannot operate properly without celebrity.[49] When President Bush urges his grieving nation to remember to 'have fun', he is recognizing that a large part of his new economy still depends on the pursuit of happiness – which must mean, in part, the gleeful consumption of celebrities. The freedom to be trivial, whim-laden and star-obsessed is a lubricant of our 'way of life'. Indeed, one might imagine it as a new patriotic injunction. Fight for your right to party, as a particularly asinine rap group once shouted.

But when it comes to celebrity we're also fighting for the right to be unequal. For Rojek, celebrity points us to 'the gap between the theory and practice of democracy'. The theory is that, after the end of monarchical rule, all citizens are now equal under the law: through our welfare institutions, we all have the same chance of 'social ascent'. The practice, however, is quite different, as any modern Orwell tramping the meaner streets of Britain or America could tell you. So one way to read the allure of celebrity is that it's a consoling myth: a pageant of can-do, go-for-it personalities, who help to turn 'meritocracy' from its original pejorative meaning into a positive buzzword for Blairites – and, in the meantime, obscure the realities of structural inequality.

The celebrity biographies of the UK pop stars Victoria Beckham and Robbie Williams are fascinating source material for Rojek's theories. Both 'Posh' and 'Robbie' regularly conjoin the humbleness of their beginnings and the intensity of their aspirations. Victoria with the requisite photo gallery of bad-hair-day family snaps, Williams with a running confessional about his insecurities under a book title that says it all – *Somebody,*

Someday. His closing words fit Rojek's theory: 'If I wasn't Robbie Williams right now, I'd probably be auditioning for the Big Brother household. I would. Some people's dreams are different: I think a huge majority of people's dreams are the same. They want to be bigger, better, they want the glamour, the fame, the celebrity.'

Rojek's most original insight is that people have been wanting this ever since the eighteenth century. He brilliantly rereads Samuel Smiles's *Self-Help* as a manual on the virtues of the celebrity – or at least, those successful exemplars of hard work and Christian discipline the good Protestant struggler should follow. But Rojek notes that the new print media that disseminated Smiles's homiletics also sold large copies of lurid sex-and-violence tomes. The new citizenry were not necessarily fascinated with the achievements of individuals, but with what Rojek calls 'the churnings of social form – the pleasures and pains of instant recognition, the moral consequences of accumulated wealth, the variation of talents, the gullibility of the public'. Which sounds like a summation of a whole sector of celebrity magazines, from *Vanity Fair* to *OK!*

Celebrities have to run cold, as well as hot, for good structural reasons. Our desires for them have to be 'abstract' and formal, rather than specific or loyal, otherwise we won't keep the conveyor belt of consumerism moving. 'As long as democracy and capitalism prevail there will always be an Olympus,' concludes Rojek, 'inhabited not by Zeus and his court, but by celebrities elevated from the mass' – bloated, often grotesque, but essentially 'an expression of social form'.

So what about those who don't wish democracy and capitalism to 'prevail'? What is their take on celebrity as the perfume (or halitosis) of democracy? Rojek can't answer this directly but he does provide some resources. And the most fertile area is the relationship between celebrity and religion.

Part of the hysteria involved in our Western pursuit of celebrity, he suggests, comes from the long-reverberating death of God. We are obsessed with the baroque forms of society that celebrities act out because we are in a general search for meaning and coherence. Their rises and falls, their tales of trial and redemption – Robbie's endless rehab, Posh's momentous love of Becks – are the only ones we believe in any more. Yet celebrity in the West is not simply about boot-strapping tales of uplift and achievement. What about our recent love of gangsterism – from *The Sopranos* to *Sexy Beast*? To a community-minded Muslim, this glorification of the petty criminal would seem pathological in the extreme. We are clearly working out some otherwise inexpressible feelings in the tapestry of Tony Soprano's life – perhaps some of the very frustrations with democracy, between the ideal of freedom and its cramped reality.

Bin Laden undoubtedly has celebrity status in the Muslim world: books, videos, portraits, the most popular boy's name in Pakistan last year (just like Kylie and Jason in the eighties). Why do we find that so inscrutable? When bandits, criminals and sociopaths can become part of our own vanity fair, what is to distinguish bin Laden from Al Capone? In a world where spirituality and transcendence are now geopolitical factors, we need to follow their traces in all cultural forms. If we want to heal our world system, we need to understand the irrationalities that cause its wounds. The pseudo-religion of Western celebrity, if we look at it properly, makes us as strange to ourselves as others may seem to us. In a moment when the clash of civilizations is forever threatened, an appreciation of our own otherness may be useful knowledge. Robbie and Posh may yet have their uses, even in wartime.

Recognizing the patterns: William Gibson

William Gibson writes a techno-thriller set in London's advertising community![50] State it this baldly, and it might seem too bathetic to be believable. Has the coiner of the term 'cyberspace' and the heir to Arthur C. Clarke as SF prophet lost his oracular nerve? Is he trying to lay the ground for a new career in corporate consultancy?

The plot of *Pattern Recognition* is altogether too tailored towards people who spend too much time punching away at machines with screens. Cayce Pollard is a freelance trend consultant who operates by intuition: she knows viscerally when a logo or brand is going to work, and gets paid unnamed fortunes for two-minute sessions. This useful trait frees her up to indulge her real obsession – charting a phenomenon called 'The Footage': these are anonymous postings of short film clips, whose enigmatic beauty is tantalizing a legion of Net-heads. One of Cayce's clients thinks they're 'the ultimate marketing strategy', and commissions her to trace them to the source.

Thus begins what sometimes seems like a combination between a frequent-flyer travel review and a gadget boy's wet dream. Those who enjoy Gibson's by now wearisomely familiar tropes and tricks – loner hero/heroine, in love with branded hi-tech, goes on quest through real or virtual space, meets/fights/fucks with galleries of urban eccentrics, talks like Raymond Chandler with laptop underarm – will enjoy this novel. Like all the most recent Gibson novels, *Pattern Recognition* presumes that seeing the world as a chaos of clashing and fusing cultures, refracted through information technology, is somehow the truest rendition of the present moment. The only difference here is that Gibson planks this in the recent past rather than the near future, when the tumble of tall towers cast a pall over all imaginings.

Yet there are some quite absurd cultural omissions from the cyber-politan sheen of this work, particularly from a writer who so evidently preens himself on the sensitivity of his zeitgeist antennae. Of course, there is the usual range of social grotesques and clichés from contemporary Japan, Gibson's preferred seam of Otherness – the sweaty geek schoolgirl fetishist, the opaquely exuberant designs and brands in neon-drenched streets, even an inscrutable and duplicitous Oriental anti-hero. Too many Western hipsters – from Barthes and *Blade Runner* onwards – have regarded the ludic excesses of Japanese consumer affluence as some kind of alien portent of the future (rather than just the usual capitalistic marketing blow out with its own Buddhist/Confucian twists).[51]

Possibly (and not surprisingly) bored with this – it's marked almost all of his previous works – Gibson instead seeks out his source of redemptive difference in contemporary Russia. The Footage isn't some awesomely clever 'viral' campaign, but the product of Nora, a crippled Moscow cineauteur. She's been sending out expensively enhanced clips of her Cannes award-winning short film, living in an old Soviet-era bohemian hangout converted to a fully staffed digital studio, all this liberally funded by a shadowy Russian property billionaire with a guilty conscience . . . and so, improbably, on.

One feels a little for Gibson's eternal-student idealism here. The marketing phenomenon that's been sending the creative classes of London and New York crazy with envy is actually an old-fashioned Romantic project. Something born of 'art, freedom and things of the spirit . . . whole universes of blood and the imagination', says Nora's sister to Cayce. In these rooms, 'people valued friendships, ate and drank . . . Now we say that everything Lenin taught us of communism was false, and everything he taught us of capitalism, true.'

However, as the ethical zenith of a novel straining for contemporary relevance, this is stunningly off-beam. Does Gibson really think, post 9/11 and now post Gulf War II, that the measure of our current chaos can be taken from an elegiac musing on the twentieth-century failures of capitalism and communism? Particularly in a work that aspires to live in the shadow of the falling towers, the complete absence of any engagement with spiritual or sacralized cultures, particularly Islam, seems less like a stylistic decision and more like a structural blindness.[52]

Was the destruction of the World Trade Center ('like watching one of her own dreams on television', recalls Cayce narcissistically) really 'an experience outside culture'? Or was it the ultimate revenge act against the semiotic dominance of Western consumerism? As Jean Baudrillard has said of the event, 'This was not the hatred felt by people from whom we have taken everything and to whom we have given nothing back, but rather the hatred felt by those to whom we have given everything, and who can give nothing in return . . . it stems from humiliation, not from dispossession or exploitation.'[53] For a novel which tiresomely vaunts its knowledge of contemporary symbols and signs, Gibson displays not the slightest inkling of the symbolic violence that the West's relentless marketing blitz wreaks on iconoclastic or reticent cultures.[54]

The subplot of Cayce Pollard's father – an old US intelligence spook who disappears on 11 September – is intended to provide the deep link between the frothy world of trendspotting and the Day That Changed Everything. Willis Pollard always warned his daughter of the dangers of 'apophenia' – the spontaneous perception of connections and meaningfulness in unrelated things. Whether it's sifting through data to find possible threats from enemies of the state or cool-hunting to find the next version of the reversed baseball cap, too much reliance on 'pattern recognition' is ultimately rendered by Gibson as a bogus knowledge. Tell that to David Blunkett and John Ashcroft, straining at the leash of civil liberties to turn all our data transactions into a search archive for 'anti-terrorism'.[55] Or to the computer gamers who are putting their ludology at the service of the American security state.[56] As Gibson's mentor William Burroughs might have put it: even literary paranoids can't know the half of what's going on, let alone anticipate it in fiction.

In a funny way, with his heroine ending the book in a spoony embrace with her new lover (and thinking of downshifting her insane career) Gibson tends to agree with the hijackers. The time for a trivially semiotic kind of play – the commercial business of 'distinguishing degrees and directions of attractiveness' – is indeed over. Gibson's alternative suggestion is that we should let love, friendship and art rule over all. Yet there are many in the world for whom Cayce's affliction – her visceral rejection of certain brands – is becoming more a rallying cry for militant and fundamentalist resistance than simply a cute way to make a living in Madison Avenue and Soho. And what might be destroyed under the onslaughts of 'regime change' aren't just the commercial trivialities of pattern recognition, but the very possibility of human recognition: the need for a genuine 'dance of civilizations', a polylogue of enriching differences conducted in peace.[57]

We have come, unsurprisingly, to the moment of 11 September again – that singular challenge to a blithe, carefree, purely 'modernist' conception of the West at play. Before we begin to take it up fully – pursuing both its political and its spiritual dimensions – we should pause for a moment, and see just how blithely the values of play *can* be invoked, deep within the comfort zones of the developed world.

For there's no business . . . like play business.

FROM BUSINESS TO 'BUSYNESS'

The Management of Play

Business is a combination of war and sport.
– André Maurois, *Memoirs*, 1970

The job of leadership today is not just to make money.
It's to make meaning.
– John Seely Brown, *Fast Company*, 1998

Glasgow: paper play

There is much hard fact to substantiate the claim that modern business has become more playful. The best evidence, in my view, is the fact that I was allowed anywhere *near* the inside of one.

Until the mid-nineties – other than taking the piss out of hippie music biz executives seated around gigantic New York dinner tables in the late eighties – I had never fully experienced the corporate world. Taking free-lance cheques from corporations is still like being a flea on an elephant, in Charles Handy's useful metaphor: you jump on, suck hard and jump off, until the next one lumbers along. You don't actually get under the skin and become part of the beast's very survival system.[1]

But one bizarre day in the late nineties, I found myself face to face with the head of a major Scottish media organization, and realized, in that very instant, that the ground was shifting under my feet. The mogul was, admit-tedly, not from the usual business school background. Gus McDonald (now Lord McDonald of Tradeston, a government minister) had been a cam-paigning left-wing journalist in television and print, yet had found himself increasingly gravitating towards management ('I always liked strategy, even in my red days,' he told me). On that windy Glasgow day in the autumn of 1996, Gus had invited me to lunch at his latest gig – managing director of Scottish Media Group, who owned the newspaper (the *Herald*) for which I was writing a weekly op-ed column.

All I was doing in that space was, literally, playing with some ideas: I was fascinated by the range of intellectual arguments around New Labour, their attempts to render a vision of modernity that might win them an elec-tion, and I tried to apply some of that theorizing to the everyday round of Scottish life. Gus had dropped me a sympathetic note about the column ('nice to see that someone else is thinking about the same things as I am, on this side of the border') and suggested a bite.

But as I sat in the leather chair on the other side of McDonald's looming desk (yes, mine was several inches lower), and as his ex-sociology-lecturer chef brought in one deliciously garlanded plate after another, I suddenly realized this was a kind of audition. For one thing, it soon became a battle of egos: the ex-trade unionist turned corporate mogul asserting his hard-won realism against the upstart ex-popstar turned post-modern chancer, who was equally hanging onto his long-nourished idealism. He dived into Scottish history, I reached up for critical theory and we both ruefully agreed that once a utopian Marxist, always a utopian Marxist – at least in terms of our belief (burnished by our mutual enthusiasm for *Wired* maga-zine at the time) that the social use of technology was always the primary force for progress. I brushed the exquisite olive-drenched breadcrumbs off my lap, took a firm grip of his hand and thought little more about it.

A few months later, after a series of rather tense meetings with the existing editorial staff, I was crow-barred by McDonald into the inner work-ings of the *Herald* newspaper, as a 'contributing editor'. They gave me a website, two pages at the back of the Saturday paper, a wild graphics designer, and a very reasonable commissioning budget – and then allowed me to do what I wanted for eight months. Now, given my experience in the music business, I know what this means: you grab all the opportuni-ties available, as long as you have the cash and latitude to do so. At least you can then point back (after they catch up with you) and say that you've brought something brand new into the world.

So that's exactly what we did. On one side of the back page was some-thing called 'E2' (short for 'Second Enlightenment') – an attempt to revive the eighteenth-century spirit of public discourse and rationality marked by the first Scottish Enlightenment, except with Net forums and global gurus. On the other side there was something called 'Scotgeist' – an attempt to do for Scottish prose what the *New Yorker* tried to do for American prose. My own assessment? Some palpable hits, some disasters, a lot of experi-mentation with topics and formats (one SMG executive mused on whether this was 'journalism for the year 3000, rather than the year 2000'). In short, my team and I seriously played, in every available rhetoric of play, with the materials before us. This was all I knew to do.

But it was only afterwards that I realized exactly what had happened. Because of the strategic fiat of a corporate executive, I had been allowed to create my own play space within a very traditional and authoritative business (a Scottish national 'newspaper of record') in the hope that it would instigate some change within the paper's then notoriously conser-vative mindset. I subsequently realized that this was an act of a 'game changer', someone who was willing to introduce some ludic turbulence into the settled patterns of a traditional workplace, then stand back and observe the changes.[2]

As I remember, the only effect I seemed to have on the *Herald*'s working practices was to generate a whistle from the gnarly, cynical-as-shit newsdesk every time I passed them on the way to my creative den. It was, without fail, the theme tune from *The Twilight Zone*.

At several points in this book, I've expressed the hope (perhaps a vain one) that the play ethic can be a possible bridge between results-driven management and meaning-driven employees in the modern enterprise or organization. Might playing together, instead of working together, be a saner, more fruitful way for highly capable 'knowledge employees' to find a liveable life within companies and institutions? What I've tried to do in moving through my existing tribes of players is to show that play values can generate legitimate forms of social order and structure, which express and sustain human potential just as effectively as 'work' (industrial *and* informational) can do. My *Herald* experience taught me an early lesson: thrusting the values of play into the heart of a deeply work-oriented situation is to risk derision and defensiveness. Soon after my corporate patron had moved on to politics, my play pages were closed down – the editor lifting my 'contribution' out of the paper's body like a lurid tumour.

Yet my second editorial experience within SMG – as one of the founding editors of their new weekend newspaper, the *Sunday Herald* – was almost a test case for the play ethic.[3] In retrospect, it was obvious: all the rhetorics of play were exactly the kinds of values we were trying to invoke with the *Sunday Herald* – play as a source of human energy; as a perpetual engagement with the world; as a mentality capable of living with uncertainty and risk; as an attractive form of collective identity; as an imaginative, symbolic freedom; as a spirit of honesty and integrity; as a saving sense of humour and subversion. A perfect editorial policy for a brand-new paper.

For a while, at least, that's exactly how it felt. We were timed to launch in the afterglow of the new Scottish Parliament, April 1999: the sense of mission, of a group of journalists being 'players' in the drama of nation-building (or at least, nation-articulating), was tangible and thrilling to us all. Our offices were the first in the world to entirely use iMacs for everyday operations – the editorial floor was a riot of blue transparent plastic – and every journalist had the world of information, both Web and database, at their fingertips. We appointed young radical feminists as executives, off-the-wall artists as overall designers; hell, even the editor – Andrew Jaspan – used to be a rock 'n' roll manager in Manchester.

Subjected to endless hours of demographic presentations and market surveys by our corporate paymasters (the 'semiotics of the segment' was undoubtedly my favourite), we were constantly reminded that our idealism, creativity and excellence were a 'play to win' – 50,000 readers by the end of year one, and a steadily rising percentage after that. For six months or so, in my role as digital and cultural editor, I felt that we were winning the play, at least in terms of the quality of the paper (the numbers were initially soft, but constantly strengthened, week by week). The spirit of exchange between and within the different elements in the enterprise – journalists, marketers/advertisers, management – was open, fertile, honest, energetic and ideas driven. The stories coming out from Silicon Valley at the time – about the vitality and vigour of 'dot-com' start-ups – resonated with my experience in Glasgow.

As every issue muscled its way onto Scottish newsstands on a Sunday morning, sharp and confident, I began to think that perhaps the 'job' – meaning a routine of duties, a fixed place of work, a constancy of colleagues and a regular wage – wasn't such an enemy of the player's life after all. The paper required us all to occupy our 'limited' and 'specific' positions in a division of labour (i.e. I couldn't do the sports editor's job, nor the business editor's job, nor they mine). But we shared enough of a common purpose and commitment – and a good enough info-structure – to allow us to generate some new ideas between us. We could maintain a kind of tensile flexibility in the face of new information, vital for a good newspaper, and exactly what the management doctors prescribe for the 'healthy' organization.[4]

In May 2000, however, I found myself voluntarily walking away from the paper I'd helped to establish. Personally, the experience of work – even 'good work' like the *Sunday Herald*[5] – created too much cognitive dissonance for me. I realized, in short, just how much of a player I really was.

The breaking point was the use of technology. The Apple Mac I used during the day to fashion a market-competitive media product (which only expressed a portion of my idealism and vision) was the same Apple Mac I was using at night – except this time, with my brother Gregory, to freely assemble our ornate neo-jazz albums, entirely according to our own dictates, whims and schedules. When you get a taste of genuinely unalienated labour then even the slightest alienation comes to seem like a temporary stay in the prison house. (One further disincentive: a swarm of overly intrusive accountants measuring every item of expenditure against a steadily tightening rule to the point of impairing basic editorial functions.)

I had no need to sustain my brief sojourn into the world of the 'proper job'. I'd acquitted myself reasonably well in the tasks before me, and I'd learned a lot about modern work. In retrospect, the reason why I lasted so long was because my particular organization was a very good example of what a 'players' workspace', within the capitalist context, might actually feel like. I had shaped it, invested myself in it, found something like a res-onant identity within it – even though it was the closely budgeted product of a publicly listed media company, whose executives were as focused on shareholder value as any of their breed. I had arranged my workplace as much like a playground as the business context would allow: more like a comfortable, resourceful toy room or a recording studio full of similarly enthusiastic and talented souls than a hard-hitting newspaper floor.

Here's the question I've been worrying at ever since: is that as much play as a business might *ever* allow? Is there always to be a gulf between the player who strikes out for the full multitude of purposes in their life – and the business organization that still, in some ultimate sense, has to 'manage' the creativity of its workers, in order to achieve strategic focus in a competitive marketplace? Does business always have to say, at some point, 'The work starts here' – and does the player always have to respond, 'My gig is ended here'?

If you were reading the business literature avidly enough, over the last few years at least, you might easily have believed that the gulf between 'worker' and 'player' was progressively closing. *Business Minds,* a book of interviews with over fifty leading management thinkers published in late 2001, is a veritable 'playbook' (as the specialist magazines are fond of say-ing) of business ludicism.[6] Leif Edvinsson urges that the knowledge worker needed 'knowledge cafes', not offices. Gary Hamel notes that the best-ever-selling business book featured the comic-strip character Dilbert, 'totally cynical about management'; while Jonas Ridderstrale gushes that though 'economies of scale and skill' should still matter for businesses, 'the new game is one of economies of soul . . . companies always need to be thinking of A&E – aesthetics and entertainment'.

On my shelves behind me are works with titles like *Jamming* ('manage-ment is a performing art', says John Kao); *The Experience Economy* (which says that all business should be reorganized like the performing arts) and *Serious Play* (where models, simulations, toys and prototypes drive business success – the slogan being, 'demo or die').[7]

If this is the tenor of the advice being thrown at major corporations in the developed West, you could be forgiven for thinking that the play ethic had already taken up residence in the strategy rooms and spring-watered canteens of higher capitalism. Indeed, from the immortally named Watts Wacker and his *Visionary's Handbook*, a 'play ethic' has already been identified in certain corporate cultures. Wacker calls it the 'paradox of leisure' where 'the line between the work and non-work world is quickly disappearing' (as evidenced by 'company softball teams, golf games with clients, cell phones at the beach and laptops on airplanes').[8]

In light of this, I think it's important to once again focus on the ethical nature of play. Just what does it mean to do ethical business in a profoundly playful world? In my fitful wanderings around the world in the early noughties, I harvested many experiences and many conversations to begin to answer that question. Yet my first briefing in the play ethics of business came from a genuinely surprising source.

Sydney: the Wizard of Oz (keeps capitalism kosher)

I went to Australia to meet the greatest living advocate of play power, and what I found was an overworked, overground management consultant who now admits to a 'strong Puritan trace' in his soul. The current thoughts of Richard Neville – sixties countercultural icon, founder of *Oz* magazine and author of the hippie classic *Playpower* – are more than just another example of youthful radical turned pension-watching conservative. The complexity of his position is worth charting. Who else might be better placed to assess whether there might be a viable play ethic for businesses and organizations?

Neville in person is still as flighty as a butterfly – greying but wiry, small framed and feline, skittering across every topic with speed and accuracy, leaving you breathless in his wake. After meeting in his endearingly cluttered terraced house, we dodged around Sydney's Glebe Point Road on a creamy Sunday morning – a lazy bohemian drag replete with brawny bookshops, baroque squats, the constant aroma of various intoxicants, and chichi houses in anything from bordello to Shaker style. It was a major achievement to fix him to a concrete bench outside the local library, shrouded from the traffic noise by a wall of eucalyptus leaves. As I brought out my PDA recorder, he drawled sneakily: 'Oh, you're such an X-er!'

If I was an X-er, Neville was at least the last quarter of the alphabet. I had purchased an original, dust-ridden copy of *Playpower* from Gould's Book Arcade on King Street in Newtown the previous day, and was (as ever) outraged and amazed by it.[9] Yes, it is a remarkably ragged work – drugs guide and traveller's memoir, post-industrial utopian tract and pansexual celebration, joke book and pop critique – and written with an insect-like attention span that I recognized in the man thirty years on. But in its very structure, *Playpower* is almost an anticipation of Web culture itself. The material cascades through its 300 pages like a printout from a powerful search engine, driven by a few keywords like 'drugs', 'sex', 'pigs', 'underground'. Like any good Web search engine, the book is a mixture of the essential, the utterly useless and the serendipitously interesting. I'd read any number of tomes which told me how much the information revolution was rooted in sixties values. But *Playpower* makes it clear that the idea of the hypertext, a system that enables any bit of information to lead to any other bit, was dreamed of by hippies decades before the first line of code was ever written.[10]

'Ah now, that would be explained by all the marijuana,' said Neville, nodding seriously. His attitude to his most famous work, from where he sits now – as the head of a futures institute regularly hired by organizations and businesses in the Australian establishment – is gently but insistently critical. He's most embarrassed by *Playpower*'s 'adolescent objectification' of women ('I have two volatile, gorgeous daughters to think about, so I'd politically correct *that* for a start'). And he regards with wry amusement its dreams of a work-free society brought about by new technology. An original example: 'Most jobs will be eliminated. Certainly all those for whom the decision-making rules can be set out in advance. Who will build the hospitals? Mr Digital Computer and his jolly gang of electronic circuits and cybernated steam shovels.'[11]

'Now in a weird sort of way,' he glosses, 'the opposite has happened ... the technology you're holding in your hand, the emails I've answered this morning, the mobile phone and pager – they aren't extending our time, they're annihilating time. It's a complete paradox. I see couples in Sydney restaurants around breakfast tables, and they're on their separate phones – but where are they to each other? The more connection, sometimes, the more disconnection. The expansion of free time hasn't happened yet. People keep saying it's just around the corner – I'm thinking I don't believe them.'

And then, the great advocate of 'the politics of play' – the 'international, equi-sexual, interracial survival strategy for the future' as the book puts it – told me how he had come to respect his own work ethic. Or more precisely, the work/leisure divide.

'To be really truthful, I have to say that pure play is only enriching and enjoyable when you've been working hard. I think you need the both. It's like night needs day, happiness needs sadness, mountains need the desert. For years I've been swimming and surfing round here, ten minutes away from Bondi – but I love it more when I've just achieved something, when I've just worked hard at writing a piece, or flown around the country making a few speeches. Play is sweeter when there's been a bit of work applied. Maybe I have a Calvinist trace in me.

'But playfulness has moved into the workplace anyway, just as *Play-power* predicted. And that's because cyber culture democratizes creativity. Back then, writers and artists were supposed to be eccentric, have long hair, wear flowing coats, maybe even have a garret, perhaps be lucky enough to get a government grant. These were special, extreme people. Now we live in an age which worships innovation and needs it to survive – even in business. So creativity is now out of the garret, and ordinary people have the chance to be honoured for their spirit of innovation. All kinds of walls are being knocked down between people in the workplace. This is happening even in *banks*, for God's sake. Wells Fargo has got a groovy cyber-office in California, where it's all long hair and jeans and people collaborating . . .' He shook his greying moptop. 'Banks!'

So Richard Neville – once sentenced to six months hard labour for bringing out *Oz*, the world's most subversive magazine, a man once described as 'the hippie counterculture's Marshall McLuhan' – was now a fully paid-up guru of the new economy. And I could easily see why the job of futurist so easily fitted him, and other post-hippies. Having lived through (perhaps even survived) a 'consciousness movement', in Neville's words, the natural next step would be to deploy that expanded mentality in the generation of 'future scenarios'. The need for 'alternative states of mind' is as relevant for a company trying to negotiate and predict a turbulent marketplace as it was for a gamine, spunky Australian boy searing a chemical trail through the squats of early seventies London. And the hippies' enthusiasm for playing around with identity and consciousness, perhaps even fusing with other minds, set them up perfectly to shape and advise the feelings and ideas-driven workplace of the early noughties. As we conversed Neville revealed himself to be fully aware of his market niche. For a ludic ex-motherfucker, he spoke the language of blue chip very well indeed.

'All these organizations say "we have great values and honour the human spirit" – nine times out of ten it's propaganda, bullshit. But the *people* in these organizations want it to be true. It would be great to just raise your peace sign and incant about Woodstock, peace and love . . . But I think you do need a bit of real economic performance.'

Neville's particular shtick was the greening of capitalism – he wanted his clients to start practising 'triple bottom line' accountancy. 'God, I never thought I'd even be mentioning the word *accountancy* . . . Yet if we want sustainability in companies – getting them to think about whether they're taking more out of the planet, or out of people, than they put back in – then it's all about measurement now. What gets measured gets done, unfortunately. But that's one way to make them responsible in an organization: you get them assessed by an independent, environmental auditor and then people who've got money to invest will say, "I'm only going to invest in socially screened or ethically screened organizations."

'We're still in the capitalist situation: that's *it*. But you can encourage people not to just think of the shareholder – because the shareholder can also be part of a wider group called society, and aborigines are also part of that. So what about a putting a bit of pre-tax profit their way? It's all about keeping capitalism kosher.'

Nothing offensive or objectionable in all this, of course. It was just that I'd heard such talk since the start of the century from a hundred different mouths, and it somewhat deflated me to find one of my countercultural heroes speaking the doxa of post-capitalism everywhere. I even heard the beginnings of a 'next work ethic' argument from him: 'If people want to be really proud of their workplaces, then they want to be helped to feel that – which is what the really ethical company can do for them. It can keep people in the building, keep them motivated.' Richard was also impeccably orthodox about anti-globalization movements. 'It's bad and good simultaneously. Why shouldn't a farmer in Kenya or Bangladesh cut out the middleman with his mobile phone, and find a decent price for his products on the market? Our Sydney protesters were tearing down McDonald signs with Nike shoes on their feet. How do you square that?'

Our conversation came to a hippie-meets-corporate zenith when Neville started to talk about 'the ability to live in paradox' being the key skill of twenty-first-century life. 'We need to cease to be surprised that things are contradictory, that they don't add up. I was brought up under the tyranny of logic – all these Scottish Presbyterian teachers rapping me over the knuckles with rulers. There's a lot going for logic, right? But really, in these times, I think the reign of logic is over.'

On this outer rim of business thinking – a vision where companies and organizations are the means whereby people can do more together than they might do as individuals, especially in the face of an endemically risky world – I'll admit that the play ethic has an obvious place. One might imagine a 'play audit' of an organization that tried to assess its ludic strengths and weaknesses: the way that it allowed the full range of play forms, ancient and modern, to be properly managed by its employees. And the ability to move through the ambiguities of play – to 'live in paradox', as Neville says – would be the primary competence.

The job of management might be to ensure that the company's play is dynamically balanced between ancient and modern forms. Emphasize purely modern play – too focused on individual development, imagination and authenticity – and the very coherence of the organization breaks down. Concentrate on purely ancient play – focusing on the collective rituals and team games that define the organization, and placing that within a highly unpredictable context – and the autonomy of the individual employees, their own sense of freedom, becomes reduced and corporatized.

This play balance was further hinted at when Neville, for all his good corporate behaviour, allowed a glimpse of those other ludic alternatives – the real 'alternative futures' – at the heart of the corporate present. And more often than not, they were still coming as reverberations from the great sixties' moment.

'A strange thing has been happening recently, when I'm meeting the CEOs. Guys come up to you and say, "You've lived an interesting life, haven't you?" I reply that really, it's not that interesting – being a bit of an outsider, you miss out on a lot of things. But then they sidle closer – they're in their Armani suit, aged somewhere between late fifties and early sixties – and they say [Neville went sotto voce], "Do you think it's OK for me to try pot?" If it was just once or twice that it happened, I'd be surprised, but . . .

'They've run a major industrial company all their lives, and it's as if they think that something's missing. Very powerful figures in public life will sidle up and tell me, "I was in Vancouver in 1970, I read *Playpower*, I lived in a commune." That happens quite a lot.

'So there's two sides to the modern corporate mentality, in my experience. I see a lot of these kinds of guys in Australia. They've led a life with a lot of absences in it – no play, no broader consciousness. That opens up an existential vacuum, and sooner or later in my more workaholic mates, I see this catching up with them. Suddenly they're fifty-nine, sixty, and they're saying "There's not much time left, I never even got to Marrakesh."'[12]

And if authoritative execs find it in their hearts to confess their countercultural past (or future) to Neville, his antennae are also still attuned enough to pick up the most powerful local resonances of all. 'The point about Australia is that we have this basic aboriginal culture, rooted utterly in gift giving – no real sense of property or proprietary relationships at all. And that's totally the Internet, isn't it? For all the commercial models that were foisted on it, the fact is that it's a gift culture where people expect to give back what they take out, without question, and with a real symmetry. You know, it's the sites where nuns are helping people with Aids that are wildly successful, not the dot-com busts.

'The world's getting better and worse, faster and faster. I think we're at a very early stage of human values. We should have the humility to realize that, and just get on with the business of making the whole process sustainable.' And with that, he skittered off down Glebe Point Road, disappearing into the melee of a street market, heading mazily towards a particularly appealing young bebop combo.

So if the most extreme sixties play radicals are now the most dutiful noughties workplace consultants – while saying, as Neville did repeatedly, 'I believe I'm still me, with a little tinkering' – then perhaps that's something to be noted. There might well be forms of business organization within which the core values of play might prosper, without being deployed as expedient techniques for team building or morale boosting. There was only one place where I knew that an explicit ideology of play had dominated its business culture: the Bay Area of San Francisco, epicentre of Silicon Valley and the dot-com boom. By the time I finally got there, as 2001 blurred into 2002, the boom had gone bust. And another explosion, on the other side of the country, had rent its damage on America. Would it challenge the play ethic too?

San Francisco: catching the conscience of kings

If anywhere could claim to be the play capital of the world, it would be San Francisco. Here is where the hippie movement transmuted its values into Silicon Valley (with the assistance of the military–industrial complex, of course) – the PC or Apple Mac as another supplement for the brain, the Net as a realization of the age of Aquarius.

Yet I arrived, in the middle of December 2001, in a strange, declining moment. The dullness and depressiveness wasn't just the result of the mild stringency of a Californian winter. A year after the beginning of the 'dot-com bust' – the great shakeout of first-wave Internet businesses throughout 2002 – and a few months after the terrorist attack on the World Trade Center, I sensed a certain torpor in the city. As I settled into my hotel, someone sent me an email from the Bay's prime futurist, the ex-Grateful Dead member John Perry Barlow. He talked about an experiment he had been conducting for the last year with his wife. They had been observing the customers in their local healthfood store, and had tried to count 'the number of genuine smiles between people – not forced, or for show, but real, spontaneous life-affirming gusts of laughter'.

Their tally? 'Seven, at most.' And as I battled my way along Market Street from the edge of the Tenderloin – trying to avoid an alarming procession of homeless men, crack dealers and psychiatric day releasers – I could only agree with Barlow. There was a head-down, jaw-clenched tenseness in the commuters as they stalked past each other. For the first time in years, I saw a street fight in a major city – a small, wiry white cyclist was facing up to a much taller black man with braids, his helmeted head barely reaching the home boy's chin. A few minutes later, like some real-life radio station going through the frequencies, I overheard a girl console

her slacker/hacker boyfriend on a concrete bench. 'Baby, at least it's a job . . .'

Yes, brief sentences from a city, their value dependent on how much you trust the city reader. But not so inaccurate, as it turns out. Employment growth had fallen from 5.9 per cent to 1.3 per cent since December 2000 in the Valley: 17,000 jobs had been lost even since 11 September.[13] Vacant office space was at its highest rate for a decade in the Bay Area.[14] IBM had just been fined for defacing the city with their software logos in a guerrilla marketing campaign; the signs marking out offices and residences 'for rent' seemed even more disfiguring in the city that drove the boom years of the new economy from 1995 onwards.[15] Maureen O'Hara, director of the Saybrook Institute for Humanistic Psychology, told me that she felt a 'dysphoria' had superseded the euphoria of the dot-com days.

It seemed like the right time – *because* it was the most inappropriate time – to start asking questions about the relationship between play and business. San Francisco and its environs had been the place where the idea of play as a positive value – as a mentality that fostered innovation, great software, cool products – had become, in the boom years, a social 'ethic': something as tangible and explicit as the Presbyterian warnings and strictures of Gordon Brown's New Labourism. The soulitarian would never have an easier climate in which to flourish – and in many ways did. The tales of basketball courts in offices, soft play areas dotted with laptops, were legendary.

Yet after the bust, and during wartime (of a kind), would these values survive? Would they disappear as management and workers alike examined their failed business models, their specious software solutions, and decided to 'return to the knitting' of defending market share? Or might the failure of the great tech dream encourage a new ethic of play – one more mature and less unthinkingly hedonistic? Could business move to busyness, from bottom line to passionate activity, in the ruins of the long boom?

All my significant leads seemed to point to one place in San Francisco: the corporate consultancy Global Business Network. Formed in 1987 by a group of ex-oil executives, media types and post-hippies, GBN had been the cheerleaders for a 'playful' model of business practice – before, during and after the dot-com rumble, boom and bust. Their particular method was known as 'scenario planning', which anticipated real world crises like the Middle East oil embargoes in 1973 two years before they happened.[16] Scenario planning was explicitly about seeing the company as a 'player'

within 'games' (in the marketplace, politics, culture and technology) whose rules were sometimes amenable to change, sometimes not. But to be aware of the range of possible outcomes of any strategic decision is, for GBN, the highest virtue.[17]

It's easy to see just how timely this kind of thinking was in the fiery years of the digital revolution in California, when the wildest scenarios (at least in terms of stock valuation) often became a reality. GBN's sensibility shaped much of the optimism and vaulting ambition around *Wired* magazine, launched in 1995 by Kevin Kelly, one of its associate members. GBN's president, Peter Schwartz, even provided the magazine with its own socio-economic paradigm – that of the 'long boom', a vision of tech-driven prosperity peaking around 2020, ushering in a new 'belle époque'.[18]

Even before 11 September, in a June 2001 interview published on the Network's website, Schwartz was already sounding gloomy about the boom's prospects: 'There was a fairly strong momentum, I believe, towards the long boom a few years ago that has fragmented to a significant extent. There are now many possibilities, which are mostly negative.'[19] When I hit the ground in SF, it turned out that Schwartz wasn't available: he was busy consulting to the White House on tactics and strategy against 'terror networks'. It was something of a comment on where the ethics of play were settling in the recessionary wartime of early noughties America.[20]

However, as I moved around their members (and ex-members: many of them having been 'let go' recently), I saw how GBN treasured an internal culture of disciplined, serious play – which didn't give their managers the ability to predict the future, but at least enabled them to be ready for most eventualities. As Napier Collyns, one of GBN's founders, put it: 'We don't try to describe a factual reality with scenarios. We are trying to brighten the perception of the system by making an imaginative leap into the future.' Management writer Art Kleiner, writing about the scenarists' approach, says that scenario makers are more like 'counsellors' than 'predictors' or 'forecasters': they 'help their audiences take advantage of whatever unthinkable events might come to pass'.[21] In terms of the one-liner that had emerged from my general theory of play – 'players need to be energetic, imaginative and confident in the face of an unpredictable, contestive, emergent world' – GBN would seem to be its perfect advocates.

And yet the deeply compromised roots of the Network's scenario-planning methods couldn't be denied: the need for a giant energy corporation to anticipate threats to its continuing levels of profit. And some of those threats (like environmental or anti-colonialist movements) might

need to be 'taken advantage of' by Shell managers in ways which, at the very least, would be ethically dubious.[22] So what were the ethics of GBN's form of play? At what point did their playing raise conflicts of value that weren't so easily resolved by drawing a wonderful 'mental map' on the wipe board?

'Yeah, we got them to step over a homeless lady in the lobby as they made their way into our "scenario dinner",' recalled the handsome, fifty-something actor before me, as we chowed through some Californian pizza. 'Boy, were they surprised when she came to the actual meal, and started poking at their plates.'

Richard Dupell, founder of the 'business theatre' company Fratelli Bologna, was describing a typical GBN stunt with at least some of the relish of the former Berkeley performance artist he was.[23] The locale for the event had been the offices of the Idea Factory, one of San Francisco's more ebullient consulting organizations (its founder, John Kao, was an ex-jazz pianist who advocated that workplace teams should 'jam' like great musicians).[24] The homeless woman was an actor who, on cue from Dupell, started picking fights with the well-heeled and increasingly unnerved corporate guests. 'She was muttering stuff like, "Hey, nice steak, how much does that cost, that could keep me in a house for a week . . ." And just at the point where things were getting uncomfortable, I stepped in and said, "Now this woman is an actor. So, what do you learn from this disorientation?"'

What effect did it have on them? 'Well, I don't know if they immediately changed their position on things, but we certainly made sure we gave them the option. There was a lot of strong discussion, a lot of major ideas welling up . . . Ultimately, I'm an actor: what we do is to put the heart and guts into these scenarios – that way they really get remembered.'

The move of a theatre company from fringe excessives to corporate consultants is characteristically San Franciscan. Yet Fratelli Bologna came to the attention of GBN's Peter Schwartz through a vicious satire of suburban consumerism, contained in their successful 1996 underground show *The Webber Family*. 'We did a parody McDonald's ad, really lampooning the people who bought the stuff,' said Dupell. 'Peter thought it was a very effective way to convey ideas and scenarios.' Fratelli carried improvisation right into the business environment. 'When we did corporate events, we'd have people appear right in their midst, characters from scenarios they knew they'd have to be ready for – a Chinese hacker, an Indian garment worker, a European woman manager.'

However, for all their impressive intellectual talk the daily reality of Fratelli Bologna isn't quite so inspiring.[25] Many of the photos on their Web brochure present them as a bunch of badly costumed actors, doing comedy turns at crass dot-com conferences. Fratelli did a lot of goofball cabaret at otherwise dull and procedural events. I happened to notice two characters in particular: one a craggy and weather-beaten middle manager called Frank; the other a kick-ass military type in khakis called General Buck Bradley. The first turned out to be Richard's meal ticket for the foreseeable future; the second, a looming ethical problem.

'Frank is just the classic bewildered management guy – always just behind the next curve, the next wave of change, and getting increasingly tired at the prospect of trying to keep up. He's very popular. I always get hirings for him from the corporate crowd. And General Buck? He goes down particularly well with the hardcore engineers and coders – all these game boys who love the idea of a real soldier shoutin' at them in the hall.'

But times were getting lean for Richard, and I couldn't help proposing my own scenario plan for Buck. Say some big local company wants to rally the employees' collective spirit and decides to play the patriotism card, in one way or another. Someone remembers Buck Bradley from the salad days of the dot-com boom era, and calls you up to do a pro-flag routine for the arm-punching boys and girls. Would you?

The man squirmed a little, and replied honestly, 'Ask me in six months time. I like to eat. And because I had such a craz-eee time in the seventies, I haven't exactly backed up my security for my old age. But man, I can't bear this flag patriotism that's going around right now – I think it's dangerous, delusionary ... So right now, no. But again, ask me in six months.'

Richard also went on to say something which made me slightly queasy. 'What we do is directed improvisation. Sometimes we use something called the "photo mask" method – we're all wearing these photocopied faces, on which are the features of the characters we're playing. They could be anybody ...'

Richard said that it was to help them get away from the predictability of 'just another middle-aged white guy' playing an exotic part. But I found this whole image disturbing. In playing with these actors – running them back and forth like video tapes, jerking them like marionettes – it allowed the assembled managers to exercise (maybe exorcise) one of their most deep-seated dreams: to make their employees act exactly the way they'd want them to act. And the face masks also encourage the idea that the actors – and by extension, all workers – are changeable and replaceable at whim.

This is one of the subtler ambiguities of play. On one side we have the imaginative, empowered, visionary play of the strategic manager, on the other, the collective, embattled and fatalistic play of the workforce. For all the hype about creativity and collaboration, they are only encouraged to play *within* the rules of the corporate plan, rather than cogitate freely about their productive life and its meaning. The playful enterprise in the new economy then begins to look like this: bosses free to play (and set the rules), employees compelled to play (only by the rules).

And in the middle, imaginatively rendering this asymmetry, is a worried middle-aged actor like Richard, who doesn't know whether he can bear doing his gung-ho general routine at the next tech conference or not. Of course, he knew that classic line from Hamlet: 'The play's the thing/wherein I'll catch the conscience of the king'? 'Yes.' He said, 'That's an interesting thought. Do you want that salad? Like I say: I like to eat.'

I went under the Bay waters that evening on the city's cavernous BART metro – filled with a carriage full of the most introverted and weary city dwellers I've ever seen – for a rendezvous with Erika Gregory, Richard's contact at GBN. Ex-GBN, as it turned out: Erika had recently been 'let go' and was 'embracing her freelance opportunities', as she dryly related to me over her aubergine salad. Erika was unusually Rubensesque for a northern Californian, and gave off the enthusiasm of a fringe-theatre producer which, she confessed, was how she started. 'Juilliard girl, shared my New York flat and my New York agent, knew pretty quickly that I wasn't going to hit any heights', as Erika briskly put it. She started her journey into organizations through a local council job, which took poor kids who were aiming for sports scholarships and tried to get them ready for the qualifying exams. 'I got very interested in the processes whereby people are enabled to learn new things – even when, especially when, they're resistant to the call.'

By a commodious route, Erika found herself on the West Coast again, working as an office assistant for GBN. One day she overheard a scenario-planning dilemma and suddenly realized that her dramatic skills could perhaps unlock the problem. Thus began her dramatizations with GBN, which then spread out into a tumult of scenario gigs for companies in the area. 'I did something for a shipping company recently – we took over a giant 100,000-square-foot ballroom, and turned it into these four separate worlds, each with its own borders. We gave the top managers a passport, and they had to move through the worlds, interact with the actors and come out of all this with three main ideas that they had to implement within the firm.'

As usual, the scenarios pushed to various extremes. What if a combination of computers, networks and local micro manufactories destroyed the markets for certain kinds of shipped components altogether? What if hijacking boats became the terrorist *acte de jour*? What if rising water levels made living on giant ships a viable opportunity for water-reclaimed communities?

It sounded to me like Disneyland meets the think tank. Erika nodded vigorously. But like Richard, at the moment she was feeling the pinch. Freelance didn't exactly imply free choice at the moment. Her current two jobs were with some 'defence contractor' and the well-paying but authoritarian Singaporean government. As far as the consulting class was concerned, it seems like the ploughshares of the dot-com boom years were turning back into swords: post 9/11, national and global security of all kinds was where the action was. She appeared untroubled by these gigs, so I asked her for more detail.

For the defence corporation, she had created a Victorian diorama. It comprised a round revolving table, around which people were precisely placed. On top of the table were several 'views on the world' – lightboxes with scenes and materials inside them, which the participants could look through. Each box represented a real player in a modern conflict: the al-Qaida terrorist, the bereaved Palestinian mother, the amoral engineer, the troubled state department official and so on. As the table slowly spun to a halt, each participant had to fully adopt the world view of the diorama. She enthusiastically went on about how this exercise 'really got these guys to think about their externalities', until I commented that working for the military industrial complex was a line I could never cross. (Only a few weeks earlier, the line had brushed my toes: after mentioning my interest in the use of play metaphors in war talk at a public meeting in London, I was approached by a nervous young man who was doing some 'scenario planning for the British Ministry of Defence ... they'd love to talk to you – all about your play ethic'. Changed times, indeed: after the privatization of everything, now the militarization of everything?)[26]

It wasn't the first time I would meet the new American patriotism on that trip. 'How could you think that an effective national defence force was a *bad* thing?' said Erika testily. 'What I feel I'm doing when I set up my little plays for these people, is I'm giving them the option of the other person's viewpoint – so they can make wiser decisions. If I feel I've gone in there and stretched their imaginations, then I've done a good thing.'

And what was she doing with the Singaporean government? 'We're working with a few hundred leading teachers on a "creativity" course, getting them into the idea of challenging accepted ways of doing things, thinking in an unorthodox manner . . .' I began to get a little impatient. Surely the best thing to encourage the forces of innovation within Singapore's technocratic oligarchy would be some old-fashioned democracy – you know, that boring old iteration of one person, one vote, exercised through just and fair elections? How could you truly preach the language of innovation in a state that still operates as a mildly authoritarian regime? 'Well, we're having to decide this week just what themes we bring into the scenario plans and dinners when we get there. It'll be . . . interesting to see what they [the government department who was hiring her] will and won't allow.'

It struck me then that this was, in essence, no different from yet another corporate gig for the highly professional Erika. Indeed, in a way, it was the ultimate opportunity for a play scenarist: dreaming a future for not just another service provider or consumer goods maker, but a whole nation. It was still corporate, in the sense that it concerned the inspirational vision of a leadership class, trying to take forward its expectant citizens/employees. This was the play of the elites – and as such, nothing to do with my idea of a play ethic.

As a parting shot, Erika made her own tart comment on the 'culture of playful collaboration' that was supposed to exist in the heyday of Bay Area capitalism. 'Oh yes, some of these companies were terribly playful – up until the point at which they were taken into bankruptcy. Then when it came to trying to get your unpaid fees out of them, well, they weren't so terribly generous and playful.'

For GBNers, scenario planning encourages the playful business manager or entrepreneur to play with different visions of the future and therefore learn to expect the unexpected. And surprisingly, according to GBN founder Stewart Brand, that makes businesses behave more responsibly in the present, as they strengthen their ability to weather all imaginable storms. To quote the futurist Paul Saffo: 'The first thing you learn in forecasting is the longer view you take, the more it's in your self-interest.'[27]

So the thrust of GBN's practice is that the purpose of business can be 'more than just the delivery of shareholder value', in the words of Eamonn Kelly, the Network's president and 'senior practitioner' of their scenario planning exercises. I caught him at their Emeryville headquarters in Oakland, just across the Bay.

'I think that over the last century, economic wisdom and moral wisdom separated. I don't mean that you couldn't do both, separately, but you could be economically wise without being morally wise. We are beginning to see a reconnection and convergence between these two wisdoms. It's being accelerated by the transparency and connectivity of ICT which empowers consumers not just to demand more from producers, but to participate in the creation of products and services, to infuse them with values from outside the organization. And I think the convergence between biotechnology and computation – in everything from cloning to food – is also compelling every business to think ethically as well as commercially.'

'Stewart Brand has a phrase about how "we are gods, and we might as well get good at it". When you read reports about the promise of regenerative medicine – that the proper manipulation of stem cells can potentially slow or even reverse the decay of our body parts – that phrase becomes more than just a throwaway line. The ethical dilemmas are staggeringly complex, particularly as we are now beginning to "play God" with ourselves. One piece of me says, that's truly remarkable, because it's possible that in fifteen years' time – I'll be in my late fifties – I might have the opportunities to turn the clock back to be as healthy as I was in my early thirties, if I'm wealthy enough. A piece of me thinks that's quite cool! But another piece of me says, "How about leaving a space on the planet for my kids?" What kind of disruption is there going to be if my life expectancy jumps from eighty to a hundred and forty years? I think we need to evolve new value systems, dialogue systems, decision-making systems, governance systems, relationship systems to truly confront those dilemmas. There's a huge challenge there, as well as an enormous opportunity.'

It's difficult not to admire the levels of ingenuity and passion that drive the GBN process. Part of that energy is required because their target audience has been American corporate culture, which over the last twenty years has been the most aggressively competitive economic machine on the planet. For US business to pursue 'sustainable growth and a better future' (as their origins statement has it), it had to be given arguments that spoke to its central purpose – the realization of profit. GBN's efforts have been largely concerned with expanding the vocabulary about what 'added value' might mean: how can a return on investment be ensured in such turbulent times? Much of that investment is now sourced in ethics and aesthetics, as much as it comes from capital or technology provided by traditional business. Answering the febrile sensibilities of 'alpha' customers and citizens is as important as paying obeisance to fund managers and shareholder interests. Added value, as Eamonn Kelly hints, is becoming *added values.*[28]

The play-ethical issue, however, is this: where do these new values and ideals come from? Surely not just from internally enlightened managers, fresh from their visionary workshops. Business should be seeking input from sources beyond the boundaries of the company or the corporation. A disquiet was growing in my mind about the easy acceptance of a certain version of the 'play ethic' in the new economy. It could be captured in a simple question: who gets to play what kind of game?

My previous four tribes of players − soulitarians, lifestyle militants, liberation teachers, neo-artists − mostly have a vision of humanity that skews towards the modern end of play's polarities: emphasizing energy, mental freedom and deep authenticity.[29]

But to regard this burgeoning mass of complex, creative humanity as merely another 'market opportunity' or a chance to reap (in Jonas Ridderstrale's words) 'more riches in niches', contradicted the spirit of progress and hope which genuinely animated people like the GBNers. I had to remember that they were a global *business* network, and not a global *busyness* network. The creative, value-rich activity that they primarily recognized was that which passed through the marketplace. Passionate, creative actions that might occur in areas beyond and before the marketplace − civic, communal, governmental, even spiritual − were only allowed into the argument if they could provide an opportunity for commodification. Yet the complexity of a play perspective requires that market and non-market be seen as part of a Moebius loop, around which the play of social forms endlessly moves − and that a non-market loop requires just as much priority as the market loop.[30]

It seemed to me that the fifty-something ex-oil executives and post-hippies of GBN had gone as far as they could go with their sensibility. They had tried to translate this distinct seventies experience − a strange fusion of oil crisis gloom and tie-dyed counterculture − into a reform practice within American corporate culture. With every structural crisis caused by technology, culture and society, the corporates became ever more amenable to the arts of the long view. Yet the step from business into 'busyness' seemed to be a conceptual limit that they couldn't or wouldn't cross. That is, from 'bottom line' and 'shareholder value' into the promotion of active, passionate, innovative humanity, out of whose general fostering all manner of civilizational (including economic) benefits would occur.[31] Who was really listening to the new players on behalf of business? Who could do the translation exercise? And was it even possible?

London 1: the saints do work

One of the first people to mail me after I first went public with the idea of the play ethic in October 2000 was a man called Phil Teer.

✉

From: pteer@stlukes.co.uk
Subject: *Observer* article

I thought your piece in the *Observer* was excellent. I'd never heard about the play ethic before. To me the key point you made was about liberating human potential. I work at an ad agency called St Luke's. We're the world's only cooperative ad agency of any size and pride ourselves on the steps we've taken to create a liberating culture at work.

We've tried to maintain a pretty flat hierarchy, spread power and responsibility as wide as possible and we've attempted to make everyone's job a creative job.

The downside is that to make this work we have to put in some pretty long hours most of the time. I heard someone say the other day that their family life kept getting in the way of their work life.

I suppose the thing is that as work becomes more like play, it becomes addictive in a different way. We've yet to discover a way of being successful while maintaining a play ethic outside of work.

These 167 words are almost a pure distillation of the strengths and limits of the play ethic in relation to business. It's worth dwelling on St Luke's as a test case in exactly how elastic business culture can be when it comes to considerations of 'liberating human potential'.

At the moment of writing (spring 2003) St Luke's, the 'most frightening company on earth' (in *Harvard Business Review*'s words), has its troubles – its founder being asked to leave by his own deputies, the company posting its first loss, on top of much ad-land rumour and recrimination. But its recent history is still worth exploring.[32] It's essentially an experiment in commercial organization, set up by a group of successful advertising executive and creatives who one day found themselves on the outside of one of America's most illustrious agencies, Chiat/Day. A thoughtful and learned bunch – particularly the classical scholar Andy Law and Oxford-educated David Abraham – they decided to grasp the opportunity to create a company from scratch, whose very structure would be dedicated to realizing the maximum creativity from its employees.

Drawing inspiration from every source – Aristotle to Third Way thinkers, complexity theory to French history – they devised a radically democratic ownership structure: every member of St Luke's, from receptionist to director, is given an equal stake in the shares of the company (retaining, however, unequal salary rates). The onus on job security in St Luke's is extremely high: benefit conditions and holiday time are set at generous levels for the industry.[33]

With that sense of 'safety' behind them, Law reasoned that the demands he could place upon these 'owners' would be total – a free out-pouring of creative commitment to the company and its projects (which were, predominantly and conventionally, pitches to corporations for substantial ad accounts). Law also argued that the whole notion of job demarcation and specialization would have to be radically challenged. In exchange for conditions of almost total security, an almost total flexibility would be expected of the St Luke's employee. Ideas must be shared freely across all departments, without cynicism or turf wars impeding the flow. Criticisms must be endured (and praise embraced) in the monthly peer review, no matter how relatively powerful your position in the company. Law presumed that people were responsible for their own actions, and their own work. This made hierarchy difficult – and also meant some extreme moments of honesty and self-critique.

From its founders' descriptions, St Luke's can sound more like an artistic or spiritual movement than a competitive ad agency, scrabbling with the best of them in a fevered, mediatized London. When you finally get to their coveted toffee-factory offices, just across from the new British Library off Euston Road, the feel is much more like a regional arts lab, or students' union cum design house, than the usual video walls and leather sofas of the successful metropolitan ad agency. There are bits of flaky art on the ceiling, luridly painted brickwork, odd scatterings of overused computers, beanbags, massage chairs and internal phones. There are glass-walled sections full of what seem like props but which are what they call 'client rooms' (comfy furnishings for the foodstuffs client, bristling tech for the telecoms client). Upstairs is a giddy, cramped warren of tottering papers, objects and files; in the basement is a down-home cafeteria which, with its injunctions to 'tidy away plates' and its rows of lockers, keeps up the post-graduate feel.

I sat around a wooden table with about ten members in the early months of 2001, and our discussions about work, play, technology and ethics were as boundary crossing and eclectic as any I've had over the last few years. On another visit, David Abraham, one of the co-founders, spared me thirty scintillating minutes (while the road was being violently dug up outside) during which we pondered the social politics of creativity at light speed; and in a subsequent discussion with Phil Teer and Neil Thompson, we drifted as easily from anti-globalization to boardroom entryism, while musing over St Luke's impending entry into Hollywood by a digital back door. To drop into the St Luke's working day is to be presented with a sea of 'open minds', as Law intended – and also some evidently well-balanced souls.

Yet although the circulation of ideas and emotions in the company is refreshingly free – at least for a medium-sized knowledge enterprise in a highly competitive marketplace – St Luke's structural tensions are all too evident. And those are largely to do with their commitment to keep each 'c' of play – communication, creativity, collaboration – corralled within the definition of 'work' (i.e. labour directed towards ends which do not fully embody the labourer's will). In the *Financial Times* report detailing their recent problems, Teer stoutly spun St Luke's reputation: 'From the outside, St Luke's has always been seen as some hippy commune. It is anything but – there has always been a strong work ethic at the heart of the agency.' Yet the attempt to play fully within this 'strong work ethic' was clearly causing major distress among its employees: according to the industry magazine *Campaign*, one internal meeting in February 2003 had 'turned into a very ugly event. Mud was slung, plates were smashed, hair was pulled and arses kicked'.[34]

Take a look at the news archives of any of the major ad industry magazines in the UK over a twelve-month period and you'll quickly see the real environment in which St Luke's swims. Like all the other agencies seeking revenue, they're pitching like crazy for the big stuff – credit card companies and car manufacturers, snack bars and home furnishing empires, massive media corporations and even more massive telecoms corporations. Some they win handsomely and famously (British Telecom putting most of their ad spend in St Luke's hands), others they lose ignominiously (IKEA deciding to remove their account, after some controversy about the ads). Some, they don't even get near. In the words of one of the *Business Minds*' gurus, Jim Collins, St Luke's doesn't use the notion of 'maximizing profits' as 'an ideological substitute for the need to find a purpose'. But profit is undoubtedly 'the blood, oxygen and nourishment' of the company: 'We are also here to make money,' said Abraham. 'Nothing we do is an enemy of that.'

Yet the gap between the founders' rhetoric and this undoubted commercial reality is occasionally preposterous. After finishing the Socratic dialogue at the end of Law's *Open Minds* – where Wittgenstein, Bill Gates, Noël Coward, Aristotle, Plato and Theodore Zeldin are quoted around the tables of the downstairs cafe: just another Monday breakfast time – I turned to some of the descriptions of recently aired St Luke's ads from magazines like *Campaign* and *Marketing Week*:

• *For IKEA's 2001 Christmas campaign* A press and radio push focusing on consumerism and a desire to 'beat the Joneses' as the real spirit behind Christmas. The campaign aims to drive pre-Christmas traffic into the stores by reminding people that IKEA sells Christmas gifts and decorations, so they can beat neighbours and relatives by having the most baubles on the tree and the best wine glasses, for example. It also urges them to 'win' the best guests by providing Ikea furniture to accommodate them . . .

• *For Tilda Rizazz, a rice product* The campaign features a supposedly busy female executive, Trudy, bumping into friends in the supermarket while buying Tilda Rizazz. They ask what she is buying, and are so impressed by her air of importance that they marvel at what it must be like to have such a hectic lifestyle. The end line says: 'Tilda Rizazz. Executive rice for busy, busy people'. A follow-up spot shows Trudy at home with a friend, still appearing frantically busy and obsessing about a big presentation she has to finish. However, she eventually cracks and admits it is all a front – at which point her friend comforts her, while taking a sly peek at her watch . . .

• *For Travelocity, a dot-com travel company* The sixty-second ad opens with a pallid man hauling himself out of bed, fully dressed, to the grating sound of an alarm clock. His day unfolds into a dreary sequence of cramped trains, an ever-increasing workload and colleagues who have no social life. The man climbs back into bed, again fully clothed, only to look forward to repeating the same process the next day. The ad is shot with a gritty, grey ambiance to convey the man's miserable lifestyle, and ends with the words 'you need a holiday' and a shot of a tropical beach . . .

Do these productions sound any less tedious, clichéd or small minded than the mainstream of television adverts, however 'neo-Marxist' and 'creative age' the process of making them might have been? St Luke's most celebrated commercial ads – the aggressive 'chuck out the chintz' series for IKEA, which challenged Britons to own up to their appalling taste in interior decoration – emboldened one of their main creatives, Andy Palmer, to define a new genre of ad. 'Co-ercials' try to 'coerce' viewers into buying products (one strapline, 'Come and see us. Or we'll come and see you' features three burly members of the 'design mafia' harassing people in their home). Indeed, one of St Luke's co-ercials – an IKEA ad in which the company's workers are forced to smell each others' armpits to appreciate the 'toil' that customers put into building their furniture – was voted 'most annoying ad' by television viewers in 2001.[35]

It's a dark thought, but I haven't been able to suppress it. Is there a continuity between that psychologically demanding 'security meets danger' workplace culture of St Luke's – 'stripping the layers of ego away' as Law puts it – and these relentlessly ironic adverts, which subject our petty insecurities and domestic vanities to scorn and exposure without pity? The continuity became even stronger in my mind when I discovered that St Luke's had been responsible for advertising Gordon Brown's welfare-to-work proposals to the nation in 1997, and had been gushingly enthusiastic about doing so.[36]

Consistent with their corporate work, St Luke's 'New Deal' ads – as well as their subsequent ads for the government on working families tax credit and adult literacy – bore down precisely upon the micro-level behaviours and decisions of ordinary people. These 'co-ercials' were much less strident in tone than the New Labour Chancellor Gordon Brown, but behind their gently challenging scenes – between fathers and sons, mothers and other mothers, across shopping queues and pub floors – the coercion of workfare was implicit: the message was, *this* is how normal the idea of 'no fifth option' could feel. That is, *if* you knuckled down.

When I visited, St Luke's was handling a government campaign to improve adult literacy – in broad terms, an unobjectionable project. But their ad narrative was typically punitive and picky. A range of stock characters are embarrassed by their inability to read – a mother unable to answer a daughter's spelling request, a young man unable to do his karaoke turn – and their embarrassment is embodied by a series of taunting little gremlins. Replace 'literacy' with 'creativity', and it almost sounds like something that could happen on the average working day at St Luke's.

To be fair to the St Lukers, when you raise any of the preceding complications with them directly, they are clear-eyed enough to admit their commercial limitations. 'We are still running a business,' said the suave but steely Abraham (now heading a major cable TV company in Europe), 'so we do as much as we can across the boardroom tables to change things. But only as much as we can.' Phil Teer is a personable, open man, but clearly has the expansion of St Luke's on his mind. And in my meetings with him, Phil was volubly anxious about whether the 'St Luke's spirit' can be maintained, as the agency opens up branches in Stockholm, Mumbai and elsewhere, and generally gears up to adopt a more 'global' role.

The limitations of trying to encompass a properly complex play ethic within a work and business context are all too obvious from the first email that Phil sent me. How genuinely liberating can 'a liberating culture at work' be? To 'make [their structure] work', as Phil put it, they have to 'put in some pretty long hours most of the time'. So family life gets in the way of work life: indeed, the workplace becomes the family and work colleagues, in this hot-house culture of compulsory creativity, become the preferred playmates.[37]

'As work becomes more like play,' says Teer, 'it becomes addictive in a different way.' From the perspective of the play ethic, Phil is a pathological player: maxing out on some play rhetorics and disregarding others. Fixated on only a few of the possible values of play, he's a modernist player (valuing human development, imagination and authenticity) caught up in finite games of commerce that limit his ludicism to a purely team-oriented model.

Indeed, Phil's closing line – 'We've yet to discover a way of being successful while maintaining a play ethic outside of work' – reveals the essential mind-set problem of the St Luke's way. The frantic over-exertion and extreme commitment that their marketplace demands force Phil into that most tired of dualities: work/leisure. His belief was that there can be a 'work that becomes more like play', and a play ethic that can be 'maintained outside of work'. Yet it's surely this very limited notion of 'success' – a success purely defined through marketplace viability – which a rich understanding of play can help to expand and deepen.

For all the evident qualities and noble intent of its founders and owners, St Luke's is a classic example of how the very vocabulary of 'work' can create a blind spot about 'human potential', even amongst the best and most energetic of us. The paradoxes are legion. How could a truly 'cooperative' culture support the kind of relentless psychological fragmentation that advertising depends on?[38] What the contortions of the St Luke's rationale show us, at the very minimum, is that business can take the potential of the play ethic only so far. Indeed, with St Luke's, their limitations are acutely ironic. This is a company that, at least internally, is committed to a pure culture of innovation. Yet it energetically accepted commissions to help spread the message of a government that is deeply suspicious of innovation – that is more interested in maintaining public order than in fomenting a bottom-up, genuinely emergent creativity.[39]

But an operation as febrile and searching as St Luke's is bound to intuit the future at some point. One of their associations – their long-term contract with British Telecom – has produced a venture that begins to point beyond the fraught conundrums that business culture gets into with the play ethic. Getoutthere.com is a well-resourced website (funded by BT) which is dedicated to the promotion of young creative talent. The site allows young creatives to upload their material to a gallery, which gets scanned and judged regularly by industry professionals; it also provides online tools for remixing music and redubbing film. Since it launched on 31 January 2000, the site has had over a million visitors: on their own website, St Luke's cite Getoutthere.com as turning around the target youth market's rather jaded vision of BT.

But I was struck by getoutthere.com as a business response to the natural players of the eighteen to thirty generation. What BT had spent several million pounds on was nothing less than a public institution for players, a networked infrastructure whereby anyone could develop and display their creativity, with no entry cost, and with professional levels of editorial and support. The usual brand paybacks were there, of course – BT's vertiginous logo twirls consistently in the top right-hand corner – and parts of the operation seemed a little thin on both participation and actual talent.

Yet the fact was that the very autonomy and strength of players' culture – all those soulitarians and lifestyle militants and neo-artists – had compelled a private corporation to get involved in public infrastructure. Only by means of a gratuitous gift of resources did they believe that they might win over the consumer loyalties of this demanding social constituency. And even with that intent, the project seemed a little forlorn: wasn't BT simply trying to emulate the kinds of open fora for creativity – from MP3 to Napster, Gnutella to Kazaa – that the Net had already spontaneously generated, and would no doubt generate again?[40]

It was typical of St Luke's ethical ingenuity that they could get a major company to part with this kind of money for this kind of venture. But it still felt patronizing, creaky, a dam erected by a corporation to generate power from flows of play it could never really understand.

London 2: *speil macht frei* (play will make you free)

He had a voice deep-fried in cynicism and world weariness. 'The problem with a play ethic is that nowadays, employers love play far too much. There are golf courses on the thirteenth floor of one US corporation I know about. It's a kind of infantilism, where we should be thinking about a proper division of labour, of rational gains in productivity. Instead we're just doing surveillance by teamwork – if you do not play, it gets noticed. It's a new totalitarianism, just as bad as the old *arbeit macht frei*. Except now, it's "You must play."'

His name was James Woudhuysen, and he was a senior strategist at the design company Seymour Powell and a battle-scarred consultant to the old and new economy. From my perch at the podium of the Institute for the Contemporary Arts in London ('a playhouse for the mind', as its 1946 mission statement puts it), I couldn't deny the pertinence of his point, and nor could the now-chuckling crowd. I didn't have much of an answer for him then, but I think I may have one now.

Over several significant pieces of public writing, Woudhuysen has shown himself to be London's foremost sceptic of the worth of the 'playful' company. But the effect he fears – the deconstruction of business into 'busyness': a place of multi-activity and meaning making, as well as efficiency and money making – is an effect that I devoutly desire. Our difference is that I wish to push the latent playfulness of the modern company to its ultimate conclusion; Woudhuysen wants to extirpate it altogether.

As a hard-headed business adviser, he has good reasons to oppose the conflation of work and play: it threatens the standard practices of competitive enterprise. The physical 'softening' of the work environment – through better ergonomics, access to facilities that 'amuse and divert', chill-out zones, team-building exercises, etc. – are 'activities that distract from wealth creation, reason and progress'.[41]

> The aim of wealth creation is blurred by an excessive focus on the psychological integrity of the workers, their 'needs, desires and loves', the quality of their human relations as groups of individuals . . . For the past two centuries, workers broadly subordinated the Self to the objectives and deadlines surrounding profitability; but there was a strict divorce between the worlds of work and play. Play was something to be done after hours. Coaches were for the pitch, not the workplace.[42]

Woudhuysen is firmly committed to the absolute separation between subject and object, rationality and nature, that allowed the birth of scientific industrialism. Given that commitment, he is right to invoke its legacy, as the growing ludicism of the workplace actively subverts this world view. A more playful vision of the universe does indeed imply that co-creation and collaboration are as important as the competitive 'survival of the fittest'. It is the interplay of both that guarantees the general health and vitality of a complex system, whether natural or social.

Again, what Woudhuysen finds objectionable from a 'work-centric' position seem like the vapours of liberated creativity from a 'play-centric' standpoint. '[Play in work] represents a relativistic retreat from the absolute certainties of the past; for when you play in a team, there is room for disagreement about how to apply the rules, there is an irrational element of Lady Luck, there is an aesthete's quest for the beautiful stroke.'[43] So what play values can bring to the division of labour in the modern workplace is a spirit of constructive dissent; a thrilling sense of unpredictability and openness; and the opportunity to make an art of one's life and labours. One is tempted to ask: what's the problem here?

Yet I agree with him that the alternative to the divisions of labour should not automatically be, as it were, the 'unity of souls' – that kind of collective, faintly coercive play that I perceived in some of St Luke's workspace culture. At the ICA event, Woudhuysen rendered it correctly as play being used to 'try and align the private self with the public self ... That's a very dangerous tendency'. The line between collective play and corporate culture has to be carefully monitored: teamwork can as easily become a surrender of the self, as well as an enrichment of it.[44]

This has to mean a new conception of organizations and enterprises. I've been calling them 'busynesses'. That is, concentrations of resource, of physical structures, of traditions of skill and practice, that are fully aware of the undoubted creativities and energies they generate – but let that spill over their boundaries. The 'play space' presumes first that it is a 'possibility machine', in Kevin Kelly's words and those who manage its boundaries have to be relaxed about the possibilities that might ensue. Busynesses provide a 'ground for players' by which they might add value promiscuously and freely throughout the terrains of their lives.

Again, the most cutting-edge management theory is edging out tentatively along this ledge, apparently ready to jump. Warren Bennis's notion of the 'post-bureaucratic organization' – where the job of management is 'to devise and maintain an atmosphere in which others can put a dent in the universe'; where companies are 'not pyramids, but structures built of energy and ideas, led by people who find their joy in the task at hand, while embracing each other, and not worrying about leaving monuments behind' – sounds like a busyness in all but name.[45]

Woudhuysen's call for a fundamentalist return to classical capitalism is perfectly understandable, given the threat to the basic model of business posed by the rise of play values. For a play ethic implies an arrangement of culture, economy and society which can both allow the maximum number of players, and also reproduce their conditions of play. Within this arrangement businesses can only do so much: indeed, it would be wrong to expect them to build the full civilizational playground entirely themselves. We need the market as an indicator of the subtle textures and unpredictable extremes of human desire: and, as an expression of some play fundamentals right across the spectrum, business is deeply useful. But we also need a context and structure around that market, which can attend to our more collective ludicisms.[46] Players need to balance freedom and security in a way that makes them feel at home in a dynamic natural and social universe.[47]

In short, the play ethic cannot be left entirely to chaos and self-determination whether generated by the market, or technological advance, or gender meltdown, or the endless mutability of signs and symbols. Thus, we enter the realm of politics – those arguments about how we order our mutually agreed realm of public action and resources to benefit the maximum number of human souls. How do we collectively ensure that everyone gets the opportunity to be a player? And yet how do we also ensure – in light of the mild authoritarianism of current market democracies – that play culture's 'multitude of purposes' isn't closed down or prejudged before it's ripe and ready? In short: what *are* the politics of the play ethic?

PLAYING FOR REAL

The Politics of the Play Ethic

No one knows who will live in this cage in the future, or whether at the end of this tremendous development entirely new prophets will arise, or there will be a great rebirth of old ideas and ideals or, if neither, mechanized petrification embellished with a sort of convulsive self-importance. For of the last stage of this cultural development, it might well be truly said: 'Specialists without spirit, sensualists without heart; this nullity imagines that it has obtained a level of civilization never before achieved.'

– Max Weber, *The Protestant Ethic and the Spirit of Capitalism*, 1904

With all the will in the world
Diving for dear life
When we could be diving for pearls.

– Elvis Costello, 'Shipbuilding', 1983

Imagine your neighbourhood playground (a good one, I hope). Now, add the hubbub and energy of children: running around in groups, huddling secretively in a corner, staring dreamily as they dangle from a bar, methodically working a chute or see-saw to its maximum tolerance. Children scheming, sharing, improvising, competing, meditating, perspiring, conspiring.

All possible human moves are contained within the iron fence: the children both defy and are limited by the equipment and conditions of the playground itself. Some children play while their primary carers are somewhere else, free as birds, defying the fears of our age: perhaps they have some snack to boost their energies, maybe even a mobile phone in their pockets to call them home. Others have their parents or minders watching them from a respectful distance, ready to intervene if a particular child isn't feisty enough to join in the melee, or falls and hurts themselves during a particularly daredevil stunt.

And all around the playground, in the broad lawns and bounded fields, other children and adults are running, throwing frisbees, cloud watching, hurtling past on bikes, kicking balls about . . . All the diversity of humans – our need for freedom and agency, and our need to be entangled in the lives of others – on display in a common space.

I've always gloried in the democratic energies of the public park. Even Glasgow is visited by high summer once in a while, and the place to be is Kelvingrove Park, in the city's university area, where all smells (from dope to ice cream), all sights (from copulation to agitation) and all sounds (from the quacking of ducks to the *hzzt*-hiss of ghetto blasters) are available, refreshing your appetite for sheer humanity. We are 'at play' here, in our officially allotted space and time: like anyone who's ever got into their groove in a moment like this, no matter your age or stage in life, you wish that it would never end.

Part of the premise of this book is that, indeed, our play time should never end – because to play is to express one's full humanity in a self-conscious and complex way. And who wouldn't want to play incessantly at that game? The urgency of the play ethic comes from the realization that a ludic civilization isn't just conceptually thinkable, but materially possible too. Who could seriously claim, in the midst of early twenty-first-century technoculture – which regularly promises us a world of resources, facilities and knowledge, and largely delivers – that we live in a world of scarcity?[1] And where there is no scarcity, no pressure to get resources and defend them bitterly, then the spirit of play – flexible, excessive, unpredictable – can flourish.

Whether in education or family life, the arts or technology, the office or the marketplace, in this book I've tried to show that our continuing self-definition as 'workers', and our lingering attachment to the dignities of the work ethic, have severely clouded our vision. The legacy of the work ethic obscures our recognition of the burgeoning richness and deeply generative power of early twenty-first-century life. And along the way, I've suggested ways in which we might begin to reform our institutions, and recalibrate our mentalities, to allow our human natures to fully express their potential.

Yet how exactly do we build our societal playground? In the age of workers, we collectively asserted our need for respite and recreation, wresting resources from the grip of industrialism. In a society where players are the primary agents of progress, we will need a new kind of collective commitment, one that can support the broad spectrum of human activities and purposes implied by a comprehensive understanding of play. And if we think of our actually existing playgrounds, we can begin to identify what the 'grounds of play' – in an structural and political sense – might be.

We need the *space* to play; we need the *time* to play; and we need *materials* to play with. And of course, we need *other people* around us, ready and willing to play too. These have specific policy consequences:

- **Play materials** We need to reimagine what we regard as our collective resources, our 'common wealth,' in the light of information technology and find a way whereby we can truly reap the benefits of our extraordinary productive powers.

- **Play time** and **Play space** We need to move from a 'welfare' system that provides our 'social security' to a new supportive system that unleashes our 'social autonomy' – specifically through a citizens' income, a reduction of employed hours and an epochal level of investment in education and public amenities.

• **Play people** We need to innovate new political forms – new ways of reciprocating and deliberating with our fellow human beings, not just within nations or continents, but globally, too. We need a 'creative democracy' that reanimates our political desires and makes us active players in shaping our societies and networks.

It's not difficult to imagine a policy platform for the play ethic in twenty-first-century Europe. So much of its essential argument – that work should be 'decentred' from its dominant ethical position in society and placed in context with other, equally value-adding activities – is already accepted, and has in some places been implemented. When the political philosopher Jurgen Habermas (a major influence on the Social Democratic Party in Germany) talks of 'conserving the great democratic achievements of the European nation-state, beyond its own limits', or when the recent French Prime Minister Lionel Jospin spoke of 'market economy, not market society', both drew some kind of line between a civilization entirely defined by work, and one in which the '*arts de vivre*' – the arts of living – are many and varied.[2]

Yet it's to the US that we turn first for our initial uncovering of the grounds of play: the digital commons revealed by the Net, and the acute need to defend these unexpected new resources.

Play materials: the comedy of the commons

They hang the man and flog the woman
That steal the good from off the common
But let the greater villain loose
That steals the common from the goose
Traditional nursery rhyme

Lawrence Lessig – professor of cyberlaw at Stanford University, scourge of Microsoft and hero to a generation of hackers – is a sight to see. If anyone wanted to draw a living cartoon of the uber-nerd, here he is: imposing forehead, tall and awkward, forensic eyes behind pebble-sized glasses. We met in the lobby of a broken-down TV warehouse in the outer hills of San Francisco. Lessig had just been grilled by a typically Bay Area phenomenon called Tech TV, where stocky men in designer kilts conducted long phone-ins about Web server software. And as we repaired to a Starbucks – wirelessly enabled, so that every table had two, sometimes three people murmuring at each other over their connected iBooks and PDAs – I readied myself for the narrow disquisitions of an academic.

Yet what I actually came away with was my first real sense that there was a tangible, contestable politics to the play ethic. There could be institutions and traditions to create and defend, and a political rhetoric to mobilize players around clear goals and targets.

Lessig's passion is to make the digital community realize that it didn't just build a communications network, it also built what he calls an 'architecture of values'.[3] The point about the Internet is that it is an 'end-to-end' structure: the most intelligent and autonomous parts of the Net are at its edges, not its centre – the structure simply ensures the transmission of rich packets of information, composed on powerful PCs by bright human users. The structure of the Net turns out to be, in a new casting of old language, a 'dot-commons' – a resource available to anyone who agrees to obey the rules that govern its use. A street, a public park, a river, a library: these are examples of 'the commons' – a shared resource to which everyone has equal access.[4]

In *The Future of Ideas*, Lessig explains further:

> Commons are features of all cultures. They have been especially important to cultures outside the United States – from communal tenure systems in Switzerland and Japan to irrigation communities within the Philippines. But within American intellectual culture, commons are treated as imperfect resources. They are the object of 'tragedy,' as ecologist Garrett Hardin famously described. Wherever a commons exists, the aim is to enclose it. In the American psyche, commons are unnecessary vestiges from times past and best removed, if possible.
>
> For most resources, for most of the time, the bias against commons makes good sense. When resources are left in common, individuals may be driven to overconsume, and therefore deplete them. But for some resources the bias against commons is blinding. Some resources are not subject to the 'tragedy of the commons' because some resources cannot be 'depleted'. (No matter how much we use Einstein's theories of relativity or copy Robert Frost's poem '*New Hampshire*', [they] will survive.) For these resources, the challenge is to induce provision, not to avoid depletion.[5]

For Lessig, the Net proves that there can be a 'comedy of the commons' for the simple reason that, while land, or oil, or forests are finite resources, information is essentially infinite.[6] Indeed, the more the Net is used, the more wealth, value and content is generated within its realm. It follows, for Lessig, that the over-zealous 'copyrighting' of the Net – that vision beloved of the major media conglomerates, where every click of down-loaded content can be charged for – destroys the very basis of the Web's innovation and vigour. So much creativity has flourished around the Web exactly because of the 'common' nature of its realm. In a real sense, every-one gets to be a 'player' on the Web: its common protocols give the pri-vate individual and the state department, the small trader and the global conglomerate, the same surface on which to pitch their tents.

Into his stride (and ignoring his eggnog latte), Lessig compared the situation with the road system. 'When the highways were built in America, did we decide that only Henry Ford's or General Motors' cars could run on them? Did we engineer the roads so that it was impossible for any other car – a Japanese car, a public bus, whatever – to drive on it? No. So we should be wary of media corporations who want to do exactly the same thing to our information superhighway – which is to limit the diversity and originality of traffic that can move through it, so that they can control the revenue from their intellectual property way beyond a proper limit. I'm not against capitalism, in its right place – in fact, I'm for that entrepreneurial, bottom-up excitement of the classic days of the Web. What I'm against are capitalists who want to own the roads.'

Lessig was very clear about how this was also a play politics. 'Look at the Apple Mac ideal, the line they promote with their technology – that you can create your own culture, or remix existing culture, use your com-puter as an expressive tool. "Rip, mix, burn" – that's the slogan. Now that's a kind of play activity that we should be supporting as a society – people being able to recombine new and existing material into compelling new visions and artworks, even products and services. The Founding Fathers of the US Constitution would have been horrified at the way in which copy-right is being extended to attack this creative culture, ensuring that all copyrighted materials are tied to their producers almost for eternity.'

Lessig told an apposite story. 'You know the book *Gone With the Wind*, by Margaret Mitchell? Sold countless millions of copies, only marginally less than the Bible. Her copyright should only have had fifty-six years of protection, but Congress decides to extend it almost perpetually, until 2032. An African-American woman writer called Alice Randall had a somewhat different view of African slavery from Ms Mitchell. So she decided to write *The Wind Done Gone* in 1997 – taking the same story, but telling it from the perspective of an African slave. Which is, of course, not a pleasant picture.

'She goes to publish it – but the Mitchell estate contacts her publisher, Houghton Mifflin, to say that Randall doesn't have the permission to do this. "This is our work, we own rights and we will not give you permission to publish a book that will embarrass the Margaret Mitchell estate." The court issues an injunction against the publishers, telling them they have to pulp the books. So here we are in the US – threatening to burn books!'[7]

'The case eventually went to the Court of Appeal, who reversed the decision under the notion of fair use. But in order for her to tell her story to the public, Randall had to hire a bunch of lawyers who were ready to spend a year litigating in the courts to defend her rights to publish a criticism of a story that was published almost, say, seventy years ago – for which the original author had already been paid.'[8]

In the case of Napster, the music-distribution service shut down by major music business laywers in 2001,[9] Lessig disagrees that the debate was about property versus theft – that is, artists and companies losing revenue to pirates and freeloaders. It was much more about an old business model trying to squash a new one. 'Napster never stood for the idea that artists should not be paid. The battle was about breaking up a very controlling and concentrated system for producing and distributing art. When five major corporations control 85 per cent of sales, that's a deeply sick market – and sick artistic decisions are getting made in that. The real challenge of peer-to-peer music sharing was this: how could you begin to produce artists and distribution in a different way? The president of Napster said, "We wanna pay for the music, so give us a compulsory licensing right. We'll pay for everything we facilitate the download of, but at least we'll have the right to get access to the music, because no labels are allowing that"'[10]

'Under that right, you'd have ten different companies develop, and those ten companies – like, say, MP3.com – would be keen not just to facilitate ways of distributing music, but also ways of producing new artists. These artists could begin to promote their art in new ways – not only through *Billboard*, *Rolling Stone* and MTV, but maybe through "preference technology", saying if you like this artist, you'll like that one, etc. A more "bottom-up" way of promotion. In that world, you've got greater competition to produce art, much greater diversity for artists, and much better deals for artists in general – they'll get paid more, not less.[11]

'My argument is not that we should have no copyright, that bands should be selling T-shirts instead of songs. It's just that the expansion of rights that exists now gives a few people the right to veto a certain development of culture – and that's wrong.'

Lessig was anxious that his position shouldn't be rendered as left versus right, but rather as old versus new. 'It's important that we don't think about these issues from a purely radical, anarchist/communist perspective to justify a play culture – we have to defend it in an appropriate way. The point is to mix the politics up, so people don't think they've heard this before, as something from the sixties and seventies. It's something different – it's about enabling creativity from the grass roots up. In America, in this tradition and culture, that's an important value we should be able to identify with.[12]

'We spent years fighting against the totalitarian menace – and now we have to fight against our own oppressive dinosaurs, who want to control the course of evolution of our digital culture. And what happens when you let dinosaurs control evolution? I can assure you that you won't end up with humans.'[13]

Lessig's legalistic passion for the foresight of his nation's founding fathers can only be admired. In his account, eighteenth-century Enlightenment wisdom still allows twenty-first-century Gen-Y dudes to 'rip, mix and burn', to play freely with their culture in the dot-commons. Indeed, one reviewer has called him the 'Paul Revere' of the Internet, crying out to anyone who'll listen that the Redcoats (or as he would put it, the 'totalitarian corporations') are coming to enclose your expressive freedoms.[14]

As a lawyer deeply in love with his own nation's civic inventiveness, Lessig's next response has been to do something that de Tocqueville would have recognized from his nineteenth-century observations of American democracy: that is, build his own institution – literally, a welcome house for players. Creativecommons.org is intended to be a space where creatives in all genres can make their own decisions about how commodified they wish their creations to be. 'Just like the hackers with Linux and other kinds of open-source coding, I think that many artists will want to experiment with the balance between ubiquity and exclusivity – how much they give their rights of use away to get themselves into the culture, and how much they might want to claw back in royalties. I think that's a decision for the artist and creator, not a huge complex of corporations, Congress and lawyers.'[15]

Lessig mentions his friend Brewster Kahle, who is also building another classic kind of institutional commons: a library. Except this library contains every page ever published on the Web since 1996, and is accessible to anyone who wants to search for a particular Web address.[16]

These are self-conscious 'defenders of the information commons' – and there will no doubt be many others to come. What the Internet has revealed is a truth we have long forgotten: that the 'commonwealth' is just as contributory to our well-being as our properties and enclosures.[17] As Lessig says, the Internet was consciously and willingly constructed as an 'innovation commons' – a shared architecture of code and values that encouraged as much creativity and experiment to flow through from its users as possible.

The question begged is obvious. If this realm was built according to a value-driven vision, can similar kinds of 'innovation commons' be built in other areas of human sociality – in education, health and welfare, science, the arts, perhaps even political democracy? How can we take the ethos of play that marks the Net and extend it to other spaces, structures and social architectures?

It's tempting to suggest that the spate of vibrant and innovative 'commons' thinking coming out of the US is partly fuelled by their impoverished and embattled sense of the public sector.[18] In the UK and Europe, there is a point where the notion of commons and state positively meet and interact. Between the remaining aspirations of the welfare state and social democracy to provide 'public services free at the point of use', and the notion of a commons that exists in a space between state and market, a mutual resource (whether rivalrous or not) tended to by active citizens, there is fertile ground.

Much of my ambivalence about the New Labour government in Britain comes from their partial recognition that some new 'innovation commons' – what Lessig also calls 'architectures of value' – do need to be built.[19] Certainly, the deployment of one form of playful energy – the love of chance that goes into mass participation in a national lottery – has resulted in the funding of some exemplary players' spaces through the various lottery funding bodies. The Tate Modern is the most notable, but there are many others (Newcastle's Baltic, Dundee's DCA, the creative sectors in Manchester and Sheffield) which qualify as creative common spaces, providing open agoras for city dwellers to meet and be stimulated by each other.[20]

The BBC has already been noted as an active constructor of 'play spaces' for the arts, along various stretches of the new digital and satellite bandwidths.[21] Indeed, much of the complaint about the BBC from its private sector competitors is that it is being *too* innovative with the commons.[22] With its budgets secured for several years under a state-run 'poll tax' – where every citizen who watches or owns a television must pay their license fee – the BBC has invested heavily in areas like its Internet operation BBCi, which is beginning to set a global standard for the open distribution of broadcast resources.

In the middle of 2003, this state-run broadcaster took the next obvious step and embraced the essential principles of commons thinking. Greg Dyke, its then Director-General, took the high-profile lecture at the Edinburgh Television Festival to announce the BBC's new creative archive – an online service that would make the thousands of programmes in the Corporation archives available to non-commercial users.[23] Reportedly inspired by conversations with Lawrence Lessig, the BBC intends the archive to be part of a more general 'peer-to-peer' approach to media in the future – where viewers should have the power to play with a broadcasters' material as freely as any other material on the Web.[24]

Furthermore, the forthcoming BBC service 'iCan' attempts to fuse Internet activism with normal television viewing patterns. The notion is that any programme evidently dealing with civic issues that might require further investigation by viewers can have its instant back-up: a button on the channel changer promises to open up a whole screen full of information, links and forums, giving the 'passive' viewer the option to be instantly 'active' in relation to what they've just seen.[25] I first heard about iCan at a conference in London, sitting beside a friend of mine who has been toiling for some years now to get NGOs interested in exactly this kind of 'social software'.[26] As the corporation's expensive and expansive plans rolled across the conference screen, he muttered a very audible imprecation: 'Bastards!' After a beat, he turned to me. 'What this really means is the BBC Can – but *I* can't.' Much of the subsequent conference comment focused on whether the BBC had a right to 'colonize' network activism in this way.[27]

Should we be churlish when parts of the state actually respond to a players' agenda? No, we shouldn't. But I'm more concerned that players shouldn't be waiting for government to 'enable' their activities, whether through direct funding or the indirect provision of infrastructure.[28] Indeed, with the BBC, it's the pressure of the soulitariat and the digital generation – whether they're hacking with open source or just channel changing furiously – that has given them the excuse to be so radical.

At minimum, the relationship between a play politics and the state should indeed be healthily tense. Official systems of power and money need to be constantly challenged by the spontaneous, spiky, self-determined activities of our 'life worlds' (the day-to-day doings of players in urban and suburban spaces).[29] We may not yet be able to identify all the kinds of 'common wealths', the spaces and architectures for free activity, that would be the political target of a play ethic. (Though those open-source mantras of 'share the goal, share the work, share the result' are beginning to migrate to other areas of society, like health, design and law.)[30] But we can make sure that the mental spaces for thinking and dreaming these futures are as open as possible. That, at least, is a domain which citizen players already occupy, and can defend with skill, articulacy and passion.

Play time: pushing back the dominion of work

So if we already have, to some extent, a 'communication commons' – ever more open to intervention and politics – then what are the socio-economic agendas that players should be pursuing to amass a constituency for their interests?[31] The first policy position would be to argue for a systematic and across-the-board reduction of working hours – initially to the thirty-five hours a week recently established by the French government, and eventually proceeding towards an ultimate target of between twenty and twenty-five hours.

From the very earliest organized protests against the mass mechanization of production, it's been understood that industrial technology held out a great promise – the minimization of 'necessary labour'.[32]

The increasing graph of productivity – machines helping humans to do more for less effort – seemed in the late nineteenth and early twentieth centuries to point towards a transformed society: a utopia where work, not leisure or recreation, would become the scarce commodity. As recently as the 1970s, thinkers and academics were worrying about the 'leisure crisis'.[33] So how did we get to our current anxiety about long working hours, when our society seems ever more technologically strident and transformatory than ever before?

One strong argument comes from the writer Richard Reeves, who argues that the desire for a shorter working week founders on the fact that work itself is moving in an ever less alienated direction. The extension of work into private life – through mobile phones in the street, networked computers in the home and so on – is understandable, says Reeves. Both our sense of community and our sense of meaning are increasingly satisfied by informational work which demands our creativity, our imagination and our empathy.[34]

After the success of the vicious but brilliant British sitcom *The Office*, it must be hard for any writer to claim that work provides a better sense of human connectedness than any other realm of experience. And much of the intent of this book has been to validate a whole range of non-working or counter-working realms – the full rhetorics of play – as equally legitimate ways of making a 'dent in the universe'.

As the steady curve of automation and acceleration of material processes impacts on our daily experience, we know that there is world enough, and time, to fully explore our own playful identities. Madeleine Bunting's acutely observed UK statistic – that more time is lost to the 'sickie' than was ever lost in the heyday of industrial dispute in the seventies – is a sign that the revolt against work is already under way in an individualized but concerted fashion: a silent collective withdrawal from the necessities of work which we would not do out of free choice.[35] But does it always have to be made in private, covertly, in bad faith and through evasion? Or could governments and business see the writing on the wall and concede the inevitable – that the ever more potentialized and individualized 'worker' wants to put work in its place; only '*one* of the moments of existence, and not a forced labour, nor the source of a permanent identity,' writes Paolo Virno.[36]

The work–life balancers concede that ceilings on working hours might well have a beneficial effect on productivity in jobs that exist. Such is the experience in France during its thirty-five-hour-week experiment.[37] (Part of the free-time bounty in France is also, delightfully, a reversal of their population decline: the shorter working week coincided with a sharp spike in the birth rate. No matter the form of familial play, French citizens were making the most of their hours.)[38] And even in America, there are regular stories of enlightened capitalists realizing that a shorter work week – along with a huge range of other pastoral benefits – can mean long-term profitability. SAS, the world's largest privately owned software firm, was featured on CBS's flagship documentary programme *60 Minutes* in April 2003:

> The company encourages people to get their work done in a thirty-five-hour week. All adhere strictly to the SAS dress code, which is no code. Laid back is the unofficial posture here, and convenience the motto – along with other perks such as onsite car detailing, a putting green and, of course, the masseur. The author of all this pampering is Jim Goodnight, a lanky, laconic billionaire, the co-founder and CEO of SAS. 'What's wrong with treating your people good?' asks Goodnight. 'All I can say is it's worked for us.'[39]

SAS is that 'company as home' that the Gores issued their faint warning about in Chapter Five, and that writers like Richard Reeves would swoon over. The ever shorter working week is the only serious response to our intensifying quest for a culture of relationships, stretching throughout the domains of our lives.[40] The virtuous circle – as SAS patently realize – is that harnessing this new sensitivity to human need and desire will undoubtedly improve the commercial performance of the company. The lifestyle-friendly company, with its crèches and gyms, in-house therapists and artists, sees these measures as a spur to productivity, not a barrier to it.

Yet the ambition of the play ethic for work is far more than just oiling the wheels of existing operations. As Goodnight says astutely, 'I guess 95 per cent of my assets drive out of the front gate every evening. It's my job to bring them back.' The more that self-determination is experienced in the free time and the common space of the new public playgrounds, the more that work will transform out of all recognition – and perhaps become politicized in an entirely new way. As Bunting notes, when early-twentieth-century American industrialists considered shortening their working week, 'They were often worried that workers with time on their hands would get mixed up in politics. Work them hard and keep them exhausted and, the thinking went, they would be less likely to have spare time for trade union meetings.'[41] Henry Ford reasoned they'd have more time to buy stuff, and for most of the consumerist twentieth century he was proved right.

Yet the question of who SAS might make software *for* – as it turns out, everyone from the US military to Victoria's Secret – would barely push its way through the cocoon of this company's culture. 'I've been here thirteen years and it's not too much yet. I think it's a good thing,' says Britt, an SAS worker who's off to the pool with her two kids, picked up from SAS childcare. 'Sometimes it does sort of feel like Disney World, but everybody likes Disney World, you know? That's good.'[42]

The company as theme park/leisure complex is clearly one way to arrange many of play's most powerful forms (play as development, play as community, play as fun) in a way that insulates many workers from its more dynamic elements (play as power, play as free thinking, play as the acceptance of openness and chance).[43] Yet the encouragement to a thirty-five-hour week is a clever move – cleverer than St Luke's, for example, requesting total commitment for complete security. SAS's human resource manager Jeff Chambers says, 'You can use all the perks, the many we have available . . . you can use none of them. The culture's very accepting that if you want to just show up, do your job and collect a paycheck, that's fine. But it's all here for you, if you want to use it.'

So the model capitalist company seeks not only to provide a sustaining infrastructure while at work, but also to keep an eye to reducing working hours – in order that the worker's autonomy is respected. Might enlightened business be a likelier ally in the push for more free and self-directed time than behaviour-obsessed governments? Certainly, the latest business thinking implicitly presumes that the 'full player' – seeking the space, and the time, to realize the creative potential of their lives – represents the future norm of both producers and consumers. And it is pumping all pistons to find a way to keep them within the commercial net.

Shoshana Zuboff and James Maxmin's *The Support Economy* makes a self-consciously revolutionary bid for a completely different model of capitalism – one that recognizes the 'psychological sovereignty' of twenty-first-century men and women. To 'service the customer' is not enough for these lifestyle militants; they need 'deep support' by companies, so that they can 'live the lives they choose':

Today's people are pioneering a new approach to consumption that we call the individuation of consumption. They want to be treated as individuals, not as anonymous transactions in the ledgers of mass consumption. They want to be heard and they want to matter. They no longer want to be the objects of commerce. Instead, they want corporations to bend to their needs. They want to be freed from the time-consuming stress, rage, injustice and personal defeat that accompany so many commercial exchanges. They seek advocacy in place of adversarialism, relationships in place of transactions. They want to take their lives in their own hands and they are willing to pay for what we call the deep support that will enable them to do so.[44]

One is tempted to rephrase Oscar Wilde's classic phrase about socialism. The new consumerism would clearly take up too many evenings, bonding with one's retail 'deep supporter' on the multimedia broadband. There is something faintly desperate about this vision of capitalism moulding itself around these 'psychological sovereigns' – particularly as the explicit context for the book is the popular disillusion with capitalism after Enron. The prospect of players using their bandwidth to spend the 'social currency' of friendship and mutual interests, perhaps more avidly than they would spend hard cash, clearly requires a drastic, neo-socialist response.[45] The Indian-born business thinker C.K. Prahalad puts it much more starkly. This new 'co-creation of value' between business and consumer, part of an 'emergent social and cultural fabric', means a huge shift in the logic of enterprise: 'Companies spent the twentieth century managing efficiencies. They must spend the twenty-first century managing experiences.'[46]

Rhetoric like this is guaranteed to ring the alarm bells of critics like Naomi Klein, Douglas Rushkoff and Jeremy Rifkin who warn of the attempt to commercialize all human experience through complex branding, real-time monitoring of customer responses and the themeing of the built environment.[47] A world 'where all life is a paid-for experience', as Rifkin's book title puts it. If there is free time, it only means 'free to consume'.[48]

So would more free time just deliver us over wholesale to ever more seductive 'experience' capitalists? This depends on whether our stories about ourselves are about agency, critique and energy, rather than a bedlam of fun and frolics – that is, about being active players rather than 'leisure classes'. Indeed, these players might respond to experience management with an even greater desire to manage experiences of their own kind. The techno-spiritual writer Erik Davis calls advertising and marketing the 'right wing of experience design': its aim is to create 'an instinctive, un-self-aware subject whose inchoate fears and desires are organized around commodities or institutions'. By comparison, the psychological explorations of media artists and spiritual literates are the 'liberal left wing' of experience design – they use their consciousness as a 'mode of expression, communication and confrontation'. The players' mentality, exactly.[49]

So from the financial bottom line to the expanding demands of our consciousness, there is much to support the reduction of working hours. The politics of the play ethic might rest satisfied with this level of enlightened regulation of capitalism.[50] The ideal role for work in the play ethic is as the means of reproducing the resources and infrastructures that support a complex society – but no more than that. Work becomes the point at which society asks that our potential for action and intention become temporarily limited and exploited, for collective benefit.

But an infinite player always looks for a way to continue the game, rather than seek a victory. Let's head for another horizon: the social wage.

Play space: the social income

When will we genuinely reap the benefits of our ever-rising techno-economic productivity? How far can we keep devising ever more efficient and ingenious ways to extract meaning and energy from our natural resources – whether they be mental or material, cultural or physical – without seriously considering the radical option? Which is: a guaranteed income, or social wage, well above the poverty line.

This would seem like the ultimate proof of the play ethic's impractical nature. Yet we have already looked at arguments from radical thinkers in social services who argue that a citizens' income might be a way to encourage genuine, 'bottom-up' social activism, to build a caring society from the grass roots.[51] A range of thinkers from across the disciplines have come to the same policy conclusion: that we simply cannot cope with the necessary and structural chaos of the information age without a completely new conception of collective welfare.

History brings us yet another confirmation that times of upheaval and revolution are the most hospitable to the deep values of play. The first-ever mention of the notion of a 'citizens' income' was in a pamphlet by the American radical Tom Paine, *1796's Agrarian Justice*. For one thing, Paine's argument shows that the notion of the commons was alive at the very beginning of the democratic experiment in America:

It is wrong to say that God made Rich and Poor; he made only Male and Female, and he gave them the earth for their inheritance . . . [the earth is] THE COMMON PROPERTY OF THE HUMAN RACE . . . Cultivation is at least one of the greatest natural improvements ever made by human invention. It has given to created earth a tenfold value. But the landed monopoly that began with it has produced the greatest evil. It has dispossessed more than half the inhabitants of every nation of their natural inheritance, without providing for them, as ought to have been done, an indemnification for that loss, and has thereby created a species of poverty and wretchedness that did not exist before.[52]

Like any decent modern reformer, Paine was keen to release his big idea in the 'heavenly opening' of post-Revolutionary America. His 'national fund', as Paine's biographer John Keane glosses, was primarily about defending 'citizens' *social* rights'. Like Lawrence Lessig, furiously trying to defend his innovation commons from both dot-capitalists and dot-communists, Paine saw the idea of a citizen's income as a mediator of necessary tensions.[53]

It is startling to realize just how consistent the position has been, from the eighteenth century to the twenty-first, on the essential reasons for a social wage. That is, as a means of securing our freedom and autonomy in the face of the 'self-destructive dynamism' of modern capitalism – a capitalism which, left to its own devices, enables some and disables others from full participation in shaping their social lives.

Thus we can turn to several substantial thinkers writing in the late nineties, both European and American, whose arguments for a social wage are no less essentially republican than Paine's – and who suggest it as the only sane response to the upheavals of our own, twenty-first-century modernity. The German sociologist Ulrich Beck, in *The Brave New World of Work*, written in 2000, sketches out a familiar landscape of an information capitalism that is dissolving the work ethic into a million fragments under the pressures of global markets, individualism and new technology. Yet must we simply live chaotically among the fragments, divided into the compulsorily over-worked or the compulsorily over-leisured? Beck says no: but 'those who wish to escape the spell of the work society must enter political society' – a place of *multi-activity*, in our families, communities, organizations and pastimes, and not a leisure zone.[54]

The basis of this new political society after the work ethic is what Beck calls 'civil labour'. He defines it as 'a state-approved exit from the market . . . Space is opened here for democratic society, as citizens give their own chosen form to themselves.' Though Beck clings to the idea of a redeemed 'work' all the way through his book, it's easy to separate a play-ful vocabulary and values from his labourist mindset.

Civil labour, as a publicly subsidized realm of non-market activism, makes community life 'more colourful and controversial' – carnivalesque, in play-ethical terms. Civil labour has, like many forms of play, a strongly voluntary element: it should 'by no means be confused with the pressure being put everywhere on benefit claimants to undertake work in the com-munity'. Civil labour is also a kind of 'organized, creative disobedience' and social 'experimentation'. When Beck comes to the issue of who should provide the resources for this realm, he is deliberately eclectic – a mixture of state and private funds, enterprising charities and light-touch public ser-vices, payment made in cash and in kind. The aim of civic money (Beck's terms for the citizens' income) is to 'establish the conditions in which democracy can be given new life, and can be acted out in people's lives, where there is no longer full employment'. Beck doesn't base his argument for a social wage upon freeing the poor from poverty, but upon the pos-sibility of attaining 'the republican ideal of a self-active civil society responsible for its own affairs'.[55]

Further to this, the veteran post-industrial utopian Andre Gorz develops three main justifications for a social wage in his most recent book, *Reclaiming Work*.[56] Firstly, because imagination, intelligence and emo-tional commitment are becoming the very 'means of production', it is very difficult to say when people are 'at work' or not 'at work'. When one comes up with a great idea, a boost to the spirits or an ideal solution while walk-ing in the park on Sunday, is one really 'at work'? Should we resent the fact that this innovation or inspiration comes to us in our 'leisure' time – or should we accept that, at our best, info-citizens are 'in play' and 'at play' all the time? The social wage becomes a recognition that this kind of mental and emotional 'labour' goes on incessantly, everywhere, and that this collective creativity needs a collective reward.

Gorz's second justification is that a guaranteed sufficient income grants people their full voluntary freedom to make their own kind of 'exit' from market society, rather than being redirected into 'third-sector' jobs that only pay support for 'socially useful' activities. Gorz says that what we should be recognizing is the value in 'activities which derive from being done for their own sake' – and that can include artistic, spiritual or self-development activities, as well as those oriented towards mutual help and social support.

Thirdly, for Gorz, a social wage actually goes with the grain of informational capitalism, in its need for ever more innovative people (even though it fears their autonomy). What the combination of free time and social income does is to 'enable individuals to develop capacities (of invention, creation, conception and intellection) which give them a virtually unlimited productivity'. The amount of training and reskilling now prevalent in companies thus becomes secularized, made into a common provision.[57]

Gorz's three justifications provoke a vision of experimental, multi-disciplinary, unalienated 'work', engaging a multiplicity of intelligences and skills.[58] They are so close to this book's understanding of play that the difference seems almost neglible.[59]

The American 'radical centrist' writer Michael Lind agrees that a high level of basic income is a 'jobs destroyer', giving employers 'an incentive to reduce their labour costs by replacing workers with more sophisticated machinery'. But he utters a most heretical thought: 'What's wrong with technological unemployment?'[60] Substituting technology for human and animal labour is 'the basis of the prosperity of advanced societies'. Lind notes that in 1800 almost everybody was a farmer, while in 2002 hardly anyone is – but all developed countries produce far more food per capita than they did 200 years ago. Yet in the service sector, too, automation is advancing and, as Lind says, quite rightly. When labour shortages in some parts of the US in the late 1990s forced grocery stores to replace cashiers with automated checkout machines, supervised by a technician, we caught a glimpse of the next wave of human replacement by machines – one that will undoubtedly extend to call centres, financial services and other standard service jobs, all susceptible to increasingly advanced automation.

If semi-skilled workers are progressively replaced by machines, where else might they find employment? Lind notes the rise in need for caring services, fuelled by both our new third and fourth agers, and our rising expectations for our health, as a possible arena. (However, his central point is far more hard-headed than this: raising labour costs compels greater automation in companies – and greater levels of automation put national communities in the forefront of global development.) Lind's argument is framed within the context of the raising of the minimum wage in America, but it also pertains to the question of how we might collectively determine the effect of something like a social wage or basic income.[61] 'By creating an incentive for employers to replace workers with robots and computers, a living wage would ultimately benefit all Americans, thanks to the spillover impact of technological progress in various industries.'[62]

There is much to debate about a social wage: the manner and timing of its introduction; the need to ensure that it takes place across a federal or confederal polity and economy (Europe is the classic test case, and particularly in terms of migration); devising the best systemic and bureaucratic solutions to its distribution and pick-up.[63] Yet the real challenge is at a much deeper, even metaphyscial level.

The Puritan presumption that the 'devil makes work for idle hands' is not just repressive, but also completely misdescribes human nature and culture at the start of this century. We already have bountiful evidence that our play can add value in a multitude of ways. Indeed, the grandest sciences now subvert the very tenets of Puritan self-loathing, that hatred of human fecundity which makes it such an opponent of play. John Calvin once memorably put it:

> If God had formed us of the stuff of the sun or the stars, or if he had created any other celestial matter out of which man could have been made, then we might have said that our beginning was honourable . . . But we are all made of mud, and this mud is not just on the hem of our gown, or on the sole of our boots, or in our shoes. We are full of it, we are nothing but mud and filth both inside and outside.[64]

Yet as Theodore Roszak points out, contemporary cosmology and biology tells us that we were precisely 'formed of the stuff of the sun or stars'. Within the Puritan logic, it follows that our material beginnings are deeply 'honourable'. To play is to express that honour, through fecundity and diversity. The challenge of shaping new institutions around our playful natures must stem from a deep shift in our evaluation of our human potential. From filth and mud, as it were, to sun and stars.

So to escape the Puritan mindset is the essential task. The question of how we establish the grounds of play then becomes a matter of political innovation and collective design. A social wage is at least worth exploring as an element of that grounding.

Play people: towards a creative democracy

The anti-corporate campaigner Susan George recently coined a fascinating new acronym. Free marketeers in the seventies and eighties were fond of proclaiming TINA – 'there is no alternative' – to a neo-liberal capitalism, which presumed that turning all of life into a commoditized experience was an unquestioned benefit. By contrast, and in the context of the new global social justice movements spanning the juncture of the twentieth and twenty-first centuries, George has suggested that we think of TATA – 'there are thousands of alternatives'. TATA suggests that there are many alternative ways for human beings to exchange goods and services, to conceive of and develop their productivity, to deploy their ingenuities, understandings and passions, than the standard capitalist globalizer's model.[65]

Yet the shift from TINA to TATA is also a supersession of the whole paradigm that underlies a work-centric society. A world in which there are thousands of models for human progress is a world in which the play drive is given centrality – our natural propensity to try and multiply our options for survival, by imagining and then enacting our possible futures. We will live in a players' republic when the overarching political structures encourage a culture of *creative democracy* – that is, a presumption that the will of human groups can be manifested in more ways than the model of one person, one vote, in periodic referenda.[66]

The third way to play?

In many ways, the greatest achievement of the work ethic was the postwar Western welfare state. Here, universally provided and democratically available, was the moral promise of work turned into reality. As a reward for subjecting yourself to the stupefying divisions of industrial labour, the basic securities of life were guaranteed: housing, health, the education of your children, the provision of public amenities for leisure and recreation and a modicum of support when capitalism – or at least, your company's part of it – failed to sustain its forward momentum.[67]

From the beginning of the labour movement in the nineteenth century to the pre-Elvis years of the mid-fifties, workers could feel they were part of a progressive raising of the standards of their lives. Yet as consumerism became ever more an expression of individual choice, an obscure sense of disappointment began to suffuse the proletarian unconscious. Was there always to be this gulf between the intense dreams of consumer culture and the dull routines of production? This angst produced its positive form in the sixties counterculture – promising (and beginning to deliver) liberation for youth, non-whites, women. And then, in one of the great accidents of history, hippie values fused with military science, creating the PC and the Internet, the basic tools of a networked society. When the oil crisis of 1973 happened and the entire energy basis of Western market democracy was put under threat, it spurred both the dissolution of our sense of social security – and the acceleration of the means of social complexity.[68]

Punk rock exploded under a social-democratic government that was rapidly losing legitimacy amongst its worker-citizens: and when Margaret Thatcher declared that there was 'no such thing as society, only individuals and families', she was only ringing her own changes on the sheer negation of collectivity that punk values had already proclaimed.[69] Thatcher promised not social 'security', but public order and private affluence. Yet cleverly, this order was regularly proclaimed to be besieged by enemies 'without' and 'within'. Order and affluence would be wonderful if achieved – but they were continually threatened by an explicit and driving social insecurity: the threat of crime, the abyss of 'dependancy'.[70]

In terms of our play rhetorics, the New Right reintroduced some of play's more ancient values into our lives – the role of competition and agonism as a way of creating social value; the need to open ourselves out to the chance and risk of a less-planned, less-predictable social universe. F.A. Hayek, in many ways the intellectual lodestar of the New Right, was also interested in play as a 'practice that led to the formation of . . . spontaneous order'.[71]

Yet the game play of the New Right was only what the intellectual precursors to New Labour called a 'regressive modernization'.[72] Thatcherism understood the dangerous, diversifying, self-creating individualism of a post-class, post-sexist, post-sixties society, and played a subtle game: unleashing some aspects of it, and constraining others. In terms of play rhetorics, the idea of careful, sustained and creative self-development – what the Blairites would later call 'education, education, education' – was rejected in favour of a learning purely geared to economic functionality.

The rhetoric of artistic expression and free imagination was frowned on, either through a moralistic attitude to art, or an active media censorship: free play in these areas was often resented and sometimes strictly policed (remember the Repetitive Beats Act?).[73] Play as authenticity and peak experience was much more problematic: Tories championed the rights of the individual, but not their right to unbridled hedonism and excess. The downfall of that government was almost certainly rooted in the 'back to basics' campaign of John Major – whose attempt to forge a common morality and ethic for Britons foundered on its perceived threat to the complexity and richness of modern lifestyles.[74]

Yet across the market democracies of the West over the last decade, the traditional political classes (and governmental functions) have faced these new 'flexi-humans', these sovereign psyches, and found them difficult to represent. I follow Manuel Castells's trinity of informationalism, feminism and environmentalism as the three great 'looseners' of industrial-age social roles and rituals.[75] As those three work out their societal logics, bringing more and more of the ability to 'style a life' to more and more men and women, the consequent social complexity will make politics as usual more and more difficult.

The Third Way solution was to set themselves a challenge: clever governments will find a way to balance 'economic dynamism' (a free-enterprise economy) with 'social cohesion' (a well-behaved and tractable society of worker-consumers). A revived 'work ethic' was the concept that would enable that balance. But as Third Way governments have risen, fallen or maintained their grip on power, one thing has become obvious: their guiding concepts are wrongly composed.

The problem of Western governments is now much more about trying to balance 'social dynamism' and 'economic cohesion', meaning the return of a much more regulated and integrated capitalism.[76] Play's diverse traditions shed a very interesting light on this tension between self-determination and collective governance, between bottom-up and top-down politics. As we know, the 'modern' definitions of play – post-Enlightenment, post-Romantic, post-psychology – are very much focused on the voluntary individual: play as an aid to development, as mental and semiotic freedom, as a realization of selfhood. The 'ancient' definitions of play are much less voluntary, much more collective, even more violent and dangerous: play as fate and chaos (gambling, luck, catastrophe – 'that's life'), play as power-and-contestation (politics, sport, war), play as collective identity (festivals, celebrations, events, mass audiences).

Contemporary governance has to be sensitive to both broad polarities of play's ambiguity – given that play forms, more than work forms, capture the behaviours and intentions of sovereign psyches. Take the ancient end of the play spectrum. As a strategy for governance, a 'New Ludenism' might ask: how can people be made ready for a chance-laden, unpredictable, endemically 'risky' society? How can they be encouraged to contest vigorously in the networks of modern life, to realize their identity as active and engaged human beings? And how and when can we feel that, although we're not sure where all this open-endedness and unpredictability is going, we're all in this together in some way?[77]

Most of this is consonant with much New Labour/New Democrat rhetoric of the nineties. On the modern side of play, the political 'modernizers' will recognize a lot too. In the UK, the efforts of cultural policy to ensure as much 'mental freedom' as possible – new national endowments, new and free museums, looser surveillance of musicians on benefit – ties in with play as imagination. Even the thrill-seeking player – the 'self-ist' – has been somewhat placated by the loosening of cannabis laws, by relaxations on sexual censorship, by the proliferation of media outlets.[78]

So has New Labour been evoking a ludic civilization – but just doesn't know it? Misrecognizing it, more like. If most of the modernizing virtues can be captured and described by the wide variety of play forms and traditions, then perhaps it's about time that modernizers become conscious of what they're doing and attend to the necessary pre-conditions of rich play. The energies, flexibilities and potentials of play are realized in play space and play time, with a security of play resources, and the presence of other players – that is, on the basis of a certain material, interpersonal and social security.

Yet recent world events have troubled what we might mean by a 'secure' society. There was a point not too long ago when the carnivals against capitalism looked as though they might force some lasting institutional reform, and very possibly a new governing logic. On the morning of 11 September 2001, the *Financial Times* – the capitalist tool to beat all capitalist tools – began a major investigative series on the protest movements. Its author James Harding began by explaining to his busy readers that the protestors' best instincts were not anti-capitalist, but 'counter-capitalist':

> It is as much a mood as a movement, something counter-cultural. It is driven by the suspicion that companies, forced by the stock markets to strive for ever greater profits, are pillaging the environment, destroying lives and failing to enrich the poor as they promised. And it is fuelled by the fear that

democracy has become powerless to stop them, as politicians are thought to be in the pockets of companies and international political institutions are slaves to a corporate agenda.[79]

The rest of the piece, and the subsequent articles, were a model of the *FT*'s journalism: accurate, representative, seeking to ascertain the truth behind the phenomenon. The series had been flagged up excitedly in preceding editions: I distinctly remember walking back from a school run in Glasgow that morning, reading the paper as I meandered to the office. I was excited that there seemed to be exactly that possibility of a 'new governing logic' opening up, right at the heart of capitalist consciousness. I was happily recalling that almost a year earlier, I had written about the possible positive relationship between the play ethic and the protest movements.[80]

And then, mid-read at my desk, I received a phone call from a gabbling friend before her television, like so many others on that September morning . . .

The *FT* series was pulled. In an article a few months later, Harding revisited the protestors, and reiterated his judgement: the 'movement of movements' was still a 'Fifth Estate', somewhat akin to the Fourth Estate of the news media: 'an unruly, unregulated and unaccountable check on corporations, politicians and the institutions of democracy'.[81] Harding's doubts about the ability of the movement to adapt to conditions of war have been answered by the range of global mass demonstrations around the Second Gulf War in 2003, which have been largely coordinated by 'counter-capitalist' protestors. Yet it's clear that 9/11 closed down the play of counter-capitalist possibilities that had been building since the original protests in 1999 – a play that has not been fully restored.

There is a bitter historical irony here. After years of lecturing to their populations about the benefits of opening themselves up to the creative destructions of the global free market, Western states are now indeed most solicitous about the 'social security' of their populations. Except that the parameters are now paranoia and fear, rather than a recommitment to the capacities and potentialities of their people. My desire in October 2000 for 'huge and visionary reinvestment in the public sector' is partly being answered – except it means more police on the streets, larger prisons and asylum apparatus and greater state surveillance of the info-commons.[82]

Is there any possibility that the leadership of the developed countries can govern in the direction of hope and play, rather than fear and control?[83] Tom Bentley, who is well acquainted with the possibilities of state government in his role as director of Demos, is gloomy:

> The irony, and perhaps the greatest obstacle [to reform], lies in recognizing that to achieve such a revolution our current generation of leaders need to make themselves redundant; that the techniques of control and command which they have used to take and retain power must give way to a more distributed, pluralistic and self-sustaining governing logic...[84]

A politician who governed in order to make him or herself redundant? The play ethic is a semi-utopian project. But it's not *that* utopian.

Playing the world game

Naomi Klein's book *No Logo* has rightly become the manifesto for a politics which rejects the play of signifiers – the branded logos and their seductive visions – in favour of the play of political forces. She attacks the hypocrisy behind the brand message of our seemingly hippest corporations. Although their marketing strategies preach the values and promulgate the images of diversity and democracy – Nike's Just Do It, Microsoft's Where Do you Want to Go Today? – their economic practices, both at home and abroad, act against diversity and democracy. Behind their dazzling post-modern displays, these 'brand bullies' distract from the poor labour conditions, anti-competitive cartelizations and sheer wastefulness that goes into the manufacture of a Gap top or Microsoft Office package.[85]

Klein has urged a new generation to say 'no logo' – to reject the brand. Her alternative is to suggest that they become *political* players, rather than just semiotic players. They should get concretely involved in building processes, institutions and commonalities which truly sustain the values of democracy and diversity, rather than just invoke them in an act of consumption.[86] Klein celebrates what she calls movements of 'self-determination' throughout the world, from the alternative summits of the World Social Forum in Porte Alegre to the cannabis-driven *centri sociale* of Milan, from the spontaneous municipalism of Argentinian communities in the wake of economic meltdown, to the south-east Asian protests against power and health policies, embodied in the activism of Arundhati Roi.[87]

From the perspective of a play politics, this movement of grass-roots, bottom-up democratic experiment is deeply encouraging. And indeed, with some of their activists, the ludic power of their activism is explicit and self-conscious. Anarchist David Graeber, writing in the *New Left Review*, outlines the rites and rituals of the protesters' 'carnivals against capitalism' – and says that they are 'attempting to invent what many call a "new language" of civil disobedience, combining elements of street theatre, festival and what can only be called non-violent warfare' – by which he means the variety of pranksterish behaviours in front of armed police, the costumed prancing and soft toy throwing typical of the usual protest. Yet this 'scrambling of the conventional categories' of street protest, this explicit deployment of play rhetorics, reveals a deeper point about the kind of society envisaged by the anti-corporate protesters.[88]

Graeber claims that the creativity and playfulness inherent in the protesters' activities is a kind of 'prefigurative politics' – a politics which gives people a tangible experience of the new society they are struggling for. In this sense, the protesters are practising a kind of 'adaptive potentiation', in the sense as defined by our general theory of play: they are testing out other worlds in their activities, yet not regarding any of these experiments as definitive programmes for social order.

So a play ethic would regard the experiments of the anti-corporate protesters as a fertile hinterland from which to draw new forms and styles of active humanity.[89] The title of Paul Kingsnorth's book on the worldwide activist movement sums it up well: *One No, Many Yesses*.[90] As Graeber says, even anarchism has something to teach those who want their organizations to be put in play, rather than torn down:

> This is a movement about reinventing democracy. It is not opposed to organization. It is about creating new forms of organization. It is not lacking in ideology. Those new forms of organization *are* its ideology. It is about creating and enacting horizontal networks instead of top-down structures like states, parties or corporations; networks based on principles of decentralized, non-hierarchical consensus democracy.[91]

So this is not the 'protest ethic' caricatured by traditional social-democrat writers – a kind of endless oppositionalism and resistance that sees no good in institutional life per se.[92] Yet I believe there needs to be a stronger connecting tissue between social-democratic and centrist political parties and administrations in the West, and the self-determinist, neo-anarchist movements that are beginning to straddle north and south.

Clearly, the players – in the most obvious sense – are taking the initiative in this. Observe the trajectory of Bono Vox, the lead singer of rock band U2: from Jubilee 2000 campaigner against global debt to hand-pumping confidant of tycoons and presidents at the World Economic Forum in 2002–3. Or note the level of artists' and performers' involvement in the protests against the Iraq War in 2003 (though we will explore the ramifications of this in the next chapter).

Manuel Castells would describes these as 'the prophets' – those 'symbol mobilizers' who can bring alternative voices and experiences right into the hearts of their societies.[93] They are not 'charismatic leaders or shrewd strategists', says Castells, but they do 'give a face (or a mask) to a symbolic insurgency so that they speak on behalf of the insurgents'. These can be good celebrities or bad cult leaders, wily national politicians (like Jordi Pujol, the ex-president of Catalonia) or inspiring revolutionaries (Subcommandante Marcos of the Zapatistas). But they are able to skate across the surface of the mediascape, making connections and building constituencies in unexpected ways: and they are prophets 'in the sense that they declare the path, affirm the values and act as symbol senders' on behalf of protesting communities.

Castells' 'prophets' are political players on the biggest of stages. This is why 'pro-play' might be as legitimate a form of players' activism as 'no logo'. A *creative* democratic politics, which presumes that startling new alliances and shifts are implicitly possible in a dynamic, emergent, networked world, could be a complement to a *defensive* democratic politics which aimed to restore social and cultural stability by pressing the pause button on dynamism, to enable a moment of reflection. The play ethic might then occupy a space between the poles of the protest ethic and the work ethic. It could help forge a language to translate the exponential demands of the former into suggestions for concrete reform that might make sense to the latter. The conditions are ripe for a major moment of social reform – if only politicians could act with the grain of the times and embrace the culture of openness and participation, diversity and creativity, that players take for granted in their lifeworlds.[94] Can business and government create 'non-alienated' spaces and times, sustainable grounds of play, commons that support innovation and creativity? And by doing this can they placate a citizenry which is clearly yearning for a new alignment, in Al Gore's words, 'between who they are, and what they do?'

*

Yet it would be wrong to assume that this alignment can simply be a matter of political understanding.

This book was always intended to conclude with a consideration of play and spirituality. The deep generative power of play in our lives has led me easily into areas of mystery and wonder about the human condition. The ancientness of play forms in our world religions also compelled me to consider just how profoundly rooted ludicism is in our species being, as an enduring survival strategy in a risky world. Most specifically, the driving religiosity of the 'Protestant ethic as a spirit of capitalism' forced me to consider that a more diverse spirituality might be fuel for a usable ethos in the age of informationalism – perhaps a 'New Age, holistic, neo-pagan' play ethic.

I was finalizing these thoughts in early September 2001. Then, to paraphrase the first lines of Thomas Pynchon's *Gravity's Rainbow*, a screaming came across the sky. And in the aftermath of 9/11, the relationships between work, play and spirituality have become almost unbearably pertinent.

THE
INFINITE
GAME

Play and
Spirituality

What do I love when I love my god? To a Buddhist, or to
a Native American, or to a contemporary eco-feminist, the
cosmos is not a blind and stupid rage, as Nietzsche
thought, but a friend, our element and matrix, the beginning
and the end, the gentle rocking of a great cosmic womb, a
friendly flux from which we take our origin and to which we
return, like the steady beat of ten thousand waves in the
sea. Then the love of God means to learn how to dance or
swim, to learn how to join in the cosmic play, to move with
its rhythms and to understand that we are each of us of no
special import other than to play our part in the cosmic ballet.
– John D. Caputo, *On Religion*, 2001

The death of God will ensure our salvation because the
death of God alone can waken the divine.
– Jacques Derrida, *Writing and Difference*, 1967

Purify your soul from all unclean things.
Completely forget something called 'this world'.
The time for play is over and the serious time is upon us.
Extract from 9/11 hijackers' letter, printed in
the *New York Times*, 27 September 2001

It's easy to see why play and spirituality might have a strong relationship. According to the linguists, the meaning of 'spirit' – 'the breath of life' – is common across three ancient languages, Latin, Greek and Sanskrit. Spirit is that which animates the inanimate, defies the determinate, flickers between order and chaos. In short, as playful as it gets.[1]

However, play and *religion* – if we conceive of religion, in terms of its linguistic roots, as the 'binding together' of people under a single spiritual tradition – have always been in tension, and often in outright opposition. At the start of this book, I described the 250-year suppression of play by the Protestant work ethic in the West – a deeply limited vision of human possibility supporting a productive system which needed those limitations to function properly. Much of the social and cultural history of the last fifty years has been about the gradual lifting of that suppression. And in many areas – from the countercultures of the sixties and seventies to the sub-cultures of the eighties and nineties, from new sexual politics to new technological habits – there has been a positive advance of profoundly playful values.[2]

In the West, much of that has been marked by the decline of organized religion – the Christian injunctions to work hard, save well and look to your salvation – and the rise of disorganized spirituality, the 'spiritual marketplace' of the post-religious era.[3] Two seemingly opposed rhetorics of play, cosmic play and personal play, come together in this moment. As the old certainties of class, nation and occupation fall away, the new proteans of the West have sought both intensely personal and intensely universal answers to their sense of confusion and disorientation. The individual – denuded of the old clothes of social positioning – must now attend to his or her self-development. If our immediate social universe is about risk, openness and opportunity, then our personal lives must be about energy, enthusiasm, health and optimism – all those capacities needed to enter the fray. There is little in the legacy of the Protestant work ethic – duty, routine, deferral of pleasures, regulation of intensities – that can provide the postmodern person with any resources for these challenges.

At the same time, we need some kind of larger consolation for this uneven, unpredictable experience of life. Again, the Protestant work ethic – with its inherent presumption that hard work in itself signifies a commitment to a higher moral order – has little to offer the dissatisfied professional, the scrabbling freelancer, the yearning working mother or father, the deeply alienated McWorker. All those who experience a gap between their interior richness and the limited expressiveness of their exterior lives – yet who suspect that a return to the old structures that might bridge that gap would be futile, even undesirable.[4]

One route to turn to is, of course, the more wildly extremist, virtual and utopian ends of popular and media culture – an ever more powerful experience of transcendence, available in the movie stalls, on a dance floor or at a console. But the other is towards a kind of spiritual vision of the universe which presumes enormity and intimacy in the same moment. Instead of salvation and redemption in the distant hereafter, it offers creativity and possibility in the perplexing and mysterious here and now.[5]

It is this vision that underpins much of the 'mind, body and spirit' culture in Western societies – a stew of Eastern and Western religions and spiritual traditions, new sciences and old activisms, which need much more careful attention than their rationalist attackers usually allow.[6] Overlapping with this phenomenon are a set of play-oriented theologians and spiritual thinkers, who represent a much-needed intellectual sharpening-up of the so-called 'New Age' movement – a movement that inspires and disheartens its friendly critics in equal measure.[7]

Strange new puritans

This chapter deliberately began with one of the most terrifying quotes about play in recent times and the greatest challenge to the notion of a play ethic as anything more than the affluent lifestyle choice of insulated Westerners. These lines from the 'discovered' letter of the suicide pilots of 9/11 speak a deeper truth about *all* religious fundamentalisms.[8] From the perspective of those who seek purity, piety and a gravely dutiful (or 'serious') human life, play is messy, this-worldly and joyful. That adaptive potentiation which humans cannot help but express, that will to variety that characterizes our existence, that endless joy of the 'influx of mind into matter', is a threat to the fundamentalist mindset – whether that fundamentalism be a Taliban regime banning all images and covering up women, or an American Christian preacher railing at the 'demonic productions' of Hollywood.[9]

Yet we must be careful to distinguish a true and complex spirit of play from the huge shifts in the West that have taken place since 11 September. What has been most fascinating about the American response to 9/11, including the war on Iraq begun in early 2003, is the way it has interrupted, and at times reversed, the move towards a more self-consciously 'fun' culture. This was represented in the nineties by the sax-playing Clinton, the creative destructions of the new economy and dot-com culture, the increasing cascade of popular culture and lifestyles.[10]

Immediately after the attack – despite a brief moment of cosmopolitan idealism – the initial response was to let the Clintonian good times continue to roll. Bush urged his population to 'spend for America', in order to avoid a consumer-led recession. Articles appeared defending the liberal culture of America (and by extension the West) against the spectre of a joyless, iconophobic, extremist Islam.[11]

The work–leisure duality that defines much of information-age America was powerfully reinforced by the attack on the Twin Towers. Those hurtling to their deaths were not in the main captains of industry, but ordinary knowledge workers in the financial sector, from over a hundred different countries – there to pick up their pay cheques, go home to their families and communities, and enjoy the fruits of their labours. The business columnist John Ellis predicted an America governed by a new cultural polarity – between a grim commitment to homeland security, and a wild compensation sought in consumer hedonism.[12] Those old 'cultural contradictions of capitalism' noted by the US sociologist Daniel Bell were being writ large, and proposed as a necessary schizophrenia.

Yet few remember that Bell's response to the self-subversion of work–leisure – the free dreams of the latter sapping the duteousness of the former – was to promote a new commitment to religion: all faces pointing towards the hereafter, in order that that excessive behaviour may be moderated in each realm (either hedonism or workaholism).[13] The high levels of belief in notions of apocalypse or demonic powers among US citizens has often been noted – America, beyond its urban centres, is a notoriously religious country – and President Bush has used his debatable mandate to reinforce a moral nationalism, backed up by the conviction of his own born-again Christianity.[14]

The possible reversion of American culture towards a more hard-line, censorious and repressive, and explicitly anti-ludic puritan culture is beyond the scope (and predictive powers) of this book. Yet one early indication might well be the levels of popular outrage at American celebrities in music, film and television, many of whom raised their voices in protest against the prospect of a war against Iraq in early 2003. Consumer boycotts were even organized against one southern country-rock act, the Dixie Chicks, whose lead singer expressed her opposition to a war in an interview with a European magazine.[15]

If anything directly attacks the notion of a more playful and creative society, it is a militant iconophobia – a distrust of those artists and creators whose semiotic productions raise too many questions and introduce too many perspectives into the domestic management of ideas and cultural consent. It would be a vast historical irony if the anti-ludic motto of the 9/11 attackers – the time for play is over, the serious time is upon us – became one of the few things that these supposedly 'clashing civilizations' could agree on.[16] How could a humane and broad play ethic defend, let alone extend itself, in a developed north becoming more obsessed with homeland security than cosmopolitan democracy?

One indirect answer might be found by exploring the ideas of some genuinely boundary-breaking thinkers on spirituality. Their backgrounds cover most of the major world religions (Judaism, Islam, Christianity, Hinduism and Buddhism) and their writing is directly interested in the structures and conditions of a players' society – its interactivity and social fluidity, its domination by sign and image, its deep grounding in new sciences and technologies.

Yet taken together, they test the inclusiveness and diversity of the notion of play – in its ancient and modern forms, as materiality and spirituality – to the extremes. Is the possibility of a play ethic merely a by-product of a certain level of affluence and prosperity, which (in the West at least) is secured through global regimes of exploitation and coercion? Or might the playful cultures of the developed world be able to participate in, and perhaps even instigate, a different kind of global conversation between cultures, communities and individuals – about values, the good life, the potential of humanity – by exploring their shared commitment to the infinite games of human spirituality?

The soul of the soulitarian

Before we explore the bigger ideas, a note of scepticism: why does a player have to concern her or himself with the spiritual, anyway? In the secular twenty-first-century world of networks, markets and lifestyles, there is surely enough rich variety in the materiality of life – of games and toys, fields and strategies – to answer any player's needs for meaning and purpose.

Yet the problem with this stance is that popular culture – the player's primary source of meaning – seems to be unable to stay away from matters of the spirit and mysticism, placed right at the heart of its most commercial projects. Many of Hollywood's lucrative movie franchises are, either explicitly or implicitly, driven by visions of a universe in which existing social or scientific rationality barely suffices to explain what happens. The *Harry Potter* series is the most out-and-out magical, in the straightforward sense of the term – positing an alternative society of wizards living secretly alongside humans, deploying supernatural powers to maintain the integrity of their own culture. *The Lord of the Rings* is a more ancient shadow world, in which supernatural powers – whether telekinesis, clairvoyance or transmutation – are the crucial forces for change and action. In this realm, humans and non-humans make alliances among themselves, engaging with equally hybrid enemies, in a Manichaean struggle for supremacy.[17]

Even the two great science-fiction franchises of the last thirty years, George Lucas's *Star Wars* and the Wachowski brothers' *Matrix* series, resonate with spiritual and theological themes. The *Star Wars* films may be far removed from us in space and time, and their mise en scène may be relentlessly technological. But their essential drama is about maintaining the spiritual balance of the universe through a medium called 'the Force'. The Force lives in all things and can be used to propel evil as well as good: those who can tap into it – the adepts known as Jedi – require many years of brutal training before they are deemed responsible enough to use it, as wise policemen, in the wider galactic society. The melange of religious traditions blended into Lucas's vision – from Buddhism to animism – has often been noted.[18]

The *Matrix* films are the most remarkable of these techno-spiritual epics, in their extreme conjunction between perennial wisdoms and just over-the-horizon futurism. As the Muslim critic Zia Sardar notes, *The Matrix* casts cyberspace as a kind of Sufi parody: humans are unknowingly trapped in a mental hallucination of reality – this world is an illusion, as the Sufi mystics would say – while their bodily energies are harvested by robots in an all-too-hellish reality. The drama of the film comes from Neo – the 'chosen one', as many of the characters whisper – who has the power to smash the hallucination from within by unravelling the code (the 'Matrix') which holds it all together. And in Sardar's words, 'like a techno Moses, Neo leads enslaved humanity to a new Zion ... we also have the techno equivalents of John the Baptist, Mary Magdalene and Judas'.[19]

Add to this best-selling computer games like *Black and White*, explicitly dramatizing their players as 'gods' whose aim is to convince the population of a territory to follow them. Or the procession of Japanese (or Japanese-inspired) cartoons that play across children's televisual media, and whose merchandise dominates their toy boxes, such as *Dragonball Z*, *Samurai Jack* or *Pokemon* and its various derivatives: all of them involve creatures with either supernatural or super-technological powers, whose narratives are about growth through challenge, the instability of existence and our need to negotiate the interventions of unseen powers.[20]

So at the most playful and ludic ends of popular culture, matter is invested with spirit in a furious and intense way. In the age of 'cut and copy, morph and paste' (whether the substance is biological or digital), we are beginning to expect that the material world is not just boringly susceptible to our own wills, but may have secret laws and agendas of its own. In terms of our play rhetorics, this is a fascinating clash. This is a mediaverse whose basic technologies encourage full exercise of the powers of the mind and will (play as imagination and freedom). Yet its main narratives and themes are obsessed with the cosmic limitations to those powers – the implicate orders within which our will and intention operates, and the implacable foes it faces (play as fate and chaos, play as contest).

Many would regard this as a creeping occultism – a surrender to the forces of irrationalism, just as our scientifically rational control of nature (whether human or non-human) is becoming ever more complete. Yet as Victoria Nelson reminds us, we should never forget how 'utterly unsophisticated the tenets of eighteenth-century rationalism have left us, believers and unbelievers alike, in that complex arena we blithely dub "spiritual"'.[21]

Is this, as Nelson and Douglas Rushkoff argue, a new version of the sixteenth-century Renaissance, where the empirical and the transcendental co-exist in a fruitful tension? As films like the *Matrix* trilogy show, it's difficult to speculate about technology these days without also invoking theology. As each advance in techno-science takes us by surprise, surely we can try to expand our reactions beyond the bottom-line fetishism of business culture, the phobic fears of eco-Luddites or the endless cheese-paring of puritan ethicists? To seek out the playful spirituality in our machines is at least a novel option.

For example, the computer giants Intel are betting their future on pla-cing a transmitting 'chip in everything' – from banknotes to milk cartons, shoes to lost keys, welfare cards to platinum cards.[22] Huizinga's definition of play as an 'influx of mind into matter' could hardly be better exempli-fied. But from a different vision of human nature, the worst is easily imag-ined. Could this enable state control and surveillance to be practised over us to a previously unimaginable extreme?

Yet pressure from consumers, citizens and the wider culture – as proved by the open source movement in software – can compel manufacturers to build their systems as much towards openness, play and interactivity, as towards paranoia work and duty. In the last months of 2003, UK owners of mobile phones equipped with the short-range wireless technology Blue-tooth have started to 'bluejack' each other – signalling to other random and nearby users their interests, their needs, their pranks. As with the phe-nomenon of flash mobs – people using their mobile phones to assemble instantly in urban locations – the initial impulse seems, well, trivially play-ful.[23] Yet this street-level compulsion to use technology to connect and touch, rather than constrain and determine, at least begs the question: might not networks and computers enable us to extend our subjectivity, as well as turn us into objects? If we yearn for communion in our com-munications shouldn't we become self-aware about this?[24]

The network path

A number of writers have engaged with the spiritual dimensions of an information age and many of them frame their arguments in terms very recognizable to a play perspective. Margaret Wertheim's *The Pearly Gates of Cyberspace* sees the digital realm as the latest version of the Christian image of 'the heavenly city' – a semi-utopian realm freed from material constraints, the only qualifications for entry being 'baptism' in the rituals of technology and coding. Yet her more profound point is that the eruption of cyberspace into late twentieth-century life is directly related to historical development. All eras' conception of space, says Wertheim (whether Medieval, Renaissance, Enlightenment or Relativistic/Post-Einstenian in the West or the numerous levels of existence in the non-West), are deeply contingent – no matter how fundamental they might seem to those operating within them. More precisely, our sense of space is always generated by what Wertheim calls a 'network of responsibility' – that is, the social agreement in a culture as to the parameters of what is real.

For postmoderns in the north, this game of truth has changed. Cyberspace 'comes into being at a time when many in the Western world are tiring of a purely physical world picture. Can it be a coincidence that we have invented new immaterial space at just this point in our history? At just the point when many people are longing once more for some kind of spiritual space?'[25]

Erik Davis is similarly alive to the spiritual dimensions of the Net and the way that the 'spirit of informationalism' might inspire humans to a more creative and transformative life. He turns backwards to the Gnostics, a heretic Christian creed of late antiquity, for whom intense self-knowledge – freed from the limitations of the body – was the route to godliness. Davis casts much of the idealism of cyberculture as an updated, console-and-keyboarded version of this ancient quest – literally, a 'techgnosis'.[26] Yet his concluding examples shift the theology of the Net into a usefully non-Christian space: the Buddhist image of the Net of Indra, with its holographic jewels representing enlightened selves, each connected to the other by immeasurable threads. As one of its scholars cites, 'each individual [jewel] is at once the cause for the whole and is caused by the whole, and what is called existence is a vast body made up of an infinity of individuals all sustaining each other and defining each other'.[27] The soulitarian vision – the techno-player in an infinite game with others – could hardly be better expressed.[28]

We can also turn to Hermann Hesse's profoundly playful novel, *The Glass Bead Game*, as another precursor of the spirituality of the information age – not so much metaphysical as 'netaphysical'. Published in 1943, this science-fictional fable has at its heart a game of knowledge. It begins initially as a kind of glass-bead abacus, but eventually evolves into an ornate interdisciplinary device which adepts devote their lives to mastering.[29]

The contemplation of the game by the players becomes a meditative practice – leading to 'the interior of the cosmic mystery, where in the alternation between inhaling and exhaling, between heaven and earth, between ying and yang, holiness is forever being created'.[30] Between Indra's Net and the glass bead game – the network as dynamic community, and the network as imaginative tool – the soul of the soulitarian, his or her 'netaphysics', may be found. Yet there is a dark side to this, Davis notes. The hero Joseph Knecht eventually leaves Castalia, the world capital of the game: he is eager to get away from the purely mental and imaginative play of this utopia and pursue a sensual life in the gritty reality of the outside world.[31]

The 'gritty world outside' brings us back, with a shudder and a jolt, to the most notorious use of a network to create 'a kind of holiness': the Islamic fundamentalism of the al-Qaida 'network', generally held to be the cause of the destruction of the Twin Towers in New York. The undeniable fact is that the movements of the terrorists, and the distribution of the technical information need to carry out their attacks, was largely coordinated by use of various technical networks – fax, web, email, mobile phone. And this has cast an ineradicable shadow over any unthinking idealism about the humanizing, never mind spiritual, powers of a 'network', in whatever shape or form.[32] What kind of 'netaphysic' is at work (and explicitly not at play) here?

The 'gulf wars' take on a different meaning when we consider the relationship between play and spirituality. The gulf that matters here is between the digitalized and diffusely spiritual players, revelling in the information societies of the West, and the angry religious militants who feel threatened by such fluidity and mutability. Can there be any common ground between them? Can the 'breath of life' be allowed to animate different cultures, practices and even uses of technology without generating antipathy and exclusive righteousness?

Davis wonders whether there could instead be a 'common groundlessness' – an acceptance that it is impossible to transcend disjunctions between belief and practice, faith and scepticism; between the consolations of the absolute and otherwordly, and the challenges and risks of our information-age lives. These tensions and conflicts could become 'dynamic and creative forces, calling us to face others with an openness that does

not seek to control or assimilate them to whatever point of view we happen to hold'.[33]

This would surely be at the core of a play ethic worth having: a 'spirit
of informationalism' that might allow all the various structures of belief
and practice in our world to find their home, their nurturance and their
playground in the network society – rather than feel exiled or reduced by
it. A 'friendly flux', indeed.[34]

Unbinding the bind:
religion in play

There are some who have already stared into the chaos and tensions of
their own contemporary faiths and tried to 'let something unexpected
bloom', in Davis's words, from the encounter between religious tradition
and 'the spirit of information'. To toy and tinker with their closed religiosity, as it were, until it can join the open play of spirituality.

Playing up to Christ: Don Cupitt

Described by one critic as the 'atheist priest', the Cambridge theologian
Don Cupitt has been trying to reconcile Western Christianity with a world
of language and signs, of social and technological flexibility, for over thirty
years. His essential position is that religions must accept what he calls the
philosophical doctrine of *interactionism*. Whatever humans take to be their
reality (whether capitalism, the reponses of their lover or God) is merely
'an interplay or conflict of individual projects and world views ... *Everything*, including all linguistic meanings, truths, values and indeed reality
itself, is a slowly evolving consensus product, the result of an interplay of
forces in the human realm ... It is human historical action rather than
divine creation that finishes the world'.[35]

In light of this position – formed out of an idiosyncratic recasting of
poststructuralism and postmodernism – Cupitt proposes that religion must

change from being 'a supernatural doctrine', to 'an experiment in self-hood'. Religion should provide us with spiritual tools for living, bringing rich symbols into our lives in exactly the same way as art does. In fact, living religiously should be a kind of 'performance art', says Cupitt in *After God* – an everyday grappling with all the consequences of our modern freedom.[36]

How can religion give us meaning, here and now? Cupitt suggests three ways. First, we should live under 'the eye of God' – 'God' being no more (and no less) than the cultural embodiment of our highest human values. Second, we can use religion to help us surrender to the unavoidable facts of ageing and death: through its rituals and practices, we can conjure up the dreamless sleep, into which we will be happy to surrender our once and only lives. Third, religion should be concerned with what Cupitt calls 'solar ethics', the aim of living expressively. We pour out our self in the service of others, and do so with an acute awareness of how humanly precarious this aim is.[37]

Again, for us, what is remarkable is how this vision of a thoroughly dedivinized Christianity is so easily framed as a play-ethical activity. Firstly, this is not a 'large-scale doctrine system and moral code', but a 'contracted vision' (the oldest idea of an ethic, Cupitt notes) that may be spoken of as 'a form of consciousness, as a spirituality, as a way of life'. Secondly, these three elements – representing 'what survives of the old religions' – are what he calls 'a small number of tricks and techniques of religious existence; ways of being a self and of relating oneself to the whole of which one is a part. These tricks can help us to love life and live well: that, now, is religion.'[38]

To describe religion as a box of handy linguistic tricks for the self – a mixture of therapy and lifestyle self-consciousness that borrows its style from a 2,000-year-old tradition – has brought Cupitt into some disrepute among his congregants.[39] But it is an extraordinarily useful position for the searching player. In *The Time Being,* Cupitt grapples with the dramatic consequences of his thoroughly ludic understanding of human experience:

> Private prayer and public worship don't happen in some privileged space outside all games, but are themselves also games that we play. So we should give up the pretence that there is a real self in there behind all the masks we wear and the games we play. No: we are theatrical all the way down. We cannot function, we cannot express ourselves and we don't even exist except within a regime of signs, a game-situation and a cultural tradition.[40]

Yet Cupitt suggests that even though we are fated to play the game of a fictionalized life, and 'not look for ways of dropping out of it', we can '*play up* a little', meaning that we can try to 'spritefully' (as well as spiritually) 'breathe new life into old texts', interpreting the old roles of religion in order to 'send them up' (the ambiguity of the phrase is deliberate).[41] Instead of 'lamenting the disappearing distinctions between sincerity and play acting, truth and fiction, reality and illusion', we should get used to 'living creatively in a very thin world'. For an ethos of play which tries to make a vision of the good life out of the real virtualities, the relentless simulations and the informational morphings of early twenty-first-century life, Cupitt's faith in 'living creatively' is of great sustenance.[42]

Cupitt's deeply performative and creative vision of religion asks us to place our faith in the incessant flux of language and discourse – signs and images being our earthly kingdom of eternal plenitude, an accessible realm in which we can exercise our spiritual liberation. At the very least, this is a religion that will chime with the most 'modern' (and perforce, postmodern) of our great play rhetorics – self-oriented play and imaginative play, directing a multimedia performance of the spirit.

Yet we live in a historical moment where an awesome magnitude of media images, spectacles and signs is showering down on the denizens of globalization – and for all the flexible joys of the developed world's lifestyle, this barrage is causing anguish to more than a few fundamentalist sects. Cupitt is aware that his critics 'are quick to point out that my own thoroughgoing culturalism and relativism goes along with all the worst features of the media-dominated consumer society'. His response is characteristically cheeky:

> Unfortunately that doesn't prove me wrong, because the modern zeitgeist machine is so all-encompassing and all-powerful that it swallows up the objectivists just as easily as it swallows up the relativists. Absolutes, certainties, foundations and authorities nowadays yo-yo in and out of fashion just as quickly as skirt lengths and trouser widths. So we're all in the same boat, and nobody can see the problem getting anything but worse. But I have the advantage, because I can better tolerate transience.[43]

Bully for Cupitt, one is tempted to say – publishing in 1995, at the very foothills of the digital boom, ready for a half decade of cut and paste, copy and morph. Yet after 9/11, some of the deeper thinking about the event has concentrated on how this postmodern sensibility might not be such a blithely positive development in consciousness and culture. The attack on the Twin Towers was, to use the classic terrorist term, a 'spectacular': violence as the means to media attention as well as mass murder. The aim was to generate an image – primed for distribution through the news network as a 'morning item' – that would shatter the psychic security of Americans and express the psychic resentment of those suffering the excesses (or the deficits) of American geopolitical intervention.[44] That the image did occasion, and still occasions, some measure of celebration in the Muslim and Arab streets of the Middle East and Africa is well documented.[45] The question asked by some of the more astute global commentators is whether this striking act of image violence was in some way brought forth by the general image domination of America and the West over non-Western cultures.

Benjamin Barber, author of the prophetic 'Beyond jihad and McWorld', has put the question most eloquently. Can Asian tea defeat Coca-Cola? Can the family meal resist fast-food grazing? Can Mexican or Indian films stand up against the violence, glamour and sentiment of Hollywood? Even in America, there are families who home-school to protect their kids from commercial culture: are they, asks Barber, an 'American Taliban' in waiting? He even doubts whether the big-city cosmopolitans really enjoy their 'screen diet' from computers, TV and cinemas. 'Terror obviously is not an answer,' concludes Barber, 'but the truly desperate may settle for terror as a response to our failure even to ask such questions.'[46]

In the framework of this book, what all this suggests is that our 'play audit' of religion and spirituality cannot afford to limit itself to purely modernist rhetorics: the untrammelled production of imagination or assertion of self. A play ethic must be about finding an appropriately dynamic equilibrium between all the modalities of play in order that a complex and capacious social life can be sustained for the maximum number. So the less voluntarist and more traditional forms of play – play as power and contest, play as identity, play as fate and chaos – must also find their correlates in the practices of faith.

Seeing around and through the spectacle: Islam and Judaism as media literacy

It might seem, at present, like the most unlikely pairing. But two brilliantly heterodox writers – one American Jewish, one British Muslim – have managed to re-engineer their religions and faiths in the context of the information age, and turn them into a different kind of 'performance art' than the free-wheeling creative Christianity of Cupitt. Indeed, they resonate far more with the darker and more compelling aspects of our play traditions – those which are about power and contest, and about the demands of identity and community.

The writers' shared battle is against a dominant image culture that imposes a uniform kind of consciousness on its audiences. They also support the right to bring their own distinct traditions to the world carnival. They regard the iconoclasm of their religions – both the Jewish and the Islamic injuctions against idols and graven images – as a form of media literacy: a way of resisting and proposing alternatives to the expensive productions of the cultural conglomerates, both inside and outside the West. Religion as 'iconocriticism', you might say.

They assert that their faith gives them an experience of difference and singularity – a tangible demonstration of what pluralism *really* means; that is, a world that can include both secularism and spirit. But reimagined, their faiths can also provide a set of critical tools to help develop the subtleties of a global consciousness. In this way, a true interplay of cultures might thrive on our planet rather than a bricolage of consumer lifestyles composed by corporations searching for 'riches in niches' and entrancing hybrids in order to stimulate jaded Western palates and intimidate non-Western cultures.

Douglas Rushkoff began his career in 1997 by charting the behaviours and rituals of the first digital generation in *Cyberia*, and moved on to become a proselytizer for the empowering nature of new media in books like *Media Virus* and *Children of Chaos* (titled *Playing the Future* in the US).[47] Yet Rushkoff came to realize that his detailed descriptions of how young people were embracing information technology – whether on the Web, or in musical raves, or in political art and activism – was being deployed as a subtle marketing tool by American big business. He went 'undercover' as a consultant for a year and charted the new 'hidden persuasions' of American advertising in *Coercion*.[48] At the same time, Ruskhoff started to reconnect with his Jewish faith, using it explicitly as a space of cultural and mental retreat from the multimedia maelstrom that he had so assiduously charted.[49]

Out of that period, Rushkoff has emerged with a 'Judaism for the information age' – and one which is self-conscious about repositioning his own earlier ethic of play on a different part of the ludic spectrum: from sheer exuberant sign play to a more sceptical awareness of the semiotic power plays of others. 'The kind of Jews I imagine emerging in the near future are Jews who are iconoclastic to the core – they reject any tendency towards mindless worship and idolatry.'[50]

Indeed, he essentially renders the formation of Judaism as a perfect example of media literacy. 'The bar mitzvah means you can read the code. Only then are you allowed to work with Torah. After you know its language, its very construction can become transparent to you. Or look at the minyan. Why do ten people need to be present when you read Torah? Because it's not supposed to be an individual's journey, but a group's.' As advertisers and TV producers scheme to keep consumers individualized, anxious and fearful, the minyan provides a model for media critique. This means you never watch alone, you compare your perceptions with immediately available friends, you remain 'emotionally distanced' from the mythology before you, whether commercial or religious. The 'graven image', in short, does not seduce you.[51]

If Cupitt 'spiritualizes' Christianity (that is, he makes the religion mobile and interpretable, a vital resource for meaning making) and thus encourages the creative impulse, Ruskhoff's open Judaism is about encouraging the critical faculty. And both creativity and critique are necessary in a society of players, whose activities become simultaneously more rewarding to themselves and more challenging to others. Rushkoff's new version of his ethic of play draws from what he regards as the Jewish contribution to the development of contemporary consciousness. 'We should use the tools of our fathers . . . to stay awake while participating in a culture that puts us to sleep . . . The awake human being is intrinsically, naturally ethical.' Rushkoff's injunction to his immediate audience is that they have few excuses not to be awake, given their general distance from need and want. And in relation to Jewish audiences in particular, their historic fears of persecution hold them back from being the full ethical players they could be.[52]

> If you start looking at life this way – as play – then you're freed up to do a lot of truly meaningful stuff. Let's say you're worried about the people starving in Rwanda and you decide you're going to fly down there and work with them. Well, for them it's survival, but for you it's 'play' because you don't have to go down there at all. Anyone who does that kind of charity work is doing it because they find it rewarding on a level of self-actualization. When you're not worried about your survival as an individual – or as a race – you have the luxury to behave ethically because it's just more fun to live that way.[53]

Rushkoff's blithe tone (exactly how cheap *is* a flight to Rwanda?) never-theless reveals one of the core assertions of a viable play ethic: that a general 'social and economic security' is required before a full ethical unfolding of our playful selves can take place. Yet as several recent studies have shown, rising affluence does not necessarily correlate with rising 'happiness' or well-being, however those terms are defined.[54] Players might find it 'fun', as Rushkoff puts it, to help others by increasing their possibilities and options. Indeed, the play ethic's aim to replace the duali-ties of work/leisure and work/life, with the continuum of play/care, is an attempt to redress the puritan prejudice: why *should* more human autonomy and self-determination means less ethics and responsibility?[55] But would those 'grounds of play' described in Chapter Ten – those 'social trampolines' that catch the players when they fall and give them the means to re-enter the fray – be enough to give them the requisite secu-rity? Perhaps more metaphysical and spiritual moorings are required. How can we feel, as the complexity thinker Stuart Kauffman puts it, truly 'at home in the universe'?[56]

Like Rushkoff, Ziauddin Sardar is also a media critic of distinction and energy. He is the author of many books on cultural studies, media studies, chaos theory, cyberfutures and postmodernism. Some of them have even been in strip cartoon form – using the old situationist technique of *detournement*, the recontextualizing of visual material, to convey complex arguments to popular audiences.[57] Writing in a witty, direct style, no one could accuse Sardar of not taking pleasure in the play of forms and lan-guage.

Yet as a Muslim, Sardar is embarked on a quest – like Ruskhoff – to equip his religion for a combative encounter with the information age, its powerful imagery and compelling narratives. And the difference between Sardar and Rushkoff is literally about information – specifically, the status of God. In a commentary about the early reception of his book, *Nothing Sacred*, Rushkoff notes that 'it's not my intention to shake the faith of those who want to believe that they are the descendants of the charac-ters populating the myths of the Bible – the 600,000 witnesses of the miracles at Mount Sinai. But the notion of an invented, evolutionary reli-gion [Rushkoff's characterization of his open-source Judaism] is, at least to the timid, incompatible with the notion of a complete and perfect trans-mission of text from the Maker himself.'[58]

For Judaism and Christianity, there has been a strong movement over the last century to historicize their religions – to turn their godly revelations into culturally constructed moments, to read their commandments as humanly composed ideals and injunctions. But there is undoubtedly a global need, particularly in the developing world, for some sense of transcendental measure. How can the entrancing images and seductive networks of Western postmodernity be assessed and reckoned with from a position which somehow resists their subtle promotions and marketing strategies? In short: for some, God cannot be a fiction (or even a 'totality of creation' that 'our brains are not yet able to process', as Ruskhoff puts it).[59] For Sardar, the power of Islam lies in its measure of transcendence and its acceptance by over a billion believers – the *umma* (collective of the faithful) – for whom the revelation of God's message to the Prophet Muhammed is a literal event.

Yet as Sardar relentlessly reminds his readers, the sacredness of a text should not close down its interpretation, but precisely make its interpretation an eternal and unfinishable process: 'the only thing that remains constant in Islam is the text of the Qur'an itself',[60] providing 'an ethical anchor for ever-changing interpretations'.[61] The grand historical mistake of Islam, in his view, came at the beginning of the Abbasid period in the fourteenth century, when the 'gates of *itijihad* were closed'.[62] *Itijihad* is a Koranic term meaning criticism, dispute, debate. The concept fell into disrepute as medieval Islamic societies began to build their power and needed to police interpretations of the holy scriptures. Thus *shari'ah*, the notion of Islamic law, came powerfully into prominence. But contemporary Muslims, casting around for some identity and solidity in the face of postmodern culture, make a fatal 'category error' in regarding the *shari'ah* as divine, says Sardar. Instead, in his view, it is merely a kind of '*fiqh* or jurisprudence, nothing more than the legal opinion of classical jurists . . . an outmoded body of law' which 'incorporates the logic of Muslim imperialism of the eight and ninth centuries', and as such is entirely inappropriate to contemporary conditions.[63]

Sardar invites us to regard the *shari'ah* as a 'problem-solving methodology' rather than law – 'a framework of values that provide Muslim societies with guidance', that are 'dynamically derived within changing contexts', not static and given. The Qur'an itself 'declares unequivocally that no one has any special privilege of interpretation: as a book of guidance, it is open to all'.[64] Yet when it is deployed by Islamic politicians as a holy law, serving naked power interests, it 'removes agency' from ordinary Muslims. The 'clergy' and *ulema* (legal scholars) who take it upon themselves to interpret and apply this ossified *shari'ah* are also, in

Sardar's view, in breach of the original tenets of Islamic scholarship. These are far from the original '*alim*, scholars, of early Islam, whose attainment of *ilm* (knowledge) was a multidisciplinary affair, with scientists and philosophers also part of the process.'[65] Indeed, as Sardar says, 'many find it surprising that over one-third of the Qu'ran is devoted to extolling the virtues of reason and the pursuit of knowledge.'[66]

Elsewhere, he notes that the ability to put reality 'into play', so proclaimed by postmodernists as our inevitable state of affairs in a 'interactionist' world, has always been accepted by Islam – particularly the variety of philosophical conditions of truth gathered under the term *Haqiqah*.[67] Yet the nihilism of values that postmodernists often derive from a world of competing truths is not, says Sardar, inevitable.

The iconoclasm of Islam, rooted in its prohibition of images of the prophet, is largely passed over by Sardar. Yet the radical Sufi writer Hakim Bey – whom Sardar quotes approvingly – has written perceptively about the way that the Islamic prohibition against imagery can be used as a kind of defence of the imagination itself (in similar terms to Rushkoff). 'We do not oppose the Image as theological iconoclasts but because we require the liberation of the imagination itself – *our* imagination, not the mediated *imaginaire* of the market,' writes Bey. 'Of course this critique of the image could just as well be applied to the word, to the book, to language itself. And of course it should be so applied. To question a medium is not necessarily to destroy it, in the name of either orthodoxy or heresy. The point is that we imagine ourselves rather than allow ourselves to be imagined; we must ourselves write ourselves or else be written.'[68]

To imagine ourselves, rather than allow ourselves to be imagined, has to be the key demand of the players' spiritual community – and particularly the complex communities of twenty-first-century Islam. Sardar is passionate about the development of a reformed Islam, and as much against Islam's own puritanical cultures (like Wahhabism) as against Western misrepresentation. The Sufi-influenced commentator on Islam, Stephen Schwartz, gives a strong sense of what a carnivalesque Islam could be like – freely determining its own communal interplay of traditions, and doing so in a variety of expressive forms. Before the Wahhabi takeover of the annual pilgrimage to Mecca, the Hajj, by the fundamentalist Saudi Arabian regime, there were 'flags and celebrations' of different national traditions, with every Islamic sect, school of jurisprudence and Sufi order represented. In Schwartz's words, the Hajj was a 'permanent county fair...

where all Muslims could come and share their traditions, their customs, their culture.'[69]

The great paradox of Sardar's own career is that, in the mediascape of the UK at least, he is what could be described as a significant player – that is, someone who deploys the technologies, screens and portals of the society of the spectacle as a means to create debate and discussion, commenting on everything from sci-fi movies to children's issues, complexity science to New Labour. He lives the unstable, category-blurring postmodern condition to the full. Yet though he is making the journey, he essentially loathes the destination.[70]

Sardar energetically occupies the semiotic, mutable condition of the play society in order to infuse it with a genuine plurality of ethics – particularly what he calls the 'integrative worldview of Islam', which 'integrates reality by providing a moral perspective on every aspect of human endeavour.'[71] It is this perspective that 'postmodern politics and economics' rejects: 'no notion of reverence, restraint, humility: no sense of limits and no ability to respond to human distress.'[72] Sardar characterizes 'the primary meaning and message of Islam' as a moral and ethical way of looking and shaping the world, 'a domain of peaceful civic culture, a participatory endeavour, and a holistic mode of knowing, being and doing'.[73]

Sardar's own self-description as a 'Muslim organic intellectual' – and his status as an ethical player – was never more bravely shown than in the article he wrote a few months after 9/11 in the *Observer* newspaper, where he declared a 'fatwa' on the terrorist network al-Qaida.[74] If this was a playful act, it was a deadly serious one: Sardar has long objected to the misuse and 'reduction' of the terms jihad and fatwa by fundamentalists – stripping away their 'spiritual, intellectual and social components', evaporating the connotations of 'personal struggle, intellectual endeavour and social construction.'[75] So Sardar's 'fatwa' was a moral challenge to bin Laden and his cohorts, to desist from their brutal and selective misinterpretation of Islam. In terms of the rhetorics of play, Sardar was deploying fatwa as a *power* play, to defend the rich collective play of Islamic cultural *identity*, in a liberal climate of *free* and *imaginative* play (the open media of the UK).

Compared to the ludic onslaught of Salman Rushdie's *The Satanic Verses* against the fixities and strictures of Islamic culture and theology – which Sardar treats disdainfully at length elsewhere[76] – Sardar's is the action of a light-footed pundit, rather than an all-encompassing novelist.

Indeed, it illustrates the extent to which we should remember to talk of 'play ethics' in the plural.

Rushdie's commitment to play as imagination and play as freedom, as described in his two great early nineties' essays, 'Is nothing sacred?' and 'In good faith', is absolute: literature is 'the one place in any society where, within the secrecy of our own heads, we can hear voices talking about everything in every possible way'[77] – including the life of the Prophet Muhammed, which brought down the Iranian fatwa on Rushdie's head. Sardar's retort is that meaning cannot be as free-wheeling as Rushdie would wish, at least for religiously defined communities whose holy writ still has a transcendant and sacred power. Though no one should be compelled to join – and indeed the Koran is explicit about there being 'no compulsion in religion' – the carnival of Islam has its rules and traditions, like any other faith. Otherwise, its sacred parade would not be definable or recognizable.[78]

The dispute between Sardar and Rushdie is at least a dispute between two evident players, with different distributions and emphases of play traditions in their approach. It is these kinds of intimate encounters, across the wide range of human purposes that a play perspective makes credible, that begin to evoke a different kind of global conversation, a conversation whose main topic Sardar calls 'the collective commitment to be humane'.[79]

The infinite game: do we play it ... or does it play us?

Play's elemental ambiguity, flexibility and adaptability, the way it insinuates itself into every corner of our existence, makes it an easy trigger for spiritual feelings and thoughts. In the Hindu vision of the universe, says Sutton-Smith, the world is played with by the gods, which includes our interior and exterior lives. 'Play, like dreams, is not a secondary state of reality as it is with us, but has primacy as a form of knowing ... for Hindus [play signifies] our multiple realities, all transformable into the other.'[80]

He quotes the work of the New York theatre director Richard Schechner on his Hindu-informed vision of play: 'It's wrong to think of playing as the interruption of ordinary life. Consider instead playing as the underlying [and] always-there continuum of experience . . . Ordinary life is netted out of playing but play continually squeezes through even the smallest holes of the work net . . . work and other activities constantly feed on the underlying ground of playing, using the play mood for refreshment, energy, unusual ways of turning things around, insights, breaks, opening and especially looseness.'[81]

This is like the *lila* or sport of the Hindu gods, where the motive of Brahman's creation of the earth is what one scholar calls 'purposeless purpose'.[82] Indeed, from an Asian-philosophical perspective, the idea of a 'play ethic' itself – a set of preferences and principles that order our play – could seem cripplingly Western. Both Buddhists and Hindus could say that, in our manifesto-like ambitions, we are merely being ignorant of the law of *karma* and the *samsaric* world. All the many strategies we have proposed, by which play can create an effect in the world and realize our purposes, could seem pointless – if our fate is to joyously (or is that carelessly? mindlessly?) participate in a cosmically playful world.[83]

Indeed, in the last lines of his magnum opus, Sutton-Smith almost admits that he has indeed fallen foul of his own karmic law. The psychologist is always, at some level, committed to human improvement and evolution: and despite his 'extensive criticisms of the rhetoric of progress', he despairs that he has merely 'invented another form of it' – that is, the notion that our brains need to maintain a perpetual state of play to keep the human organism adaptable for any circumstance or challenge.[84] There are also 'neurological descriptions,' suggests Sutton-Smith, 'that prompt us to see a brain at play that is as universal as that kind of play envisaged for the gods and for the physical universe' (i.e. the indeterminate and unpredictable universe theorized by quantum physicists).[85]

In any case, whether we see the brain as primal player, or the universe, there is more than enough evidence to support a powerful intuition here: that our personal playfulness might harmonize with, or at least be analogous to, a more cosmic and constitutive playfulness in ways that we must accept are not entirely in our control. Yet the notion that we are played by our universe, as much as we play with our universe, is still a mighty challenge to the Cartesian-Christian mindset.

It seems impossible to assert the primacy of one form of play without the others crowding in upon it: and spirituality would seem to be no different than any other realm we have dealt with. Yet even as a broad and deep spirituality tries to subsume the player into the cosmic play, I must let the individual player try to make her last, complex stand. James Carse's *Finite and Infinite Games* is probably the most brilliant attempt to deal with the spiritual consequences and contradictions of play. It proceeds from the very notion that one can be a conscious and intending player; there is a set of actions and strategies that one can take to live 'a life of possibility'. Yet this is a playful self which is far from smug, impregnable or narcissistic, simply projecting its simulations and parlaying its games onto the world. Carse calls this kind of self a 'finite' player – for whom every game entered into (whether cultural or economic, sexual or political) is one which must be won or lost.

The character of the infinite player can be read from this summary of Carse's own hypnotic syllogisms:

Finite players play within boundaries; infinite players play with boundaries.

Finite players are serious; infinite players are playful.

Finite players win titles; infinite players have nothing but their names.

A finite player plays to be powerful; an infinite player plays with strength.

A finite player consumes time; an infinite player generates time.

The finite player aims to win eternal life; the infinite player aims for eternal birth.

The philosopher David Loy puts Carse's statements into the context of Indra's Net, that vision of a universe where individuals exist both in themselves and in relation to every other individual. 'The difference is between a player struggling to ground himself in the Net, and a player who plays with the Net because she has realized that she *is* the Net.' Loy goes on: 'We are to play not because there is nothing else to do, not because the lack of some higher meaning means we just while away our time, but because play is implied by the nature of meaning and time...'[86]

So the infinite player begins to sound like the state of selflessness, the loss of self-preoccupation, that Buddhists often aim for – that 'stepping out from the house of ego' that connects a person to a deeper universal order.[87] But Carse's vision always sounds far less contemplative than that, far more witty and risky – like that of a high-stakes gambler, or a racing driver:

> To be playful is not to be trivial, or frivolous, or to act as if nothing of consequence will happen. On the contrary, when we are playful with each other we relate as free persons, and the relationship is open to surprise;

everything that happens is of consequence. It is, in fact, seriousness that closes itself to consequence, for seriousness is a dread of the unpredictable outcome of open possibility. To be serious is to press for a specified conclusion. To be playful is to allow for possibility *whatever the cost to oneself* [my emphasis].[88]

Whatever the cost to oneself: this is the essential challenge that any ethic of play must make to anyone who considers the ludic life. To be a player is to make a commitment to a kind of fully conscious, everyday activism that can literally 'put into play' all the structures, routines, accepted roles and embedded understandings of your life – in technology and education, families and communities, businesses and organizations, politics and spirituality, culture and consciousness. And this has consequences which, as I've tried to show, are often revolutionary and transformative in nature. Once you begin to explore and develop your own ethos of play, there's no knowing where you'll end up. Or who you'll end up becoming.

If the world is composed of suffering it is because the world is essentially free. Suffering is the necessary consequence of the free play of the parts of the system. You should know that, and say so.

– Michel Houellebecq, *The Elementary Particles*, 2000

IN SOME FUTURE ECCENTRIC PLANET:
Where Wit may sparkle all its rays,
Uncurst with Caution's fears;
And Pleasure, basking in the blaze,
Rejoice for endless years!

– Robert Burns, 'Letter to William Smellie', 1835

As it is outlined here, the play ethic is neither unlikely, nor outlandish, nor even unduly impractical. I'm partly making that claim on the basis of the kinds of people who have sought me out over the last few years, and the kinds of conversations we've had. From primary teachers in Melbourne to Cabinet Office gurus in Whitehall; from hackers and telecom executives in Helsinki to humanistic psychologists and comic improvisers in San Francisco; from wildly idealistic students in Shannon to weary social workers in Dundee; from perplexed jazz musicians in a dingy Glasgow bar to unimpressed ad executives in a converted London biscuit factory; and many, many others. I have learned from them all, and I hope they have learned something from me.

But one thing that has become obvious is that a play ethic only addresses some problems, while leaving others almost entirely untouched. Apart from the last chapter, and some elements of the general theory of play, my analysis has sought out the player mostly within the institutions and locales of Western modernity – the school, the office, the laboratory or studio, the democratic political arena, the bohemian enclave, the media outlet, the nuclear and post-nuclear family. My argument has been that, as the great unsettling forces of informationalism, feminism and environmentalism have rattled these institutions apart, forcing them to question their very premises and goals, we have been in need of a new social rationale. Not to restore these structures to their former solidity – the ambition of the Third Way communitarians in Europe and America in the nineties – but to help them deconstruct themselves into new forms: a new way for parents and children to be with each other, a new way for technology's benefits to be accessible and empowering, a new way for organizations to bring people together to put 'a dent in the universe', as Warren Bennis puts it.

'Play' – as a noun, a verb, a reality, an emotion, a memory, an intensity – rouses people to think about their lives in a way which somehow makes chaos and uncertainty seem natural, inevitable, fertile: the 'life of possibility', in James Carse's words. And a 'play ethic' – the idea that there might be some consistent principles to adhere to, some rules of thumb whereby the openness and unpredictability of the times might be confidently, rather than fearfully, faced – seems to attract many people. Whether I've contributed to the change, or whether I've just been particularly alive to the topic at a moment of speedy cultural evolution, I'm not exactly sure. But I conclude this book in early 2003 with a growing sense of the legitimacy of the players' perspective in the developed West – whether as an intellectual topic, as a possible identity for the productive and creative life, or as a growing emotional zone in which men and women can further explore their new equalities and vulnerabilities.[1]

'What is the ethical foundation of informationalism?' wondered Manuel Castells in 1996. 'And does it need an ethical foundation at all?' When I first read that, I wanted to answer that play was its foundation, and that it was indeed sorely needed. Looking at his suggestive notes towards what a 'spirit of informationalism' might look like, it seems more than exemplified by the research and interviews that have gone into this book. 'It is a culture, indeed,' says Castells, 'but a culture of the ephemeral, a culture of each strategic decision, a patchwork of experiences and interests, rather than a charter of rights and obligations.'[2]

Yet I have tried to move on from that patchwork, and to suggest that we might well have obligations and rights in a play culture. The *right to play* – with the state, market and third sector supporting our desires to compose a richly satisfying and value-creating life – is counterbalanced by the *obligation to care*: the same institutions expecting that the inevitable fragility of human beings be directly addressed by players. How we ensure those obligations are met is the most difficult topic this book could address – and I eagerly invite your responses. Sometimes I believe that the more the existential freedom and non-alienation of the player becomes a mass opportunity, the more altruism and care will become a natural element in our repertoire of self-expressions, simply one of our 'response abilities'. This is the hope of substantial thinkers like Beck, Bauman and Rushkoff.[3] Sometimes, in a less sanguine mood, I think that there might have to be some limited measure of conditionality, some evident tripwire whereby the support systems for the full player are progressively reduced, or some compulsion to at least offer an explanation for destructive or self-destructive behaviour.[4]

Yet my deepest faith – which is no less justifiable than the suspicious distrust of human nature held by many politicians and business leaders – is that the angels will make work for idle hands in the players' republic, not the devils. And in the true spirit of play, I think we should try to build our playgrounds among ourselves in the first place – rather than try to iron out all problems of rights and obligations in advance, or wait for enlightened system-steerers to see the error of their ways. We should forge the ethics of play in practice as much as in theory.

This is already happening. Players are building their own institutions and constitutions, enabled by the wired and wireless Net, to answer the yearning for meaning that is the most dominant human response to the upheavals of the early twenty-first century. These can be about private yearnings – say, to reconnect yourself to the playful identities of your childhood, answered by websites like Classmates.com or Friendsreunited.com. Or they can be very civic and public yearnings – the notion that an 'emergent democracy' might come to fruition, through some orchestration of the many articulate voices now expressing themselves through social software, like blogging and affinity networks, wikipedia and open-source. I very much hope that the rhetorics and justifications for more playful forms of life outlined by this book are taken up by these digital constituencies, and 'hacked' into better, worse or at least more interesting shapes by their passionate engagements. 'We are an enterprise of mortals, disdaining to protect ourselves against surprise; living in the strength of our vision, we eschew power and make joyous play of boundaries.' Amen to that, Brother Carse.

Yet as the previous chapter indicated, we no longer live in a world where the 'developed West' can presume that its gossamer webs of informationalism will remain intact. Nor that its powers to 'rip, mix and burn', to morph signs and simulate experiences, will always meet with global approval.

Play can only really flourish, whether at the level of the body or the body politic, if an appropriate level of security and sustainability can be guaranteed. A society where small ads now appear in newspapers for chemical-proof bunkers or anthrax-detection kits; where citizens walk the streets in surgical masks to protect themselves from the season's lethal infection; where national leaders carefully orchestrate war fever against disobedient client states in order to tide them over to the next plebiscite . . . No, this is not a society that could readily support the vision of the play ethic: a vision that presumes mutual reciprocation, acceptance of difference and otherness, an open commons of resources and information.

On my last invitation to the Cabinet Office in London in 2003, I was happy to tell them that all their 'institutional reforms' would mean nothing if some angry young Middle-Eastern men finally got themselves organized enough to either irradiate or bioterrorize a major British conurbation within the next few years, and thus unravelled the social web of civility that still persists on these islands. British popular culture, in all its irreverent playfulness, is actually one of the few attractive melodies to be heard in the advancing cacophony of the 'clash of civilizations'. It is difficult to imagine a mighty war between the 'free West' and 'Islam as the new communism' in Britain, for example, when the cinema halls are showing movies like *East is East* or *Bend It Like Beckham*, when the evening television runs comedies like *The Kumars at Number 42*, and the book-stalls are filled with capacious multicultural best-sellers like Zadie Smith's *White Teeth*.

This is a consciousness question more than it is a technology question: the real lethality lies in the intent to cause mass destruction, more than the capability to do so. The quality of the global conversation has to improve urgently. Governments who believe that force, might and violence prepare the way for democracy, civility and peace need to be reminded, by the imaginative activism of their citizens, that their logic is deeply flawed. If the play ethic enabled in Westerners and northerners a greater self-consciousness about the multiple truths that might pertain in a truly globalized world; if it encouraged us to be aware of diversity not as an act of tolerance but as an imaginative empathy that puts you in the shoes of the other, respecting their games and the integrity of their rules – then it might be more than a shuffle of the chairs on the deck of the *Titanic*, however fascinating, innovative, even preferable these rearrangments might be in the short-term.

If the play ethic can moderate the resurgence of the panicky, paranoid, commanding and controlling tendencies of Western societies, post 9/11 by raising a steady voice for the rights of individuals to order their time, space and resources in a humane and generative manner, then it will have been more than a mere 'media intervention', a 'cultural meme', 'this season's talker'. It will have increased the peace, as the activists say. For all the exciting diversity of lifestyles, technologies and organizations both described and prescribed in the preceding pages, there could be no greater ambition.

So I bid you: *lego!* and play well. Or preferably, as the Indo-Europeans once said: *engage yourself.*

ACKNOWLEDGEMENTS

I know this book has changed at least *one* person's life. It's brushed, tickled and thumped quite a few other lives, some of whom need to be acknowledged.

My immediate thanks to Jeremy Trevathan, who commissioned the book, Bill Hamilton, who closed the deal, and most of all to my editor, the smart and patient Stuart Evers. Other editors who have paid me to flesh out these ideas in their news and review pages since the late nineties must also receive their due: Mark Douglas-Home, George McKechnie, Harry Reid, Andrew Jaspan, Boyd Tonkin, Louise France and John Mulholland.

The response of many organizations and institutions to my play ethic project has been heartening, and sometimes even rent-paying. My thanks to Bartle Bogle Hegarty, Lowe Lintas, St Luke's, the International Society for the Performing Arts, Aula, Acorn, Demos, ICA, Victoria Innovation Schools Commission, Zack Lynch's Brainwaves, the Scottish Executive, Royal Museum of Scotland, ADSW and especially the International Futures Forum.

It may seem nerdish in the extreme, but I have to single out some software for specific gratitude. Since 2000, Ari Paparo's Blink site (www.blink.com) has allowed me to roam the world, yet take my research library with me, available and updatable at any Web cafe. Brewster Kahle's Wayback Machine (www.archive.org) retrieved much deleted Web content for me. I'd also like to commend the *Guardian*, the *Telegraph*, the *Scotsman* and the BBC for resisting the move to paid-for online archives. We freelance intellectuals need our commons: they held their nerve against the accountants.

Thinkers and writers who have commented helpfully on parts of this text are: Rebecca Abrams, Tom Bentley, Jeremy Brown, Mihaly Cziksentmihalyi, Mark Earls, Brian Goodwin, Christopher Harvie, Pekka Himanen, Stephen Linstead, Zack Lynch, Paul Miller, Geoff Mulgan, Richard Reeves, Douglas Rushkoff, Matt Statler, Jane Taylor, Phil Teer, May Miles Thomas, Michael Thomsen, Stephen Turner, Robert Wallsten and James Woudhuysen.

Particular thanks are due to Indra Adnan for including me in her range of forums and think tanks over the years (including Power of the Arts, Poiesis, the S-Word and New Integrity), for her crucial engagement with this book in its closing stages and for her love and understanding.

My brothers Gregory and Garry John Kane have kept me in orbital contact with my singing career: I hope to land again on that planet very soon. Through their unstinting willingness to love and care for my children (and me), John and Mary Kane, and the McAlpine family, are as constitutive of *The Play Ethic* as anyone. As a mother, a professional and a friend, Joan McAlpine knows how important she was to this book's eventual emergence. For all that, my profound thanks.

And as daughters to a father, Grace and Eleanor McAlpine-Kane are at the inexpressible end of things. Girls, I hope this book is a mirror to your idealism, energy and sheer embrace of the world: you are the most natural players I know. I love you both, and I couldn't have written this without you.

NOTES

INTRO: TOWARDS THE PLAY ETHIC

1 See Bartleby.com, American Heritage Dictionary,
http://www.bartleby.com/61/roots/IE112.html

2 No, I did not support the war – for reasons which I hope become clear at the end of this book.

3 Philip Stephens and Cathy Newman, 'Blair warns Chirac on the future of Europe', *Financial Times*, 28 April 2003.

4 Ian Traynor, 'New Europe gets shock lesson in realpolitik', *Guardian*, 28 April 2003.

5 Dan Plesch, 'Without the UN safety net, even Japan might go nuclear', *Guardian*, 28 April 2003.

6 On play as agonism, see Johan Huizinga, *Homo Ludens: A Study of Play In Culture*, Beacon Press, 1971.

7 Jackie Ashley, 'Tough, yes, but at least he is not in the awkward squad', *Guardian*, 28 April 2003.

8 Jean Eaglesham, 'Labour and Tories vie to play down expectations', *Financial Times*, 28 April 2003.

9 Sarah Hall, 'Blair brother tells of family trauma', *Guardian*, 28 April 2003.

10 And some have: see Leo Abse, *Tony Blair: behind the smile.* Robson, 2003.

11 Michael Howard, 'Fighting is over but the deaths go on', *Guardian*, 28 April 2003.

12 See D.W. Winnicott, *Playing and Reality*, Basic, 1971, and Erik H. Erikson, *Toys and Reasons: Stages in the Ritualisation of Experience*, Marion Boyars, 1978.

13 James Carse, *Finite and Infinite Games*, Ballantine, 1986, p. 4.

14 Terrence Deacon, *The Symbolic Species: the Co-Evolution of Language and the Brain*, Norton, 1997.

15 See 'On camp', in Susan Sontag, *A Susan Sontag Reader*, Penguin 1983.

16 See http://www.bbc.co.uk/innovationnation and http://www.nesta.org.uk

17 See Richard Florida, *The Rise of the Creative Class: and How It's Transforming Work, Leisure, Community and Everyday Life*, Basic, 2004, and website http://www.creativeclass.com

18 See Winnicott note above.

19 My favourite recent slogan from the anti-capitalist movement was from their Mayday 2003 celebrations, urging supporters to occupy the streets of London

creatively: 'Mayday is our weapon of mass construction. Use it!'
http://www.wombles.org.uk/actions/mayday2003.php

20 See Max Weber, *The Protestant Ethic and the Spirit of Capitalism*, Routledge, 1985. For a useful history of the work ethic, see Richard Donkin, *Blood Sweat and Tears: the evolution of work*, Texere, 2002.

21 See Boris Frankel, *The Post-Industrial Utopians*, Polity, 1987.

22 For a splendidly (but intelligently) conspiratorial narrative of the suppression of seventies' utopianism, see Brian Holmes, 'The flexible personality', http://amsterdam.nettime.org/Lists-Archives/nettime-l-0201/msg00012.html

23 See Stuart Hall, *The Hard Road to Renewal: Thatcherism and the Crisis of the Left*. Verso, 1988.

24 See Pat Kane, 'The angels do make work for idle hands', *Scotland on Sunday*, 5 January 1997.

25 See Alfonso Montuori, 'Creativity, complexity and improvisation in daily life', California Institute of Integral Studies, http://www.ciis.edu/faculty/articles/montuori/creativityandimprov.pdf

26 Brian Sutton-Smith, *The Ambiguity of Play*. Harvard, 1999.

27 On the link between 'renascence/renaissance' and 'reframing', see Douglas Rushkoff, *Open Source Democracy*, Demos, 2003, http://www.demos.co.uk/opensourcedemocracy_pdf_media_public.aspx

28 For humour and play, see Simon Critchley, *On Humour*, Routledge, 2002.

29 See Helen's website, http://www.genderquake.org

30 Peter Reason and Brian Goodwin, 'Toward a science of qualities in organizations: lessons from complexity theory and postmodern biology', *Concepts and Transformations*, 1999, 4(3), pp. 281–317. http://www.bath.ac.uk/~mnspwr/Papers/sciencequalities.htm

31 Anthony Giddens, *The Future of Radical Politics*, Polity, 1994, p. 101.

ONE / NEXT MOVE

1 My first ever essay on the play ethic was in *Scotland on Sunday*, 5 January 1997, 'When angels guide the hands of idleness', p. 16.

TWO / A GENERAL THEORY OF PLAY

1 The rhetorics of play are taken from Sutton-Smith's magnum opus *The Ambiguity of Play* (Harvard, 1997). Sutton-Smith regards these rhetorics in a similar fashion to Michel Foucault's notion of 'discourses' – i.e. they are ways of speaking and thinking about play that represent various power interests (e.g. educators interested in play as progress, artists and creatives in play as imagination, politicians and sports people in play as power and contest, etc.). Sutton-Smith's perspective is academic and dispassionate,

though driven by a belief in the evolved primordiality of play as a kind of perpetual process of necessary innovation for advanced mammals. My own interest in the rhetorics, taken together as a broad typification of human cultural behaviour, is in the complexity and dynamism of the social order they describe – a social order which is already beginning to flourish in the developed West as its populations move towards a 'post-scarcity' condition. A 'play ethic', as this chapter endeavours to show, is partly an exercise in auditing the existing balance of play forms and rhetorics in any social phenomenon, and then an invitation to find a way to address any excessive emphases or debits. This 'play audit' will then apply itself to the various domains of social order recognizable to modernity – technology, education, family and community, the arts, business and politics.

2 Sutton-Smith talks of a seventh value system or rhetoric of play, play as frivolity – the reduction of play enacted by the work ethic, into a 'waste of time, idleness, triviality' (Chapter 11, 'Rhetorics of frivolity', *Ambiguity of Play*). His book (and this one) is an attempt to defy the Puritan injunction and map out the full range of playful forms and values. But Sutton-Smith holds out for a 'playfulness' – a 'metaplay, which plays with normal expectations of play itself' (1997, p. 147). This can justify the historical tradition of the court jester, the feast of fools, the Rabelasian reversals of power and status, and its contemporary correlates in satire and humour, the political cartoon, the 'dumb and dumber' youth media (MTV's *Jackass*, the Farelly brothers' films), even the political 'custard-pieing' of contemporary global figures like Bill Gates (see http://news.bbc.co.uk/1/hi/uk/629352.stm). Don Handleman has talked of 'playfulness as the very openness that enables us to frame play, and to enter into its realities . . . it is so important precisely because it is itself not framed. A condition of being in the world on its way to becoming someone or something else, playfulness is more embodied feeling and aesthetic than it is cognition . . . Playfulness is the simultaneity of multiplicity.' (From Handleman, 'Framing, braiding and killing play', *Focaal: European Journal of Anthropology*, no. 37, 2001, pp. 145–6). Part of the development of the play rhetorics in this book is that playfulness, in that sense of the 'simultaneity of multiplicity' – the reality that there are different realities before us – is actually an *ontological* diversity. Our science, both social and natural, is revealing a universe which is deeply mutable, open to possibility, irreducibly 'in play'. In short, if we laugh, we laugh *with* the playful universe – not *at* it.

3 John Brockman, ed., *The Third Culture*, Simon and Schuster, 1997. Also see his website, http://www.edge.org

4 Whitney Houston, 'The Greatest Love of All', written by Michael Masser and Linda Creed.

5 'After all, play itself is not a figure of speech, not a trope, not a metaphor: play is at first a kind of biological, prelinguistic enactment with its own claims on human existence, no matter how metaphorized it is in other

claims.' Sutton-Smith, *The Ambiguity of Play*, p.143. Also see *Ambiguity*, Chapter 2, 'Rhetorics of animal play' and Chapter 3, 'Rhetorics of child play'.

6 See the classic collection of essays in J.S. Bruner, A. Jolly and K. Sylva, *Play: Its Role in Development and Evolution*, Penguin, 1976; also A.D. Pellegrini, *The Future of Play Theory*, SUNY Press, 1995; and for the play of higher mammals, see Jane Goodall, *The Chimpanzees of Gombe*, Harvard UP, 1986. Also see Patrick Bateson and Paul Martin, *A Design For Life: How Behaviour Develops*, Jonathan Cape, 1999, Chapter 11, 'Everything to play for'; Edward P. Fisher, 'The impact of play on development: a meta-analysis', *Play and Culture* 5.2 (May 1992), pp. 159–81; Kim A. McDonald, 'The secrets of animal play', *Chronicle of Higher Education*, 13 January 1995; E.C. Mouledoux, 'The development of play in childhood: an application of the classifications of Piaget and Caillois in developmental research', *Studies in the Anthropology of Play: Papers in Memory of B. Allen Tindall*, ed. P. Stevens, Leisure Press, 1977, pp. 196–209; F.B. Oakley, 'Methodological considerations for studies of play in primates', *The Anthropological Study of Play: Problems and Prospects*, eds. D.F. Lancy, and B.A. Tindall, Leisure Press, 1976. 173–8; C. Trevarthen and F. Grant. 'Infant games and the creation of culture', *Not Work Alone: A Cross-Cultural View of Activities Superfluous to Survival*, eds. J. Cherfas and R. Lewin, London, England: Temple Smith, 1980, pp. 33–44.

For a general and combative overview of the continuities between animal and human play see Marc Bekoff, 'The evolution of animal play, emotions and social morality', *Zygon: Journal of Religion and Society*, December 2001, vol. 36, no. 4, pp. 615–66. Also, Marek Špinka, Ruth C. Newberry and Marc Bekoff, 'Mammalian play: Training for the unexpected', *The Quarterly Review of Biology*, Volume 76, Number 2, June 2001: 'Our major new functional hypothesis is that play enables animals to develop flexible kinematic and emotional responses to unexpected events in which they experience a sudden loss of control. Specifically, we propose that play functions to increase the versatility of movements used to recover from sudden shocks such as loss of balance and falling over, and to enhance the ability of animals to cope emotionally with unexpected stressful situations. To obtain this "training for the unexpected", we suggest that animals actively seek and create unexpected situations in play through self-handicapping; that is, deliberately relaxing control over their movements or actively putting themselves into disadvantageous positions and situations.'

7 See Philippe Aries, *Centuries of Childhood*, Cape, 1962: 'In medieval society the idea of childhood did not exist; this is not to suggest that children were neglected, forsaken or despised. The idea of childhood is not to be confused with affection for children: it corresponds to an awareness of the particular nature of childhood, that particular nature which distinguishes the child from the adult, even the young adult. In medieval society this awareness was lacking. That is why, as soon as the child could live without the constant solicitude of his mother, his nanny or his cradle-rocker, he belonged to adult society' p. 125. 'Medieval art until about the twelfth century did not know

childhood or did not attempt to portray it. It is hard to believe that this neglect was due to incompetence or incapacity; it seems more probable that there was no place for childhood in the medieval world' p. 31.

8 Rousseau quotes taken from Cohen, *The Development of Play*, Routledge, 1993, p. 23. In many ways, *Emile* was a major marker of the transition from Enlightenment to romanticism – romanticism both as a cultural mood and as a period of civic activism and reform: 'If the philosophy of the Enlightenment brought to eighteenth-century Europe a new confidence in the possiblity of human happiness, special credit must go to Rousseau for calling attention to the needs of children. For the first time in history, he made a large group of people believe that childhood was worth the attention of intelligent adults, encouraging an interest in the process of growing up, rather than just the product. Education of children was part of the interest in progress which was so predominant in intellectual trends of the time.' P. Robertson, 'Home as a nest: middle-class childhood in nineteenth-century Europe' in L. DeMause (ed.), *The History of Childhood*, London, Souvenir, 1976, p. 407.

9 'This new privileged status of childhood entailed more than a percieved separateness of child and adult. From the time of the Romantic poets onwards it is not uncommon to see childhood as a repository of inheritances and attributes which were often lost or blunted in adulthood. The more adults and society seemed bleak, urbanized and alienated, the more childhood came to be seen as properly a garden, enclosing within the safety of its walls a way of life which was in touch with nature and which preserved the rude virtues of earlier periods of the history of mankind.' H. Cunningham, *The Children of the Poor: Representations of Childhood since the Seventeenth Century*, Oxford, 1991, p. 43.

10 See entries on Froebel, Montessori and Pestalozzi in *Fifty Major Thinkers on Education: from Confucius to Dewey*, ed. J.A. Palmer, Routledge, 2001.

11 See Janet Moyles, *The Excellence of Play*, Open University Press, 1994. John Dewey, who is usually seen as the foremost American advocate of a child-centred education, had a complicated and contradictory attitude to play, possibly due to the historical strength of the Protestant work ethic in the US. 'Perhaps realizing that he can't advocate work while simultaneously holding on to such human-centered views as democracy and interest, Dewey decided simply to redefine work to mean something more like play, that is, voluntary, spontaneous, authentic, and purposeful. As he put it regarding his description of work activities, "[t]he dictionary does not permit us to call such activities work." His view of work, then, is that it is play, except it seems to be more social, purposeful, and utilitarian. He calls other types of work that are not intrinsically motivated drudgery, toil, or labour.' From 'Reinterpreting Dewey: some thoughts on his views of science and play in education', Alexander Makedon, Chicago State University. (http://webs.csu.edu/~bigoama/articles/JohnDewy.html

12 'Throughout the 1860s and 1870s, groups of middle-class reformers had come to see that it was not enough to simply forbid most forms of leisure,

especially as this strengthened the attractions of the public house. Thus the emphasis shifted more towards the provision of alternatives, designed to supplant more immoral forms . . . The real success of the "rational recreationists" [was in] the active involvement of the new local authorities in leisure provision.' From 'Passing the time away: the historical development of leisure', in John Clarke and Chas Critcher, *The Devil Makes Work: Leisure in Capitalist Britain*, London, Macmillan, 1985, pp. 64, 65.

13 See James Woudhuysen, 'Play as the main event in international and UK culture', *Cultural Trends 43/44*, 2001.

14 Sutton-Smith's critique of Piaget remains devastating, accusing the great thinker of an impossibly narrow conception of how play forms affect adults throughout their lives. 'Piaget on Play: a critique', *Psychological Review 73*, pp. 104–10 (1966), and 'Piaget on play: revisited', in *The Relationship Between Social and Cognitive Development*, ed. W.F. Overton, Erlbaum, 1982.

15 The two scientists most identified with the rooting of adult play in solid psychological research are Mihaly Csikszentmihalyi, *Creativity: Flow and the Psychology of Discovery and Invention*, New York, Harper Collins, 1996, and Howard Gardner, *Art, Mind and Brain*, New York, Basic Books, 1982.

16 Hara Estroff Marano, 'The power of play', *Psychology Today*, July/August 1999, pp. 36–42.

17 'Whatever happened to play?', *Time*, 30 April 2001; Bryant Furlow, 'Play's the thing', *New Scientist*, 9 June 2001, p. 30.
http://www.geocities.com/multiculturalhouse/G_play.htm

18 The concept of the 'human motor' comes from Anson Rabinbach. 'The displacement of work from the centre to the periphery of late twentieth-century thought can thus be understood by the disappearance of the system of representations that placed the working body at the juncture of nature and society – by the disappearance of the "human motor" . . . The disappearance of work is a consequence of the declining power of an intellectual discourse that places energy and fatigue at the centre of social perception.' *The Human Motor: Energy, Fatigue and the Origins of Modernity*, Berkeley, University of California Press, 1992. Yet the modern rhetorics of play clearly lead towards a new conception of what makes people active and productive in a post-work age – a new 'human motor', tapping into a much less exhaustible set of human resources (the desiring rather than labouring body; the active rather than routine mind). But, as we shall see, a *modern* rhetoric of play is only half the story of a truly playful civilization – including the 'ethic' that might help make it worth living in.

19 Sutton-Smith, *The Ambiguity of Play*, Harvard, 1997, Chapter 8, 'Rhetorics of the imaginary'. In their revulsion at the greyness and standardization of early industrial society, the Romantics proclaimed their belief in the playful potential of the human mind. No one exemplifies the notion that art could make the universe a playground more than William Blake. His poetry is always zooming in and out of perspective, like a powerful computer game, using verbal form to open out new worlds: 'To see a world in a grain of

sand/And a heaven in a wild flower/Hold infinity in the palm of your hand/And eternity in an hour', William Blake, 'Augaries of Innocence' in *Selected Poetry*, OUP, 1998, p. 173.

20 Percy Bysshe Shelley, 'In Defence of Poetry', 1821, available at http://www.bartelby.com/27/23.html; Friedrich von Schiller, 15th letter in *On the Aesthetic Education of Man*, Clarendon Press, 1983.

21 On the ethic of intersubjectivity, see Jurgen Habermas, *The Philsophical Discourse of Modernity*, Polity, 1986.

22 A reference to Jean-Luc Godard's great aphorism about avant-garde cinema, '*Ce n'est pas une image juste, c'est juste une image?*' ('It's not a just image, it's just an image'), *Vent d'Est* (film), 1970; Robert Burns, 'To a Louse' in *Selected Poems*, Penguin, 1994.

23 Breton quote is from André Breton, *Manifestoes of Surrealism*, translated by Richard Seaver and Helen R. Lane, University of Michigan Press, 1969.

24 Ekow Eshun, 'Surrealism and advertising', http://www.bbc.co.uk/arts/tate/surrealism/ekow1.shtml

25 James Woudhuysen, 'The magic of mobile', *Spiked-online*, 9 May 2001, http://www.spiked-online.com/Articles/00000002D0A7.htm, and 'Team players', 12 April 2001, http://www.spiked-online.com/Articles/000000005560.htm. See also Chapter 8, this volume.

26 Howard Gardner, *The Disciplined Mind*. See also Chapter 6, this volume.

27 See Lawrence Lessig, *The Future of Ideas*, and the interview in this volume, Chapter 9.

28 Johan Huizinga, *Homo Ludens: A Study of Play in Culture*, Beacon Press, 1971.

29 Sutton-Smith, *The Ambiguity of Play*, Harvard, 1997, Chapter 10, 'Rhetorics of the self'.

30 Take the emblematic image of transatlantic pop in 2000: the musician Moby, leaping ecstatically into space on the cover of his best-selling album, called 'Play', or the satellite channel, showing music and comedy, which urges an entire nation to go ludic with the title UK Play. For a full range of examples, see Woudhuysen, 'Play as the main event', *ibid.*, pp. 102–36.

31 Woudhuysen, *ibid*.

32 A.K. Nardo, *The Ludic Self in Seventeenth Century English Literature*, SUNY, 1991.

33 Sutton-Smith, *The Ambiguity of Play*, Harvard, 1977, pp. 177–8.

34 See Andrew Hussey, *The Game of War*, Jonathan Cape, 2001.

35 See Richard Neville's *Playpower*, Paladin, 1970, and his later memoir, *Hippie Hippie Shake*, Bloomsbury, 1997. One of the most ironic manifestations of play as freedom comes from the post-hippie fallout. American writer David Brooks has recently described the rise of the 'bobos' – 'bourgeois bohemians' – in American society who have turned freedom to play with reality into freedom to play with commodities. They have used their bourgeois affluence to express their subjectivity through bohemian consumer lifestyles – exotic toys, detailed personal therapies, ever more exclusive

experiences. Indeed, Brooks builds his own 'play ethic' out of a blend of all three modernist play rhetorics: 'We Bobos have taken the bourgeois imperative to strive and succeed, and we have married it to the bohemian impulse to experience new sensations. The result is a set of social regulations constructed to encourage pleasures that are physically, spiritually and intellectually useful while stigmatizing ones that are useless or harmful. In this way the Protestant Work Ethic has been replaced by the Bobo Play Ethic, which is equally demanding. Everything we do must serve the Life Mission, which is cultivation, progress and self-improvement.' Brooks, *Bobos In Paradise*, 2001.

36 Howard Gardner, *Developmental Psychology* and *Art, Mind and Brain*, both Little, Brown, 1982.

37 A modernist play ethic could be understood as the ultimate end point of the Renaissance humanist tradition. The fifteenth-century Florentine philosopher Pico della Mirandola wrote that 'man is an animal of diverse, multiform and destructible nature . . . it is given to man to have that which he chooses and to be that which he wills'. We must infuse the world with our playful imaginings: 'It is ignoble', says Pico, 'to give birth to nothing from ourselves.' from Richard Sennett, *The Corrosion of Character*, W.W. Norton, 1998, p. 101. Between the Renaissance philosopher and the player exulting in the technological and cultural playgrounds of the developed world, there would seem to be an enduring and consistent conversation.

38 For a recent assessment of the split between modern and ancient rhetorics of play, see Brian Sutton-Smith, 'Foreword', in *Focaal: European Journal of Anthropology*, no. 37, 2001, pp. 7–9, special section on 'Playful power and ludic spaces: studies in games of life'. Summary article by Galina Lindquist, 'Elusive play and its relations to power', available online at http://www.focaal.box.nl/previous/intro_37.pdf

39 For background to the British National Lottery, see http://society.guardian.co.uk/lottery

40 Subsequent adverts have also evoked the sheer irrational disruptiveness of a lottery win: the sense that one stroke of luck will change your life irreversibly, forever – but unpredictably. In one ad, a giant 'thunderball' suddenly bursts out of the cinema screen, moving awesomely down the aisles at great speed – threatening to crush the audience members, but actually only ruffling their hair. Some even look over their shoulders wistfully as it thunders away. The suppressed violence, the surrender to implacably awesome forces in these images, is terrifying. Also see Plato, *Laws*, Princeton University Press, 1969, p. 1300: 'One might be moved to say . . . that no law is ever made by a man, and that human history is all an affair of chance . . . and yet there is something else which may be said with no less plausibility . . . *That God is all, while chance and circumstance, under God, set the whole course of life for us.*'

41 See Chapter 10, 'The infinite game', this volume.

42 Don Handelman, 'Passages to play: paradox and process', *Play and Culture*, 5 (1), pp. 1–19, 1992.

43 See Gerda Reith, *The Age of Chance: Gambling and Western Culture*, Routledge, 2002. 'The appeal of gambling has often been obscured by the involvement of money, with explanations for the former (especially given its modern commercialization) concentrating heavily on the latter. This is misleading, however, for the ancient and widespread popularity of the activity taps into more fundamental human concerns – not the desire to be rich, but the desire to be *secure* . . . Under this interpretation, the concept of chance is sacralized, once more becoming a sign of metaphysical meaning through which gamblers can infer something of their status – not only in the game, but also in the wider world . . . In an Age of Chance, surrounded by a multitude of risks and existing precariously in a general climate of ontological insecurity, the actions of the gambler have implications for existence that extend far beyond the individual game being played' (pp. 183–4).

44 Sutton-Smith, *Ambiguity of Play*, pp. 72–3.

45 Alessandro Falassi, *Time out of Time: Essays on the Festival*, University of New Mexico Press, 1967, p. 3.

46 Matthew Collin, *Altered State: the Story of Ecstasy Culture*, Serpent's Tail, 1997.

47 Jeremy Rifkin, *Age of Access: the New Culture of Hypercapitalism, Where All of Life Is a Paid-for Experience*, Penguin, 2001.

48 Huizinga continues: 'From the life of childhood right up to the highest achievements of civilisation, one of the strongest incentives to perfection, both individual and social, is the desire to be praised and honored for one's excellence . . . The point is that all these contests, even when fantastically depicted (in legend and story) as mortal and titanic combats, still belong to the domain of play', *Homo Ludens*, p. 3 See also Roger Callois, *Man, Play and Games*, University of Illinois Press 1961.

49 '"Assert myself to eliminate the hurt": black youth in urban America', Marcyliena Morgan, Harvard University, contribution to Aspen Instutute Round Table, http://www.aspenroundtable.org/5Morgan.pdf. Also see Loic Wacquant, 'From slavery to mass incarceration: rethinking the "race question" in the US', *New Left Review* 13, January–February 2002, http://www.newleftreview.net/NLR24703.shtml

50 And the seventh – the trivial and humorous – allows us, always, the possibility of laughter as the last defence against the oppressions of reality.

51 Social theory might also see the divide between modern and ancient play as a version of its own notable duality – play as agency versus play as structure. See Zygmunt Bauman, *Postmodern Ethics*, Polity, 1996.

52 Of course, the subversive impact that the Second World War had upon the authority of the machine metaphor – from the all too mechanistic horrors of the American atom bomb, to the Nazi death camps proclaiming that '*arbeit macht frei*' (work liberates) – is still being calculated. Yet the effect that

Notes

machine consciousness had on the cultures of play, from the eighteenth century to the mid-twentieth, was to caricature them as messy, extraneous, incalculable: something that literally 'gummed up the works'. Art and literature, whether popular or avant garde, certainly had a powerful role in reasserting the power of play in the midst of an ever more industrializing society. Indeed, there is an argument that the seeds of capitalism's crises in the twentieth century have largely been sown by ludic uprisings of one kind or another, from surrealism to advertising, the sixies hippies to the nineties anti-capitalist carnivaleers – all raising demands that the system could not contain.

53 On the notion of 'moebius' thinking, see Handleman, *ibid.*, pp. 150–3. Also Charles Hampden-Turner and Fons Trompenaars, *Mastering the Infinite Game*, Chapter 2, Wiley.

54 Prigogine and Stengers, *Order Out of Chaos: Man's New Dialogue with Nature*, Bantam, 1984.

55 For example, Einstein's remark to Niels Bohr: 'You believe in the dice-playing god, and I in the perfect rule of law' (P.A. Schlipp, ed., *Albert Einstein: Philosopher-Scientist*, Open Court, 1949, p. 176). Einstein also wrote to Cornelius Lanczos, one of his biographers: 'It is hard to sneak a look at God's cards. But that He would choose to play dice with the world . . . is something that I cannot believe for a single moment.' And in a letter to James Frank: 'But that there should be statistical laws with (in)definite solutions, i.e., laws that compel God to throw dice in each individual case, I find highly disagreeable.' (Letter to Cornelius Lanczos, 21 March 1942, expressing his reaction to quantum theory, which refutes relativity theory by stating that an observer can influence reality, that events do happen randomly; Einstein Archive 15–294; quoted in Hoffmann, *Albert Einstein: Creator and Rebel*, Chapter 10; Frank, *Einstein: His Life and Times*, pp. 208, 285; Pais, *Einstein Lived Here*: *Essays for the Layman*, OUP, 1994, p. 114.) Physicist Niels Bohr is said to have told Einstein, 'Stop telling God what to do.'

The idea that 'for every quantum object, we have probability; we do not have certainty', in the words of Nobel-prize-winning US physicist Leon Lederman, drove Einstein to distraction: for the last thirty years of his life he battled against what came to be known as the 'Copenhagen interpretation' of quantum physics, promulgated by Niels Bohr and Werner Heisenberg. His language remained distrustful of the ludic: in a letter to his biographers, Einstein wrote that 'most of them simply do not see what sort of risky game they are playing with reality'. But physicists today still have to respect the fact that, in lieu of a Theory of Everything (TOH), God does still seem to 'play dice' with certain kinds of material phenomena in the universe. Lederman sums up the position well: '[Quantum reality] gives us an indeterminate world, which in some sense frees us from the old classical world of Newton, where everything is predetermined, everything goes according to forces and positions, so that in principle some all-knowing mind

or super-supercomputer could predict the entire world. In classical theory, if you knew all the data, you could toss a coin and predict the outcome with certainty. But now we know that's not so. There is a fundamental quantum nature that in some sense frees us from this determinism', Leon Lederman in transcript, *Closer to Truth* (PBS), Show 207, 'Why is quantum physics so beautiful?'
http://www.closertotruth.com/topics/universemeaning/207/207transcript.html)

56 Mikail Spariosu, *Dionysus Reborn*, Cornell University Press, 1989, p. 275.

57 Spariosu, *ibid.*, p. 224. Also see Manfred Eigen and Ruthild Winkler, *Laws of the Game: How the Principles of Nature Govern Chance*, Princeton University Press, 1993.

58 This also has a spiritual dimension. So many twentieth-century physicists turned to Eastern religions and mythologies, and their relaxation with creative paradox, for some kind of solace: the Hindu cosmology of Shiva's dance, a permanent weaving and reweaving of matter and form, or the Buddhist notions of karma and its sublime interconnectedness, appealed to many of those who had tried to get their 'animal brains' around the quantum. A universe that seethed with a creative, transformative potential required a spiritual vision somewhat more fulfilling than linear Protestantism, unproblematically connecting soul to God via rationally good works.
A 'quantum culture' has undoubtedly developed out of the science of quantum physics – answering the need for what Andrew Ross has called a 'kinder, gentler science', during a century in which scientific industrialism nearly brought life on earth itself to an explosive end. (See Danah Zohar, *The Quantum Self, The Quantum Society* and *Spiritual Intelligence*, all on Bloomsbury; and Andrew Ross, 'New age: a kinder, gentler science?', in *Strange Weather: Culture Science and Technology in an Age of Limits*, Verso, 1991.)

Often allied with New Age therapies, or sometimes with countercultural movements like feminism or anarchism, quantum culture tries to found its vision of an unalienated, non-exploitative humanity on the quirks and quarks of subatomic behaviour. Yet the shadow of the atomic bomb has always fallen over quantum idealism, never quite escaping its culpability. The rise of environmentalism also forced a shift in scientific focus – a need to think about systems, habitats, ecospheres and networks at levels higher than the subatomic; to examine the connections between elements in a living, breathing and struggling world. (See Pat Kane, 'There's method in the magic', *New Statesman & Society*, 23 August 1996.)

The question of what causes scientific change, the shift from one 'paradigm' to another, is a thorny one. But there is no doubt that the twentieth century – an era in which industrial society reached its greatest triumphs and plumbed its most terrible depths – has undergone a fundamental revolution, away from the primacy of the machine metaphor and towards new ones: more holistic, more fluid, more aesthetic. So much of the development of physics in the twentieth century has not been towards increasing certainty, but at best a sense of the marvellous creativity and fecundity of the physical universe. (See Stuart Kauffman, *At Home in the Universe*, Allen Lane, 1996; Fritjof Capra, *The Hidden Connections*, Penguin, 2002.)

59 Brian Goodwin, 'Complexity, Creativity and Society', *Soundings*, Issue 5, Spring 1997.

60 As Goodwin says, a typhoon is, after all, a very specific and ordered event. But it is also a 'possible pattern' that might occur from that small disturbance: a typhoon, a high-pressure region with sunny skies, a low-pressure front with rain, etc. We don't know what it will be – but we can guess what it might be: the weather system 'combines both order and chaos'.

61 Adrian Woolfson, 'How did the slime mould cross the maze?', *London Review of Books*, 21 March 2002.

62 We shouldn't make the mistake of counterposing these evolutionary processes – competition and survival versus creative emergence. The latter views the dynamics of the whole, the former expresses the perspective of a part. It's difficult to understand this through a machine metaphor of science – where each part interlocks precisely with every other part. Instead, we have to think through 'an apparent contradiction', says Goodwin, a 'paradoxical condition' – one where 'maximum freedom of the parts' goes together with 'coherence of the whole'. We turn to the paradoxes of quantum mechanics again, and to ambiguity and paradox in general. Again, it is the 'play' in complex systems – that flexibility and unpredictability which governs the behaviour of its constituent parts – which twentieth- and twenty-first-century scientists seem forever fated to discover.

63 The quote continues: 'Play is chaotic and unpredictable, but out of it order keeps emerging: it also appears to share properties with the type of chaos-to-order transitions that are seen in social insects such as ants. Humans may be manifesting a particular form of behaviour in creative activity that shares basic dynamic properties with life in general, so that our creativity is essentially similar to the creativity that is the stuff of creation. Life at the edge of chaos does express with remarkable accuracy our current experience of social and economic disintegration as we move towards some new form of global culture ... A biology that has at its centre the dynamics of emergent creativity will be rather more helpful in giving the insights into the tortuous turns on this path than one that is based upon selfish genes and competition. It is also a good deal more optimistic, since it recognizes that cultural disorder, together with more extensive fields of interaction and communication, can give rise to new levels of coherent, integrative order.' Brian Goodwin, *How The Leopard Changed Its Spots*, Pheonix, 1996.

64 Robert Wright, *Non-Zero: the Logic of Human Destiny*, Little, Brown, 2000.

65 Kant explores the tension in modern humans between what Chris Rojek calls 'the egoistic needs of the individual and the social needs of labour'. As Kant puts it: 'through the desire for honour, power or property, it drives him to

seek status among his fellows, whom he cannot bear yet cannot bear to leave ... He therefore expects resistance all around, just as he knows of himself that he is in turn inclined to offer resistance to others. It is this very resistance which awakens all of man's powers, and induces him to overcome his tendency to laziness ... Thus, the first true steps are taken from barbarism to culture – a continued process of enlightenment.' Cited in Chris Rojek, *Decentring Leisure, Rethinking Leisure Theory*, Sage, 1995, p. 190.

66 Robert Wright, 'Two Years Later, a Thousand Years Ago', *New York Times*, 11 September 2003, available at http://www.nonzero.org/nyttwoyears.htm.

67 Geoffrey Miller, *The Mating Mind*, Penguin, 2002, pp. 394–403.

68 *Ibid.*, p. 417.

69 Stuart Kauffman, *Investigations*, Allen Lane, 2001.

70 For example see Fritjof Capra, *The Hidden Connections*, Allen Lane, 2002. Recent studies on networks try to analyse the points at which their loose connectedness suddenly becomes a kind of order or hierarchy – when one node, or pathway of connections, becomes dominant in any particular network environment. Books on this include Mark Buchanan, *Nexus: Small Worlds and the Groundbreaking Science of Network,* Norton, 2002; Duncan J. Watts, *Six Degrees: The Science of a Connected Age*, Heinemann, 2003; Malcolm Gladwell, *The Tipping Point*, Little, Brown, 2001.

71 As the great theorist of the network society, Manuel Castells puts it: 'When nodes become redundant, networks tend to reconfigure themselves, deleting nodes and adding new productive ones. Nodes increase their importance for the network by absorbing more information and processing it more efficiently. The relative importance of a node does not stem from its specific features but from its ability to contribute valuable information to the network. In this sense, the main nodes are not centres but switches and protocols of communication, following a networking logic rather than a command logic in their performance. Networks work on a binary logic: inclusion/exclusion. As social forms, they are value free. They can equally kiss or kill: nothing personal.' Castells, 'Informationalism and the network society', in Pekka Himanen, *The Hacker Ethic and the Spirit of the Information Age*, Secker and Warburg, 2001, p.167.

72 'The network is the least structured organization that can be said to have any structure at all. In fact, a plurality of truly divergent components can only remain coherent as a network. No other arrangement – chain, pyramid, tree, circle, hub – can contain true diversity working as a whole ... The Atom represents clean simplicity, the Net channels the messy power of complexity.' Kevin Kelly, *Out of Control: the New Biology of Humans and Machines*, Fourth Estate, 1996, p. 25.

73 For a useful overview of what an activist (as opposed to passivist) politics might be in the network society, see Paul Miller, *Open Policy: threats and opportunities in a wired world*, Forum for the Future, 2002. Copy available for free download at http://www.theforumelab.org.uk/uploadstore/OpenPolicy.pdf

74 On the parasitism of work upon play – or in their terms, of capital upon the energies of the 'multitude' – see Antonio Negri and Michael Hardt's *Empire*, Harvard, 1999, and its discussion in Chapter 4 of this book.

75 In *The Ambiguity of Play*, Sutton-Smith defines play's function as 'the reinforcement of the organism's variability', so that its evolved behaviours don't become too rigid and predictable. This variable behaviour goes from 'the actual to the possible' – that is, from physical play to the play of the mind. Psychologically, Sutton-Smith defines play as 'a virtual simulation characterized by staged contingencies of variation, with opportunities for control engendered by either mastery or further chaos'.

To state all this simply: play is an act of the imagination that raises a whole spectrum of scenarios and options for the player, who can decide to either follow one option or allow them to generate more options. Sutton-Smith goes on: 'Clearly, the primary motive of players is the stylized performance of existential themes that mimic or mock the uncertainties and risks of survival, and in so doing, engage the propensies of mind, body and cells in exciting forms of arousal' (*Ambiguity of Play*, p. 231). So all the varieties of play we have considered – some of them teetering on self-contradiction or mutual subversion – are stamped with one characteristic: they 'mimic or mock the uncertainties and risks of survival'.

Sutton-Smith adds another scientific twist. Play can also be understood as 'a lifelong simulation of the key neonatal characteristics of unrealistic optimism, egocentricity and reactivity, all of which are guarantors of persistence in the face of adversity' (*ibid.*). Again, this is overly compressed, but can be easily unravelled. 'Neonates' – young children – can be unreasonably happy, self-obsessed beyond measure and supremely sensitive to all stimuli and input: and what that state of being does is to keep them going, maintain their gulping enthusiasm for life, push them forward to the next stage of mastery. Again, what modern adult does not admire the indefatigability of the child in their environment? And how liberating might it feel to know that when we play as adults – recognizing all of play's varieties and forms as legitimate – we are recovering some of that early, awesomely constitutive energy?

76 'Speech given by the chancellor, Gordon Brown, to the Urban Summit in Birmingham', *Guardian*, Friday, 1 November 2002. http://politics.guardian.co.uk/economics/story/0,11268,824105,00.html

77 See Wendy Wheeler, *A New Modernity?*, Lawrence and Wishart, 1999, particularly pp. 103–31 on the 'managerialism' of New Labour.

THREE / THE ANGELS MAKE WORK

1 Speech by Chancellor of the Exchequer to the Institute of Directors, 15 November 2001, HM Treasury website (http://www.hm-treasury.gov.uk/ newsroom_and_speeches/press/2001/press_125_01.cfm)

2 These are largely taken from a helpful archive of Gordon Brown's major speeches as Chancellor of the Exchequer from 1997–2003, available on the HM Treasury website 'Newsroom and Speeches' section, at http://www.hm-treasury.gov.uk/newsroom_and_speeches/speeches/ chancellorexchequer/speech_chex_index.cfm. Other sources include: 'Brown says Labour is party of business', *Epolitx.com*, Monday, 14 May 2001, http://www.epolitix.com/bos/epxnews/a5c656bfb1819f47913a12f95cf75b350000 003855f8.htm, 'Getting ready to spend', *Observer*, 15 April 2001. Interview with Brown, http://www.observer.co.uk/business/story/0,6903,473201,00.html; 'Britain learns America's lesson', Gordon Brown, *The Wall Street Journal*, 19 June 2001. Available at http://www.britainusa.com/economy/xq/asp/SarticleType.1/Article_ID.1516/qx/ articles_show.htm

3 William P. Quigley , 'The quicksands of the Poor Law: poor relief legislation in a growing nation, 1790–1820', *The Northern Illinois University Law Review*, Fall, 1997.

4 Pekka Himanen, *The Hacker Ethic*, Secker and Warburg, 2002, p.13.

5 *Ibid.*, pp. 16–17.

6 From 'The Protestant work ethic rules', http://www.tartanplace.com/tartanhistory/protestantrules.html

7 Thomas Carlyle, *Past and Present*, Book 3, Chapter 11, 'Labour'. http://dspace.dial.pipex.com/town/terrace/adw03/readings/carlyle/3–11.htm

8 Andrew Gowers, Robert Chote and Robert Peston, 'Gordon Brown's progress', *Financial Times*, 18 February 1998.

9 Isaac Watts, 'Against idleness and mischief', from his *Divine Songs, Attempted in Easie Language for the Use of Children* (1715). Cited in *The Oxford Companion to Children's Literature*, Humphrey Carpenter and Mari Prichard, eds, Oxford University Press, 1984, p. 536.

10 Cited in Rebecca Abrams, *The Playful Self*, Fourth Estate, p. 67.

11 Max Weber, *The Protestant Ethic and the Spirit of Capitalism*, Routledge, 1992.

12 Speech by the Chancellor to the Yale Club, New York, 26 July 2001, HM Treasury website http://www.hm-treasury.gov.uk/newsroom_and_speeches/ press/2001/press_91_01.cfm

13 Writes Anthony Dworkin: 'There were a number of stages in Bell's diagnosis of decline [of the Protestant work ethic]. One was the advent of cultural modernism, which drew on the same individualist energies as business enterprise. It broke the bonds of artistic tradition and asserted the centrality of the self. Modernist culture promoted "the idea of boundless experiment . . . of unconstrained sensibility, of impulse being superior to order, of the imagination being immune to merely rational criticism".' At first these were the values of the avant garde, confined to an urban elite. However, the coming of mass society in the twentieth century allowed them to permeate popular culture and led to the excesses of the 1960s. At the same time, social changes such as urbanization, mass communication and

easy credit were turning the US into a consumer society. People came to define themselves through spending as much as working, and consumerism encouraged them to gratify their every desire. The deferred gratification of early capitalist production yielded to the instant gratification of later capitalist consumption. Thus, cultural and economic forces conspired to undermine the restraint and morality that had given birth to capitalism and were needed to hold it together. Social values were no longer concerned with 'how to work and achieve, but how to spend and enjoy', Bell wrote. 'When the Protestant ethic was sundered from bourgeois society, only hedonism remained . . . the elements that provide men with common identification and effective reciprocity' – family, Church and community – lost their hold, and people's "capacity to maintain sustained relations with each other" was destroyed.' 'Daniel Bell', *Prospect*, October 2000.

14 'Just do it' is the Nike slogan from the mid-nineties; 'Search for the hero inside yourself' was the title of a song by pop band M-People, used extensively in a UK television ad campaign for Peugeot cars, also in the mid-nineties.

15 For a fascinating insight into how direct action groups have actually 'blagged' the New Deal in order to turn it into a 'troublemakers' training scheme', see 'Running to stand still: globalization, blagging and the dole', from the anarchist magazine *Do or Die* (available at http://www.eco-action.org/dod/no9/dole.htm). 'Some have been able to turn the New Deal to their own advantage by getting on an otherwise pricey mountaineering, Desk Top Publishing or Web Design course – all handy skills when you want to set up a road camp, occupy buildings or produce political magazines and websites.'

16 Ulrich Beck talks of the need to subsidize 'creative disobedience' through the welfare system, in order to restore the very legitimacy of the civil realm itself. *The Brave New World of Work*, Polity, 1999. See also Chapter 9, this volume.

17 See Chris Rojek, *Decentring Leisure*, Routledge, 1998: 'Because work was regarded as the fundamental human need and the centre of social existence, communication, play and sociality were marginalized, thus exacerbating the individual's sense of homelessness. Leisure became an artificial realm of freedom in which the pursuit of escape routinely ended in anti-climax and where fantasy and illusion flourished. It was therefore no accident that leisure practice under modernity became ever more dominated by the dream world of advertising. Escape and freedom became qualities of experience which could only be realized through images. The fantasy world of *homo faber* was necessarily over-heated, and distorted because the rewards of satisfaction, fulfilment, excitement and release that leisure was meant to provide was never more than gestural. It was not that people failed to experience these qualities in leisure. Rather they experienced them in a momentary, fragmented form which only emphasized the illusory character of "authentic" escape under modernity' (p. 184).

18 See essays in E.P. Thompson, *Customs in Common*, Merlin, 1991.

19 Chas Critcher and John Clarke, *The Devil Makes Work: Leisure in Capitalist Britain*, Macmillan 1985.

20 Mark Dery summarizes Ewen's analysis: 'Robbed of the social practices whereby they had traditionally constructed meaning and set adrift in a machine age in which seasonal and circadian rhythms were shattered by the time clock, urban laborers soon grew restive. As dissent spread, industrialists came gradually to realize that "human engineering" in the workplace was not enough, that their purview must be extended beyond the sweat shop and the assembly line, into the cultural arena. Only a value system consonant with a market economy, in which puritan denial was supplanted by secular indulgence, agrarian conservation by industrial exploitation, familial bonds by corporate fealty, and the veneration of a shared history by a fetishizing of the modern, would ensure the smooth functioning of an anomic workforce geared towards mass production. "It was within such a context that the advertising industry began to assume modern proportions and that the institution of a mass consumer market began to arise," Ewen observes. "The business community now attempted to present an affirmative vision – a new mechanism – of social order in the realm of daily life to confront the resistance of people whose work lives were increasingly defined by the rigid parameters of industrial production and their corporate bureaucracies. Advertising was to develop as a tool of social order whose self-espoused purpose was the 'nullification' of the customs of ages; to break down the barriers of individual habits. It defined itself as at once the destroyer and creator in the process of the ever-evolving new. Its constructive effort was to superimpose new conceptions of individual attainment and community desire; to solidify the productive process while at the same time parrying anti-corporate feeling." Corporate capitalists used advertising, its impact heightened by newly arrived technologies of reproduction and replication such as photography and chromolithography, to promote an ideology of consumption. The transformation of these 19th-century captains of industry into twentieth-century captains of consciousness was well under way.' http://www.levity.com/markdery/ewen.html

21 On pop culture's subversive energies, see Simon Frith, *Performing Rites: Evaluating Popular Music*, Oxford, 1998; and Greil Marcus, *Lipstick Traces*, Harvard, 1990.

22 See George McKay, *Senseless Acts of Beauty: Cultures of Resistance Since the Sixties*, Verso, 1996.

23 Richard Donkin, *Blood Sweat and Tears: the Evolution of Work*, Texere, 2002, last chapter.

24 As Schiller said in the eighteenth century: 'The mental state of most men is, on the one hand, fatiguing and exhausting work and, on the other, debilitating pleasure.' Friedrich von Schiller, *On Naïve and Sentimental Poetry*, Ungar, 1979.

25 Tom Bentley, 'Will we blow apart society?', *New Statesman*, Special Supplement on the theme 'Knowledge is power!', 27 September 1999, pp. xvii–xix.

26 The great synthesizer of these themes is Geoff Mulgan, founder of Demos and until recently head of the UK Government's Strategy Unit, the key volumes are *Politics in an Anti-Political Age*, Polity, 1996; *Connexity: How to Live in a Connected World*, Vintage, 1999, and *Life After Politics*, Demos, 2000.

27 On this 'control culture', see Larry Elliot and Dan Glaister, *The Age of Insecurity*, W. N. Norton, 1998.

28 Richard Sennett, *The Corrosion of Character: the Personal Consequences of Work in the New Capitalism*, W.N. Norton, 1998.

29 Sennett, *Corrosion of Character*, p. 10.

30 Sennett, *ibid.*, p. 148.

31 Sennett, *ibid.*, pp. 32–45, pp. 52–3.

32 The rise of 'post-materialist values' is associated with the work of Ronald Inglehart, a US sociologist who has been tracking the rise of such values globally for over three decades, via something called the 'World Values Survey', http://wvs.isr.umich.edu/index.html. An introduction to his work is from the *Washington Monthly*, Winter 2000 – 'Globalization and postmodern values', http://www.twq.com/winter00/231Inglehart.pdf. Inglehart's website is http://wvs.isr.umich.edu/ringlehart/publications.html

33 See Chapter 5, this volume.

34 Kate Hilpern, 'I won't be in today – I'm ill', *Guardian*, 2 December 2002. The article cites that one in three days taken for sick leave in the UK are 'bogus' – and that the cost to employers is £500 per employee, or £12 billion pounds a year to the economy.

35 Charlotte Denny, 'Brown's productivity challenge', *Guardian*, 17 March 2003.

36 The Work Foundation are even on the search to define the word 'workful' as a new and positive adjective, describing a vision of work as transformation. For my sceptical view on this, see PlayJournal, http://www.playjournal.com. http://journalscape.com/playjournal/2003–06–12–22:29

37 Stephen Overell, 'The search for corporate meaning', *Financial Times*, 12 September 2002.

38 On the organizational implications of the homeostat metaphor, see Andy Pickering, 'Cybernetics and the mangle: Ashby, Beer, and Pask', at http://www.uiuc.edu/unit/STIM/pickering1.pdf.; Geoff Bowker, 'Synchronization4': Hermes, Angels and the Narrative of the Archive', at http://www.uiuc.edu/unit/STIM/bowker2.pdf; and Max Boisot and Jack Cohen, 'Shall I compare thee to . . . an organisation?', *Emergence*, 2(4) 2000.

39 Overell, *ibid.*, my emphasis. In the same article, Norman Bowie, a professor of ethics at the University of Minnesota, gives another equilibrial definition: 'Meaningful work is work that is freely entered into, that allows the worker to exercise their autonomy and independence; that enables the worker to develop their rational capacities; that provides a wage sufficient for physical

welfare; that supports the moral development of employees and that is not paternalistic in the sense of interfering with the worker's conception of how they wish to obtain happiness.'

40 See Philip Brown and Hugh Lauder, 'Capitalism and social progress', *Guardian*, 18 June 2001: '. . . The breakdown of established patterns of family life, work and leisure; demographic changes in childbirth, marriage, divorce, employment and mortality rates . . . and greater freedom about how we construct our personal identities – all [these have] placed greater demands on us to be more "reflexive" about our lives, as little can be taken for granted . . . Much of what was part of our everyday routines now requires a greater level of conscious decision-making.'

41 Howard Gardner, William Damon, Mihlay Csikszentmihalyi, *Good Work: When Exellence and Ethics Meets*, Basic Books, 2001.

42 *Ibid.*

43 See Chapters 5 and 9, this volume.

44 Gardner, *Chronicle, ibid.*

45 http://www.seriousplay.com/what.html

46 *Ibid.*

47 Kate Lovell, 'Give me back my ball', *Guardian*, 31 March 2003. http://jobs.guardian.co.uk/officehours/story/0,9897,925916,00.html

48 Rebecca Abrams, *The Playful Self: Why Women Need Play in Their Lives*, Fourth Estate, 1997.

49 Seriousplay.com, *ibid.*

50 *Ibid.*

51 '"Aint misbehavin": taking play seriously in organizations', Working Paper 5 (2002), Imagination Lab Foundation, www.imagilab.org (available on request).

52 Simon London, 'The next core competence is getting personal' (interview with C.K. Prahalad), *Financial Times*, 13 December 2002. Larry Elliot, 'Analyse this: corporate culture is in a midlife crisis', *Guardian*, 31 March 2003. See also Jeremy Rifkin, *Age of Access*.

53 James Moore, 'The Second Superpower rears its beautiful head', http://cyber.law.harvard.edu/people/jmoore/secondsuperpower.html. James Moore's weblog, documenting reactions to his thesis, is at http://blogs.law.harvard.edu/jim/

54 See Joe Dominguez, Vicki Robin, *Your Money or Your Life: Transforming Your Relationship With Money and Achieving Financial Independence*, Penguin USA, 1999; Duane Elgin, *Voluntary Simplicity*, Quill, 1998; and Polly Ghazi and Judy Jones, *Getting a Life: the Downshifter's Guide to Happier, Simpler Living*, Hodder and Stoughton, 1997.

55 See excerpt, 'What is social complexity?', from the website supporting Richard Wright's *Non Zero: the Logic of Human Destiny*, Vintage, 2001, at http://www.nonzero.org/app2.htm

56 See Francis Fukuyama, *The Great Disruption: Human Nature and the Reconstitution of Social Order*, Free Press, 1999.

57 Kirkpatrick Sale, *Rebels Against the Future – the Luddites and Their War on*

Notes

the Industrial Revolution: Lessons for the Computer Age, Perseus, 1996. See also Kevin Kelly's extraordinary 'Interview with the Luddite', a dialogue with Sale, in Wired, June 1995, http://www.wired.com/wired/archive/3.06/saleskelly_pr.html

58 For a discussion of poiesis, see George Steiner, Grammars of Creation, Faber, 2001.

FOUR / THE RISE OF THE SOULITARIANS

1 Hue and Cry, 'The only thing (more powerful than the boss)', Remote (CD), Circa Records, 1989.

2 Marshall McLuhan, Understanding Media: the Extensions of Man, MIT Press, 1994.

3 The full quote, from the 1972 edition of the Whole Earth Review is: 'We are as gods and might as well get good at it. So far remotely done power and glory – as via government, big business, formal education, Church – has succeeded to the point where gross defects obscure actual gains. In response to this dilemma and to these gains, a realm of intimate, personal power is developing – the power of individuals to conduct their own education, find their own inspiration, shape their own environment, and share the adventure with whoever is interested. Tools that aid this process are sought and promoted by the Whole Earth Catalog.' http://www.well.com:70/0/WER/manifesto

4 Any of the pronouncements of the British Labour Minister for Trade and Industry, Patricia Hewitt, illustrate of both these approaches. See her collected speeches at http://www.dti.gov.uk/ministers/ministers/hewitt.html

5 For an overview of this tendency, see Douglas Rushkoff, 'The people's net: the Internet is back, alive and well', Yahoo Internet Life, July 2001. Available at http://www.rushkoff.com/features/peoplesnet.html

6 See Gary Rivlin's interview with Linus Torvalds, 'Leader of the free world', Wired, November 2003, http://www.wired.com/wired/archive/11.11/linus.html

7 See Wired, February 2003, special on music downloading: http://www.wired.com/wired/archive/11.02/

8 John Arquilla, David Ronfeldt (eds), Networks and Netwars: the Future of Terror, Crime, and Militancy, Rand Corporation, 2001. Available for free download at http://www.rand.org/publications/MR/MR1382/

9 Felix Stalder and Jesse Hirsh, 'Open source intelligence', First Monday, v.7, no.6, June 2002, http://firstmonday.org/issues/issue7_6/stalder/index.html

10 At the point of completing this book (April 2003), there are many signs of this next phase-shift in cyberspace heading towards a real soulitarian politics. See Joi Ito's 'Emergent democracy', http://joi.ito.com/static/emergentdemocracy.html, which argues that the fusion of weblogs, mobile phones and activism will create a new public sphere. A similar position is taken by Howard Rheingold's book Smart Mobs: the Next Social Revolution

(Perseus, 2002), with its supporting weblog at http://www.smartmobs.com. And Stanford University Law Professor James Moore's essay, 'The second superpower raises its beautiful head', ups the ante on digital activism even further, http://cyber.law.harvard.edu/people/jmoore/secondsuperpower.html

11 A sparky and witty overview of the latest stats on ICT (information and communication technologies) is the regularly updated weblog at the UK's Work Foundation, I-Wire, at http://www.theisociety.net

12 Apart from Alex Garland's novel (and subsequent film) *The Beach*, another excellent evocation of the soulitarian lust for experience and transcendence comes from Decca Aitkenhead's *The Promised Land: Travels in Search of the Perfect E*, Fourth Estate, 2002.

13 'Time, work discipline and industrial capitalism', in E.P. Thompson, *Customs in Common: Studies in Traditional Popular Culture*, Merlin, 1991.

14 Richard Barbrook is the irrepressible theorist of dot- or cyber-communism – an audacious attempt to politicize the first generation of militant digital players. His key texts are 'A cybercommunist manifesto', available at Nettime, http://www.nettime.org/Lists-Archives/nettime-l-9909/msg00046.html. Further refinements – explictly relating to download culture and code sharing – come in 'The regulation of liberty: free speech, free trade and free gifts on the Net', available from the University of Westminster's Hypermedia Centre, at http://www.hrc.wmin.ac.uk/hrc/theory/regulationofliberty/t.html

15 John Knell, *Most Wanted: the Quiet Birth of the Free Worker*, The Work Foundation, 2000. For an interesting distinction between the soulitarian as 'wired', and the soulitarian as 'entrepreneurial', see Fernando Flores and John Gray, *Entrepreneurship and the Wired Life: Work in the Wake of Careers*, Demos, 2000.

16 See Michael Lewis, *The Future Just Happened*, Coronet, 2002, for an early account of just how self-propellingly smart the smart workers are going to be – and how play, in all its rhetorics and forms, is their natural expression of self in the world.

17 Robert Reich, *The Work of Nations*, Vintage, 1991. Excerpt at http://distance-ed.bcc.ctc.edu/econ/kst/BriefReign/symbanalydef.htm

18 'Do we think of computers as things that exist in their own right, or do we think of them as conduits between us? We should treat computers as fancy telephones, whose purpose is to connect people. Information is alienated experience. Information is not something that exists. Indeed, computers don't really exist, exactly; they're only subject to human interpretation. This is a strong primary humanism I am promoting. As long as we remember that we ourselves are the source of our value, our creativity, our sense of reality, then all of our work with computers will be worthwhile and beautiful.' From Chapter 17, 'The prodigy', in John Brockman's *Digerati: Conversations with the Digital Elite*, HardWired, 1996. Available at http://www.edge.org/documents/digerati/Lanier.html

19 Both ads are viewable at http://www.playmore.com, after registration.

20 Marc Pesce, 'The Xbox: 1,000,000,000,000 operations per second', *Wired*, May 2001, http://www.wired.com/wired/archive/9.05/xbox.html

21 Wagner James Au, 'Burn down the shopping malls!' *Salon.com*, 22 February 2002, http://archive.salon.com/tech/feature/2002/02/22/state_of_emergency/index.html

22 Naomi Klein, 'Signs of the times', *The Nation*, 22 October 2001.

23 There is the beginnings of an 'auteurs' movement' in video games, led by designers who are interested in defining (and defending) a video game aesthetic. A good portal site is http://www.ludology.org: the most noted 'ludologist' is Henry Jenkins at MIT. His pieces are available at http://web.mit.edu/21fms/www/faculty/henry3/publications.html#articles

24 Tom Peters, 'The brand called you', *Fast Company*, August/September 1997, http://www.fastcompany.com/online/10/brandyou.html

25 Pat Kane, 'Flitter-brained pseud-heads' (review of Coupland's *Microserfs*), *Independent*, 21 December 1996.

26 The latest news on Will Wright's deep sense of social order: he's helping the CIA to anticipate threats to American security. Kevin Maney, 'Military strategists could learn a thing or two from the Sims', *USA Today*, 2 April 2003, http://www.usatoday.com/money/industries/technology/2003–04–01–sims_x.htm

27 Howard Rheingold, 'Helsinki's Aula: where geospace, sociospace, and cyberspace meet . . .' *The Feature*, 17 July 2002, http://www.thefeature.com/index.jsp?url=article.jsp?pageid=15435

28 Andrew Leonard, 'Finland: the open source society', The Free Software Project, *Salon*, http://archive.salon.com/tech/fsp/2000/04/20/chapter_six_part_1/

29 Andrew Leonard, 'Life, liberty and the pursuit of free software', *Salon*, 15 February 2001, http://dir.salon.com/tech/log/2001/02/15/unamerican/index.html

30 Pekka Himanen, *The Hacker Ethic*, Secker and Warburg, 2001.

31 Ilkka Hannula and Risto Linturi, '100 phenomena', http://www.linturi.fi/100_phenomena/index.html

32 William Shaw, 'In Helsinki virtual village . . .', *Wired*, May 2001, http://www.wired.com/wired/archive/9.03/helsinki.html

33 Antti Kasvio, 'Towards a wireless information society: the case of Finland', from Dept of Information Studies, University of Tampere, http://www.info.uta.fi/winsoc/engl/lect/progr.html

34 Manuel Castells, Pekka Himanen, *The Information Society and the Welfare State: The Finnish Model*, Oxford, 2002, Chapter 7, 'Conclusion'.

35 Castells and Himanen, *Information Society*, Chapter 6.

36 'Scores of social systems are abstracted from their locally knowable basis. Communities are distributed; exchange has many new (or revived) forms; relationships, health, security, and education are all shifting to new models. It is not that anything and everything "has a Web site" – well beyond that. What matters now is that "anything and everything" is or is on the verge of being loosed from locality and distanced by its systemization and

abstraction.' Rick Robinson, 'Capitalist tool, humanist tool', *Design Management Journal*, Spring 2001. See also my pamphlet, *Designing an E-Future*, Design Council, 2001.

37 Antonio Negri and Michael Hardt, *Empire*, Harvard, 2001, p. 52.

38 There is a huge literature on the destruction of industrial militancy by informational capitalism in a global context, but the source most consulted by this book is *The Rise of the Network Society* by Manuel Castells (Blackwell, 2000), particularly Chapters 2–4.

39 Ursula Huws, 'The making of a cybertariat? Virtual work in a real world', in *Socialist Register: Working Classes, Global Realities*, Merlin Press, 2001.

40 Nate Bolt has described these workers as part of the 'binary proletariat': 'The call centers of 2,000 telemarketers who sell the drone of their authentic human voices make up the Binary Proletariat. The cubicled floor space of start-ups turned agglomerates make up the Binary Proletariat. The 3,500 temporary workers at Microsoft, subject to the slightest change in the new global market, are part of the Binary Proletariat.' Nate Bolt, 'The binary proletariat', vol. 5, no 5 (May 2000), http://firstmonday.org/issues/issue5_5/bolt/index.html

41 Huws, *ibid*. Douglas Rushkoff expresses some hope that the first clear instance of digital class consciousness will come from programmers, who he urges to form a 'global programmers union'. 'Exodus: from pyramid-building to a global programmers union', May 2001, http://www.rushkoff.com/cgi-bin/columns/display.cgi/exodus.

42 See Daniel Pink, *Free-Agent Nation: the Future of Working for Yourself*, Warner, 2001.

43 Andrew Ross's researches are gathered together in the book *No-collar: the Hidden Cost of the Humane Workplace*, Basic, 2003.

44 From a publishers' Q&A, posted by Ross to the Nettime website, 27 December 2002, http://amsterdam.nettime.org/Lists-Archives/nettime-l-0212/msg00121.html

45 Andrew Ross, 'Techno-sweatshops', *Tikkun*, January/February 2000, http://www.tikkun.org/magazine/index.cfm/action/tikkun/issue/tik0001/article/000115c.html

46 See Will Hutton, *The World We're In*, Abacus, 2003, on the difference between US and European labour regulations.

47 Ross, *No-Collar*, p. 250.

48 Himanen, *The Hacker Ethic*, p. 80. See the activist site http://www.via3.net, as an attempt to enlist the energies of networked activists to mutual benefit, in an electronically organized barter community. Two good portal sites for these kinds of initiatives are http://www.ethicalmedia.org and http://www.vitamin-e.net

49 See 'Trotsky at Saatchi's', in Chapter 7, p. 230, this volume.

50 Negri and Hardt, *Empire*, p. 53.

51 This has also been called 'aesthetic labour' by the Glasgow researcher Chris

Warhurst. See *Looking Good, Feeling Good: Style Counseling in the New Economy* (with Dennis Nickson), Work Foundation, 2001.

52 Negri and Hardt, *Empire*, pp. 386, 388.

53 Quote from Negri in Mark Leonard, 'The Left should love globalization' (interview with Negri), *New Statesman*, 28 May 2001.

54 Gopal Balakrishnan captures their position well, and with some sarcasm: 'Running through the work is the fervent belief that contemporary capitalism, although seemingly impervious to anti-systemic challenge, is in fact vulnerable at all points to riot and rebellion. The increasing importance of immaterial, intellectual labour in high value-added sectors of the economy is shaping a collective labourer with heightened powers of subversion. An ineradicable plebeian desire for emancipation is stoked by the increasingly apparent malleability of all social relationships and permeability of all borders. This global multitude, embracing all those who work, or are just poor, from computer scientists in Palo Alto to slum-dwellers in São Paulo, no longer imagines communities as integral nations.' 'Virgilian Visions', *New Left Review*, September/October 2000, http://www.newleftreview.net/NLR23909.shtml

55 There is a fascinating theological element to Negri's writings, or at least an attempt to deal with the transgressive and boundary-bursting nature of the dynamic processes of the information society. Here are the closing words to *Empire*, invoking an 'ancient legend' to illustrate what 'communist militancy' might mean – turning 'a rebellion into a project of love'. We are asked to consider St Francis of Assisi: 'To denounce the poverty of the multitude he adopted that common condition and discovered there the ontological power of a new society . . . Francis, in opposition to nascent capitalism, refused every instrumental discipline, and in opposition to the mortification of the flesh (in poverty and in the constituted order) he posed a joyous life, including all of being and nature, the animals, sister moon, brother sun, the birds of the field, the poor and exploited humans, together against the will of power and corruption. Once again in postmodernity we find ourselves in Francis's situation, posing against the misery of power the joy of being . . . This is the irrepressible lightness and joy of being communist' (p. 413).

Elsewhere, Negri has mused on the materialist theory of eternity: 'There is no immortality of the soul, but there is the eternity of your actions . . . Each of us is responsible for his or her singularity, for his or her present, for the intensity of life, for the youth or age that each of us brings to it. And this is the only way to avoid death: seize time, hold it, and fill it with responsibility. And every time that you lose it in routine or in habit or weariness, depression, or anger, you lose the "ethical" sense of life. This is eternity. Eternity is our responsibility with respect to the present, in every moment and every instant. A complete ethical responsibility, in which we have to invest all of our beauty, or sometimes our meanness, but in either case with sincerity. I am proposing nothing less than a secular and atheistic Franciscanism.' (Transcript of video interview with Negri, available at http://lists.village.virginia.edu/~forks/exile.htm). For more read Negri's essay 'Alma Venus', in *Time for Revolution*, Continuum, 2002. Chapter 10, this volume, develops this theme of the relationship between play, technology and spirituality.

56 See Chapter 10, this volume.

57 Tom Savigar, *Born Clicking: Are Kids Smarter than Adults?*, ICA/Sense Network, 2002, available at http://www.ica.org.uk/index.cfm?articleid=1081

FIVE / LIFESTYLE MILITANTS

1 See Steven Pinker on his critique of early years education, interview by Tim Radford, 'Have you heard? It's in the genes', *Guardian*, 25 September 2002, at http://education.guardian.co.uk/print/0,3858,4508138–110865,00.html. An alternative perspective comes from Janet Moyles (ed.), *The Excellence of Play*, Open University, 1994.

2 Frank Furedi, *Paranoid Parenting: Abandon Your Anxieties and Be a Good Parent*, Allen Lane, 2001. Matthew and Laurie Taylor, *What Are Children For?*, Short, 2003.

3 See David Aaronovitch, 'What's so smart about being childish?', *Independent*, 6 June 2001.

4 Marc Pesce, *The Playful World: How Technology is Transforming Our Imagination*, Ballantine, 2000. See also http://www.playfulworld.com

5 See Marc Pesce, 'Toys and the playful world', a talk for Women in Toys, New York City, 14 February 2001, http://www.hyperreal.org/~mpesce/WIT.html

6 Sherry Turkle, 'Cyborg babies and cy-dough-plasm: ideas about self and life in the culture of simulation', in Robbie Davis-Floyd and Joseph Dumit (eds), *Cyborg Babies: from Technosex to Technotots*, Routledge, 1998. Also available at http://web.mit.edu/sturkle/www/cyborg_babies.html

7 Turkle, 'Cuddling up to cyborg babies', *Unesco Courier*, September 2000, http://www.unesco.org/courier/2000_09/uk/connex.htm

8 'Robot care bears for the elderly', *BBC Online News*, 21 February, 2002, http://news.bbc.co.uk/1/hi/sci/tech/1829021.stm

9 See also Turkle, 'Who am we?', *Wired*, January 1996, http://www.wired.com/wired/archive/4.01/turkle_pr.html

10 Jenny James, 'Tech comes to toyland', *Time Europe*, 11 December 2000.

11 Mike Anderiesz, 'Crisis of conscience', *Guardian*, 27 March 2003, http://www.guardian.co.uk/online/story/0,3605,922338,00.html

12 Daniel Bell, *The Coming of Post-industrial Society*, Basic, 1973, p.28.

13 For the history of the golem, see 'The ghosts in our machines', Pat Kane, *Independent*, 16 March 2002, a review of Victoria Nelson's *The Secret Life of Puppets* (Harvard, 2002). Available at http://enjoyment.independent.co.uk/books/reviews/story.jsp?story=274877

14 'LEGO Toys Named "Product of the Century"', *Business Wire*, 2 December 1999, http://www.findarticles.com/cf_0/moEIN/1999_Dec_2/57890114/print.jhtml

15 For a slightly more academic treatise on the semiotics of Lego, see Roger Said, Matt Statler and Johan Roos, 'Lego speaks!', at Imagilab Working Papers, http://www.imagilab.org/working_papers_pdf/WP%202002-7.pdf

16 See Seymour Papert's Web page, http://www.papert.org

17 David Shenk, 'Use technology to raise smarter happier kids', *Atlantic*, 7 January 1999, http://www.theatlantic.com/unbound/digicult/dc990107.htm

18 For example, see discussion on the hacker site Slashdot, at http://slashdot.org/article.pl?sid=01/08/29/1257205&mode=thread

19 Lego is a remarkably powerful metaphor for sci-tech types, like the award-winning chemist Susan Gibson. 'As Gibson talks, the world starts to seem a tremendously complicated Lego set, with people discovering how to fit it together in new ways every year', Andrew Brown, 'Welcome to the chemistry set', *Guardian*, 10 April 2003, http://education.guardian.co.uk/print/0,3858,4644457-108966,00.html

20 On 'middlescence', see Gail Sheehy, 'New passages', *U.S. News & World Report*, 9 June 1995; on 'adultescence', see Frank Furedi, 'The children who won't grow up', *Spiked-Online*, 29 July 2003, http://www.spiked-online.com/Printable/00000006DE8D.htm

21 Quoted in Bel Mooney, 'Paging all kidults', *Nationwide News Proprietary* (Australia), 28 September 2002.

22 Dominic Utton, 'Dad, I've got just what you wanted', *Sunday Times*, 19 January 2003.

23 Pat Kane, 'Magic, mystery and the quest for universal truth', *Sunday Herald*, 12 September 1999.

24 See http://www.friendsreunited.co.uk and http://www.schooldisco.co.uk

25 The ultimate kidult toy in terms of personal mobility has to be Dean Kamen's Segway – a gyroscopic motorized pavement scooter that threatened to make all walking redundant. Or, as it turned out, not.

26 On epistemophilia, see Monica Rudburg, 'The epistemophilic project', in Kathy Davis, *Embodied Practices: Feminist Perspectives on the Body*, Sage, 1997, pp. 182-3.

27 Brian Sutton-Smith, 'Play as adaptive potentiation', in P. Stevens (ed.), *Studies in the Anthropology of Play*, Leisure Press, 1977.

28 Gillian Thomas and Gina Hocking, 'Other People's Children', Demos, 2003, http://www.demos.co.uk/otherpeopleschildren_pdf_media_public.aspx

29 My personal favourite (along with my daughter's) is the Powerpuff Girls on Cartoon Network. See Robert Lloyd, 'Beyond good and evil', *LA Weekly*, 24-30 November 2000, http://www.laweekly.com/ink/01/01/features-lloyd.php

30 See Dave Hill, 'The kids aren't alright', *Guardian*, 11 November 2003, http://media.guardian.co.uk/advertising/story/0,7492,1082222,00.html

31 'Kids becoming fast food TV nation', *Guardian*, 23 September 2003, http://media.guardian.co.uk/advertising/story/0,7492,1049673,00.html

32 Thomas and Hocking, *Other People's Children*, p. 23.

33 See Frank Furedi, *Paranoid Parenting*, Penguin, 2001.

34 See http://www.babyeinstein.com

35 Thomas and Hocking, *ibid.*, p.22.

36 On scaffolding, see Paul Martin and Patrick Bateson, *Design for a Life*, Chapter 8, 'Sensitive periods'.

37 Thomas and Hocking, *ibid.*, p. 54–5.

38 *Ibid.*, p. 55.

39 *Ibid.*, p. 56.

40 See Walter Truett Anderson, *The Future of the Self: Inventing the Postmodern Person*, Tarcher/Putnam, 1997.

41 See Chapter 10, this volume.

42 Suzie Mackenzie, 'Fathers and sons', *Guardian*, 18 January 2003, http://books.guardian.co.uk/departments/politicsphilosophyandsociety/story/0,6000,875903,00.html

43 I prefer the art-rock band Radiohead's (perhaps unwitting) formulation, Kid A – who is represented in the album artwork as a wild smiling icon, making sense of a demanding, mutable world. Kid A gets three cheers.

44 Thomas and Hocking, *ibid.*, p. 29.

45 Al and Tipper Gore, *Joined at the Heart: the Transformation of the American Family*, Henry Holt, 2002.

46 Gore, *Joined at the Heart*, p. 229.

47 *Ibid.*, pp. 211–2.

48 *Ibid.*, pp. 204–5.

49 *Ibid.*, pp. 215–16.

50 *Ibid.*, p. 230.

51 See Ulrich Beck, *The Normal Chaos of Love*, Polity, 1995; Anthony Giddens, *The Transformation of Intimacy*, 1992; Theodore Zeldin, *An Intimate History of Humanity*, Minerva, 1995.

52 See Chapter 7, this volume.

53 Melanie Howard and Michael Wilmott, 'The networked family', *New Times*, March 2000.

54 On 'doing family', see David Morgan, 'Risk and family practices: accounting for change and fluidity in family life', in E.B. Silva and C. Smart (eds.), *The New Family?*, Sage, 1999, pp. 13–30.

55 *Lilo & Stitch*, Disney DVD, 2002.

56 David Denby, 'The speed of light' (on George Gilder's Evernet), *New Yorker*, 27 November 2000.

57 Sylvia Ann Hewlett and Cornel West, 'Caring for crib lizards', *The American Prospect*, 1 January 2001, http://www.prospect.org/print/V12/1/hewlett-s.html

58 Ben Summerskill, 'Sorry, no children', *Observer*, 30 July 2000, http://www.observer.co.uk/review/story/0,6903,348485,00.html

59 For a sceptical take on voluntary complexity, see Landgon Winner, 'The voluntary complexity movement', *Tech Knowledge Revue*, 1.3, 14 September 1999, http://www.praxagora.com/stevet/netfuture/1999/Sep1499_94.html

60 Sarah Hall, 'Fathers "scared" to ask for flexible hours', *Guardian*, 14 January 2003. Also see Fathers Direct at http://www.fathersdirect.co.uk

61 Dave Hill, 'Being there is not enough', *Guardian*, 15 January 2003.

62 Anthony Clare, Chapter 7, 'Man the father', in *On Men: Masculinity in Crisis*, Chatto, 2000.

63 Bill Elias, 'Gadget-loving dad', *Tech TV*, 1 June 2001, http://www.techtv.com/products/fathersday/story/0,23008,3330068,00.html

64 Scott Kirsner, 'From the war front to home, finding jobs for robots', *New York Times*, 27 December 2002.

65 Rebecca Abrams, Chapter 7, 'Eve's legacy', in *The Playful Self: Why Women Need Play in their Lives,* Fourth Estate, 1997.

66 Rebecca Abrams, 'Let's all go out to play', *New Statesman*, 13 November 2000.

67 Rebecca Abrams, Chapter 7, 'Eve's legacy', in *The Playful Self: Why Women Need Play in their Lives*, Fourth Estate, 1997.

68 Abrams, *ibid.*, p. 114.

69 Abrams, Chapter 6, 'The imperative of service', *ibid*.

70 See C. Hampden-Turner's and Fons Trompenaar's, *The Seven Cultures of Capitalism*, Piatkus, 1995, and *Mastering the Infinite Game*, Capstone, 1997, as studies in the global diversity of work ethics.

71 For visions of the technological plenitude that awaits us in the twenty-first century, see Michio Kaku, *Visions*, Bantam, 1999; Ray Kurzweil, *The Age of Spiritual Machines*, Penguin USA, 2000.

72 See the many works of Hazel Henderson on the diversity of economic models necessary for a 'win-win world', researchable at http://www.hazelhenderson.org. Also see the New Economics Foundation (http://www.neweconomics.org) for more detailed studies.

73 Abrams, *The Playful Self*, p. 223.

74 Zygmunt Bauman, 'Am I my brother's keeper?', *European Journal of Social Work*, vol. 3, no. 1, pp. 5–11, 2000.

75 Paul Feyerabend, *The Conquest of Abundance: a Tale of Abstraction Versus the Richness of Being*, Chicago, 1999; Zygmunt Bauman, *Postmodern Ethics*, Polity, 1995.

76 Abrams, *The Playful Self,* pp. 106–7.

77 On non-duality, see the works of Ken Wilber and in particular David Loy's *Non-Duality: a Study in Comparative Philosophy*, Humanity, 1999.

78 See the 'Reimagining social work', Powerpoint, April 2003, at http://www.reimaginingsocialwork.org, '*Session material*', page.

79 See http://www.reimaginingsocialwork.org, and http://www.newintegrity.org

80 For much intelligent discussion on these debates see http://www.communitycare.co.uk. Also, see Andrew Cooper, Rachael Hetherington and Ilan Katz, *The Risk Factor: Making the Child Protection System Work for Children*, Demos, 2003, http://www.demos.co.uk/theriskfactor_pdf_media_public.aspx

81 See Nigel Parton and Patrick O'Byrne, *Constructive Social Work: Towards a New Practice*, Palgrave, 2000.

82 Carolyn Taylor and Susan White, 'Knowledge, truth and reflexivity: the

problem of judgement in social work', *Journal of Social Work*, 1(1), 2001, p. 51.

83 See Chapter 9, this volume.

84 Bill Jordan, *Social Work and the Third Way: Tough Love as Social Policy*, Sage, 2002, p. 199.

85 This is similar to the 'zero-work' option for a social wage, in the 'Alternatives' chapter of Nick Dyer-Witherford's *Cyber-Marx: Cycles and Circuits of Struggle in High Technology Capitalism*, University of Illinois Press, 1999, pp. 426–37, http://www.fims.uwo.ca/people/faculty/dyerwitheford/Chapter8.pdf

86 Bauman, 'Am I my brother's keeper?', *ibid.*, p. 5.

87 *Ibid.*, p. 10.

88 6.5 million working days lost to work-related stress or depression; one in seven adults off work for at least six months due to illness or injury; and a cost of £11 billion a year to employers. In the public sector, employees are five times more likely to be off sick than in the IT sector. Stephen Bevan, *Attendance Management*, Work Foundation, 2003. See http://www.theworkfoundation.com/newsroom/pressreleases.jsp?ref=107
Also Bevan, 'Sickness absence: a cost worth managing', at http://www.employment-studies.co.uk/news/126art1.php. On the war for talent, see John Knell, *Most Wanted*, The Work Foundation, 2001.

89 The chief executive of the banking giant Lloyds TSB, Peter Ellwood, puts it authoritatively: 'When an employee leaves a company, the average cost to the business is more than £3,000. Stress-related sick leave costs UK industry £370m a year, yet employers are more likely to offer counselling than flexible work options that might prevent the stress in the first place. Of the employers surveyed by the DTI, 56 per cent had never considered flexible working locations, such as working from home, and 57 per cent had never considered offering job-sharing schemes – two common ways to reduce workplace stress.' See Ellwood's pieces on http://www.employersforwork-lifebalance.org.uk/ellwood.htm

90 See Ellwood's pieces on http://www.employersforwork-lifebalance.org.uk/ellwood.htm

91 See Thomas Frank, *One Market Under God*, Penguin, 2002.

92 Madeleine Bunting, 'New year, same grind', *Guardian*, 6 January 2003.

93 Alexandra Frean, 'Flexible hours are preferred to pay rise', *The Times*, 2 January 2003.

94 For a recent survey of European working time regimes, see 'Working time developments – 2002', at EIRO (European Industrial Relations Observatory) http://www.eiro.eurofound.ie/2003/03/update/tn0303103u.html

95 'Charles Leadbeater, 'Welcome to the amateur century', *Financial Times*, 23 December 2002. See also his *Up the Down Escalator: Why the Global Pessimists Are Wrong*, Penguin, 2002.

96 On the need for social dissensus, see Jean-François Lyotard's *The Postmodern Condition: a report on knowledge*, Manchester UP, 1985.

1 'Success begins deep in the heart and soul', Ewan Aitken. *Times Educational Supplement*, 1 November 2002, p. 24.

2 'The bruiser is really a softie', *ibid.*, p. 7.

3 'Absence of phonic irritation aids the playful Finns', *Times Educational Supplement*, 22 November 2002, p. 21. There is some evidence that a more play-centred early years educational approach is coming back into fashion, though in the Celtic peripheries of Wales and Scotland. See BBC Online News, 'More "play", less work in early years', 12 February 2003, http://news.bbc.co.uk/1/hi/wales/2752895.stm

4 Janet R. Moyles (ed.), *The Excellence of Play*, Oxford University Press, 1994. See in particular the opening chapter by Peter K. Smith.

5 Moyles, *Excellence of Play*, p. 7.

6 BBC Online News, 'Clarke backs competitive sport', 23 May 2003, http://news.bbc.co.uk/2/hi/uk_news/education/2932680.stm

7 Alex Moore, 'Citizenship education in the UK: for liberation or control?', Institute of Education, University of London, http://ec.hku.hk/kd2proc/proceedings/fullpaper/Theme2FullPapers/AlexMoore.pdf

8 Ivan Illich, *Deschooling Society*, Marion Boyars, 1996, p.103.

9 See Pekka Himanen, 'The net academy', in *The Hacker Ethic*, Vintage, 2001.

10 See Richard Florida, 'The Post-scarcity effect', in his *The Rise of the Creative Classes*, Basic, 2002; and George Moyser, 'Post-scarcity radicalism in the US', *Government and Opposition* (2000), 35 (1), pp. 119–22.

11 On the dialectic between counterculture and policy, see Virginia Postrel, 'One best way', in *The Future and its Enemies*, Free Press, 1999. For a historical account of the effects of the US counterculture, see Peter Braunstein and William Micheal Doyle, *Imagine Nation: the American counterculture of the 1960s and '70s*, Routledge, 2002. For the UK, see Sheila Rowbotham, *Promise of a Dream: Remembering the Sixties*, Verso, 2001.

12 For more on Spinoza's radical idea of education, see Antonio Negri, Michael Hardt, *The Savage Anomaly: the Power of Spinoza's Metaphysics and Politics,* Minnesota, 1991.

13 See Ross McKibben, 'Nothing more divisive', *London Review of Books*, 28 November 2002, http://www.lrb.co.uk/v24/n23/contents.html.

14 The earliest statement of this hope was Buckminster Fuller's 'Education automation', available at http://www.bfi.org/education_automation.htm. But it informs much of the 'leisure age' literature of the early to late seventies. For a useful overview see Ian P. Henry, *The Politics of Leisure Policy*, Palgrave Macmillan, 2001.

15 David Docherty, 'Why I quit', *Guardian*, 2 December 2002, http://media.guardian.co.uk/mediaguardian/story/0,7558,852024,00.html

16 See Tina Bruce, 'Play, the universe and everything!', in Moyles, *The Excellence of Play*, *ibid.*

17 This is backed up by Howard Gardner's notions of 'education for

The Play Ethic

understanding' as outlined in *The Disciplined Mind*, Penguin, 2000. To truly understand a great topic like evolution or the Holocaust, one must apply a range of intelligences – and some of those might be the physical, the musical, the interpersonal and the intra-personal (the classic intelligences of the arts, and of carnival). However, a play ethic would see the power of carnival and collective performance as being more than a specific teaching tool and as a means to children becoming properly socialized in a post-work, proto-play society.

18 Kathleen Roskos and James Christie, 'Examining the play-literacy interface: a critical review and future directions', *Journal of Early Childhood Literacy*, vol 1 (1), 2001, pp. 59–89.

19 'Adolescence lost/childhood regained: literacy and the rise of the techno-subject', Allen and Carmen Luke, *Journal of Early Childhood Literacy*, 1 (1), 2000, pp. 90–120.

20 'Adolescence', Luke, *ibid.*, p. 95.

21 See Andrew Pettegree, Alastair Duke and Gillian Lewis, *Calvinism in Europe, 1540–1620*, Cambridge University Press, 1997.

22 'Adolescence', Luke, *ibid.*, p. 104.

23 BBC Online, 'Video games "stimulate learning"', 18 March 2002, http://news.bbc.co.uk/1/hi/education/1879019.stm

24 'Children get smart with their computer games', John Paul Flintoff, *Financial Times*, 14/15 December 2002, p. 11. For more research, see Seymour Papert's home page, http://www.papert.org

25 'Most secondary school systems remain geared up for dual pathway certification: tracking and streaming students towards either vocation or university education. Yet students increasingly are crafting life pathways that constitute a kind of educational bricolage. Some students mix some vocational certification and hands-on skilling, alongside one or two requisite tertiary degrees, in preparation for emergent and yet unheard of jobs, for which the "multiple entry" stamps on the educational passport constitute the new barcodes on the swipe card into a flexible and unstable job market. Lifelong learning, horizontal occupational mobility, generic textual and semiotic skills that can be quickly reinterpreted and cross-applied to a variety of jobs – these are among the new generational scenarios.' 'Adolescence', Luke, *ibid.*, p. 109.

26 'Adolescence', Luke, *ibid.*, pp. 115–17.

27 'Adolescence', Luke, *ibid.*, p. 102.

28 See Pat Kane, 'Media studies: how to read the signs', *The Herald*, 10 December 1998.

29 For the latest research see Nesta Future Lab, http://www.nestafuturelab.org/

30 See Gardner's lecture, 'An education for the future: the foundation of science and values'. Paper presented to The Royal Symposium. Convened by Her Majesty, Queen Beatrix, Amsterdam, 13 March 2001, http://www.pz.harvard.edu/Pls/HG_Amsterdam.htm

31 Lella Gandini, 'The Reggio Emilia story: history and organization', in J. Hendrick (ed.), *First Steps Towards Teaching the Reggio Way*, Merril/Prentice-Hall, 1997.

32 Norma Morrison, 'The Reggio approach: an Inspiration for inclusion of children with "special rights"', http://www.milligan.edu/ProfEducation/NMorrison/fpworkshop/dkgreggio200.htm.

33 Carlina Rinaldi, 'Staff development in Reggio Emilia', in G. Lillian, *Reflections on the Reggio Emilia Approach*. Urbana, 1994.

34 Morrison, 'The Reggio approach', *ibid*.

35 Morrison, *ibid*.

36 Leila Gandini, *ibid*.

37 '*Shkole* did not mean just "having time", but also a certain relation to time: a person living an academic life could organize one's time oneself – the person could combine work and leisure the way that he wanted.' Pekka Himanen, *The Hacker Ethic*, Secker and Warburg, 2001, pp. 33–4, 76.

38 *Ibid.*, p. 78.

39 BBC Online News, 'Homework for cheats', 25 September 1998, http://news.bbc.co.uk/1/hi/education/180241.stm

40 See essays available in *Children and Computer Technology*, Fall/Winter 2000, http://www.futureofchildren.org/pubs-info2825/pubs-info.htm?doc_id=69787

41 See discussion on Linux in Chapters 4 and 9, this volume.

42 See essays in *Experiencing Reggio Emilia: Implications for Pre-School Provision*, edited by Lesley Abbott, Open University Press, 2001.

43 On Finland, see Pekka Himanen and Manuel Castells, *The Information Society and the Welfare State: The Finnish Model*, Oxford 2002. On Emilia-Romagna, see Irene Rubbin, *Italy's Industrial Renaissance*, Comitate Regionale Dell Emilia Romagna, 1986.

44 See Will Hutton, *The World We're In,* 2002, Vintage.

45 The only wrong note in the movie is the absence of video games and the Internet.

46 Matthew Boyle and Graham Leicester, *Changing Schools Education in a Knowledge Society*, Scottish Council Foundation, August 2000, http://www.scottishcouncilfoundation.org/pubs_more.php?p=33

47 George Davie, *The Crisis of the Democratic Intellect*, Birlinn, 1989.

48 Immanuel Wallerstein, 'Uncertainty and Creativity', talk at *Forum 2000: Concerns and Hopes on the Threshold of the New Millennium*, Prague, 3–6 September 1997. http://fbc.binghamton.edu/iwuncer.htm

49 Manuel Castells, 'Epilogue', in Pekka Himanen's *The Hacker Ethic*, *ibid.*, p. 167.

50 See the international critical reaction to Sweet Sixteen at http://www.metacritic.com/video/titles/sweetsixteen/

51 On 'real virtuality', see Castells, *ibid.*, p.170.

52 Douglas Ruskhoff, *Playing the Future: What We Can Learn from Digital Kids*, Riverhead, 1999.

53 'During the normal life of a historical system, even great efforts at

transformation (so-called 'revolutions') have limited consequences, since the system creates great pressures to return to its equilibrium. But in the chaotic ambience of a structural transition, fluctuations become wild, and even small pushes can have great consequences in favouring one branch or the other of the bifurcation [branching of options]. If every agency operates, this is the moment.' Immanuel Wallerstein, 'A Left politics for an age of transition', 2001, http://fbc.binghamton.edu/iwleftpol2.htm

54 See http://www.internationalfuturesforum.com

55 Howard Gardner puts it more eloquently: 'We live at the first time in history where we will have machines that are in many ways at least as smart as we are. Machines that can plan economies, wage diplomacy, alter politics, and, for all I know, manage our leisure life, our love life, the place and manner of our deaths, and rebirths, how and whether we will be remembered. There will be experiments in cloning organs or whole human beings, and there will be attempts to merge humans and robots, for example, through the implanting of silicon chips in our brains; some will even hope to achieve immortality in that way, by downloading the wet brains into a vast dry database. I will leave it to you to determine whether this prospect of indefinite lives more closely approximates a dream or a nightmare!

'I'm not saying that these issues – what used to be the stuff of science fiction – should dominate the curriculum of the school. I am saying something more radical – that they are already beginning to constitute the curriculum of life each day. Students won't have to learn in school about cloned organs and organisms or silicon implants in the hippocampus because they will see them on television or surf past them on the Internet, or hear them argued about around the dinner table at night or at the cyber café around the corner.

'And so the tasks of educators will become dual and dually challenging: on one hand, to inculcate the traditional disciplines and ways of thinking as I have described them; and, on the other hand, to help students cope with and perhaps take an active role in deciding how to deal with these dazzling developments, which, as I say, are no longer restricted to the pages of science fiction.' Gardner, 'An education for the future: the foundation of science and values', *ibid.*

56 The question of what an education in the light of the 'new sciences' might be is tentatively explored by Fritjof Capra in his Centre for Ecoliteracy, http://www.ecoliteracy.org/

57 The Cosmic Rough Riders is the name of a Scottish rock band. http://www.cosmicroughriders.com/

58 James Carse, *Finite and Infinite Games*, Ballantine, 1986, section 17.

59 Carse, *ibid.*, pp. 52–3

60 Scott Lash's *Critique of Information*, Sage, 2002, proposes that 'communication' has replaced 'society' as the proper object of study for the human sciences – and that play is the characteristic mode of the 'communicator', pp. 157–64.

61 See 'Intellects', in Nick Dyer-Witherford, *Cyber-Marx, Cycles and Circuits of Struggle in High Technology Capitalism*, Illinois, 1999, http://www.fims.uwo.ca/people/faculty/dyerwitheford/Chapter9.pdf. *On Davie*, see *note 47, this chapter*.

62 See Chapter 9, this volume.

63 The Steven Spielberg film *Minority Report* (2002) features many of the plausible near-future innovations in communications technology – hardly surprising, as Spielberg consulted over twenty futurists in the pre-production phase. For a somewhat jaundiced view of the process from one of the participants, see Jaron Lanier, 'A minority within the minority', *21C*, http://www.21cmagazine.com/minority.html

64 See Howard Rheingold's Smart Mobs website (http://www.smartmobs.org) for a regular update on the challenges presented by always-on connectivity.

SEVEN / THE PLAY AESTHETIC

1 To make this obvious: you're looking for the new forms in the confusion; you're seeking the order at the edge of chaos. But the theories, as usual in pop music, only come after the discovery.

2 See my previous book, *Tinsel Show: Pop, Politics and Scotland*, Polygon, 1992 for stories of pop-life frustration.

3 There is a thriving research culture exploring the relationship between the arts and everyday life, communities and organizations. See, for example, the think tank Poiesis (http://www.poiesis.org) and its 'Power of the arts' strand; and the Aesthetics, Creativity, and Organization Research Network (http://acorn.lld.dk/).

4 James Carse, *Finite and Infinite Games*, Ballantine, 1994, p. 76.

5 Sutton-Smith, *Ambiguity of Play*, pp. 133–4.

6 Hans-Georg Gadamer's work in phenomenology is also useful here – the meaning of art as the interplay of object and spectator, art as an open and infinite process of meaning. See Gadamer, *The Relevance of the Beautiful*, Cambridge University Press, 1986.

7 Karl Groos, *The Play of Man*, quoted in Sutton-Smith, *Ambiguity*, p. 135.

8 See Howard Gardner, *Art, Mind and Brain*, Basic, 1984, and Daniel Berlyne, *Aesthetics and Psychobiology*, Appleton, Century, Crofts, 1971.

9 The classic essay which explores the status of a delimited and authored 'work of art' in a modern media age is Walter Benjamin's 'The work of art in the age of mechanical reproduction', *Illuminations*, Schocken, 1968.

10 For more on Joseph Beuys, see the Social Sculpture Unit at Oxford Brookes University, http://www.brookes.ac.uk/schools/apm/social_sculpture/

11 Though for different take on a 'universal aesthetic', see Steven Pinker, *The Blank Slate: the Denial of Human Nature*, Penguin, 2002.

12 On the 'movie-like' and scripted nature of consciousness itself, see Peggy La

Cerra and Roger Bingham, *The Origin of Minds: Evolution, Uniqueness, and the New Science of the Self*, Harmony Books, 2003.

13 See Virginia Postrel, *The Substance of Style*, Harper Collins, 2003. A useful interview is on the *Atlantic Monthly* website, http://www.theatlantic.com/unbound/interviews/int2003–08–27.htm

14 For an exploration of the roots/routes metaphor, see Paul Gilroy, 'Roots and routes: black identity as an outernational project', in Herbert W. Harris, Howard C. Blue and Ezra E.H. Griffith, eds, *Racial and Ethnic Identity: Psychological Development and Creative Expression*, Routledge, 1995.

15 Simon Frith, *Performing Rites: on the Value of Popular Music*, Harvard, 1998, final chapter.

16 Manuel Castells, *The Internet Galaxy*, Oxford, 2002, pp. 204–5.

17 http://www.guardian.co.uk/arts/turnerpeoplespoll/story/ 0,13945,1073508,00.html

18 'The classical avant-gardes provide a repository of ideas, tactics and strategies that are now played out in a radically enlarged context; no longer the context of art itself, but that of the network society . . .' Eric Kluitenberg, 'Transfiguration of the avant-garde: the negative dialectics of the Net', on Nettime, http://amsterdam.nettime.org/Lists-Archives/nettime-l–0201/ msg00104.html

19 James Doherty, 'After 44 days, David Blaine's out of his box', *Scotsman*, 20 October 2003, http://www.news.scotsman.com/uk.cfm?id=1158142003

20 For marketing, see Watts Wacker and Ryan Matthews, 'Deviants. Inc', *Fast Company*, March 2002, http://www.fastcompany.com/online/56/deviant.html. For conceptual arts, see the artist-group Inventory, note 32, below.

21 Chapter available at http://www.marxists.org/archive/trotsky/works/1924/ lit_revo/cho7.htm

22 Marx's point was that, eventually, capitalism makes us all global players: 'the bourgeoisie has through its exploitation of the world market given a cosmopolitan character to production and consumption in every country . . . [There is] intercourse in every direction,' Marx noted further – not just in material, but also in 'intellectual' production. 'The intellectual creations of individual nations become common property. National one-sidedness and narrow-mindedness become more and more impossible . . .' Hard not to think that Herr Marx, transported to the early twenty-first century, wouldn't be sitting in the local Starbucks, his nose in copies of *Wallpaper*, *The Economist* and *Wired* magazines. (Marx was also a geek: when he praised the bourgeoisie's 'immensely facilitated means of communication' that 'draws all nations, even the most barbarian, into civilisation', you know that he'd be down with the hackers, arguing for an open global network. The great bearded one actually was a soulitarian long before he identified with the proletarians.)

23 'One can say with certainty that collective interests and passions, and individual competition, will have the widest scope and the most unlimited opportunity. Art, therefore, will not suffer the lack of any such explosions of

collective, nervous energy, and of such collective psychic impulses which make for the creation of new artistic tendencies and for changes in style. It will be the aesthetic schools around which "parties" will collect, that is, associations of temperaments, of tastes and of moods. In a struggle so disinterested and tense [. . .], the human personality, with its invaluable basic trait of continual discontent, will grow and become polished at all its points.' Trotsky, 'Communist Policy Towards Art', in *Literature and Revolution*, available at http://www.marxists.org/archive/trotsky/works/1924/lit_revo/cho7.htm

24 Stefan Courtois et al., *The Black Book of Communism: Crimes, Terror, Repression*, Harvard, 1999.

25 On the connections between hackerism and socialism, see the works of Columbia University Law School's Eben Moglen, in particular 'The dotCommunist manifesto', January 2003, available at http://moglen.law.columbia.edu/publications/dcm.html. Also see Richard Barbrook, 'Cyber-communism: how the Americans are superseding capitalism in cyberspace', http://www.hrc.wmin.ac.uk/theory-cybercommunism.html

26 On the idea of the 'adjacent possible' in any fixed situation – the way that autonomous agents (and artists are certainly those) 'push their way into novelty' in both nature and culture, see Stuart Kauffman, *Investigations*, Oxford, 2002, p. 22.

27 Michael Foucault, *Ethics: Subjectivity and Truth*, Penguin, 2002, p.262.

28 Since this moment, the BBC have radicalized the entire broadcasting ecology, with their idea of the 'creative archive' – turning over BBC copyrighted broadcast material to the public realm for use. See Chapter 9, this volume.

29 See 'Collective: ICA Beck's Futures', *BBC Online*, http://www.bbc.co.uk/dna/collective/A1019819

30 Lucy Skaer's two contributions are so risible and aleatory that they almost defy anyone – let alone an avant-garde art competition – to take them seriously. In one moment, she simply leaves a scorpion and a diamond on a pavement in Amsterdam: in another, she tricks a Glaswegian dignitary into ceremonially laying a paving slab that she has recently levered out of the same pavement.

31 See BBC Online, 'Collective', on Beck's Futures 2003, http://www.bbc.co.uk/dna/collective/A1019819

32 This is exemplified by the French situtationist Guy Debord's quote: 'It was modern poetry for the last 100 years that had led us to this place. We were a handful who thought that it was necessary to carry out its programme in reality and to do nothing else.'

33 Inventory, 'Fierce sociology', http://www.infopool.org.uk/inventor.htm

34 Peter Wollen, 'Thatcher's artists', *London Review of Books*, October 1997.

35 'Semiocracy' is a pejorative term coined by the French thinker Jean Baudrillard in *Symbolic Exchange and Death* (Sage, 1993, p. 78), to describe a society which rules by the power of the sign, the simulation and the image. A 'liberal semiocrat' – apart from being not a bad pun on the Liberal

Democrats, a significant party in the UK political system – is someone who wields the power of their significations (like a player-artist) to emancipate and liberate.

36 Technologies like the hard-drive video recorder TiVo promised that kind of flexibility in the short term, recording programmes on a vast hard disk and attempting to repond to a viewer's taste patterns. The mass-market launch at the end of 2003 of Sky Television's SkyPlus box in the UK – which reproduces most of the TiVo's functions and sells itself on the slogan, 'Create your own TV channel' – shows that the consumer impetus to 'become the auteur' is genuinely strong.

37 I take the notion of 'system' from the social theorist Jurgen Habermas, and his notion of the inevitable yet generative tensions between 'system' and 'lifeworld' – the latter being that realm of emotion, culture, community and human relationships that must always exceed the operations of power and money. Out of many works, see J. Habermas, *Autonomy and Solidarity*, Verso, 1986. And 'cash from chaos' was the slogan of the situationist manager of the Sex Pistols, Malcolm McLaren. See Jon Savage, *England's Dreaming: Anarchy, Sex Pistols, Punk Rock and Beyond*, St Martin's Press, 2002, p. 536.

38 For a sobering account of the costs of artistic commitment and creativity, see Mickey Z., *The Murdering of My Years: Artists and Activists Making Ends Meet*, Soft Skull, 2003.

39 Richard Florida, 'The rise of the creative class', *Washington Monthly*, May 2002, http://www.washingtonmonthly.com/features/2001/0205.florida.html

40 Robert Samuelson, 'But does it own the means of production?', Review of 'The rise of the creative classes', *Los Angeles Times*, 14 September 2002. Peter Drucker coined the phrase 'knowledge worker' in the late 1940s.

41 'Talented people seek an environment open to differences. Many highly creative people, regardless of ethnic background or sexual orientation, grew up feeling like outsiders, different in some way from most of their schoolmates. When they are sizing up a new company and community, acceptance of diversity – and of gays in particular – is a sign that reads "non-standard people welcome here" . . . [Diversity] is spoken of so often, and so matter-of-factly, that I take it to be a fundmental marker of creative class values. Creative-minded people enjoy a mix of influences – they want to hear different kinds of music and try different kinds of food. They want to meet and socialize with people unlike themselves, trade views and spar over issues.' Florida, 'Creative class', *ibid*.

42 Florida quotes taken from Terence Blacker, 'I'm depressed by this creative view of economics', *Independent*, 10 June 2002.

43 Richard Florida, 'The New American Dream', *Washington Monthly*, March 2003, http://www.washingtonmonthly.com/features/2003/0303.florida.html

44 Sherry Ruth Anderson and Paul Ray, *The Cultural Creatives: How 50 Million People Are Changing the World*, Harmony, 2000, and website: http://www.culturalcreatives.org

45 http://www.senseworldwide.net

46 Salman Rushdie, 'In good faith', *Imaginary Homelands*, Granta 1991.

47 For example, see World Bank, *Culture Counts: Financing, Resources, and the Economics of Culture in Sustainable Development*, Florence, October 1999.

48 For the notion of the non-player, see Ashis Nandy, *Exiled at Home*, Oxford, 1998, 'If beating the West at its game is the preferred means of handling the feelings of self-hatred in the modernized non-West, there is also the West constructed by the savage outsider who is neither willing to be a player or a counterplayer ... [this] "West" is not merely a part of an imperial world view; its classical traditions and its critical self are sometimes a protest against the "modern West" ... the modern West has produced not only its servile imitators and admirers, but also its circus-tamed opponents and its tragic counterplayers, performing their last gladiator-like acts of courage in front of appreciative Caesars. The essays in this book are a paen to the non-players, who construct a West which allows them to live with the alternative West, while resisting the loving embrace of the West's dominant self ...' pp. 143–4 and 161.

49 Chris Rojek, *Celebrity*, Reaktion, 2002.

50 William Gibson, *Pattern Recognition*, Penguin, 2003.

51 See Masao Miyoshi, H.D. Harootunian (eds), *Postmodernism and Japan*, Duke, 1989.

52 Frederic Jameson, in an otherwise perceptive essay on Pattern Recognition, says that the absence of Islam is 'a welcome relief, in a moment in which it is reality, rather than culture or literature, that is acting on the basis of that particular stereotype'. Yet surely this vitiates his description of it as an 'inventory of the world-system' at the beginning of the twenty-first century? Jameson, 'Fear and loathing in globalisation', *New Left Review*, September–October 2003, http://www.newleftreview.net/NLR25706.shtml

53 From Jean Baudrillard, 'The despair of having everything', *Le Monde Diplomatique*, November 2002, available at http://amsterdam.nettime.org/Lists-Archives/nettime-l-0211/msg00067.html

54 See discussion of the work of Ziauddin Sardar, Chapter 10, this volume.

55 See *BBC Online News*, 'Blunkett outlines ID card plans', 12 November 2003, http://news.bbc.co.uk/1/hi/uk_politics/3259285.stm. Though even in the US, there is some claw-back on the Bush government's panoptical ambitions. See Jim Lobe, 'Congress defunds controversial "total information" program', *Common Dreams*, 26 September 2003, http://www.commondreams.org/headlines03/0926-02.htm

56 See Bill Gertz, 'CIA pursues video game', *Washington Times*, 29 September 2003, http://washingtontimes.com/national/20030929-123116-1145r.htm. See also Henry Jenkins, 'War games', *MIT Technology Review*, 7 November 2003, http://www.technologyreview.com/articles/print_version/wo_jenkins110703.asp

57 On polylogue, see Ziauddin Sardar, Merryl Wyn Davies and Ashis Nandy, *Barbaric Others: a Manifesto on Western Racism*, Pluto, 1993.

1 Charles Handy, *The Elephant and the Flea*, Arrow, 2002. Review by Pat Kane, 'Look back in anger management', *Independent*, 20 September 2001, http://www.independent.co.uk/low_res/story.jsp?story=94950&host=5&dir=207

2 On the 'game-changers' at Royal Dutch Shell, see Gary Hamel, 'Innovation now!', *Fast Company*, December 2002, http://www.fastcompany.com/online/65/innovation.html

3 'Scotland heralds a new Sunday paper', *BBC News Online*, 7 February 1999, http://news.bbc.co.uk/1/hi/uk/273216.stm

4 Reference on tensile flexible companies in Sennett, *Corrosion of Character*, Norton, 1998.

5 See the Good Work project, http://www.goodworkproject.org//, *on journalism as 'good work'*.

6 Tom Brown, Stuart Crainer, Des Dearlove and Jorge Nascimento Rodrigues, *Business Minds: Management Wisdom Direct from the World's Greatest Thinkers*, *Financial Times* Prentice Hall, November 2001.

7 John Kao, *Jamming the Art and Discipline of Business Creativity*, Diane, 1996; James H. Gilmore and B. Joseph Pine II, *The Experience Economy*, Harvard Business School Press, 1999; Michael Schrage, *Serious Play: how the Best Companies Simulate to Innovate*, Harvard Business School Press, 1999.

8 'Welcome to a world where anything is possible – unless it isn't', Watts Wacker, at *First Matter* website (http://www.firstmatter.com/pr/vh_pr.asp)

9 Richard Neville, *Playpower*, Paladin, 1971.

10 Another notable anticipation of the Web from the same era was Pete Townshend's image of 'The Grid', which he turned into a musical in 2002. See http://www.wdkeller.com/lhcln.htm

11 Neville, *Playpower*, p. 221.

12 Peter Drucker notes this mid-life angst in the knowledge worker, and recommends a solution that sounds like a multi-rhetoric vision of play – both artistic and sociable, agonistic and aerobic: 'The upward mobility of the knowledge society, however, comes at a high price: the psychological pressures and emotional traumas of the rat race. There can be winners only if there are losers. This was not true of earlier societies. The son of the landless labourer who became a landless labourer himself was not a failure. In the knowledge society, however, he is not only a personal failure but a failure of society as well . . . Given this competitive struggle, a growing number of highly successful knowledge workers of both sexes – business managers, university teachers, museum directors, doctors – 'plateau' in their 40s. They know they have achieved all they will achieve. If their work is all they have, they are in trouble. Knowledge workers therefore need to develop, preferably while they are still young, a non-competitive life and community of their own, and some serious outside interest – be it working as a volunteer in the community, playing in a local orchestra or taking an active part in a small town's local government. This outside interest will give them the

opportunity for personal contribution and achievement.' Drucker, 'The next society: the next workforce', *The Economist*, 3 November 2001.

13 'California facts', California State of the State Conference, available at http://web .archive.org/web/20011121052520/http://www.milkeninstitute.org/sos2001/facts.cfm [Wayback retrieval].

14 Sue McAllister, 'Bay Area's office vacancy rates climb', *Silicon Valley.com*, 19 July 2001, http://web.archive.org/web/20010725112921/http://www.siliconvalley.com/docs/news/svfront/commo72001.htm [Wayback retrieval].

15 James Niccolai, 'IBM's graffiti ads run afoul of city officials', *CNN.com*, 19 April 2001, http://www.cnn.com/2001/TECH/industry/04/19/ibm.guerilla.idg/index.html?s=8

16 Arie De Geus, 'Planning as learning', *Harvard Business Review*, March–April 1988. De Geus suggests that the consultant is like Winnicott's notion of the transitional object – the toy that the child plays with in order to engage more skilfully with its environment (p.5). For more on Pierre Wack, the founder of the Group Planning Department, see Art Kleiner, 'The man who saw the future', *Strategy and Business*, Spring 2003, http://www.strategy–business.com/press/article/?art=29406251&pg=0. A‹???›

17 And continues to be, perpetual war or not: see Jamais Cascio, 'Shall we play a game?', GBN website, February 2003, http://www.gbn.com/ArticleDisplayServlet.srv?aid=3000

18 Peter Schwartz and Peter Leyden, 'The long boom: a history of the future, 1980–2020', *Wired*, July 1997, http://www.wired.com/wired/archive/5.07/longboom.html?topic=&topic_set=

19 'The new view on the next decade: a conversation with Peter Schwartz', interview conducted by Peter Leyden, GBN website, August 2001, http://www.gbn.com/ArticleDisplayServlet.srv?aid=3400

20 Though Schwartz has come up with another era-defining paradigm – the hydrogen economy. See 'How hydrogen can save America', *Wired*, April 2003, http://www.wired.com/wired/archive/11.04/hydrogen.html

21 Art Kleiner, 'Consequential heresies' , GBN website, May 1996, http://www.gbn.com/ArticleDisplayServlet.srv?aid=185

22 John Vidal, 'When disaster strikes' [on Shell's brand rebuilding, in the face of oil spills, and the assassination of Ken Saro-Wiwa in Nigeria], *Guardian*, 9 July 2001, http://www.guardian.co.uk/Archive/Article/0,4273,4218124,00.html

23 See their website, http://www.fratellibologna.com/

24 Ethan Watters, 'Kao's theory', *Business 2.0*, September 1999, http://www.business2.com/articles/mag/0,1640,13133,00.html

25 http://www.fratellibologna.com/NewPages/improvmatrix.html

26 The Ministry of Defence finally heaved forth their scenario plan in 2003. 'Strategic trends', Military of Defence website, http://www.mod.uk/jdcc/trends.htm

27 Quotes from Stewart Brand, *The Clock of the Long Now: Time and Responsibility*, Weidenfield and Nicolson, 1999. Brand continues: 'In the long

run, saving yourself requires saving the whole world . . . We don't know what's coming. We do know we're in it together.'

28 Much of this thinking is extended in Eamonn Kelly, *What's Next? Exploring the New Terrain for Business*, Wiley, 2002.

29 The games that these tribes want to play are predominantly 'infinite' rather than 'finite games', in the James Carse sense – the first played for the purpose of continuing the game, the second 'played for the purpose of winning the game'. The soulitarian wants to take the possibilities of technology and see how far they can be extended. Men and women want to throw off all the inherited weight of outdated gender stereotypes and see how effective an 'emotional democracy' can be. The educator wants to focus as much time and resources on the flowering of minds and souls, and test the limits of human potential. The neo-artist wants to shape symbols using all the facilities and opportunities of the age in order to gauge what the real 'power of the arts' might be.

30 On Moebius strip as a metaphor for business, see Charles Hampden-Turner and Fons Trompenaars, *Mastering the Infinite Game*, Capstone, 1997, pp. 27–30.

31 Though one of GBN's founders, Jay Ogilvy, is beginning to question the undoubted rule of market values in his contributions to *What's Next? Exploring the New Terrain for Business*, ibid., 2002. After outlining what he regarded as the two great Reformations of modernity – from Church to state, and from state to market – he speculates on the coming third Reformation: 'If I were to throw out a guess for the successor to the religious-to-political-to-economic era, my candidate would be aesthetic or environmental. Here the sources of value are not religious. It's not about political categories like justice or the freedom of the slaves or colonies. It's not just economic categories either – value in wealth as we would ordinarily measure it in terms of head of cattle or acres of land or tons of steel. The sources of value would really be more aesthetic: beauty, laughter, and cultural and artistic value. But that's too ridiculously long off to entertain.'

32 Daniel Rogers, 'What next for St Luke's?', *Financial Times* (Web version), 10 March 2003.

33 See Andy Law's two books on St Luke's – *Open Minds*, Orion, 1998, and *Experiment at Work: Explosions and Experiences at the Most Frightening Company on Earth*, Profile, 2003.

34 Rogers, *What next?*, ibid.

35 Owen Gibson, 'Ikea gives St Luke's the elbow', *Guardian*, 1 November 2001, http://media.guardian.co.uk/advertising/story/0,7492,584778,00.html

36 'Work was important to us. We felt it could be liberating . . . David Abraham made it clear that this was personally important to every single person at St Luke's . . . We were awarded £18 million to persuade every businessman in Great Britain to address the loathsome spectre of unemployment, to solve it as a shared duty, and to put vigour and pride back into the jobs of

thousands, possibly millions of people all over the country. It was a dream come true.' Law, *Open Minds*, pp. 237–9.

37 For an often absurdly upbeat paen to 'work as community', see Richard Reeves, *Happy Mondays*: *Putting the Pleasure Back into Work*, Momentum, 2001; for his early engagement with the ideas in this book, see pp. 109–12.

38 'Senior industry figures are now predicting the death of St Luke's trademark co-operative structure – in which each employee is allocated the same number of shares each year and everyone has a say in how the company is run. When St Luke's was set up Rupert Howell, founder of HHCL & Partners and former chief executive of Chime, famously said: 'Democracy is laudable, but I'm not sure communism is.' TBWA's Beattie says: 'Something that was invented as an antidote to office politics has been brought down by office politics.' Another London agency boss agrees: 'It's very difficult to run an agency along the lines of a kibbutz.' Law's guarantee to employees of 'a job for life' certainly seems to fly in the face of common sense in a downsizing industry. Andy Medd, partner of Mother, the agency which has assumed St Luke's mantle as 'Britain's hottest ad agency' says: 'The problem with a commune is that in principle no one ever leaves.' Law says: 'On reflection, the cooperative is not the interesting thing about St Luke's. Instead it is the way we combined creative talent. If co-operatives aren't careful they turn into mutual funds.' Rogers, 'St Luke's', *Financial Times*, *ibid*.

39 St Luke's founder Andy Law's latest book, *Experiment at Work* (Profile, 2003), only compounds the paradoxes. As a reviewer quips: 'I'd tend to be a little sceptical of things like the agency's claims to have done away with basic human instincts like "fear, greed and ego" by the simple method of outlawing them in the contract of employment, particularly since the author himself has just resigned after "a difference of opinion" in the boardroom to spend more time on a music-business venture with Anita Roddick and Dave Stewart.' Warwick Cairns, 'St Luke's gospel', *Management Today*, 22 April 2003.

40 Indeed, BT's failed attempt to claim copyright over the highlighted links that appear on websites – the feature that ensures the full connectivity of material on the Web – shows that their understanding of the deep forces of play culture is vestigial at best. 'BT loses Web links battle', *BBC News Online*, 23 August 2002, http://news.bbc.co.uk/1/hi/technology/2212203.stm

41 James Woudhuysen, 'All play and no work', *IT Week*, 15 January 2001, http://web.archive.org/web/20010501114329/http://www.zdnet.co.uk/itweek/columns/2001/02/woudhuysen.html [Wayback retrieval].

42 James Woudhuysen, 'Team players', *Spiked Online*, 12 April 2001, http://www.spiked-online.com/articles/00000005560.htm

43 Woudhuysen, 'Team players', *ibid*.

44 The 'management of play', in other words, can be about forcibly reducing the inherent ambiguity of play to one expedient set of traditions and rhetorics – a mix of, say, play as power and play as identity – rather than keeping open the flow and flux between and around them.

45 Bennis in Des Dearlove, Tom Brown and Stuart Craines, *Business Minds: Management Wisdom Direct from the World's Greatest Thinkers*, *Financial Times* Prentice Hall, 2001. Another, much darker vision of the players' organization comes from the sociologist Scott Lash. He describes the 'disorganization': 'Organisations make rational choices (usually), with unintended consequences (side effects). Disorganisations . . . often are the side effects and unintended consequences of organisations . . . Organizations are the props, the struts, the joists that sustain ideology, that sustain the symbolic, [that reproduce] economic and social relations. Disorganisations are the enemies of reproduction. They are involved in the *pro*duction of economy, of culture'.

The examples Lash gives are 'youth cultures, say BritPop subcultures or Brazilian skateboarding and surf wear culture. The *new* new social movements. Ghetto youth gangs, excluded from the information and communication structures of the global information culture. The tribes of gangster capitalism involved in today's illegal circulations of drugs, weapons, immigrants and body parts. The neo-families of our transformed intimacy. The flexibly networked work associations in the new sectors – bio-tech, software, multimedia'. Lash, *Critique of Information*, Sage, 2002, pp. 39–48. The environment of 'violence', 'tribalism' and 'archaism' which disorganizations can thrive in must be reckoned with as the possible underside of a play-dominant culture – and makes the need for a play ethic, as a conscious ordering of our ludic potentialities, ever more urgent. Castells also makes a similar point about the 'perverse connection' – criminal and terror networks – as the obverse of the information age, in Chapter 3, *End of Millenium*, Blackwell, 2000.

46 Note on culture-determined markets see Bill Cope and Mary Kalantzis, *Productive Diversity: A New, Australian Approach to Work and Management*, Pluto Australia, 2000.

47 Our information networks are often the only means wherby 'fluid moderns' (as philosopher Zygmunt Bauman calls players) can strike that balance between freedom and security: 'Those who tilt the balance too far to freedom, are often to be found by Bauman rushing for home, desperate to be loved, eager to re-establish communities. But that's not to say that the liquid moderns want their old suffocating security back. They want the impossible: to have their cake and eat it, to be free and secure . . . Sisyphus had it easy. The work of the liquid modern is likewise never done, but it takes much more imagination. Bauman finds his hero working everywhere – jabbering into mobile phones, addictively texting, leaping from one chat room to another, Internet dating (whose key appeal, Bauman notes, is that you can always delete a date without pain or peril). The liquid modern is forever at work, forever replacing quality of relationship with quantity . . .

'What's the significance of all this anxious work? For Bauman, the medium isn't the message – the new gadgets we use hardly determine who we are. Nor are the messages that people send each other significant in themselves;

rather, the message is the circulation of messages. The sense of belonging or security that the liquid modern creates consists in being cocooned in a web of messages. That way, we hope, the vexing problem of freedom and security will disappear. We text, argues Bauman, therefore we are. "We belong," he writes, "to the even flow of words and unfinished sentences (abbreviated, to be sure, truncated to speed up the circulation). We belong to talking, not what talking is about . . . Stop talking – and you are out. Silence equals exclusion." Derrida was on to something when he wrote "Il n'y a pas dehors du texte," though not for the reason he supposed. It is that the fear of silence and the exclusion it implies makes us anxious that our ingeniously assembled security will fall apart.' Stuart Jeffries, 'Pump-house of the heart' [review of Zygmunt Bauman's Liquid Love, Polity, 2003], *Guardian*, 19 April 2003, http://books.guardian.co.uk/review/story/0,12084,938792,00.html

Yet Bauman can often take too gloomy a view of the players' condition. See my *Independent* review of his *Globalisation: the Human Consequences* (Polity, 1998), 'The dark side of the global dream', 11 August 1998. 'What if the culture of the globalisers – hybrid, restless, pluralistic – were not just an elite affair? Pop culture, and the techno-creativity that the Cool Britannia scam tried to exploit, joyously embraces the global. It emphasises routes rather than roots, mixing utopia and realism, both vagabond and tourist. Is it possible that a younger generation might forge its own "world ethic", deploying the same flexible processes – digital technology, computer networks, cheap travel – which are what Bauman deplores?'

NINE / PLAYING FOR REAL

1 For example, see Ray Kurzweil's archive on the 'Singularity' – the coming exponential explosion of developments in technologies and society – on his website,
http://www.kurzweilai.net/meme/frame.html?main=memelist.html?m=1%23584

2 Jurgen Habermas, 'Why Europe needs a constitution', *New Left Review*, Sept-Oct 2001, http://www.newleftreview.net/NLR24501.shtml; on Jospin, see Lionel Barber, 'Europe seeks a third way to prosperity', *Financial Times*, 15 January 2001, http://specials.ft.com/europereinvented1/FT3VDDT1WHC.html

3 See Lessig, *The Future of Ideas: the Fate of the Commons in a Connected World*, Vintage, 2002. Lessig's work on constitutional law in the months after the break-up of the Soviet Union were similarly about an architecture of value – the political structures appropriate to new democracy. In an interview on PBS, Lessig compares this constitutionalism to the 'constitutionalism of the Internet – both of them are about a structuring of space so that democracy can emerge'. *The Charlie Rose Show*, 4 January 2002, audio clip at http://media5.bloomberg.com:443/cgi-bin/getavfile.cgi?A=4487421

4 Garrett's Tragedy of the Commons at
http://www.members.aol.com/trajcom/private/trajcom.htm

5 'A "commons" is a resource to which everyone within a relevant community has equal access. It is a resource that is not, in an important sense, "controlled". Private or state-owned property is a controlled resource; only as the owner specifies may that property be used. But a commons is not subject to this sort of control. Neutral or equal restrictions may apply to it (an entrance fee to a park, for example) but not the restrictions of an owner. A commons, in this sense, leaves its resources "free".' All from Lessig, 'The Internet under siege', http://www.foreignpolicy.com/issue_novdec_2001/lessig.html.

6 Or to use the language of commons theory: land is a 'rivalrous' resource, where many compete for a limited amount, while information is a 'non-rivalrous resource' – anything that exists can be copied, or reinterpreted, and new information thus endlessly generated. Lessig, *The Future of Ideas*, pp. 20–1.

7 Lessig in *NY Times*, http://barbara.simons.org/lessig.html

8 Lessig also notes the absurdity of Disney suing for extended copyright, when most of their early movies were a 'rip, mix and burn' of European literary classics – the Brothers Grimm, Jules Verne. Even Steamboat Willie, Mickey's original incarnation, was admitted by Disney to be a parody of a Buster Keaton movie. See Free Culture transcript, http://www.oreillynet.com/lpt/a/2641

9 Napster reopened in 2003, as a pay-service. See Katie Dean, 'New Napster off to a solid start', *Wired News*, 3 November 2003, http://www.wired.com/news/digiwood/0,1412,61023,00.html

10 Brad King, 'Napster's assert go for a song', *Wired News*, 28 November 2002, http://www.wired.com/news/digiwood/0,1412,56633,00.html

11 See debates and material on Future of Music Coalition, http://www.futureofmusic.org/. More context at Charles Mann, 'The year the music died', *Wired Magazine*, November 2002, http://www.wired.com/wired/archive/11.02/dirge_pr.html

12 'Life, liberty and the pursuit of copyright', *Atlantic*, http://www.theatlantic.com/unbound/forum/copyright/intro.htm. Also see Lessig's 'Cyberspace and Constitution', http://cyberlaw.stanford.edu/lessig/content/articles/works/AmAcd1.pdf

13 Since this interview, Lessig has been involved in a failed Supreme Court constitutional challenge to the Sonny Bono Copyright Term Extension Act. The history of the case is available here http://eldred.cc/. For his reaction to the case, see Lawrence Lessig, 'Protecting Mickey Mouse at art's expense', *New York Times*, 18 January 2003. For background, see 'Lessig's showdown', *Wired Magazine*, http://www.wired.com/wired/archive/10.10/lessig_pr.html

14 Though Lessig rails at hackers' inability to affect law on this matter. For an impassioned plea, see his presentation, 'Free Culture', at the O'Reilly Open Source Conference, 24 July 2002, http://randomfoo.net/oscon/2002/lessig/

15 See Creative Commons at http://www.creativecommons.org, for its recent background, see report at http://www.austinchronicle.com/issues/dispatch/2003-02-28/screens_feature.html.

16 Kahle has added to the archive by including out-of-copyright stretches of TV, films and videos He already has an extraordinary archive of world TV coverage of 9/11, from the point of impact to a week later. It should also be noted that many of the researched links in this book have been retrieved using Kahle's archive, at http://www.archive.org – material that would otherwise be unavailable, except on expensive commercial databases like Lexis Nexis or Reuters.

17 See the work of James Boyle, 'The second enclosure movement and the construction of the public domain', http://www.law.duke.edu/pd/papers/boyle/pdf, and 'The opposite of property', http://www.law.duke.edu/boylesire/foreword.pdf. For a fascinating analysis of Roman law as a template for a commons-sensitive legal framework, see Carol Rose, 'Romans, roads, and romantic creators: traditions of public property in the information age', *Law and Contemporary Problems*, Winter/Spring 2003, paper available at http://papers.ssrn.com/sol3/delivery.cfm/SSRN_ID293142_code020426530/pdf?abstractid=293142

18 See David Bollier's site on 'Reclaiming the American Commons' (http://ww.bollier.org/reclaim.htm), in particular his essay 'Renaissance of the Commons' (with John Clippinger).

19 For an inside view of the relationship between bottom-up volunteering and top-down control by government, see David Boyle, 'Rules of Engagement', *Guardian*, 2 June 2003, available at http://society.guardian.co.uk.volunteering/story/0,8150,967299,00.html

20 For the ambiguous effect of these spending programmes, see Muzira Mirza, 'Impoverished Aims', *Spiked-Online*, 30 May 2002, http://www.spiked-online.com/Printable/00000006D910.htm

21 See Chapter 7 this volume

22 See David Cox, 'Can pay – but why should we?', *New Statesman*, 11 November 2002.

23 'Dyke to open up BBC archive', 24 August 2003, *BBC News Online*, http://news.bbc.co.uk/1/hi/entertainment/tv_and_radio/3177479.stm

24 See Danny O'Brien, 'Auntie's digital revelation', *Guardian*, 28 August 2003, http://www.guardian.co.uk/online/story/0,3605,1030176,00.html, and 'TV's tipping point: why the digital revolution is only just beginning', text of the speech by Ashley Highfield, Director of BBC New Media & Technology, at the Royal Television Society on 6 October 2003, http://www.paidcontent.org/stories/ashleyrts.shtml

25 Sian Kevill, 'The BBC's plans for digital democracy', *Open Democracy*, 20 February 2003, http://www.opendemocracy.net/debates/article.jsp?id=8&debateId=85&articleId=995

26 Martyn Perks, 'Social software – get real', *Spiked-Online*, 20 March 2003, (http://www.spiked-online.com/Printable/00000006DCF1.htm).

27 'Where now for the digital economy? Think tanks join forces for London conference', IPPR press release, 7 November 2002, http://www.ippr.org.uk/press/index.php?release=163. For an example of this

scepticism, see Martyn Perks, 'What I can can't do', *Spiked-Online*, 20 November 2003, http://www.spiked-online.com/articles/ooooooo6DFD3.htm

28 Much of this critical challenge to government is evident in the activities of centre-left think tanks and advocacy groups in London. For examples of attempts to take the argument of an informational commons to the heart of government policy, see James Wilsdon, *The Politics of Bandwidth: Network Innovation and Regulation in Broadband Britain*, Demos, 2002; Paul Miller, *Open Policy: Threats and Opportunities in a Wired World*. Forum for the Future, 2002 (free download available at http://www.forumforthefuture.org.uk/publications/ default.asp?pubid=24).

James Crabtree, a veteran of e-democracy, takes a sceptical line about involvement of the state in e-politics: 'This should become the ethic of e-democracy: mutual-aid and self-help among citizens, helping to overcome civic problems. It would encourage a market in application development. It would encourage self-reliance, or community-reliance, rather than reliance on the state. Such a system would be about helping people to help themselves. It would create electronic spaces in which the communicative power of the Internet can be used to help citizens help each other overcome life's challenges. Most importantly, by making useful applications, it would help make participatory democracy seem useful too.' Crabtree, 'Civic hacking: a new agenda for e-democracy', *Open Democracy*, 6 March 2003, http://www/opendemocracy.net/debates/article-8-85-1025.jsp

29 The tension between 'system' and 'lifeworld', or state/market and everyday life, comes from the German philosopher Jurgen Habermas. The best confrontation of players' culture and official philosophy I know of is Habermas's tussle with Bataille, 'Between eroticism and general economics', in Chapter 8 of his *The Philosophical Discourse of Modernity*, MIT Press, 1987.

30 See Thomas Goetz, 'Open Source Everywhere', *Wired Magazine*, November 2003, http://www.wired.com/wired/archive/11.11/opensource_pr.html

31 For the 'communication commons', see Nick Dyer-Witherford, Chapter 8, 'Alternatives', in *Cyber-Marx: Cycles and Circuits of Struggle in High Technology Capitalism*, University of Illinois Press, 1999. Book available free online at http://ww.fims.uwo.ca/people/faculty/dyerwitheford/index.htm

32 Karl Marx did get the argument for reduced working time absolutely right, as this quotation from *Capital* shows: 'The real wealth of society and the possibility of a constant expansion of its reproduction process does not depend on the length of surplus labour but rather on its productivity and on the more or less plentiful conditions of production in which it is performed. The realm of freedom really begins only where labour determined by necessity and external expediency ends: it lies by its very nature beyond the sphere of material production proper. Just as the savage must wrestle with nature to satisfy his need, to maintain and reproduce his life, so must civilised man, and he must do so in all forms of society and under all

possible modes of production. This realm of natural necessity expands with his development, because his needs do too; but the productive forces to satisfy these expand at the same time. Freedom, in this sphere, can consist only in this, that socialised man, the associated producers, govern the human metabolism with nature in a rational way, bringing it under their collective control instead of being dominated by it as a blind power; accomplishing it with the least expenditure of energy and in conditions most worthy and appropriate for their human nature. But this always remains a realm of necessity. The true realm of freedom, the development of human powers as an end in itself, begins beyond it, though it can only flourish with this realm of necessity as its basis. The reduction of the working day is the basic prerequisite.' Marx, *Capital*, vol 3, pp. 958–9. Much of this argument has been taken up by Negri and Hardt in *Empire*.

33 For an account of why the leisure society never materialized, see Gary Cross, *Time and Money: the Making of Consumer Culture*, Routledge, 1993.

34 Richard Reeves, *Happy Mondays*, Momentum, 2001.

35 The educational philosopher John White calls this 'heteronomous work' (as opposed to autonomous work – work we would choose to do freely). See his *Education and the End of Work*, Open University, 1999.

36 Paulo Virno, 'Some Notes Towards the Proposal of a "General Intellect",' *Futur Anteriur*, 10, 1992, p.47.

37 See Charlotte Thorne, *Another Country: France Versus the Anglo-Saxon Economists*, Work Foundation, 1999.
http://web.archive.org/web/2003042415442/
http://www.theworkfoundation.com/pdf/Another_Country.pdf

38 'Babies galore for the broody French: Paul Webster in Paris reports that big family benefits and a 35-hour week are reversing the Europe-wide trend', *Observer*, 15 December 2002,
http://www.observer.co.uk/focus/story/0,6903,860208,00.html

39 Morely Safer, 'Working the good life', *CBS Sixty Minutes*, 20 April, 2003,
http://www.cbsnews.com/stories/2003/04/18/60minutes/main550102.shtml

40 See Theodore Zeldin, *An Intimate History of Humanity*, Vintage, 1994, and Zygmunt Bauman, *Liquid Love*, Polity, 2003.

41 Madeleine Bunting, 'Why aren't we taking more time?', *Guardian*, 10 March 2003, http://money.guardian.co.uk/work/workinglives/story/
0,12886,902044,00.html

42 Is it conceivable that no SAS worker, however caressingly they are laboured and sumptuously 're-created', has no ethical view on the end users of their software? Does the play of their cognitive imaginations hit the rubber boundaries of the SAS cocoon, and reverberate no further? 'Somebody said that someone got filled in/for saying that people get killed in/the result of this shipbuilding,' sang Elvis Costello once – and for shipbuilding replace coding. Might the company as health spa stop coders developing their hacker ethic? Max Weber was as prescient as ever: 'The idea of duty in one's calling prowls around in our lives like the ghost of dead religious beliefs.

Where the fulfilment of the calling cannot directly be related to the highest spiritual and cultural values, or when, on the other hand, it need not be felt simply as economic compulsion, the individual generally abandons the attempt to justify it at all. In the field of its highest development, the United States, the pursuit of wealth, stripped of its religious and ethical meaning, tends to become associated with purely mundane passions, which often actually give it the character of sport. ' Max Weber, *The Protestant Ethic*, p. 182.

43 Though see Cory Doctorow's *Down and Out in the Magic Kingdom* (2003) for a clever satire on a post-scarcity future where daily existence is like living in a theme park, and the only currency is 'reputation'.

44 'Deep support is not just an enhanced version of conventional customer service. It is an entirely new way of doing business, a radically different approach to the realization of value in which the very purpose of commerce is redefined around the objective of supporting individuals. Deep support enables psychological self-determination. It produces time for life. It facilitates and enhances the experience of being the origin of one's life. It recognizes, responds to and promotes individuality. It celebrates intricacy. It multiplies choice and enhances flexibility. It encourages voice and is guided by voice. Deep support listens and offers connection. It offers collaborative relationship defined by advocacy. It is founded on trust, reciprocity, authenticity, intimacy, and absolute reliability.' From http://www.thesupporteconomy.com

45 On the notion of social currency, see Douglas Rushkoff, 'Social currency: content as a medium for interaction,' January 2001, http://www.rushkoff.com/cgi-bin/columns/display.cgi/social_currency

46 Simon London, 'The next core competence is getting personal' (interview with C.K. Prahalad), *Financial Times*, 13 December 2002. Examples given of companies that co-create with their customer, reports London, include 'Harley-Davidson, the motorcycle manufacturer that excels at cultivating goodwill among owners, and John Deere, the maker of agricultural machinery that has promoted virtual communities among farmers with similar interests. Then there is Lego, which chose to encourage rather than sue computer enthusiasts who were messing with the operating system of its programmable Mindstorm products, and International Business Machines, which was quick to embrace Linux, a heavyweight computer operating system developed by the worldwide community of software enthusiasts. The common thread is that these companies are trying to engage with customers, open their doors and their processes and tap into that quivering mass of ad-hoc communities known as the Internet.' An extended paper on Prahalad's ideas is 'The co-creation connection', C.K. Prahalad and Venkatram Ramaswamy, *Strategy + Business*, issue 27, http://www.strategy-business.com/media/pdf/02206.pdf

47 Rifkin, *Age of Access*; Klein, *No Logo*; Rushkoff, *Coercion*.

48 Rifkin himself advocates a 'play ethos' at the end of the *Age of Access*. But it is interesting to compare his work with that of another American writer on play who comes from the libertarian tradition, Virginia Postrel ('Fields of Play' in *The Future and its Enemies*, Free Press, 1998). For Postrel, the social order that play values encourage is one that she calls 'dynamist' – a bottom-up, self-organizing, choice-driven world, in which experiment and innovation is paramount, and an openness to the future is the most necessary mindset. Yet she also identifies what she calls 'enemies of the future', and even gives them a generic name. Against the dynamists like her are 'stasists' – top-down bureaucrats, know-better politicians and control-obsessed corporate heads, for whom the creative energies of the ludic masses are nothing but trouble and interference. Stasists believe in the work ethic, and in the vision of a clockwork universe which undergirds its morality. For them, 'progress is a machine. Turn the crank, and innovation pops out. The future is predictable, controllable, and inevitable. There is one best way, and that way is perfectly obvious. There is no need for experimentation, novelty, or surprise – all of which encourage dangerous impulses. In this linear model, play represents disruption, a threat to the social order.'

For Postrel, the nature of play justifies an anti-statist (as well as an anti-stasist) politics. There is nothing that public institutions can do, which private actors – freely experimenting and innovating, in their 'fields of play' – couldn't do better. Thus for Postrel – deeply inspired by the new biology, by Hayek's libertarianism, and by the digital capitalism of the late nineties – a 'play ethic' justifies a deregulated, highly marketized society, in which social diversity isn't thwarted by considerations of social equality. No wonder *The Future and Its Enemies* became something of a cult amongst the rapacious dot-com boomers of California.

On the other side of the political spectrum – and richly abused by Postrel in her book – Rifkin also invokes play as the basis of an entirely new social order. Except this time, his 'play ethos' justifies an extensive reregulation of society. This is an 'age of access', where electronic networks of all kinds bring services and information to consumers and citizens. Rifkin's fear is that some won't get access to necessary resources, because of the predominant commercialism of these networks.

Rifkin gives us a choice. Either allow the corporations to dominate this new infrastructure and make our every use of it a 'paid-for experience'. Or, reclaim and regulate the same networks, and put them at the service of the values of play – which, in Rifkin's understanding, are described as 'collective, empathetic, community-based and deeply voluntary'. Rather than play being a disruptive force that helps us to break through the routines and conventions of life (as Postrel desires), for Rifkin play is the way we build our most meaningful experiences with each other – a way of constructing a natural 'common culture' that precedes the marketplace. And thus his political requests are for regulatory limits to be placed on capital and markets. Property rights should be recast as the right to share in common resources, as well as the right to possess them exclusively (as in Lessig's notion): there should be a public stake established within privatized networks. (Much of this is developed by Zuboff in her support economy – with businesses joining federations that subsume competitiveness for customer responsiveness.) Education should be aimed at the civic qualities of the child, rather than simply their market readiness, expanding their capacity for sociable interaction and co-creation, as well as individual self-assertion. Thus, says Rifkin, will 'deep mature play' be ensured.

I find myself divided between these two American visions of a play politics. Or rather, I somehow want them both to pertain. Play itself is a zone of ambiguity and complexity, a driving force for both our individualist and our collective urges, a capaciously infinite game of life, in which a multitude of finite games can exist. Few writers seem to be aware of the rhetorical construction of their theories of play. Postrel errs too much on play as imagination, chance and agonism, downgrading the ways in which play also provides zones of nurturance and stability in our lives (the need to treasure the playful child, the collective celebrations of sport and nation). Rifkin overly emphasizes play as authenticity, developmental health and cultural carnival – strangely denying those material excesses, those sometimes dangerous explorations of human sensuality and creativity, which play also drives.

Postrel exults in the 'creative destructions' of the American system, defending its ultra-individualism and competitive energies against all manner of heavy-handed planners and banners. For her, the declaration's injunction to seek 'life, liberty and the pursuit of happiness' is the play ethic incarnate – a delightfully impure and energetic basis for national life. Yet Rifkin, faced with such a culture, can only adopt a defensive position: for him, the purity of play – its unforced reciprocity between humans – is something to be defended against the alienating matrix of markets and technologies, forcing him to sound like a most regretful Luddite. The seemingly playful dynamist faces the seeming playful stasist, and each paralyses and mutually defines the other.

49 'Altered states of consciousness are real, and as our media technologies get better at drawing us in and out of them, artists and other non-coercive proponents of the human spirit (or whatever you want to call it) need to become familiar with these states . . . By recognizing that the material that we are now focused on is not technology but human experience itself, then we take a step closer to that strange plateau where our inner lives unfold into an almost collective surface of shared sensation and reframed perception – a surface on which we may feel exposed and vulnerable, but beginning to awake.' Erik Davis, 'Experience design', available at his website, http://www.techgnosis.com/experience.html. For more on Erik Davis, see Chapter 10, this volume.

50 But remember the Di Lampudesa strategy. As the wise old Left historian Immanuel Wallerstein recently noted. 'One has to ask: what are the likely

reactions of different political forces in such a situation? The easiest to predict is the reaction of the upper strata of the world-system. They are of course a complex mix and do not constitute an organized caucus. But they probably can be divided into two main groups. The majority will share in the general confusion and will resort to their traditional short-run politics, perhaps with a higher dose of repressiveness insofar as the politics of concessions will not be seen as achieving the short-run calm it is supposed to produce . . . And then there is the small minority among the upper strata who are sufficiently insightful and intelligent to perceive the fact that the present system is collapsing and who wish to ensure that any new system be one which preserves their privileged position. The only strategy for such a group is *the Lampedusa strategy – to change everything in order that nothing change* [my emphasis]. This group will have firm resolve and a great deal of resources at their command. They can hire intelligence and skill, more or less as they wish. They will do so. They may have already been doing so.' Wallerstein, 'A Left Politics for the Twenty-first Century? Or, Theory and Praxis Once Again', 1999,
http:www?http://fbc.binghamton.edu/iwleftpol.htm

51 See Bill Jordan, *Social Work and the Third Way: Tough Love as Social Policy*, Sage, 2002, and the discussion in Chapter 5.

52 Tom Paine, *Agrarian Justice*. Quoted in John Keane, *Tom Paine: A Political Life*, Bloomsbury, 1996.

53 Keane writes: 'Paine favoured the preservation of a private-property, market-driven economy, but he argued that its self-destructive dynamism – its tendency to generate wealth by widening the income gap between classes – could be tamed by institutionalising the basic principle of each person's entitlement to full citizen's rights . . . That universal guarantee of a right to a basic citizens' income would then require – contrary to the spirit of the new 1795 constitution – a universal franchise.' Keane, *Tom Paine*, p.427.

54 Ulrich Beck, *The Brave New World of Work*, Polity, pp. 125–6.

55 'It is thus a self-grounding act of political society, and not a hand-out to the poor: it allows society to give itself a new material foundation . . . to gain *a new political creativity* [my emphasis],' Beck, *ibid.*, p. 144. In *Empire*, Negri and Hardt note that their immaterial labourers – those I've called the 'soulitariat' – 'produce in all their generality all day long . . . labour power has become increasingly collective and social . . . [it cannot] be individualized and measured'. And so, because 'the entire multitude produces' – that huge miasma of emotional and intellectual activities that makes up our lives, enabled by information technology, which we allow business to use and exploit – then all should receive an equal benefit of that productivity, 'an equal compensation such that a social wage is really a guaranteed income. Once citizenship is extended to all, we could call this guaranteed income a citizenship income, due each as a member of society' (p. 403). When Hardt and Negri argue for the 'irrepressible lightness and joy of being communist', they are followers of Friedrich von Schiller down to the last letter: the

entirety of *Empire* is an 'ode to Joy' – the joy, also, of true play. For them, reality does indeed 'lose its seriousness . . . when necessity becomes light'. Their exaltation of the 'productive excess' (p. 357) of the information age leads, unsurprisingly, to a social policy which recognizes the only collective way to harness that excess – the social wage.

56 Andre Gorz, *Reclaiming Work: Beyond the Wage-based Society*, Polity, 1999.

57 Gorz lays out his vision: 'The ultimate goal to which the unconditional grant of a basic income points is that of a society where the necessity of work is no longer experienced as such, because each person, from childhood onwards, will be involved in, and feel the attraction of, a general proliferation of artistic, sporting, techno-scientific, artisanal, political, philosophical, ecosophic, relational and co-operative activities all around him or her; a society in which means of production for self-providing are accessible to everyone at any time of day, just as databanks and teleworking resources already are; in which exchanges are principally exchanges of knowledge, not of commodities, and do not therefore need to be mediated by money . . . Once it has been eliminated as a separate, autonomised power, productive work will consist mainly in the capacity to take advantage of accumulated knowledge, to enrich and exchange it, without the valorization [making valuable] of that knowledge imposing itself on individuals as an alien demand, without it dictating to them the nature, intensity, duration and hours of their work.' Gorz, *Reclaiming Work*, p.92.

58 There is another possible fourth justification for the social wage from Gorz. How might we be productive in a world in which we have been liberated to choose between our professional and our voluntary labours? Gorz is not necessarily opposed to the 'flexibility' and 'discontinuity' of employment demanded by modern business of its workers – yet he is opposed to that condition being 'passively suffered'. How can these be 'transformed into opportunities to choose and self-manage discontinuity and flexibility'? Gorz cites the Danish and Dutch systems, with their endless varieties of working-time schemes, as harbingers of the future. Yet as the productive powers of techno-science increase, the question becomes more urgent: when do we recognize the extent to which we have been 'liberated from labour', and start to organize our societies accordingly?

59 Gorz's desire to 'reclaim work' is heartfelt. For him, a post-market work is something that can be reconciled with 'a culture of daily life, an art of living, which it would both extend and nourish, instead of being cut off from them'. It must be 'appropriated' differently, from childhood onwards – no longer 'suffered as a penance, but lived as an activity merged in the flow of life, a path to the full development of senses, towards power over oneself and the external world, and as a bond with others'. Children would understand work as 'the linking of the acquisition of knowledge with a pride in being able to do things . . . "Work" might then become quite naturally one of the dimensions of life, accompanied by and alternating with a range of other activities in which "productivity" is not a consideration, though those

activities would contribute indirectly to the productivity of labour, by way of the creative, imaginative and expressive capacities they developed.'
Reclaiming Work, pp. 98–99.

Yet if this is a new 'ethic' for work – work as one of the 'arts of living' – Gorz still seems unable, or unwilling, to see the wider circle within which work exists. At one point he sees this vision as a 'culture-based' rather than 'work-based' society. Yet his attack on cyber culture in the epilogue – as a virtualization of human labour, a dethroning of the power of community based in physical co-presence – is the point at which Gorz remains tied to the 'metaphysic of labour' (pp. 113–15). A play ethic makes the crucial shift beyond distrusting the symbolic and the semiotic, the babel of voices and the generation of imagination: cyber culture only gives the natural tendencies of the 'symbolic species' new impetus. See *The Symbolic Species*. Terence Deacon, Norton 1998.

60 Michael Lind, 'The case for a living wage', *New Leader*, 1 October 2001. Available at http://www.newamerica.net/index.cfm?pg=article&pubID=564

61 'A case can be made, then, that the replacement of labour by machinery as a result of a higher minimum wage (or anything else that increases labour costs) is a positive step, not an evil to be avoided . . . What difference does it make for the economy as a whole whether grocery store checkout stations are automated or not? The economic powers of the 21st century will be the "robot powers". Despite all the chatter about globalization, the corporations that dominate world commerce in such fields as automobiles and aerospace remain those that can use their superiority in the vast domestic markets of populous nations like the U.S., Japan and Germany as springboards for expansion into foreign markets. Obviously the home market for national robot industries will be much greater in countries where employers in many traditionally labour-intensive sectors are compelled to invest in ever more sophisticated robots by high wages and tight labor markets . . . Lind, *ibid*.

62 *Ibid*.

63 The best available symposium on basic income and social wage schemes is the *Boston Review*'s special edition on 'Delivering a basic income', October/November 2000. With a lead essay from Philippe Van Parijs, and replies from Emma Rothschild, Claus Offe, William Galston and others, http://bostonreview.mit.edu/ndf.html#Income

64 Theodore Roszak, 'What a piece of work is man: humanism, religion, and the new cosmology', *Scientific and Medical Network*, http://www.datadiwan.de/SciMedNet/library/articlesN71+/ N71humanism_Roszak.htm

65 Katherine Ainger, 'Trade wars: the battle in Seattle', *Red Pepper*, November 1999, http://www.redpepper.org.uk/intarch/xwto.html

66 There is much 'creativity' in the field of e-democracy. See Joi Ito's 'Emergent democracy', http://joi.ito.com/static/emergentdemocracy.html, which argues that the fusion of weblogs, mobile phones and activism will create a new public sphere. A similar position is taken by Howard Rheingold's book *Smart*

Mobs: the Next Social Revolution (Perseus, 2002), with its supporting weblog at http://www.smartmobs.com. Stanford University Law Professor James Moore's essay 'The second superpower raises its beautiful head' ups the ante on digital activism even further, http://cyber.law.harvard.edu/people/jmoore/secondsupperpower.html

67 Zygmunt Bauman, 'Chasing the elusive society', in *Society Under Siege*, 2002, pp. 25–51.

68 See Manuel Castells, *The Power of Identity*, Blackwell, 1996.

69 See Jon Savage, *England's Dreaming*, Faber and Faber, 1992.

70 See Zygmunt Bauman, *Work, Consumerism and the New Poor*, 2001.

71 Citing Johan Huizinga's *Homo Ludens* approvingly, Hayek noted that game play was a 'clear instance of a process wherein obedience to common rules by elements pursuing different and even conflicting purposes results in overall order', even in some games an 'overall increase of productivity'. F.W. Hayek, 'Play, the school of rules', in *The Fatal Conceit: the Errors of Socialism*, Routledge, 1989.

72 Stuart Hall (ed.), *New Times*, Lawrence and Wishart, 1985.

73 See Matthew Collin and John Godfrey, *Altered State: the Story of Ecstasy Culture and Acid House*, Serpent's Tail, 1997; and George McKay, *DIY Culture: Party and Protest in Nineties' Britain*, Verso, 1998.

74 See 'Major goes back to the old values', *Guardian*, 9 October 1993, http://politics.guardian.co.uk/politicspast/story/0,9061,801926,00.html

75 Manuel Castells, *The Network Society*, Blackwell, 1996.

76 Tom Bentley, 'Letting go: complexity and the left', *Renewal*, Winter 2002. When Zuboff in *The Support Economy*, Viking, 2002, talks of 'infrastructure convergence', where federations of companies 'build digital platforms to eliminate the replication of administrative activities across their enterprises', she is anticipating a level of economic cohesion which is light years from the neo-liberal savagery of an open marketplace. Faced by the 'psychological self-determination' of twenty-first-century man and woman, Zuboff says we need to 'fundamentally alter the orientation, purpose, and economics of commerce . . . the only thing that stands in the way of infrastructure convergence today is the old enterprise logic of managerial capitalism and the ways in which it prescribes organizational boundaries and antiquated conceptions of ownership' (see http://www.thesupporteconomy.com). Libertarian critics in the US think they recognize this kind of collectivism when they see it. 'Call it Marxism for the Information Age: What's yours is mine, and if you're not willing to share it, the State will expropriate it for communal use and toss you a few pennies for your investment. Such a regulatory ethos is wholly corrupt and completely at odds with foundations of a free and just capitalist system. Sadly, however, morality-based arguments don't get very far in Washington these days. We can only hope that policymakers will at least take into account the economic downside of infrastructure sharing.' Adam Thierer and Clyde Wayne Crews Jr, 'EchoStar-DirecTV merger critics propose infrastructure socialism in outer space',

Techknowledge (at the Cato Institute), issue 41, 8 October 2002, http://www.cato.org/tech/tk/021008-tk.html

77 See my presentation to the Strategy Unit at the Cabinet Office, 'Government and play', June 2002, available at http://www.theplayethic.com

78 Warren Hoge, 'Britain to stop arresting most private users of marijuana', *New York Times*, 11 July 2002.

79 James Harding, 'Globalisation's children strike back', *Financial Times*, 11 September 2001.

80 'Once the dust settles, what might the anti-capitalists bring to the politics of a play ethic? They might ask for fair trade, not free trade. For the use of information networks to co-ordinate global democracy, not just to facilitate the movements of global capital. For news media to reflect a much wider range of societal viewpoints. For marketing to talk about the efficiency, design and reusability of products – rather than emphasizing the way they'll be the answer to our dreams. For political authority always to be justified, its legitimacy tested against the will of autonomous citizens rather than assumed. What's the alternative? That an aggressive, business-driven order provokes further resistance – which could be a destructive mixture of cyber-terrorism and social intolerance, the computer virus and the fundamentalist commune. A ghastly prospect. But not improbable . . . In the face of anti-capitalism, we have to devise a credible post-capitalism, a new balance between markets and society which can absorb all (or at least most) of the discontents that we all feel – from manager to tree-hugger, from worried mother to stressed worker. As a new "spirit of capitalism" (to borrow from Max Weber), directing the new economy and its powers in the direction of human liberation, the play ethic has at least an even chance of striking that balance.' Pat Kane, 'Play for today', *Observer*, 22 October 2000, http://www.observer.co.uk/life/story/0,6903,386013,00.html

81 James Harding, 'The anti-globalisation movement', *Financial Times*, 10 October 2001. See also Mike Bygrave's *Observer* articles and responses, 21 July 2002, http://www.observer.co.uk/worldview/story/0,11581,759233,00.html

82 See Wendell Berry, 'A citizen's response to the national security strategy of the United States', available at http://www.commondreams.org/views03/0209-11htm; Nick Cohen, 'Darkening of a Nation', *Observer*, 26 October, 2003, http://observer.guardian.co.uk/libertywatch/story/0,1373,1071505,00.html

83 See 'Ten things to do in conceptual emergency', available from the International Futures Forum, http://www.internationalfuturesforum.com

84 'The inequality and powerlessness already caused by globalisation cannot be easily addressed within a decade. But the prize is to create movements and systems whose momentum is unstoppable even after their original leaders have retired from the scene. The possibility of shaping such change comes at the price of giving up the attempt to control it.' Bentley, *Renewal, ibid.*

85 See Naomi Klein, *No Logo*, Flamingo, 2000.

86 Naomi Klein, 'Empowering people', *Superhumanism* conference, 29 May 2001,

http://www.dandad.org/content/super/speakers/speaker naomi.html; and Klein,
'The do mentality', *Financial Times*, 29 May 2001.

87 Naomi Klein, *Fences and Windows*, Flamingo, 2002.

88 'Why is it that, even when there is next to no other constituency for
    revolutionary politics in a capitalist society, the one group most likely to be
    sympathetic to its project consists of artists, musicians, writers, and others
    involved in some form of non-alienated production? Surely there must be a
    link between the actual experience of first imagining things and then bringing
    them into being, individually or collectively, and the ability to envision social
    alternatives – particularly, the possibility of a society itself premised on less
    alienated forms of creativity?' Graeber, 'The new anarchists', *New Left Review*,
    13, January–February 2002, http://www.newleftreview.net/NLR24704.shtml

89 Says Antonio Negri, 'Representative democracy has been neutralized or, if
    you like, expropriated by television and mass communications . . . we have to
    move from "representative democracy" to "expressive democracy"' – by
    which Negri means the 'flexible multitudes, trading on their intellect rather
    than their capital . . . a politics based on direct participation rather than
    representation through parties, trade unions or other groups'. Mark Leonard,
    'The Left should love globalisation' (interview with Negri), *New Statesman*,
    28 May 2001.

90 Paul Kingsnorth, *One No, Many Yesses: A Journey to the Heart of the Global
    Resistance Movement*, Free Press, 2003.

91 'Ultimately, it aspires to be much more than that, because ultimately it
    aspires to reinvent daily life as a whole. But unlike many other forms of
    radicalism, it has first organized itself in the political sphere – mainly
    because this was a territory that the powers that be (who have shifted all
    their heavy artillery into the economic) have largely abandoned.' Graeber,
    ibid.

92 John Lloyd, *The Protest Ethic: How the anti-globalisation movement
    challenges social democracy*. Demos, 2001,
    http://www.demos.co.uk/theprotestethic_pdf_media_public.aspx

93 Castells, *The Power of Identity*, pp. 361–2.

94 Says the media thinker Douglas Rushkoff: 'A growing willingness to engage
    with the underlying code of the democratic process could eventually manifest
    in a widespread call for revisions to our legal, economic, and political
    structures on a scale unprecedented except in the cases of full-fledged
    revolution. Transparency in media makes information available to those who
    never had access to it before. Access to media technology also empowers
    those same people to discuss how they might want to change the status
    quo. Finally, networking technologies allow for online collaboration in the
    implementation of new models, and the very real-world organization of social
    activism and relief efforts. The good news, for those of you within the power
    structure today, is that we are not about to enter a phase of revolution, but
    one of renaissance. We are heading not toward a toppling of the democratic,
    parliamentary, or legislative processes, but toward their reinvention in a new,

participatory context. In a sense, the people are becoming a new breed of wonk, capable of engaging with government and power structures in an entirely new fashion. The current regime, in the broadest sense, will have ended up being the true and lasting one – if it can get its head and policies around these renaissance modalities of increased dimensionality, emergence, scalability, and participation ... Our marketing experts tell us that they are failing in their efforts to advertise to Internet users and "cultural progressives" because this new and resistant psychographic simply wants to engage, authentically, in social experiences. This should sound like good news to anyone who, authentically, wants to extend our collective autonomy.' Rushkoff's advice to politicians? 'Don't beat them; let them join you. This population is made up not of customers to whom you must sell or even constituents to whom you must pander, but partners on whom you can rely and with whom you can act. Treat them as such, and you might be surprised by how much you get done, together.' Douglas Rushkoff, *Open Source Democracy*, Demos, 2003,
http://www.demos.co.uk/opensourcedemocracy_pdf_media_public.aspx

TEN / THE INFINITE GAME

1 'Spirit (Hebrew: ruach; Greek; pneuma; Latin: spiritus) is very different from soul in that it is not normally embodied. Rather it is an active, free-ranging supernatural power, often winged and almost always exceedingly busy, delivering messages, causing trouble, helping, chivvying and tormenting. Notice here a big difference between a god and a spirit: whereas a god typically sits enthroned, over the cosmos on a mountaintop or in a temple where he receives worship and hands out the law, a spirit is seldom portrayed seated, and never legislates.' Cupitt, *After God: the Future of Religion*, Weidenfield and Nicolson, 1997, pp. 4–5. Also note Fritjof Capra, *The Hidden Connections*, Penguin 2002, Chapter 5.

2 Historian Niall Ferguson notes the decline of work-ethic values in Europe, and makes some contentious points about the decline of Protestantism in particular countries, compared to the continued religiosity of American society (where productivity rates prove that people are willing to work harder). 'How Weber's "Protestant ethic" explains U.S. edge over Europe', *New York Times*, 9 June 2003,
http://rasa.iht.com/cgi-bin/generic.cgi?template=articleprint.tmplh&ArticleId=98903

3 See Wade Clark Roof, *Spiritual Marketplace: Baby Boomers and the Remaking of American Religion*, Princeton 2001; and Mick Brown, *The Spiritual Tourist*, Bloomsbury, 1998.

4 The integral philosopher Ken Wilber maps out the full crisis of the internal and external realms of modern spirituality in books like *Integral Psychology* (2002) and *A Theory of Everything* (2002), both on Shambhala.

5 This is John Caputo's vision of the play of the cosmos, in us and through us,

the 'friendly flux and matrix' from which we emerge and to which we return, and in the midst of which we do our best to dance and perform our lives. Caputo, *On Religion*, Routledge, 2001, p.139.

6 Pat Kane, 'There's method in the magic', from *The Politics of Risk Society*, Jane Franklin (ed.), Polity, 1997.

7 Pat Kane, 'New Ageism: science or a tree-hug too far?', *Independent*, 15 June 2000.

8 'Full text of notes found after hijackings', *New York Times*, 29 September 2001, http://www.nytimes.com/2001/09/29/national/ 29SFULL-TEXT.html?ex=1069563600&en=e54bc2366adba6a7&ei=5070. The respected Middle-East journalist Robert Fisk has cast scepticism on this letter, or at least its translation. 'What Muslim would write: "The time of fun and waste is gone"?', *Independent*, 29 September 2001

9 See Tariq Ali, *The Clash of Fundamentalisms: Crusades, Jihads and Modernity*, Verso, 2003.

10 See Greil Marcus, *Double Trouble: Bill Clinton and Elvis Presley in a Land of No Alternatives*, Henry Holt, 2000; and Andrew Ross, *No Collar: the Humane Workplace and its Hidden Costs*, Basic Books, 2002.

11 See Charles Paul Freund, 'In praise of vulgarity: how commercial culture liberates Islam – and the West', *Reason*, March 2002, http://reason.com/0203/fe.cf.in.shtml

12 Ellis's comments remain remarkably astute: 'The flip side of the market created by the Age of Fear is escapism. The transition from a television culture to a more escapist Internet and interactive-gaming culture, which is already under way in the younger demographic, will accelerate. Fear requires respite, something that relieves anxiety. As New Yorkers (especially) and Americans (generally) learned from September 11, the television can drive you mad. You have to get out of your own head, your own thoughts, and connect. New Yorkers did (and still do) this by going out to restaurants, but young people can't afford to go out every night. Yet their need to connect is made even greater by the Fear. And so games and Internet connections will prosper and thrive as never before. And the games that sell best will be the kind that resonate within the new zeitgeist.' John Ellis, 'Digital matters', *Fast Company*, December 2001, http://www.fastcompany.com/magazine/53/jellis.html

13 Anthony Dworkin, 'Daniel Bell', *Prospect*, October 2000.

14 Jane Lampman, 'New scrutiny of role of religion in Bush's policies', *CS Monitor*, 17 March 2003, http://www.csmonitor.com/2003/0317/p01s01-uspo.html

15 Andrew Gumbel, 'Hollywood revives McCarthyist climate by silencing and sacking war critics', *Independent*, 21 April 2003, http://www.commondreams.org/headlines03/0421-02.htm

16 Slavoj Zizek ponders whether a generation of young Arab Muslims 'dreaming of becoming suicide bombers' would force the US government to 'impose a permanent state of emergency at home' – and allows himself 'a slightly

paranoid reflection ... What if the people around Bush know this? What if this "collateral damage" is the true aim of the entire operation? What if the real target of the 'war on terror' is the disciplining of the emancipatory excesses in American society itself?' Zizek then goes on to discuss the many debates in the US media suggesting the legitimate torture of al-Qaida suspects. *London Review of Books*, 3 April 2003.

17 A.O. Scott, 'Fantasy feeds youthful need to triumph over evil', *The Age* (Australia), 15 July 2002, http://www.theage.com.au/articles/2002/07/14/1026185138465.html

18 See David Wilkinson, *The Power of the Force: the Spirituality of Star Wars*, Lion, 2000.

19 Ziauddin Sardar, 'Playing the game', *New Statesman*, 26 April 1999. For more on the spirituality of *The Matrix*, see Erik Davis, 'The *Matrix* way of knowledge', *Salon*, 12 May 2003, at http://www.techgnosis.com/matrixre.html, and Gregory Benford, 'Theological science fiction: why the *Matrix* matters', *Reason*, 23 May 2003, at http://www.reason.com/hod/gb052303.shtml

20 On *Black and White*, see James Wagner Au, 'Playing God', 10 April 2001, http://dir.salon.com/tech/review/2001/04/10/black_and_white/index.html. For a regular update of the impact of Japanese pop culture on the West, see the online fanzine, *Giant Robot,* http://www.giantrobot.com

21 Review of Victoria Nelson's *The Secret Life of Puppets* (Harvard), 'The ghosts in our machines', Pat Kane, *Independent*, 16 March 2002.

22 Brendan Koerner, 'Intel's tiny hope for the future', *Wired*, December 2003.

23 'New mobile message craze spreads', *BBC Online News*, 4 November 2003, http://news.bbc.co.uk/2/hi/technology/3237755.stm. For information on flash mobs and other startling uses of mobile technology, see Howard Rheingold's site, http://www.smartmobs.com.

24 See Ray Kurzweil, *The Age of Spiritual Machines*, Penguin, 2000.

25 Margaret Wertheim, *The Pearly Gates of Cyberspace: a History of Space from Dante to the Internet*, Virago, 1999, p. 304.

26 Erik Davis, *Techgnosis: Myth, Magic and Mysticism in the Age of Information*, Fourth Estate, 1998, pp. 93–101.

27 Francis Cook, *Hua-yen Buddhism*, Pen State Press 1977, p. 3.

28 See also David Loy, 'Indra's postmodern Net', *Philosophy East and West*, vol 43, no 3, July 1993, pp. 481–510, http://ccbs.ntu.edu.tw/FULLTEXT/JR-PHIL/ew25326.htm

29 'All the insights, noble thoughts and works of art that the human race has produced in its creative eras, all that subsequent periods of scholarly study have reduced to concepts and converted into intellectual property – on all this immense body of intellectual values the Glass Bead Game player plays like an organist on an organ. And this organ has attained an almost unimaginable perfection; its manuals and pedals range over the entire intellectual cosmos; its stops are almost beyond number. Theoretically this instrument is capable of reproducing in the Game the entire intellectual

content of the Universe.' Hermann Hesse, *The Glass Bead Game*, Vintage, 2000, pp. 6–7.

30 From Davis, *ibid.*, p. 332.

31 *Ibid.*, pp. 332–3

32 For example, see John Arquilla and David Ronfeldt's 'Fighting the network war', *Wired*, December 2001, http://www.wired.com/wired/archive/9.12/netwar.html.

33 Davis, *Techgnosis*, *ibid.*, p. 334.

34 John D. Caputo, *On Religion*, Routledge, 2001, p. 131.

35 D. Cupitt, *After God: the Future of Religion*, Phoenix, 1998, p. 66.

36 Cupitt, *ibid.*

37 'Like the sun, we must live and die at the same time . . . giving out an enriching warmth.' Cupitt, *ibid.*

38 *Ibid.*, p. 104.

39 See S. Cowdell, *Atheist Priest? Don Cupitt and Christianity*, SCM Press, 1988.

40 'It is still not easy to take in the really true truth [*sic*] about the human condition, which is that we are in an outsideless language-evoked flux of becoming, a flux which is always at once a coming-to-be and a passing-away. The unbearable lightness of being – our post-Buddhism of the sign, our fictionalism . . . Our philosophical and religious traditions used to claim that it was possible for us to step out of all language games and role-playing and become pure, naked, recollected selves. But [. . .] life is theatre. In the late Baroque and Rococo, the Catholic religion visibly admits its own theatricality, and makes the crucial acknowledgement that the line separating the real from the fictional is itself a fiction.' Don Cupitt, *The Time Being*, SCM, 1992, pp. 158–60.

41 'And we should get used to a new distinction, between the various stereotyped and unsatisfactory roles that culture gives us to play, and our own efforts to reinterpret them, subvert them, laugh at them and, in the long run, remake them . . . Can you imagine a religion that is consistent not in a solemnization of the status quo, but in a mood of laughter added to life?' *ibid.*, p. 161.

42 Although Cupitt tries to maintain his distance from the New Age, the 'Creation Spirituality' of the Franciscan monk Matthew Fox almost entirely passes over into that realm. Fox's dissolution of Christianity into the 'sea of faith', as Cupitt once put it, is militantly and expansively playful: 'To recover the wisdom that is lurking in religious traditions we have to let go of more recent religious traditions – specifically, an exclusively fall/redemption model of spirituality . . . It is a dualistic model [separating the sacred and profane] and a patriarchal one; it begins its theology with sin and original sin, and it generally ends with redemption. Fall/redemption spirituality does not teach believers about the New Creation or creativity, about justice-making and social transformation, or about Eros, play, pleasure and the God of delight.' Matthew Fox, *Original Blessing*, Bear and Co. 1983, p. 9. Those who are stained by the image of original sin, says Fox elsewhere, have 'no ego, no

self-respect, no tolerance for diversity, no love of creation, no sense of humour, [and] no sense of sexual identity or joy.' Fox, *The Coming of the Cosmic Christ*, Harper and Row, 1988, p. 182.

43 Cupitt, *The Last Philosophy*, SCM, 1995, p. 108.

44 Jean Baudrillard,'The spirit of terrorism'. *Le Monde*, 2 November 2001, available in English at http://amsterdam.nettime.org/Lists-Archives/nettime-1-0111/msg00083.html

45 Asad Latif, 'Muslims are returning to sources of Islam to clarify the meaning of their actions', *Straits Times*, 12 September 2002, http://straitstimes.asia1.com.sg/sept11/story/0,1870,142639,00.html

46 'Jihad may grow out of and reflect (among other things) a pathological metastasis of valid grievances about the effects of an arrogant secularist materialism that is the unfortunate concomitant of the spread of consumerism across the world. It may reflect a desperate and ultimately destructive concern for the integrity of indigenous cultural traditions that are ill-equipped to defend themselves against aggressive markets in a free-trade world. It may reflect a struggle for justice in which Western markets appear as obstacles rather than facilitators of cultural identity.' Benjamin Barber, 'Beyond jihad and McWorld', *The Nation*, 21 January 2002, http://www.thenation.com/doc.mhtml%3Fi=20020121&s=barber

47 *Cyberia: Life in the Trenches of Cyberspace*, Clinamen, 2002; *Playing the Future: What We Can Learn from Digital Kids*, Riverhead, 1999; *Media Virus! Hidden Agendas in Popular Culture*, Ballantine, 1996.

48 Pat Kane, 'The double agent who fled Cyberia just in time', *Independent*, 19 April 2000, http://enjoyment.independent.co.uk/books/reviews/story.jsp?story=46224

49 Douglas Rushkoff, 'Remember the Sabbath: an argument for a day off', December 1999, at http://www.rushkoff.com/cgi-bin/columns/display.cgi/remember_the_sabbath

50 Interview with Douglas Ruskhoff at Clal: the Jewish Public Forum, http://www.rushkoff.com/interviews/clal.html. See also Rushkoff's *Nothing Sacred: the Truth About Judaism*, Basic Books, 2003.

51 Rushkoff, Clal: Jewish Public Forum, *ibid.*

52 'An ethical sensibility is internalized only by people who have the luxury and ability to move out of survival mode. Many Jews are unnecessarily caught in survival mode: even though they are financially fine, and anti-Semitism is at an all-time low, they are worried about their survival because they think the Cossacks or the Nazis are going to come around the corner. They are worried about the survival of Jews as an officially listed "people." When they're stuck in survival mode people don't have fun, and can't touch the beauty of existence. They experience only existential despair.' Ruskhoff, Clal, *ibid.*

53 *Ibid.*

54 See Richard Reeves, 'Life's good. Why do we feel bad?', *Observer*, 19 May 2002; 'Money and happiness' (with Richard Layard), *The Talk Show*, BBC4, transcript at http://www.bbc.co.uk/bbcfour/talkshow/features/transcripts/

money_happiness.pdf; and David Wessel, 'Sad little rich country', *Washington Monthly*, November 2003, http://www.washingtonmonthly.com/features/2003/0311.wessel.html

55 See Chapter 5, this volume.

56 Stuart Kauffman, Chapter 7, 'The promised land', in *At Home in the Universe*, Penguin, Oxford, 1996.

57 See Zardar's books for Icon's *Introducing . . .* series, on Chaos, Mathematics, Islam and Cultural Studies.

58 See Rushkoff's website, Open Source Judaism, http://www.opensourcejudaism.com/articles.html

59 Rushkoff, Clal, *ibid*.

60 Ziauddin Sardar, 'Rethinking Islam', http://www.islamfortoday.com/sardar01.htm

61 Ziauddin Sardar, 'The agony of a 21st century Muslim', *New Statesman*, 17 February 2003. Though one wonders whether Sardar would agree with Rushkoff's formulation, 'everything is sacred, but nothing is sacrosanct'. http://www.rushkoff.com/2003_05_01_archive.php

62 Sardar, 'Rethinking Islam', *ibid*.

63 Sardar, 'The agony of a 21st century Muslim', *ibid*.

64 Sardar, 'The agony of a 21st century Muslim', *ibid*.

65 Sardar, *Understanding Islam*, *ibid*.

66 Sardar, 'The true meaning of Islam's holy book', *Express on Sunday*, 30 September 2001. He continues: 'That's the message that terrorists like Osama Bin Laden are trying to suppress.'

67 Sardar, *Postmodernism and the Other: the New Imperialism of Western Culture*, Zed, 1998, pp. 41–2.

68 'One can reject the authoritarianism of the [Islamic] ban on imagery without necessarily rejecting its intentionality. We could interpret it in a sufistic manner: a voluntary self-restraint vis-a-vis imagery and representation (a sublimation of the image) can result in a flow of power to the autonomous ("divinized") imagination . . . The purpose of such an exercise, from a sufi perspective, would be to channel the "creative imagination" toward the realization of spiritual insight: for example, revealed or inspired texts are not merely read but re-created within the imaginal consciousness. Clearly this directly experienced aspect of imaginal work may raise the question of one's relation with orthodoxy and mediated spiritual authority. In some cases, values are not merely re-created, but created: that is, values are imagined. The possibility appears that orthodoxy may deconstruct itself, that ideology may be overcome from within. Hence the ambiguous relation between Islamic authorities and Islamic mystics. The sufi critique of the Image can certainly be "secularized".' Hakim Bey, 'The obelisk', http://www.to.or.at/hakimbey/obelisk.htm

69 From C-Span's 'Booknotes' show, Brian Lamb interviewing Stephen Schwartz, 2 February 2003, http://www.booknotes.org/Transcript/?ProgramID=1713

70 Pat Kane, 'Drawing strength from the ruins of certainty', review of Sardar's *The A to Z of Postmodern Life*, in the *Independent*, 28 May 2002.

71 Sardar, 'Understanding Islam', *ibid*.

72 Zia Sardar, 'Faith, diversity and dignity in a global age', *Independent*, 6 September 2002.

73 Sardar, 'Understanding Islam', *ibid*.

74 Sardar, 'My fatwa on the fanatics', *Observer*, 23 September 2001, http://observer.guardian.co.uk/comment/story/0,6903,556545,00.html.

75 *Ibid*.

76 Sardar, *Postmodernism and the Other*, pp. 181–97

77 Salman Rushdie, 'Is nothing sacred?', in *Imaginary Homelands*, Granta, 1991.

78 Brian Sutton-Smith reminds us of the coercive element of play as identity – the community pressure to participate – in Chapter 6 of the *Ambiguity of Play*.

79 See Pat Kane's review of Sardar's *The A to Z of Postmodern Life* (Icon, 2002) in the *Independent*, 28 May 2002, http://enjoyment.independent.co.uk/books/reviews/story.jsp?story=299798

80 Schechner quoted in Sutton-Smith, *Ambiguity of Play*, pp. 55–6.

81 Richard Schechner, 'Playing', in *Play and Culture*, 1(1), 1988, pp. 16–18.

82 K.R. Sundararajan, 'Playful and purposive creation – A comparative study of Hinduism and Christianity', available from http://web.sbu.edu/theology

83 K.R. Sundararajan, 'Self-consciousness in Ramanuja's Vedanta', http://www.here-now4u.de/eng/self-consciousness_in_ramanuja.htm. See also David Loy in 'Indra's postmodern Net', *ibid.*, quoting the Zen scholar Hee-Jin Kim: '[N]ot-to-commit-any-evil is neither the heteronomous "Thou shalt not" nor the autonomous "I will not," but is non-contrivance, ... When morality becomes effortless, purposeless, and playful, it becomes a non-moral morality which is the culmination of Zen practice of the Way in which morality, art, and play merge together. When *ought* becomes *is* in the transparency of *thusness*, only then do we come to the highest morality.' As Loy explains: 'This is the non-moral morality of the bodhisattva, who, having nothing to gain or lose, is devoted to the welfare of others. Contrary to popular belief, this is not a sacrifice. Indra's Net implies that, insofar as I am caused by the whole universe, it exists for my benefit; but insofar as I am the cause of the whole universe, I exist for it. This dilemma is resolved by realizing that there is no real distinction between the terms: when I am the universe, to help others is to help myself. The bodhisattva knows that no one is saved until we're all saved.'

84 Sutton-Smith, p. 231. See also note 6, Chapter 2, this volume.

85 Edelman, Damasio, previous paper on consciousness. Mikal Spariosu, *Dionysus Reborn*, Ithaca, 1989.

86 'So the grand destiny of humanity is ... to play? Does our incredulity reflect the absurdity of the proposal, or how far we have fallen from the Garden of Eden? Perhaps the predominantly negative connotations of the word reveal less about play than about us: our self-importance, our need to stand out

from the rest of creation (and from the rest of our fellows) by accomplishing great things.' Loy, 'Indra's postmodern Net', *ibid*.

87 See Walter Truett Anderson, 'Liberation from the self: where East meets West', *The Future of the Self*, Tarcher/Putnam, 1997.

88 James Carse, *Finite and Infinite Games*, Ballantine 1986, p. 19.

OUTRO / BEYOND THE PLAY ETHIC

1 On the intellectual front, I'm delighted to see that an entirely new academic discipline called 'ludology' – the study of play games – has emerged almost spontaneously from within the games sector itself. The portal for this material is http://www.ludology.org, and the earliest of the academic and peer-reviewed journals is http://www.gamestudies.org

2 Manuel Castells, *The Network Society*, Blackwell, 1996, p. 198.

3 Ulrich Beck, 'Zombie categories', in Jonathan Rutherford (ed.), *The Art of Life*, Lawrence and Wishart, 2001; Zygmunt Bauman, *Postmodern Ethics*, Polity, 1992; Douglas Rushkoff, *Nothing Sacred*, Basic Books, 2003.

4 For similar agonizings, see Nick Dyer-Witherford, 'Alternatives', in *Cyber-Marx*, 1999, Illinois.

Notes

SELECTED BIBLIOGRAPHY

Aaronovitch, David, 'What's so smart about being childish?', Independent, 6 June 2001

Abbott, Lesley (ed.), *Experiencing Reggio Emilia: Implications for Pre-School Provision*, Open University Press, 2001

Abrams, Rebecca, *The Playful Self: Why Women Need Play in their Lives*, Fourth Estate, 1997

— 'Let's all go out to play', New Statesman, 13 November 2000

Abse, Leo, *Tony Blair: Behind the Smile*, Robson, 2003

Aitkenhead, Decca, *The Promised Land: Travels in Search of the Perfect E*, Fourth Estate, 2002.

Ali, Tariq, *The Clash of Fundamentalisms: Crusades, Jihads and Modernity*, Verso, 2003

Anderson, Sherry Ruth and Ray, Paul, *The Cultural Creatives: How 50 Million People Are Changing the World*, Harmony, 2000

Anderson, Walter Truett, *The Future of the Self*, Tarcher/Putnam, 1997

Andre, Breton, *Manifestos of Surrealism*, translated by Richard Seaver and Helen R. Lane, University of Michigan Press, 1969

Aries, Philippe, *Centuries of Childhood*, Cape, 1962

Arquilla, John and Ronfeldt, David, 'Fighting the network war', *Wired*, December 2001

— *Networks and Netwars: The Future of Terror, Crime and Militancy*, Rand Corporation, 2001, http://www.rand.org/publications/MR/MR1382/

Au, James Wagner, 'Playing God', Salon.com, 10 April 2001

— 'Burn down the shopping malls!', Salon.com, 22 February 2002

Balakrishnan, Gopal, 'Virgilian visions', *New Left Review*, Sepember/October 2000, http://www.newleftreview.net/NLR23909.shtml

Barabsi, Albert-Laszlo, *Linked*, Plume, 2003

Barber, Benjamin, 'Beyond jihad and McWorld', *The Nation*, 21 January 2002

Barbrook, Richard, 'A cybercommunist manifesto', http://www.nettime.org/Lists-Archives/nettime-l-9909/msg00046.html — 'Cyber-communism: how the Americans are superseding capitalism in cyberspace', http://www.hrc.wmin.ac.uk/theory-cybercommunism.html

— 'The regulation of liberty: free speech, free trade and free gifts on the Net', http://www.hrc.wmin.ac.uk/hrc/theory/regulationofliberty/t.html

Baudrillard, Jean, *Symbolic Exchange* and Death, Sage, 1993

— 'The spirit of terrorism', *Le Monde*, 2 November 2001, available in English at http://amsterdam.nettime.org/Lists-Archives/nettime-l-0111/msg00083.html

— 'The despair of having everything', *Le Monde Diplomatique*, November 2002

Bauman, Zygmunt, *Postmodern Ethics*, Polity, 1992

— 'Am I my brother's keeper?', *European Journal of Social Work*, vol. 3, no. 1, 2000, pp. 5–11

— *Work, Consumerism and the New Poor*, OUP, 2001

— 'Chasing the elusive society', in *Society Under Siege*, Polity, 2002, pp. 25–51

— *Liquid Love*, Polity, 2003

Beck, Ulrich, *The Normal Chaos of Love*, Polity, 1995

— *The Brave New World of Work*, Polity, 2001

— 'Zombie categories', in Jonathan Rutherford (ed.), *The Art of Life*, Lawrence and Wishart, 2001

Bell, Daniel, *The Coming of Post-Industrial Society*, Basic, 1973

Benford, Gregory, 'Theological science fiction: why *The Matrix* matters', *Reason*, 23 May 2003

Benjamin, Walter, 'The work of art in the age of mechanical reproduction', *Illuminations*, Schocken, 1968

Bentley, Tom, 'Will we blow apart society?', *New Statesman*, 27 September 1999

— 'Letting go: complexity and the left', *Renewal*, Winter 2002

Berlyne, Daniel, *Aesthetics and Psychobiology*, Appleton, Century, Crofts, 1971

Berry, Wendell, 'A citizen's response to the national security strategy of the United States', http://www.commondreams.org/views03/0209-11.htm

Bevan, Stephen, *Attendance Management*, Work Foundation, 2003

Bey, Hakim, 'The obelisk', http://www.to.or.at/hakimbey/obelisk.htm

Boisot, Max, and Cohen, Jack, 'Shall I compare thee to . . . an organization?', *Emergence*, 2(4) 2000

Bollier, David, 'Reclaiming the American commons', http://www.bollier.org/reclaim.htm

Bolt, Nate, 'The binary proletariat', *First Monday*, vol. 5, no. 5, May 2000, http://firstmonday.org/issues/issue5_5/bolt/index.html

Bowker, Geoff, 'Synchronization 4: Hermes, angels and the narrative of the archive', http://www.uiuc.edu/unit/STIM/bowker2.pdf

Boyle, James, 'The second enclosure movement and the construction of the public domain', http://www.law.duke.edu/pd/papers/boyle.pdf

Brand, Stewart, *The Clock of the Long Now: Time and Responsibility*, Weidenfield and Nicolson, 1999

Braunstein, Peter and Doyle, William Michael, *Imagine Nation: the American Counterculture of the 1960s and '70s*, Routledge, 2002

Brockman, John, *Digerati: Conversations with the Digital Elite*, HardWired, 1996

Brooks, David, *Bobos in Paradise*, Simon and Schuster, 2001

Brown, Gordon, speech to the Yale Club, New York, 26 July 2001, HM Treasury website,http://www.hmtreasury.gov.uk/newsroom_and_speeches/press/2001/press_91_01.cfm

Brown, Mick, *The Spiritual Tourist*, Bloomsbury, 1998

Brown, Philip, and Lauder, Hugh, 'Capitalism and social progress', *Guardian*, 18 June 2001

Brown, Tom and Crainer, Stuart (et al.), *Business Minds: Management Wisdom Direct from the World's Greatest Thinkers, Financial Times*, Prentice Hall, November 2001

Buchanan, Mark, Nexus: *Small Worlds and the Groundbreaking Science of Networks*, Norton, 2002

Bunting, Madeleine, 'New year, same grind', *Guardian*, 6 January 2003

— 'Why aren't we taking more time?', *Guardian*, 10 March 2003

Callois, Roger, *Man, Play and Games*, University of Illinois Press, 1961

Capra, Fritjof, *The Hidden Connections*, Penguin, 2002

Caputo, John D., *On Religion*, Routledge, 2001

Carlyle, Thomas, *Past and Present*, bk 3, ch. 11, 'Labour', http://dspace.dial.pipex.com/town/terrace/adwo3/readings/carlyle/3-11.htm

Carse, James, *Finite and Infinite Games*, Ballantine, 1986

Castells, Manuel, *The Network Society*, Blackwell, 1996

— *The Power of Identity*, Blackwell, 1996

— *End of Millenium*, Blackwell, 2000

— *The Internet Galaxy*, Oxford, 2002

Clare, Anthony, *On Men: Masculinity in Crisis*, Chatto, 2000

Cohen, David, *The Development of Play*, Routledge, 1993

Cohen, Nick, 'Darkening of a nation', *Observer*, 26 October 2003

Collin, Matthew, *Altered State: the Story of Ecstasy Culture*, Serpent's Tail, 1997

Cook, Francis, *Hua-yen Buddhism*, Pen State Press, 1977

Cooper, Andrew, Hetherington, Rachael and Katz, Ilan, *The Risk Factor: Making the Child Protection System Work for Children*, Demos, 2003

Courtois, Stefan et al., *The Black Book of Communism: Crimes, Terror, Repression*, Harvard, 1999

Cowdell, S., *Atheist Priest? Don Cupitt and Christianity*, SCM Press, 1988

Crabtree, James, 'Civic hacking: a new agenda for e-democracy', *Open Democracy*, 6 March 2003, http://www.opendemocracy.net/debates/article-8-85-1025.jsp

Critcher, Chas and Clarke, John, *The Devil Makes Work: Leisure in Capitalist Britain*, Macmillan, 1985

Critchley, Simon, *On Humour*, Routledge, 2002

Cross, Gary, *Time and Money: the Making of Consumer Culture*, Routledge, 1993

Csikszentmihalyi, Mihaly, *Creativity: Flow and the Psychology of Discovery and Invention*, Harper Collins, 1996

Cunningham, H., *The Children of the Poor: Representations of Childhood since the Seventeenth Century*, Oxford, 1991, p.43

Cupitt, Don, *The Time Being*, SCM, 1992

— *The Last Philosophy*, SCM, 1995

— *After God: the Future of Religion*, Phoenix, 1998

Davie, George, *The Crisis of the Democratic Intellect*, Birlinn, 1989

Davis, Erik, *Techgnosis: Myth, Magic and Mysticism in the Age of Information*, Fourth Estate, 1998

— 'Experience design', 2003, http://www.techgnosis.com/experience.html

— 'The matrix way of knowledge', *Salon.com*, 12 May 2003

De Geus, Arie, 'Planning as learning', *Harvard Business Review*, March–April 1988

Doctorow, Cory, *Down and Out in the Magic Kingdom*, Tor, 2003

Dominguez, Joe and Robin, Vicki, *Your Money or Your Life: Transforming Your Relationship with Money and Achieving Financial Independence*, Penguin USA, 1999

Donkin, Richard, *Blood Sweat and Tears: the Evolution of Work*, Texere, 2002

Drucker, Peter, 'The next society: the next workforce', *The Economist*, 3 November 2001.

Dworkin, Anthony, 'Daniel Bell', *Prospect*, October 2000

Dyer-Witherford, Nick, *Cyber-Marx: Cycles and Circuits of Struggle in High Technology Capitalism*, University of Illinois Press, 1999

Eigen, Manfred and Winkler, Ruthild, *Laws of the Game: How the Principles of Nature Govern Chance*, Princeton University Press, 1993

EIRO, 'Working time developments – 2002', http://www.eiro.eurofound.ie/2003/03/update/tn0303103u.html

Elgin, Duane, *Voluntary Simplicity*, Quill, 1998

Elliot, Larry and Glaister, Dan, *The Age of Insecurity*, Norton, 1998

Ellis, John, 'Digital matters', *Fast Company*, December 2001

Erikson, Erik H., *Toys and Reasons: Stages in the Ritualization of Experience*, Marion Boyars, 1978

Eshun, Ekow, 'Surrealism and advertising', http://www.bbc.co.uk/arts/tate/surrealism/ekow1.shtml

Falassi, Alessandro, *Time out of Time: Essays on the Festival*, University of New Mexico Press, 1967

Ferguson, Niall, 'How Weber's "Protestant ethic" explains U.S. edge over Europe', *New York Times*, 9 June 2003

Feyerabend, Paul, *The Conquest of Abundance: a Tale of Abstraction versus the Richness of Being*, Chicago, 1999

Flores, Fernando and Gray, John, *Entrepreneurship and the wired life: work in the wake of careers*, Demos, 2000

Florida, Richard, 'The rise of the creative class', *Washington Monthly*, May 2002

— 'The new American dream', *Washington Monthly*, March 2003

— *The Rise of the Creative Class: And How It's Transforming Work, Leisure, Community and Everyday Life*, Basic, 2004

Foucault, Michael, *Ethics: Subjectivity and Truth*, Penguin, 2002

— *The Coming of the Cosmic Christ*, Harper and Row, 1988

Fox, Matthew, *Original Blessing*, Bear and Co., 1983

Frank, Thomas, *One Market Under God*, Penguin, 2002

Frankel, Boris, *The Post-Industrial Utopians*, Polity, 1987

Freund, Charles Paul, 'In praise of vulgarity: how commercial culture liberates Islam – and the West', *Reason*, March 2002

Frith, Simon, *Performing Rites: Evaluating Popular Music*, Oxford, 1998

Fukuyama, Francis, *The Great Disruption: Human Nature and the Reconstitution of Social Order*, Free Press, 1999

Furedi, Frank, *Paranoid Parenting*, Penguin, 2001

— 'The children who won't grow up', *Spiked-Online*, 29 July 2003, http://www.spiked-online.com/Printable/00000006DE8D.htm

Gadamer, Hans-Georg, *The Relevance of the Beautiful*, Cambridge University Press, 1986

Gandini, Lella, 'The Reggio Emilia story: history and organisation'. In J. Hendrick (ed.), *First Steps Towards Teaching the Reggio Way*, Merril/Prentice-Hall, 1997

Gardner, Howard, *Developmental Psychology*, Little, Brown, 1982

— *Art, Mind and Brain*, Basic, 1984

— *The Disciplined Mind*, Penguin, 2000

— 'An education for the future: the foundation of science and values'. Paper presented to The Royal Symposium, convened by Her Majesty, Queen Beatrix, Amsterdam, 13 March 2001, http://www.pz.harvard.edu/Pls/HG_Amsterdam.htm

— 'Good work, well done: a psychological study', *Chronicle of Higher Education*, 22 February 2002, http://chronicle.com/free/v48/i24/24b00701.htm

Gardner, Howard, Damon, William and Csikszentmihalyi, *Good Work: When Excellence and Ethics Meet*, Basic Books, 2001

Ghazi, Polly and Jones, Judy, *Getting a Life: The Downshifter's Guide to Happier, Simpler Living*, Hodder and Stoughton, 1997

Gibson, William, *Pattern Recognition*, Penguin, 2003

Giddens, Anthony, *The Transformation of Intimacy*, Polity, 1992

— *The Future of Radical Politics*, Polity, 1994

Gilmore, James H.B, and, Pine II, Joseph, *The Experience Economy*, Harvard Business School Press, 1999

Gilroy, Paul, 'Roots and routes: black identity as an outernational project', in Harris, Blue, and Griffith (eds.) *Racial and Ethnic Identity: Psychological Development and Creative Expression*, Routledge, 1995

Goodwin, Brian, *How the Leopard Changed Its Spots*, Phoenix, 1996

Goodwin, Brian and Reason, Peter, 'Toward a science of qualities in organizations: lessons from complexity theory and postmodern biology', *Concepts and Transformations*, 4(3), 1999, 281–317, http://www.bath.ac.uk/~mnspwr/Papers/sciencequalities.htm

Gore, Al and Tipper, *Joined at the Heart: the Transformation of the American Family*, Henry Holt, 2002

Gorz, Andre, *Reclaiming Work: Beyond the Wage-Based Society*, Polity, 1999

Gowers, Andrew, 'Gordon Brown's progress', *Financial Times*, 18 February 1998

Graeber, David, 'The new anarchists', *New Left Review* 13, January–February 2002

Habermas, Jurgen, *Autonomy and Solidarity*, Verso, 1986

— 'Between eroticism and general economics', *The Philosophical Discourse of Modernity*, MIT Press, 1987

Hall, Stuart (ed.), *New Times*, Lawrence and Wishart, 1985

— *The Hard Road to Renewal: Thatcherism and the Crisis of the Left*, Verso, 1988

Hamel, Gary, 'Innovation now!', *Fast Company*, December 2002

Hampden-Turner, Charles and Trompenaars, Fons, *The Seven Cultures of Capitalism*, Piatkus, 1995
— *Mastering the Infinite Game*, Capstone, 1997
Handelman, Don, 'Passages to play: paradox and process', *Play and Culture*, 5 (1), 1992, pp. 1–19
— 'Framing, braiding and killing play', *Focaal: European Journal of Anthropology*, no 37, 2001, pp. 145–6
Handy, Charles, *The Elephant and the Flea*, Arrow, 2002
Harding, James, 'Globalization's children strike back', *Financial Times*, 11 September 2001
— 'The Anti-Globalization movement', *Financial Times*, 10 October 2001
Hayek, F.W., 'Play, the school of rules', *The Fatal Conceit: the Errors of Socialism*, Routledge, 1989
Henry, Ian P., *The Politics of Leisure Policy*, Palgrave Macmillan, 2001
Hesse, Hermann, *The Glass Bead Game*, Vintage, 2000
Hewlett, Sylvia Ann and West, Cornel, 'Caring for crib lizards', *The American Prospect*, 1 January 2001, http://www.prospect.org/print/V12/1/hewlett-s.html
Himanen, Pekka, *The Hacker Ethic*, Secker and Warburg, 2001
Himanen, Pekka and Castells, Manuel, *The Information Society and the Welfare State: The Finnish Model*, OUP, 2002
Holmes, Brian, 'The flexible personality', http://amsterdam.nettime.org/Lists-Archives/nettime-l-0201/msg00012.html
Howard, Melanie and Wilmott, Michael, 'The networked family', *New Times*, March 2000
Hue and Cry, 'The Only Thing (More Powerful Than The Boss)', *Remote* (CD), Circa Records, 1989
Huizinga, Johan, *Homo Ludens: a Study of the Play Element in Culture*, Beacon Press, 1971
Hussey, Andrew, *The Game of War*, Jonathan Cape, 2001
Hutton, Will, *The World We're In*, 2002, Vintage
Illich, Ivan, *Deschooling Society*, Marion Boyars, 1996
Inglehart, Ronald 'Globalisation and postmodern values', *Washington Monthly*, Winter 2000, http://www.twq.com/winteroo/231Inglehart.pdf
International Futures Forum, *Ten Things to Do in a Conceptual Emergency*, IFF, 2003
Ito, Joi, 'Emergent democracy', http://joi.ito.com/static/emergentdemocracy.html
Jameson, Frederic, 'Fear and loathing in globalization', *New Left Review*, September–October 2003
Jenkins, Henry, 'War games', *MIT Technology Review*, 7 November 2003
Jordan, Bill, *Social Work and the Third Way: Tough Love as Social Policy*, Sage, 2002
Kaku, Michio, *Visions*, Bantam, 1999
Kane, Pat, *Tinsel Show: Pop, Politics and Scotland*, Polygon, 1992
— 'The angels do make work for idle hands', *Scotland on Sunday*, January 1997
— 'Play for today', *Observer*, 22 October 2000

Kao, John, *Jamming the Art and Discipline of Business Creativity*, Diane, 1996

Karl Groos, *The Play of Man*, Ayer, 1976

Kasvio, Antti, 'Towards a wireless information society: the case of Finland', Department of Information Studies, University of Tampere, http://www.info.uta.fi/winsoc/engl/lect/progr.html

Kauffman, Stuart, At Home in the Universe, Penguin, 1996

— *Investigations*, OUP, 2002

Keane, John, *Tom Paine: A Political Life*, Bloomsbury, 1996

Kelly, Eamonn (ed.), *What's Next? Exploring the New Terrain for Business*, Wiley, 2002

Kelly, Kevin, 'Interview with the Luddite', *Wired*, June 1995, http://www.wired.com/wired/archive/3.06/saleskelly_pr.html

— *Out of Control: the New Biology of Humans and Machines*, Fourth Estate, 1996

Kevill, Sian 'The BBC's plans for digital democracy', *Open Democracy*, 20 February 2003, http://www.opendemocracy.net/debates/article.jsp?id=8&debateId=85&articleId=995

Kingsnorth, Paul, 'The global backlash', *New Statesman*, 28 April 2003

– *One No, Many Yesses: A Journey to the Heart of the Global Resistance Movement*, Free Press, 2003

Klein, Naomi, *No Logo*, Flamingo, 2000

— 'The do mentality', *Financial Times*, 29 May 2001

— 'Empowering people', Superhumanism conference, 29 May 2001, http://www.dandad.org/content/super/speakers/speaker_naomi.html

— 'Signs of the times', *The Nation*, 22 October 2001

— *Fences and Windows*, Flamingo, 2002

Kleiner, Art, 'Consequential heresies', *GBN*, May 1996, http://www.gbn.com/ArticleDisplayServlet.srv?aid=185

— 'The man who saw the future', *Strategy and Business*, Spring 2003

Kluitenberg, Eric, 'Transfiguration of the avant garde: the negative dialectics of the Net', http://amsterdam.nettime.org/Lists-Archives/nettime-l-0201/msg00104.html

Knell, John, *Most Wanted*, Work Foundation, 2001

Kurzweil, Ray, *The Age of Spiritual Machines*, Penguin USA, 2000

Lanier, Jaron, 'A minority within the minority', http://www.21cmagazine.com/minority.html

Lash, Scott, *Critique of Information*, Sage, 2002

Latif, Asad, 'Muslims are returning to sources of Islam to clarify the meaning of their actions', *Straits Times*, 12 September 2002

Law, Andy, *Open Minds*, Orion, 1998

— *Experiment at Work: Explosions and Experiences at the Most Frightening Company on Earth*, Profile, 2003

Layard, Richard, 'Money and happiness' *The Talk Show*, BBC4, 7 April 2003, transcript at http://www.bbc.co.uk/bbcfour/talkshow/features/transcripts/money_happiness.pdf

Leadbeater, Charles, *Up The Down Escalator: Why The Global Pessimists Are Wrong*, Penguin, 2002

— 'Welcome to the amateur century', *Financial Times*, 23 December 2002

Leicester, Graham and Boyle, Matthew, *Changing Schools Education in a Knowledge Society*, Scottish Council Foundation, 2000, http://www.scottishcouncilfoundation.org/pubs_more.php?p=33

Leonard, Andrew, 'Finland: the open source society', The Free Software Project, 20 April 2000, Salon, http://archive.salon.com/tech/fsp/2000/04/20/chapter_six_part_1/

— 'Life, liberty and the pursuit of free software', *Salon*, 15 February 2001

Leonard, Mark, 'The Left should love globalization', *New Statesman*, 28 May 2001

Lessig, Lawrence, 'The Internet under siege', *Foreign Policy*, November/December 2001, http://www.foreignpolicy.com/issue_novdec_2001/lessig.html.

— 'Free culture', at the O. Reilly Open Source Conference, 24 July 2002, http://randomfoo.net/oscon/2002/lessig/

— *The Future of Ideas: the Fate of the Commons in a Connected World*, Vintage, 2002

Lewis, Michael, *The Future Just Happened*, Coronet, 2002

Lindquist, Galina, 'Elusive play and its relations to power', *Focaal: European Journal of Anthropology*, no 37, 2001, http://www.focaal.box.nl/previous/intro_37.pdf

Linturi, Risto and Hannula, Ilkka, '100 Phenomena', http://www.linturi.fi/100_phenomena/index.html

Lloyd, John, *The Protest Ethic: How the Anti-globalization movement challenges social democracy*, Demos, 2001

Loy, David, 'Indra's postmodern Net', *Philosophy East and West*, vol 43, no 3, July 1993, pp. 481–510, http://ccbs.ntu.edu.tw/FULLTEXT/JR-PHIL/ew25326.htm

— *Non-Duality: A Study in Comparative Philosophy*, Humanity, 1999

Luke, Allen and Carmen, 'Adolescence lost/childhood regained: literacy and the rise of the techno-subject', *Journal of Early Childhood Literacy*, 1 (1), 2000, pp. 90–120

Lyotard, Jean-François, *The Postmodern Condition: A Report on Knowledge*, Manchester University Press, 1985

Makedon, Alexander, 'Reinterpreting Dewey: Some Thoughts on His Views of Science and Play in Education', Chicago State University, http://webs.csu.edu/~bigoama/articles/JohnDewy.html#of

Marcus, Greil, *Lipstick Traces*, Harvard, 1990

— *Double Trouble: Bill Clinton and Elvis Presley in a Land of No Alternatives*, Henry Holt, 2000

Marx, Karl, *Capital: Vol. 3*, Lawrence and Wishart, 1998

McKay, George, *Senseless Acts of Beauty: Cultures of Resistance Since the Sixties*, Verso, 1996

— *DIY Culture: Party and Protest in Nineties' Britain*, Verso, 1998

McKibben, Ross, 'Nothing more divisive', *London Review of Books*, 28 November 2002, http://www.lrb.co.uk/v24/n23/contents.html.

McLuhan, Marshall, *Understanding Media: The Extensions of Man*, MIT Press, 1994

Micheal Lind, 'The case for a living wage', *New Leader*, 1 October 2001, http://www.newamerica.net/index.cfm?pg=article&pubID=564

Miller, Geoffrey, *The Mating Mind*, Penguin, 2002

Miller, Paul, *Open Policy: threats and opportunities in a wired world*, Forum for the Future, 2002

Miyoshi, Masao and Harootunian, H.D. *Postmodernism and Japan*, Duke, 1989

Moglen, Eben, 'The dotCommunist manifesto', January 2003, http://moglen.law.columbia.edu/publications/dcm.html.

Montuori, Alfonso, 'Creativity, complexity and improvisation in daily life', California Institute of Integral Studies, http://www.ciis.edu/faculty/articles/montuori/creativityandimprov.pdf

Moore, Alex, 'Citizenship education in the UK: for liberation or control?', Institute of Education, University of London, http://ec.hku.hk/kd2proc/proceedings/fullpaper/Theme2FullPapers/AlexMoore.pdf

Moore, James 'The second superpower raises its beautiful head', http://cyber.law.harvard.edu/people/jmoore/secondsuperpower.html

Morgan, David. 'Risk and family practices: accounting for change and fluidity in family life', in E.B. Silva and C. Smart (eds), *The New Family?*, Sage, 1999, pp. 13–30

Morrison, Norma, 'The Reggio approach: an inspiration for inclusion of children with "Special Rights"', http://www.milligan.edu/ProfEducation/NMorrison/fpworkshop/dkgreggio2oo.htm

Moyles, Janet R. (ed.), *The Excellence of Play*, Oxford University Press, 1994

Moyser, George, 'Post-scarcity radicalism in the US', *Government and Opposition*, 35 (1), 2000, pp. 119–122

Mulgan, Geoff, *Politics in an Anti-Political Age*, Polity, 1996
— *Connexity: How to Live in a Connected World*, Vintage, 1999
— *Life After Politics*, Demos, 2000

Nandy, Ashis, *Exiled at Home*, Oxford, 1998

Nardo, A.K., *The Ludic Self in Seventeenth Century English Literature*, SUNY, 1991

Negri, Antonio, *Time For Revolution*, Continuum, 2002

Negri, Antonio and Hardt, Michael, *The Savage Anomaly: The Power of Spinoza's Metaphysics and Politics*, Minnesota, 1991
— *Empire*, Harvard, 2001

Nelson's Victoria, *The Secret Life of Puppets*, Harvard, 2002

Neville, Richard, *Playpower*, Paladin, 1970
— *Hippie Hippie Shake*, Bloomsbury, 1996

O'Brien, Danny, 'Auntie's digital revelation', *Guardian*, 28 August 2003

Palmer, J.A. (ed.), *Fifty Major Thinkers on Education: from Confucius to Dewey*, Routledge, 2001

Parton, Nigel and O'Byrne, Patrick, *Constructive Social Work: Towards a New Practice*, Palgrave, 2000

Perks, Martyn, 'Social software – get real', *Spiked-Online*, 20 March 2003, http://www.spiked-online.com/Printable/ooooooo6DCF1.htm

— 'What I-can can't do', *Spiked-Online*, 20 November 2003, http://www.spiked-online.com/articles/ooooooo6DFD3.htm

Pesce, Marc, *The Playful World: How Technology is Transforming Our Imagination*, Ballantine, 2000

— 'Toys and the playful world', Talk for women in Toys, 14 February 2001, New York City, http://www.hyperreal.org/~mpesce/WIT.html

Peters, Tom, 'The brand called you', *Fast Company*, August/September 1997, http://www.fastcompany.com/online/10/brandyou.html

Pettegree, Andrew, Duke, Alastair and Lewis, Gillian, *Calvinism in Europe, 1540–1620*, Cambridge University Press, 1997

Piaget, Jean, *Play, Dreams and Imitation in Childhood*, Norton, 1962

Pickering, Andy, 'Cybernetics and the mangle: Ashby, Beer, and Pask', available at http://www.uiuc.edu/unit/STIM/pickering1.pdf.

Pink, Daniel, *Free-Agent Nation: the Future of Working for Yourself*, Warner, 2001

Plato, *Laws*, Princeton University Press, 1969

Postrel, Virginia, 'Fields of Play', *The Future and its Enemies*, Free Press, 1998

— *The Substance of Style*, Harper Collins, 2003

Prahalad, C.K. and Ramaswamy, Venkatram, 'The co-creation connection', *Strategy + Business* 27, 2002, http://www.strategy-business.com/press/article/18458?pg=D

Prigogine, Ilya and Stengers, Etienne, *Order Out of Chaos: Man's New Dialogue with Nature*, Bantam, 1984

Quigley, William P., 'The quicksands of the Poor Law: poor relief legislation in a growing nation, 1790–1820', *The Northern Illinois University Law Review*, Fall, 1997

Rabinbach, Anson, *The Human Motor: Energy, Fatigue and the Origins of Modernity*, University of California Press, 1992

Reeves, Richard, *Happy Mondays*, Momentum, 2001

— 'Life's good. Why do we feel bad?', *Observer*, 19 May 2002

Reich, Robert, *The Work of Nations*, Vintage, 1991

Reith, Gerda, *The Age of Chance: Gambling and Western Culture*, Routledge, 2002

Rheingold, Howard, *Smart Mobs: The Next Social Revolution*, Perseus, 2002

— 'Helsinki's aula: where geospace, sociospace, and cyberspace meet . . .' *The Feature*, 17 July 2002, http://www.thefeature.com/index.jsp?url=article.jsp?pageid=15435

Rifkin, Jeremy, *Age of Access: The New Culture of Hypercapitalism, Where All of Life Is a Paid-for Experience*, Penguin, 2001

Rinaldi, Carlina, 'Staff development in Reggio Emilia', in G. Lillian, *Reflections on the Reggio Emilia Approach*, Urbana, 1994

Rivlin, Gary, 'Leader of the free world', *Wired*, November 2003,
http://www.wired.com/wired/archive/11.11/linus.html

Robertson, P., 'Home as a nest: middle class childhood in nineteenth century Europe', in DeMause, L. (ed.), *The History of Childhood*, Souvenir, 1976

Robinson, Rick, 'Capitalist tool, humanist tool', *Design Management Journal*, Spring 2001

Rogers, Daniel, 'What next for St Luke's?' *Financial Times* (Web version), 10 March 2003

Rojek, Chris, *Decentring Leisure*, Routledge, 1998

— *Celebrity*, Reaktion, 2002

Roof, Wade Clark, *Spiritual Marketplace: Baby Boomers and the Remaking of American Religion*, Princeton, 2001

Rose, Carol, 'Romans, roads, and romantic creators: traditions of public property in the information age', *Law and Contemporary Problems*, Winter/Spring 2003,
http://papers.ssrn.com/sol3/delivery.cfm/SSRN_ID293142_code020426530.pdf?abstractid=293142

Roskos, Kathleen and Christie, James, 'Examining the play-literacy interface: a critical review and future directions', *Journal of Early Childhood Literacy*, vol 1 (1), 2001, pp. 59–89

Ross, Andrew, *Strange Weather: Culture, Science and Technology in an Age of Limits*, Verso, 1991

— 'Techno-sweatshops', *Tikkun*, January/February 2000,
http://www.tikkun.org/magazine/index.cfm/action/tikkun/issue/tik0001/article/000115c.html

— *No Collar: the Humane Workplace and its Hidden Costs*, Basic Books, 2002

Roszak, Theodore, 'What a piece of work is man: humanism, religion, and the new cosmology', in Hermann, Robert, *Expanding Humanity's Vision of God: New Thoughts on Science and Religion*, Templeton Press, 2001. Essay available at
http://www.datadiwan.de/SciMedNet/library/articlesN71+/N71humanism_Roszak.htm

Rowbotham, Sheila, *Promise of a Dream: Remembering the Sixties*, Verso, 2001

Rubbin, Irene, *Italy's Industrial Renaissance*, Comitate Regionale Dell Emilia Romagna, 1986

Rudburg, Monica, 'The epistemophilic project', in Kathy Davis, *Embodied Practices: Feminist Perspectives on the Body*, Sage, 1997, pp. 182–3

Rushdie, Salman, 'Is nothing sacred?', in *Imaginary Homelands*, Granta, 1991

Rushkoff, Douglas, *Media Virus! Hidden Agendas in Popular Culture*, Ballantine, 1996

— Children of Chaos: Surviving the End of the World As We Know It, Flamingo, 1997.

— 'Remember the Sabbath: an argument for a day off', December 1999, at
http://www.rushkoff.com/cgi-bin/columns/display.cgi/remember_the_sabbath

— 'Social currency: content as a medium for interaction', January 2001, http://www.rushkoff.com/cgi-bin/columns/display.cgi/social_currency
— 'Exodus: from pyramid-building to a global programmers union', May 2001, http://www.rushkoff.com/cgi-bin/columns/display.cgi/exodus,
— 'The people's net: the Internet is back, alive and well', Yahoo Internet Life, July 2001, http://www.rushkoff.com/features/peoplesnet.html
— *Cyberia: Life in the Trenches of Cyberspace*, Clinamen, 2002
— *Nothing Sacred*, Basic Books, 2003
— *Open Source Democracy*, Demos, 2003
— interview, at Clal: The Jewish Public Forum, 2000, http://www.rushkoff.com/interviews/clal.html
Sale, Kirkpatrick, *Rebels Against the Future – The Luddites and Their War on the Industrial Revolution: Lessons for the Computer Age*, Perseus, 1996
Sardar, Ziauddin, Davies, Merryl Wyn and Nandy, Ashis, *Barbaric Others: A Manifesto on Western Racism*, Pluto, 1993
— 'Playing the game', *New Statesman*, 26 April 1999
— 'My fatwa on the fanatics', *Observer*, 23 September 2001
— 'The true meaning of Islam's holy book', *Express on Sunday*, 30 September 2001
— 'Faith, diversity and dignity in a global age', *Independent*, 6 September 2002
— 'The agony of a 21st century Muslim', *New Statesman*, 17 February 2003
Savage, Jon, *England's Dreaming*, Faber and Faber, 1992
Savigar, Tom, *Born Clicking: Are Kids Smarter than Adults?*, ICA/Sense Network, 2002, available at http://www.ica.org.uk/index.cfm?articleid=1081
Schechner, Richard, 'Playing', *Play and Culture*, 1(1), 1988, pp. 16–18
Schiller, Friedrich von, *On Naïve and Sentimental Poetry*, Ungar, 1979
— *Letters on the Aesthetic Education of Man*, Oxford, 1983
Schrage, Michael, *Serious Play: How the Best Companies Simulate to Innovate*, Harvard Business School Press, 1999
Schwartz, Peter and Leyden, Peter, 'The long boom: a history of the future, 1980–2020', *Wired*, July 1997
Sennett, Richard, *The Corrosion of Character: the Personal Consequences of Work in the New Capitalism*, Norton, 1998
Shaw, William, 'In Helsinki virtual village . . .', *Wired*, May 2001, http://www.wired.com/wired/archive/9.03/helsinki.html
Shenk, David, 'Use technology to raise smarter happier kids', *The Atlantic*, 7 January 1999 http://www.theatlantic.com/unbound/digicult/dc990107.htm
Sontag, Susan, 'On camp', *A Susan Sontag Reader*, Penguin 1983
Spariosu, Mikail, *Dionysus Reborn*, Cornell University Press, 1989
Stalder, Felix and Hirsh, Jesse, 'Open source intelligence', *First Monday*, vol 7, no 6 June 2002, http://firstmonday.org/issues/issue7_6/stalder/index.html
Statler, Matt, Roos, Johan and Said, Roger, 'Lego speaks!', at Imagilab Working Papers, 2002 http://www.imagilab.org/working_papers_pdf/WP%202002-7.pdf
Statler, Matt, Roos, Johan, and Victor, Bart, '"Aint misbehavin": taking play seriously in organizations', Working Paper 2002–5, Imagination Lab

Foundation,
http://www.imagilab.org/working_papers_pdf/Roos%20&%20Statler%202002-5a.pdf

Steiner, George, *Grammars of Creation*, Faber and Faber, 2001

Sundararajan, K.R, 'Playful and purposive creation – a comparative study of Hinduism and Christianity', presented at the World's Parliament of Religions at Cape Town, South Africa, on 4 December 1999. Paper available at http://web.sbu.edu/theology/ Sundararajan/My Papers Creation.doc.

Sundararajan, K.R., 'Self-consciousness In Ramanuja's Vedanta', http://www.here-now4u.de/eng/self-consciousness_in_ramanuja.htm.

Sutton-Smith, Brian, 'Piaget on play: a critique', *Psychological Review* 73, 1966, pp. 104–10

— 'Play as adaptive potentiation', in P. Stevens (ed.), *Studies in the Anthropology of Play*, Leisure Press, 1977

— 'Piaget on play: revisited', in W.F. Overton (ed.), *The Relationship between Social and Cognitive Development*, Erlbaum, 1982

— *The Ambiguity of Play*, Harvard, 1999

— 'Foreword', *Focaal: European Journal of Anthropology*, no 37, 2001

Taylor, Carolyn and White, Susan, 'Knowledge, truth and reflexivity: the problem of judgement in social work', *Journal of Social Work*, 1(1), 2001, p.51

Taylor, Matthew and Laurie, *What Are Children For?*, Short, 2003

Thomas Goetz, 'Open Source Everywhere', *Wired*, November 2003

Thompson, E.P., 'Time, work discipline and industrial capitalism', in *Customs in Common: Studies in Traditional Popular Culture*, Merlin, 1991

Thorne, Charlotte, *Another Country: France Versus the Anglo-Saxon Economists*, Work Foundation, 1999

Trotsky, Leon, 'Communist policy towards art', in *Literature and Revolution*, http://www.marxists.org/archive/trotsky/works/1924/lit_revo

Turkle, Sherry, 'Who am we?', *Wired*, January 1996, http://www.wired.com/wired/archive/4.01/turkle_pr.html

— 'Cyborg babies and cy-dough-plasm: ideas about self and life in the culture of simulation', in Davis-Floyd, Robbie and Dumit, Joseph (eds), *Cyborg Babies: From Technosex to Technotots*, Routledge, 1998

— 'Cuddling up to cyborg babies', *Unesco Courier*, September 2000, http://www.unesco.org/courier/2000_09/uk/connex.htm

Ursula Huws, 'The making of a cybertariat? Virtual work in a real world', in Panitch, Leo, *Socialist Register: Working Classes, Global Realities*, Merlin Press, 2001

Van Parijs, Philippe, et al., 'Delivering a basic income', *Boston Review*, October/November 2000, http://bostonreview.mit.edu/ndf.html#Income

Virno, Paulo, 'Some notes towards the proposal of a "general intellect"', *Futur Antereur*, 10, 1992

Vygotsky, Lev, *Educational Psychology*, Blackwell, 1995

Wacker, Watts, 'Welcome to a world where anything is possible – unless it isn't', *First Matter*, 1 February 2000, http://www.firstmatter.com/pr/vh_pr.asp

Wacker, Watts and Matthews, Ryan, 'Deviants Inc', *Fast Company*, March 2002

Wallerstein, Immanuel, 'Uncertainty and creativity', Talk at Forum 2000: Concerns and Hopes on the Threshold of the New Millennium, Prague, 3–6 September 1997, http://fbc.binghamton.edu/iwuncer.htm

— 'A left politics for the twenty-first century? Or, Theory and praxis once again', 1999, http://fbc.binghamton.edu/iwleftpol.htm

— 'A left politics for an age of transition', Ferdinand Braudel Centre, 2001, http://fbc.binghamton.edu/iwleftpol2.htm

Warhurst, Chris and Nickson, *Dennis, Looking Good, Feeling Good: Style Counselling in the New Economy*, Work Foundation, 2001

Watts, Duncan J., *Six Degrees: The Science of a Connected Age*, Heinemann, 2003

Watts, Isaac, 'Against idleness and mischief', from his *Divine Songs, Attempted in Easie Language for the Use of Children* (1715), cited in Carpenter, Humphrey and Prichard, Mari, *The Oxford Companion to Children's Literature* (eds), Oxford University Press, 1984, p.536

Weber, Max, *The Protestant Ethic and the Spirit of Capitalism*, Routledge, 1985

Wertheim Margaret, *The Pearly Gates of Cyberspace: A History of Space from Dante to the Internet*, Virago, 1999

Wessel, David, 'Sad little rich country', *Washington Monthly*, November 2003, http://www.washingtonmonthly.com/features/2003/0311.wessel.html

Wheeler, Wendy, *A New Modernity?*, Lawrence and Wishart, 1999

White, John, *Education and the End of Work*, Open University, 1999

Wilber, Ken, *A Theory of Everything*, 2002, Shambhala
— *Integral Psychology*, 2002, Shambhala

Wilkinson, David, *The Power of the Force: the Spirituality of Star Wars*, Lion, 2000

Wilsdon, James, *The Politics of Bandwidth: Network Innovation and Regulation in Broadband Britain*, Demos, 2002

Winner, Landgon, 'The voluntary complexity movement', *Tech Knowledge Revue*, 1.3, 14 September 1999, http://www.praxagora.com/stevet/netfuture/1999/Sep1499_94.html

Winnicott, D.W., *Playing and Reality*, Basic, 1971

Woolfson, Adrian, 'How did the slime mould cross the maze?', *London Review of Books*, 21 March 2002

World Bank, *Culture Counts: Financing, Resources, and the Economics of Culture in Sustainable Development*, October 1999

Woudhuysen, James, 'All play and no work', IT Week, 15 January 2001
— 'Play as the Main Event in International and UK Culture', *Cultural Trends*, 43/44, 2001
— 'Team players', *Spiked-Online*, 12 April 2001, (http://www.spiked–online.com/articles/00000005560.htm

Wright, Richard, *Non Zero: the Logic of Human Destiny*, Vintage, 2001

Zezima, Michael, (ed.) *The Murdering of My Years: Artists and Activists Making Ends Meet*, Soft Skull Press, 2003

Zeldin, Theodore, *An Intimate History of Humanity*, Vintage, 1994

Zuboff, Shoshana and Maxmin, James, *The Support Economy*, Viking, 2002

INDEX